Proceedings of the
First Pacific-Asia Conference on
Knowledge Discovery and Data Mining

KDD: TECHNIQUES AND APPLICATIONS

Proceedings of the
First Pacific-Asia Conference on
Knowledge Discovery and Data Mining

KDD: TECHNIQUES AND APPLICATIONS

23–24 Feb 97

editors

Hongjun Lu
MIS

Hiroshi Motoda
Osaka Univ.

Huan Liu
NUS

World Scientific
Singapore • New Jersey • London • Hong Kong

Published by

World Scientific Publishing Co. Pte. Ltd.
P O Box 128, Farrer Road, Singapore 912805
USA office: Suite 1B, 1060 Main Street, River Edge, NJ 07661
UK office: 57 Shelton Street, Covent Garden, London WC2H 9HE

British Library Cataloguing-in-Publication Data
A catalogue record for this book is available from the British Library.

First published 1997
First repint 1998

KNOWLEDGE DISCOVERY AND DATA MINING: TECHNIQUES AND APPLICATIONS
Proceedings of the 1997 Pacific Asia Conference

~~ISBN 981-02-2919-4~~

Printed in Singapore.

Foreword

Welcome to the inaugural Pacific Asia Conference on Knowledge Discovery & Data Mining (PAKDD) that is being held in Singapore. The PAKDD seeks to provide a forum for researchers and practitioners from the Pacific Asia region as well as world-wide in KDD research and development.

The data glut, brought about by the pervasive use of computers, has caused many organizations to lament, "Computers promised us a fountain of wisdom but delivered a flood of data." The advent of KDD has provided data analysis tools to cope with the massive databases that have ensued. The scientific challenges for KDD, coupled with a practical orientation, have ignited the interest of both the academic and user communities. This, in turn, has provided the motivation to create PAKDD for the two communities to interact.

The generous support of sponsors as well as the cooperation extended by many agencies and professional bodies, which have made PAKDD '97 possible, is highly appreciated.

We are also grateful to Hongjun Lu, Hiroshi Motoda and the dedicated members of the PAKDD '97 Program Committee who have put together an outstanding opportunity for sharing the results of research and development in KDD.

On behalf of the Organizing Committee, I welcome those of you who come from the four corners of the world to Singapore.

Lee Hing Yan
General Chair

Preface

Knowledge Discovery in Databases (KDD) is a complex process involving data collection, data cleaning, dimensionality reduction, rule induction, pattern recognition, data/result analysis, and evaluation. The sharp increase in use of computers and related technologies makes acute the "data-rich but knowledge-poor" problem. Data accumulates all over the world at an inconceivable speed. Business people want to find out if accumulated data can help them make better decisions; engineerers want data to tell them what they can improve further; and scientists want to make discoveries based on data they have. In short, KDD has become a multi-disciplinary field of research and development where people search for solutions in answering all sorts of tough questions of KDD.

PAKDD'97, the First Pacific-Asia Conference on Knowledge Discovery and Data Mining, is the first conference dedicated to KDD in the Pacific-Asia region. It is also among the first few such conferences and workshops in the world. The relatively young field of KDD has been attracting many researchers and practitioners from databases, machine learning, pattern recognition, and statistics. Much work has been done, new approaches have been suggested, practical systems built, and novel applications attempted. In order to take best advantage of these achievements, PAKDD is organized to provide a platform for researchers and developers in the region as well as in the world to exchange ideas, discuss problems, and share experiences. PAKDD also serves a role as the continued regional effort to promote creative research and solid development and to move forward the frontier of KDD.

This inaugural conference has been well received by countries in the region as well as in Europe. The statistics of the 26 papers accepted for presentation reveal some interesting patterns (isn't it a simple KDD task?): The authors of 26

papers come from 12 countries and regions, including Japan, USA, Australia, Singapore, Hong Kong, Canada, China, Germany, Ireland, Israel, Taiwan, and UK. Four papers out of 26 are from Europe, outside of the region. In this proceedings, you will find all aspects of research and development in KDD. We group the papers into six major categories: (i) Clustering Techniques (4 papers), (ii) Classifiers and Classification Techniques (8 papers), (iii) Concept Learning and Rule Discovery (4 papers), (iv) Learning Association Rules and Patterns (4 papers), (v) Visual Data Exploration (2 papers), and (iv) KDD Applications (4 papers).
As a matter of fact, if we recall the complex process of KDD, the 26 papers cover from pre-processing, processing, to post-processing in KDD. You may find interesting discretization techniques and prior knowledge injection as examples of pre-processing, or induction of association and classification rules, unsupervised learning in large databases, and knowledge discovery for processing, or identification of missing patterns for post-processing, or data visualization in the process of KDD. In addition, you can also read about applications of KDD in World-Wide-Web, Real-Time Tele-Marketing Operations, etc. This conference is only the starting point of further collaboration of research efforts in KDD. We sincerely hope that researchers will get to know each other better through this proceedings, establish a base for future communication, and be better equipped to face the challenges ahead.

Hongjun Lu, Hiroshi Motoda, and *Huan Liu*
in Singapore

Conference Organization

Organizing Committee

General Chair:	Hing-Yan Lee (Japan-Singapore AI Centre)
Programme Co-Chairs:	Hongjun Lu (National University of Singapore) Hiroshi Motoda (Osaka University, Japan)
Exhibition:	Lynica Foo (Japan-Singapore AI Centre)
Treasurer:	Kwok-Leong Hui, JSAIC (Japan-Singapore AI Centre)
Publicity:	Huan Liu (National University of Singapore)
Secretariate:	Hwee-Leng Ong (Japan-Singapore AI Centre)
Local Arrangements:	Angeline Pang (Japan-Singapore AI Centre) Bing Liu (National University of Singapore)

Programme Committee

Arbee L. Chen, National Tsing Hua University, Taiwan
David Cheung, Hong Kong University, Hong Kong
Roger Chiang, Nanyang Technological University, Singapore
Son Dao, Hughes Research Lab., USA
David Dowe, Monash University, Australia
Jiawei Han, Simon Fraser University, Canada
Se Jung Hong, T.J. Watson IBM Lab., USA
Steven H. Kim, KAIST, Korea
Masaru Kitsuregawa, Tokyo University, Japan

Organising and Supporting Bodies

PAKDD'97, The First Pacific-Asia Conference on Knowledge Discovery and Data Mining is organized by

Information Technology Institute
Department of Information Systems and Computer Science, National University of Singapore

in cooperation with

National computer Board, Singapore
Singapore Computer Society AI Chapter
Singapore Federation of the Computer Industry
Japanese Society for Artificial Intelligence
Korean Advanced Institute of Science & Technology
Korea Expert Systems Society

PAKDD'97 is sponsored and supported in kind by

Computer Power Group (Singapore) Pte Ltd
IBM Singapore Pte Ltd
Integral Solutions (Asia) Pte Ltd
Lee Foundation
NCR Corporation
Pilot Software Pte Ltd
SAS Institute (Singapore) Pte Ltd
Software AG (Singapore) Pte Ltd

Contents

Chapter 1

Clustering Techniques

KNOWLEDGE REPRESENTATION AND DISCOVERY BASED ON LINGUISTIC ATOMS

DEYI LI, JIAWEI HAN
School of Computing Sciences, Simon Fraser University
Burnaby, British Columbia Canada V5A 1S6
{dli,han}@cs.sfu.ca

EDMOND CHAN, XUEMEI SHI
Department of Computing
Hong Kong Polytechnic University, Kowloon, Hong Kong
{csmcchan,csxshi}@comp.polyu.edu.hk

An important issue in Knowledge Discovery in Databases is to allow the discovered knowledge to be as close as possible to natural languages to satisfy user needs with tractability on one hand, and to offer KDD systems robustness on the other. At this junction, this paper describes a new concept of linguistic atoms with three digital characteristics: expected value Ex, entropy En, and deviation D. The mathematical description has effectively integrated the fuzziness and randomness of linguistic terms in a unified way. Based on this model a method of knowledge representation in KDD is developed which bridges the gap between quantitative and qualitative knowledge. Mapping between quantitatives and qualitatives becomes much easier and interchangeable. In order to discover generalized knowledge from a database, we may use virtual linguistic terms and cloud transforms for the auto-generation of concept hierarchies to attributes. Predictive data mining with the cloud model is given for implementation. This further illustrates the advantages of this linguistic model in KDD.

1 Background and Motivations

Knowledge discovery in databases (KDD) is considered to be the non-trivial extraction of implicit, previously unknown, and potentially useful knowledge from large numbers of small, very specific instances [10]. The laboriousness of the development of realistic KDD applications, previously reported examples of knowledge discovery in the literature and our experience in real world knowledge discovery situations all lead us to believe that knowledge discovery is a representation-sensitive, human-oriented task consisting of friendly interactions between a human and a discovery system. Unfortunately, most existing discovery systems have been motivated more by a novel discovery technique than by representation of discovery tasks and discovered knowledge. Current work in KDD uses some form of (extended or modified) SQL as the data mining query language and some variant of predicate calculus for the discovered results. The variants frequently contain some form of quantitative modifier, such as confidence, support, threshold, and so forth [3]. This tends to lead to discovered rules such as:

With 54.1% of support and 12.7% of confidence, customers who have delayed payment of their card charges more than 32.1 days, can be characterized as people with the average age of 20.124 years old, whose balance is lower than $5,180 (Canadian).

rather than the qualitative representation:

Generally speaking, customers who have delayed payment of their card charges of about one month are relatively young people whose balance is low.

This is, however, more than a simple issue of semantics and friendliness. The former rules are not robust under change to the underlying database, while the latter ones are. In a real very large database, data are often infected with errors due to the nature of the collection. In addition, an on-line discovery system supporting a real database must keep up with changing data. It does not make much sense if a very precisely quantitative assertion is made about the behavior of an application domain based on such a database. It may be necessary, to some extent, to abandon the high standards of rigor and precision used in conventional quantitative techniques. As this moment, a piece of qualitative knowledge extracted may be more tolerant and robust. Clearly, quantitative results such as confidence and support cannot remain constant under conditions of any change. By contrast, qualitative representation will remain true until there is a substantial change in the database.

On the other hand, quantitative knowledge discovered at some lower levels of generalization in KDD may still be suitable, but the number of extracted rules increases. In contrast, as the generalization goes up to a higher level of abstraction, the discovered knowledge is more strategic. The ability to discover quantitative and yet significant knowledge about the behavior of an application domain from a very large database diminishes until a threshold may be reached beyond which precision and significance (or relevance) become almost mutually exclusive characteristics. That is to say that, if the generalization to a very large database system exceeds a limit, the reality and exactness of its description become incompatible. This has been descibed as the principle of incompatibility [13, 12]. To describe phenomena qualitatively we take linguistic variables and linguistic terms [14] and show how quantitative and qualitative inference complement and interact with each other in a simple mechanism.

In the remainder of this paper we will present a new concept of linguistic atoms and show its relationship to fuzzy logic and probability theory in sections 2–3. We will then show how the representation of discovery tasks and discovered knowledge are comprehensible and directly interpretable in natural languages and relate quantitative and qualitative concepts in an integrated fashion in section 4. We then explore applications of the model to KDD, showing, in section , virtual linguistic terms and cloud transforms are used to generate concept hierarchies for attributes, and, in section 6, cloud generators are implementeded to make prediction from the data stored in the related attributes respectively. Finally, we close with conclusions and some suggestions for future work.

2 Linguistic Atoms and Compatibility Functions

2.1 Linguistic Atoms

Our point of departure in this paper is to represent linguistic terms in logical sentences or rules. We imagine a linguistic variable that is semantically associated with a list of all the linguistic terms within a universe of discourse. For example, "age" is a linguistic variable if its values are "young," "middle age," "old," "very old," and so forth, rather than the natural numbers. In the more general cases, a linguistic variable is a quintuple:

$$\{X, T(x), U, S, C_X(u)\} \tag{1}$$

X is the name of the variable. $T(x)$ is the term-set of X; that is, the collection of its linguistic values. U is a universe of discourse. S is a syntactic generator which generates the terms in $T(x)$. $C_X(u)$ is a compatibility function. It denotes the relationship between a term x in $T(x)$ and U. More precisely, the compatibility function maps the universe of discourse into the interval $[0, 1]$ for each u in U.

It is important to understand the notion of compatibility functions. Consider a set of linguistic terms T in a universe of discourse U — for example, the linguistic term *"young"* in the interval $U = [0, 100]$. T is characterized by its compatibility function $C_X : u \rightarrow [0, 1]$. The statement that the compatibility of, say 28 years old, with *"young"* is 0.7, has a relationship both to fuzzy logic and probability.

In relation to fuzzy logic, the correct interpretation of the compatibility value "0.7" is that it is an indication of the partial membership to which the element "age-value 28" belongs to the fuzzy concept of the label *"young."* The compatibility function of the linguistic term at this time does not create a dichotomy in the universe of discourse. Rather, it maps the universe of discourse into the real-valued interval [0,1] instead of the set {0,1}. The partial membership value describes the degree to which the particular element u of the universe of discourse satisfies the property that characterizes the linguistic term.

To understand the relationship with probability on the other hand, the correct interpretation of the compatibility value"0.7," given by one's conception, is that it is merely subjective indication. Human knowledge does not conform to such a fixed crisp membership degree "0.7" at the "age-value 28." There does not exist any unique partial membership functions, which could be universally accepted by human beings to the universe of discourse U. But there is always a tendency showing that the membership degree at "age-value 28" is a stable random number, behind which a subjective probability distribution is obeyed. The degree of compatibility takes on random values itself. This type of randomness is adhered on the fuzziness.

Regarding syntactic generation, we shall usually assume that a linguistic variable is structured in the sense that it is associated with two rules. The first is the atom generator rule. It specifies the manner in which a linguistic atom, which cannot be spliced into any smaller parts, may be generated. The second, the semantic rule, specifies a procedure for computing composite linguistic terms, based on linguistic atoms.

In addition to linguistic atoms, a linguistic term may involve connectives (such as *"and," "or," "either"* and *"neither"*), the negation (*"not"*) and the hedges (such as *"very," 'more or less," "completely," "quite," "fairly," "extremely"* and *'somewhat"*). The linguistic connectives, hedges and negation may be treated as (some form of) soft operators which modify the meaning of their operands, linguistic atoms, in a soft computing fashion to become composite linguistic terms. That is the business of the semantic rule.

2.2 Compatibility Functions

Following the important characteristics of linguistic variables and terms, we define a new concept of compatibility clouds to represent linguistic terms.

Let U be the set, $U = \{u\}$, as the universe of discourse, and T a linguistic term associated with U. The membership degree of u in U to the linguistic term T, $C_T(u)$, is a random number with a stable tendency. $C_T(u)$ takes the values in [0,1]. A compatibility cloud is a mapping from the universe of discourse U to the unit interval [0,1]. That is,

$$\begin{aligned} C_T(u): \quad & U \rightarrow [0,1] \\ & \forall u \in U \;\; u \rightarrow C_T(u) \end{aligned}$$

The concept of compatibility clouds is often pictured as two-dimensional graphs with the universe of discourse represented as one dimensional. The geometry of compatibility clouds is a great aid in understanding the uncertainty and defining the cloud concept related to linguistic terms. Visualizing this geometry may by itself be the most powerful argument for fuzziness and randomness. Figure 1 shows appropriate compatibility clouds for the linguistic terms *"about 20," "teenager"* and *twenty-something"* from the term-set of the linguistic variable *"Age."*. It is important to see the properties of the clouds.

First of all, the mapping from all $u \in U$ to the interval [0,1], is a one-point to multi-point transition, producing a compatibility cloud, rather than a

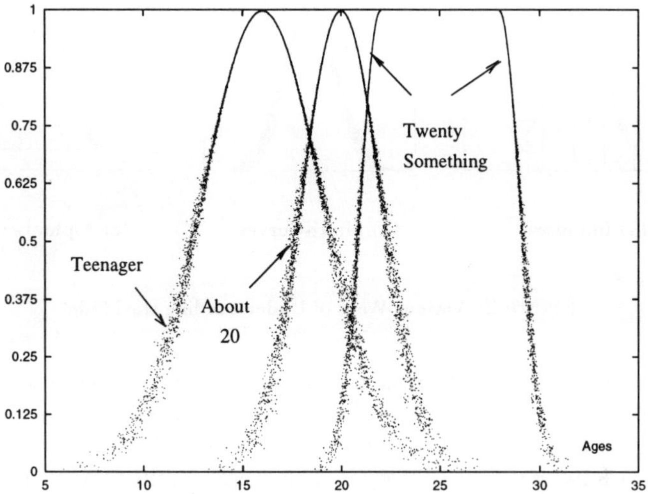

Figure 1: **Various Linguistic Terms for the Linguistic Variable *"Age"***

membership curve. Traditionally, the membership function of a fuzzy set is a one-point to one-point mapping from a space u to the unit interval [0,1]. After the mapping the uncertainty of an element belonging to the fuzzy concept becomes certain to that degree, a precise number. The uncertain characteristics of the original concept are not passed on to the next step of processing at all. This is not in keeping with the fuzzy thinking of a human being. However, with the model of compatibility clouds, soft computing may be implemented to exploit the tolerance and inheritance for uncertainty and imprecision. Secondly, any particular drop of the cloud may be paid little attention to. However, the total shape of the cloud, which is visible, elastic, boundless and movable, is most important. That is why we use the terminology "cloud" to name it. Thirdly, the mathematic expected curve (MEC) of a compatibility cloud may be considered as its membership function from the fuzzy set theory point of view. Finally, the definition has effectively integrated the fuzziness and randomness of a linguistic term in a unified way. In the cloud, fuzziness lies at the center, and there may be nothing to do with probability, but there is a probability adhered on the fuzziness from the statistical point of view. The degree of membership of u to T is a probability distribution rather than a fixed value.

There are various ways to interpret the concept of compatibility clouds. It was said that the membership function frequently takes on fuzzy values itself.

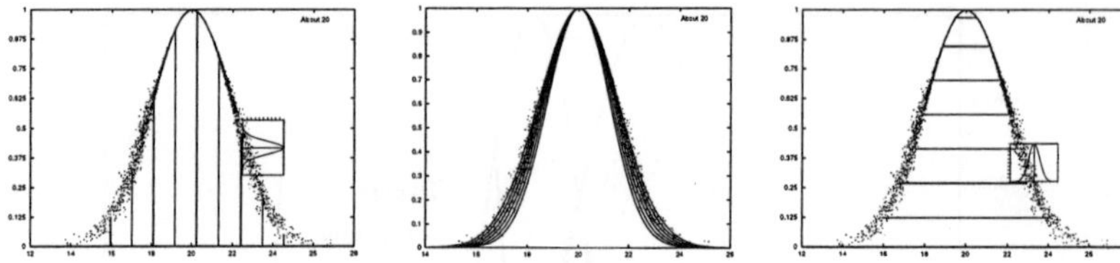

(a) Impulses (b) Multi-Curves (c) Alpha Levels

Figure 2: Various Ways of Understanding the Model

This type of fuzzy set is called the ultrafuzzy set, level 2 fuzzy set, or interval-valued fuzzy set [2, 7, 11, 4]. The cloud model combines all these ideas into a whole. Figure 2(a) illustrates the role of a compatibility cloud for a linguistic term T in a universe of discourse U. The membership degrees at each u are all random numbers showing the deviation but obeying certain probability distributions. The thickness of the cloud is uneven; near the top and bottom of the cloud, the standard errors are smaller than that in the middle. While Figure 2(b) shows a cluster of membership functions given individually and subjectively by a group of people. The deviations from one to another may appear to be random, but there is a regularity in the whole showing that at the waist part of the cluster, it scatters most, and at the top and the bottom of the cluster, it is more focused. The cluster turns into a compatibility cloud when the number of membership functions becomes infinite. Figure 2(c) illustrates the understanding of the compatibility cloud in a new way. If we use the family of its α-level sets to present the members of the linguistic term at the membership degree α respectively. The left and right limits of one of the α-level sets give the position of the linguistic term at the degree of α, and the width of the α-level set is related to the coverage of the linguistic term in the universe of discourse. But the width itself becomes random showing the deviation which obeys a certain probability distribution.

Of course, there may be some other ways to see the model. Whichever way the cloud is viewed, we can see the integrated uncertainty of fuzziness and randomness and the convergent properties of the cloud model.

The concept of linguistic variables provides a means of approximate characterization of linguistic concepts, which are too complex, rich, or soft (with tolerance) to be amenable to description in precise quantitative terms, but which may be more naturally and easily comprehensible by a human being. It offers a more elastic framework for constructing composite linguistic terms based on linguistic atoms. Soft computation with linguistic terms requires the solution of qualitative reasoning and should lead to results which are able to simulate human thinking in a qualitative way [15]. Therefore, the representation of linguistic atoms becomes an essential and fundamental issue in knowledge discovery. If we are able to develop soft computations of linguistic terms, soft computing may be considered as a qualitative generalization and specification, which could be of use in a wide variety of practical applications in KDD.

3 Modeling on Compatibility Clouds

A wide variety of linguistic terms put obstacles in the way of unifying the representation of qualitative knowledge. However, a complicated or composite linguistic concept may be considered as some kind of soft computation based on the primary or atomic terms which cover qualitative characteristics in common sense, such as fuzziness and randomness. For example, "young" and "old", are served as linguistic atoms in the composite linguistic term "not very young and not very old". And the hedges, such as"very," "quite" and "extremely," as well as the connectives, "and" and "or," are treated as soft operators which modify the meaning of operands in a specified fashion. Therefore, it is worthwhile to first set up a linguistic model for those linguistic atoms. The concept of compatibility clouds provides a means of both qualitative and quantitative characterization of linguistic atoms.

3.1 Digital Characteristics

The bell shape of compatibility clouds called normal compatibility clouds are based on normal distributions, which have been supported by results in every branch of both social sciences (such as psychology, industry, commerce, and linguistics) and natural sciences. The normal compatibility clouds with the most popularity are most useful in representing linguistic atoms. A normal compatibility cloud characterizes the qualitative meaning of a linguistic atom with three digital characteristics:

$$A(Ex, En, D) \tag{2}$$

where Ex, En, and D are the expected value, entropy and deviation of the cloud respectively. A given set $\{Ex, En, D\}$ uniquely defines a particular compatibility cloud A.

The expected value Ex of a compatibility cloud is the position at U corresponding to the center of gravity of the cloud. In other words, the element Ex in the universe of discourse is fully compatible with the linguistic atom A. It is very easy to determine Ex in practical applications.

The entropy En of a linguistic atom is a measure of the fuzziness of the concept within the universe of discourse. The entropy of a linguistic atom

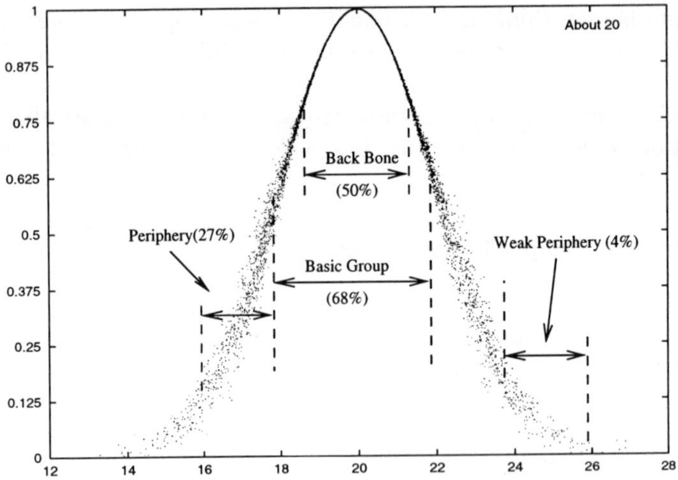

Figure 3: Contributions of Different Groups

is defined by the bandwidth of the mathematical expected curve (MEC) of the normal compatibility cloud showing how many elements in the universe of discourse could be accepted to the linguistic atom. The MEC of the normal compatibility cloud to a linguistic atom A is:

$$MEC_A(u) = e^{-\frac{(u-Ex)^2}{2En^2}} \tag{3}$$

The deviation D is a measure of the randomness of compatibility function. Looking at the normal compatibility cloud in detail we see that its thickness is uneven. Close to the waist, corresponding to the center of gravity $(Ex, \frac{\sqrt{2}}{4})$, the degree of compatibility is most dispersed, while at the top and bottom the focusing is much better. Therefore, the maximum deviation D really comes from the randomness of the compatibility degree at the waist part of the cloud.

It should be noticed that the top, bottom, and waist of a cloud, however, do not need to be precisely defined at all. The three digital characteristics are good enough to represent a bell-shaped cloud.

3.2 Contribution Measurements

Let δ_{contr} be the contributions of a small group δ_g of elements u in the universe of discourse of a linguistic atom A:

$$\delta_{contr} = C_A(u)\frac{\delta_g}{\sqrt{2\pi}En} \tag{4}$$

then the total contributions $CONTR$ of all u in the universe of discourse are:

$$CONTR_A = \frac{\int_{-\infty}^{\infty} C_A(u)du}{\sqrt{2\pi}En} = 1 \tag{5}$$

It is easy to calculate the contributions of any group to a linguistic atom A, as shown in figure 3. If there is a need to randomly pick up some elements from the universe of discourse to represent a linguistic atom, those elements closed to the expected value Ex will have priority as they make the greatest contribution to the linguistic term. The probability distribution of an average of such independent measurements is approximately normal, and the approximation can be made as closely as desired by increasing the size of the population. That is why we can take the Gaussian probability distribution in calculating the contributions of a group to a common sense concept. Let P be the priority of an element u in the universe of discourse U. The priority of u to represent the linguistic atom is equivalent to the Gaussian probability density distribution with the random variable of U:

$$Priority(u) = Probability(u) = \frac{1}{\sqrt{2\pi}En} e^{-\frac{(u-Ex)^2}{2En^2}} \tag{6}$$

A critical factor is that the important link between probability distributions and compatibility functions related to common sense concepts has been set up in this way. The universal applicability of linguistic atoms remarkably relieves the heavy burden in many areas of research and applications related to commonsense knowledge representation. The consistence profiles fills the gap between quantitative and qualitative knowledge well.

3.3 Half Clouds and Trapezoidal Clouds

It should be noted that, though the bell shape of clouds, is most useful in representing linguistic atoms, the cloud model does not restrict to the only full bell shape. When the expected value reaches the left or the right boundary of the universe of discourse, the bell shape of the cloud becomes a half-down or half-up bell cloud. But it may still be characterized by the three parameters: Ex, En, and D. For example, the linguistic atom "close to 100%" just takes the shape of half-up bell with Ex=100%, and certain values of En and D, as his representation; while "very close to 100%" may be represented by modification of the representation of "close to 100%", such as the same Ex, little changes of En and D. The representation of half-bell-shape clouds does make sense to some linguistic atoms where available. However, if there is a need to represent the compatibility function of a linguistic term in a fuzzy trapezoidal shape, we may think it consists of a half-up and a half-down clouds plus the middle part with the membership degree of 1, such as was shown for the case of

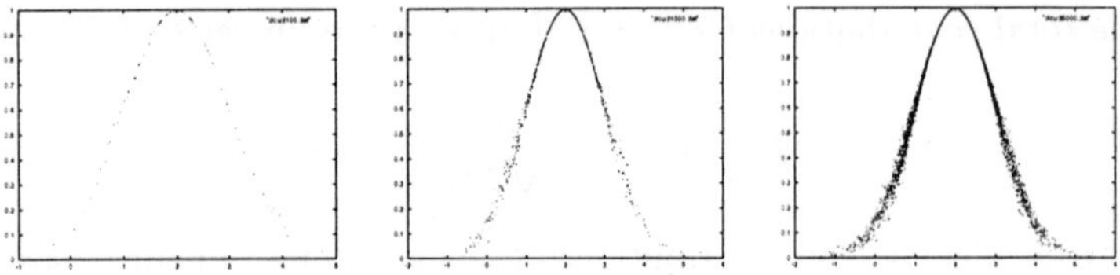

(a) 100 Drops (b) 1000 Drops (c) 5000 Drops

Figure 4: Clouds with Various Drops

"twenty-something" in figure 1. Along the same line, asymmetrical clouds are all considered, such as positive and negative skewed shape clouds which can be represented by the Gamma compatibility functions. Nevertheless, the bell-shaped cloud model is the basic one to compose others.

4 Qualitative Representation Based on Atom Models

Mapping between quantities and qualitatives becomes much easier and interchangeable based on the model of linguistic atoms. A series of linguistic atom generators have been implemented both in hardware and software.

4.1 Linguistic Atom Generators

Given three digital characteristics Ex, En, and D, to represent a linguistic atom *"about 2"* the generator could produce as many drops of the cloud as you like. All the drops obey the properties described above. Figure 4 shows the total shapes with 100, 1000, and 5000 drops generated respectively with the same parameters Ex = 2.0, En =1.0 and D = 0.04.

Cloud-drops may be generated on conditions. Figure 5(a) shows the generator producing drops under a given numerical value u in the universe of discourse, U; while figure 5(b) shows the generator under the condition of a given membership degree μ. All the drops generated in Fig 5(a) have the same value of u in the universe of discourse, and Gaussian distributed membership degrees μ_i; whereas all the drops generated in Fig5(b) have the same membership degree μ, and Gaussian distributed numerical values u_i in the universe of discourse.

It is natural to think about the generator mechanism in an inverse way. Given a limited set of drops, $drop_i$(u,C_x), as samples of a compatibility cloud, the three digital characteristics Ex, En, and D could be produced to represent the corresponding linguistic atom (see Figure 6). The two kinds of atom gener-

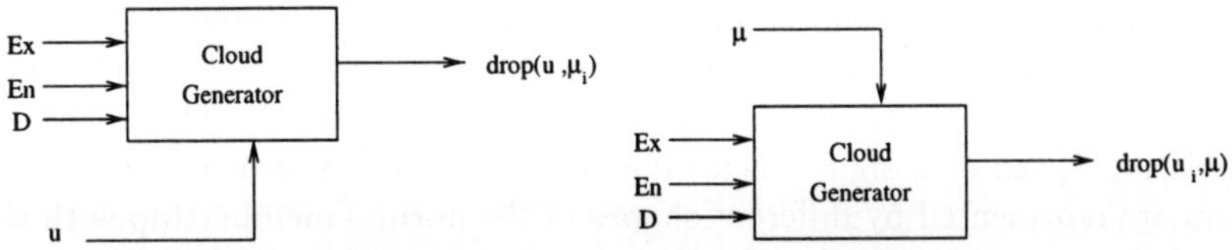

(a) On the condition of "u" (b) On the condition of "μ"

Figure 5: Generators on Conditions

ators may be called forward and backward generators respectively. The atom generators implemented in both hardware and software have been a patented invention in China[8, 9]. The combination of the two kinds of generators can be used interchangeably to bridge the gap between quantitative and qualitative knowledge.

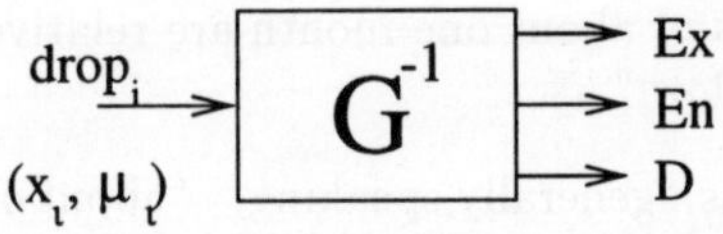

Figure 6: A Backward Cloud Generator

4.2 Linguistic Quantifiers

There are originally in first order logic two quantifiers: the universal quantifier $\forall$ and the existential quantifier $\exists$. In addition to these quantifiers, there is also a numerical quantifier that expresses quantitative information about the objects satisfying an expression. With a statistical approach we could use [0%, 100%] to cover all the cases. However, the concept of linguistic quantifiers enters into qualitative representation by treating "quantifier" as a linguistic variable with a finite or infinite term-set such as shown below:

T(quantifier) = {rarely, occasionally, generally speaking, frequently ...,}

For certain application domains we may define some synonymous atoms. For example, the term "basically" will be assumed to be more or less synonymous with "generally speaking" and "unlikely" with "rarely" and so on.

The linguistic atom model provides a basis for defining linguistic quantifiers. To simplify our exposition we shall assume that all atomic linguistic quantifiers are related to the universe of discourse [0%,100%]. Thus, any point in [0%,100%] can be assigned as a value to U. Different atomic linguistic quantifiers are represented by different shapes of the normal membership with their digital characteristics: A(Ex, En, D).

It should be observed that, when the cloud is floating from left to right over the universe of discourse, some part of the cloud may be cut beyond the region [0%, 100%], and the three parameters may also change from time to time, depending on which particular linguistic quantifier represented. With this understanding, we may even extend the representation to any atomic linguistic quantifier by creating a new linguistic label which will match the shape of the cloud.

It becomes a nontrivial improvement when the quantifiers in data mining tasks and in the description of discovered knowledge are linguistic in nature. For example, when a piece of discovered knowledge states:

> it "Generally speaking, customers who have delayed payment of their card charges of about one month are relatively young people whose balance is low."

The qualitative concepts "generally speaking," "about one month," "relatively young" and "balance is low" may be well matched with quantitative notions of support, confidence, day, age, and balance.

5 Auto-Generation of Concept Hierarchies in Attributes

To discover general knowledge from very large databases we must fuse data into high level concepts (for example, see [5, 1]). The concept hierarchy in an attribute is a useful mechanism for achieving this purpose. The discovered concept, or abstraction, usually implies a certain context, thus providing more general information than the raw data in that attribute. However, any concept hierarchy acts as a filter, and if that filter is not suitable for the data (which is particularly likely if it is static), the generalization will be skewed. For this reason we need a data distribution-dependent, auto-generated, flexible concept hierarchy to an attribute. While some work has been done in this area (*eg.* [6]), it is limited to numeric attributes. The refinement component is also limited, and does not always allow the appropriate merging or splitting of concepts. The larger goal will require the modification of generalization algorithms to take into account the flexibility of the hierarchy, and also the ability to provide an arbitrary partial order, rather than simply a tree. Our purpose at present, however, is simply to show how we may automatically generate a concept hierarchy. To achieve this purpose we interpret attributes

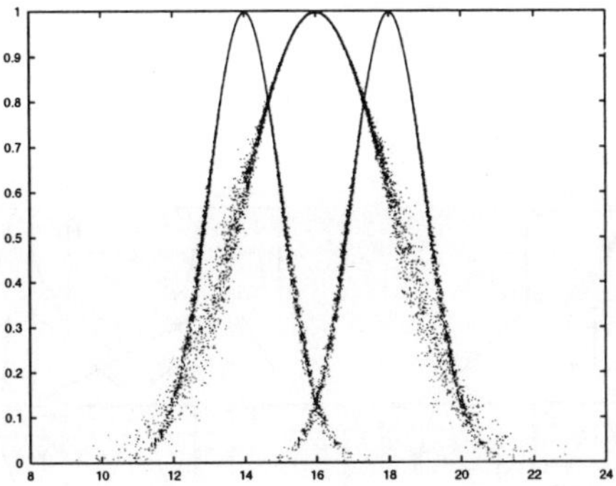

Figure 7: Generalizing *"about 14"* and *"about 18"* to *"teenager"*

to be generalized as linguistic variables and attribute values as linguistic terms. The universe of discourse is the domain of the attribute.

Suppose we have two linguistic atoms, $A_1(Ex_1, En_1, D_1)$ and $A_2(Ex_2, En_2, D_2)$, over the same universe of discourse U. A ***virtual linguistic atom***, $A_3(Ex_3, En_3, D_3)$, may be created by synthesizing the two using the following definition:

$$\begin{aligned} Ex_3 &= \frac{Ex_1 \times En_1 + Ex_2 \times En_2}{En_1 + En_2} \\ En_3 &= En_1 + En_2 \\ D_3 &= \frac{D_1 \times En_1 + D_2 \times En_2}{En_1 + En_2} \end{aligned} \tag{7}$$

From a geometrical point of view, this definition satisfies the property that the torques of A_3 (which are the products of the center of gravity of A_3 and the perpendicular distances to the horizontal and vertical axes respectively) is equal to the sum of torques of A_1 and A_2. The linguistic atom A_3 can be considered as the generalization of A_1 and A_2. To make this concrete, figure 7 shows how the concepts *"about 14"* and *"about 18"* may be generalized to that of *"teenager"*. This definition can be conveniently extended to the synthesis of many linguistic atoms. The price paid is that the entropy of the generalized linguistic atom increases, which reflects the more general information coverage.

It is a short step to move from a virtual linguistic atom to a concept hierarchy. Consider an attribute to be generalized with a frequency distribution $f(u)$ over a domain of discourse U. We define the cloud transform (CT) for this distribution as:

$$f(u) = \sum_{i=0}^{\infty} \alpha_i A_i(Ex_i, En_i, D_i) \tag{8}$$

The essential meaning of the CT is that by using enough linguistic atoms we can (approximately) represent the frequency distribution of the values in

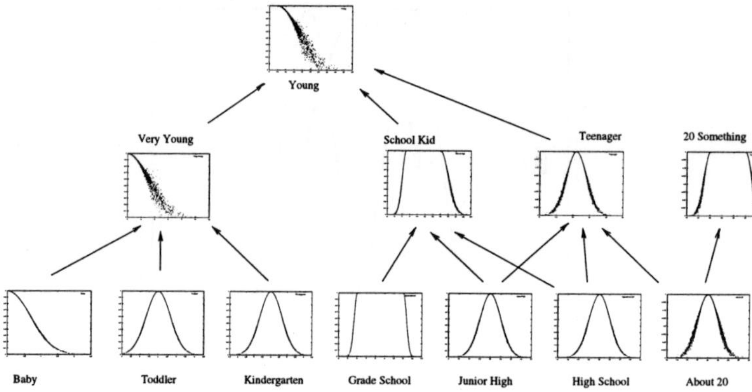

Figure 8: A Hierarchy for the linguistic variable "age"

that attribute. That is to say, we can think of any frequency distribution as consisting of the weighted sum of linguistic atoms $A_i(Ex_i, En_i, D_i)$.

Using the concept of the virtual linguistic terms, we generalize the CT to reduce the number of linguistic atoms. This effectively allows us to move to a higher level in the concept hierarchy by synthesizing the closest atoms to new terms over the universe of discourse. Thus

$$\begin{aligned} f(u) &\simeq \textstyle\sum_{i=0}^{N_1} \alpha_i A_i(Ex_i, En_i, D_i) \\ &\simeq \textstyle\sum_{i=0}^{N_2} \beta_i B_i(Ex_i, En_i, D_i) \\ &\simeq \textstyle\sum_{i=0}^{N_3} \gamma_i C_i(Ex_i, En_i, D_i) \\ &\simeq \ldots \end{aligned} \tag{9}$$

where $N_1 > N_2 > N_3 \ldots$. The attribute is generalized to $A_i(Ex_i, En_i, D_i)$ which is generalized to $B_i(Ex_i, En_i, D_i)$ which is generalized to $C_i(Ex_i, En_i, D_i)$ and so forth. We use the (fuzzy) notions of "overlapping" and "closeness" to pick appropriate virtual linguistic atoms to merge when generating the concept hierarchy. Preliminary implementation work has been very encouraging. For example, we are able to move from histogramming given age data through to notions such as "about 20" at a lower level to "twenty-something" to "young" at higher levels. A sample concept hierarchy is shown in figure 8. The reader should note that the labels attached are *not* generated by the auto-generation method, but are produced by the syntactic generator of the linguistic variable as described in section 2. The hierarchy generated is orthogonal to the labels placed on the nodes, which are for human convenience, not for the discovery system.

We may also make the CT in a top-down way to get a conceptual hierarchy, if the CT is done in the order of $N_1 < N_2 < N_3 \ldots$. That is to split linguistic atoms from generalization to specification. The auto-generation of concept hierarchies allows the coverage of a broad spectrum of concept granularity spreading from that of a very qualitative concept down to that of the numerical character with the lowest granularity possible. The concept cloud transform offers a smooth and seamless transition between different level of the concept hierarchy.

6 Predictive Data Mining with the Cloud Model

In predictive data mining, a predictive task would be to predict an unknown value in the predicted attribute based on the given data in the relevant attribute(s). Since we here focus on the application of the cloud model to prediction, only one relevant attribute is considered for simplicity. Suppose we are going to predict the salary for a person, whose working background (working years) is given.

Followed by the above section, the concept hierarchies in the predicted attribute, Salary, and the relevant attribute, WorkingYear, could be automatically generated by cloud transforms respectively, based on the given data in the two attributes.

We roll-up the generalization to discover the correlation rule between the relevant attribute and the predicted attribute. such as "If A then B," where A and B are linguistic concepts represented by the cloud model. We then use two forward cloud generators to construct the correlation rule since the digital characteristics of the linguistic concepts A and B in that correlation rule are discovered (see Figure 9). When an input value, x_i, representing the predictive condition (working years of the person in this example) which belongs to the concept A enters, the compatibility degree, μ_i, produced by the generator CG_A, represents the activated strength of the rule which controls the generator CG_B to produce a set of drops y_i quantitatively. A significant advantage over the conventional prediction in data mining is that there is inherent uncertainty in the case of chaining rules. The uncertain characteristics have passed on to the next step for further processing, since y_i is an uncertain value rather than a fixed one to the given input x_i. The output uncertainty in responding to the same input value is a feature which actually happens with predictions given by domain experts.

Generally speaking, there are a set of correlation rules discovered. These correlation rules very often put the focus on the nonlinear characteristics to a specific database. Therefore, all the activated rules will make contributions to the given predictive condition if more than one rule is fired by an input value while making the prediction. These facts shed a new light on our uncertainty reasoning strategy done by cloud generators. We could have an implementation

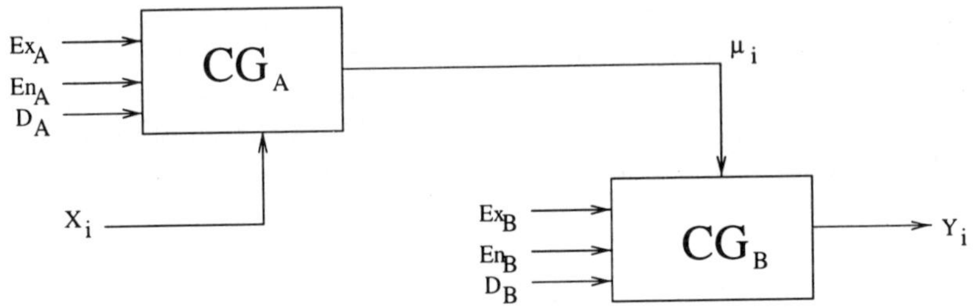

Figure 9: A Fuzzy Rule Implemented in Hardware

by using a self learning backward cloud generator, MCG_B^{-1}, to take such a job if there are N correlation rules related to the predictive condition (see Figure 10) The linguistic terms used in the predictive condition description will decide how high the rolling-up generalization goes to.

7 Conclusion

Knowledge representation for discovery tasks and discovered knowledge is one of fundamental issues in KDD theory. While mainstream research concentrates on data mining methods and algorithms, an alternative aspect of KDD is adopted in this paper. Qualitative modeling and analysis has been developed into a research area concerned with discovering qualitatively about the behavior of database systems. A new linguistic model based on a characterization of both the structure of linguistic concepts and the uncertainty distribution of examples in knowledge acquisition is presented by using the concept of compatibility clouds, integrating randomness and fuzziness with three digital characteristics Ex, En, and D. A systematic approach has been developed to capture the qualitative knowledge contained in a quantitative way. The fundamental achievements of the linguistic cloud theory are:

1. The introduction of linguistic variables and terms into a qualitative knowledge representation is presented to explain how human communication with linguistic words in everyday life when such labels are used instead of numerical values.

2. A well defined mathematical representation of linguistic atoms with only three digital parameters for uncertainty modeling is given to explore the essential uncertainty with both fuzziness and randomness.

3. The atom generators implemented in both hardware and software have been a patented invention in China. By using the combination of for-

ward and backward generators, the mapping between quantitatives and qualitatives becomes much easier and interchangeable.

4. The idea of virtual linguistic terms and cloud transforms given in this paper plays an important role in the auto-generation of concept hierarchies, when an attribute is considered as a linguistic variable, while attribute values as linguistic terms. We think that the auto-generation of concept hierarchies is one of foundations of the discovery mechanism in KDD.

5. The use of cloud models and cloud transforms for predictive data mining is given based on discovering correlation rules. The predictive process is performed with the combination of forward and backward linguistic generators.

However, to develop sound foundations of knowledge representation and discovery mechanism in KDD systems will require a lot of work. Various forms of domain-specific linguistic patterns have been used for interpretation of concepts in KDD. The model of linguistic atom could be extended to more complicated linguistic patterns, such as multi-dimensional one.

Another possible direction for future work is soft computing based on the atom model. Hopefully, this paper will lead to comparative studies, something that has been lacking in previous reports.

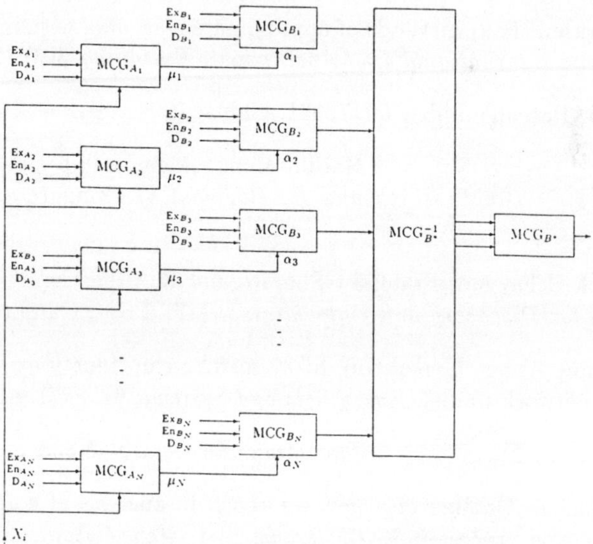

Figure 10: Prediction with Linguistic Generators

References

[1] Yandong Cai, Nick Cerone, and Jaiwei Han. An attribute-oriented approach for learning classification rules from relational databases. In *IEEE Intl. Conf. on Data Engineering*, pages 281–288, 1990.

[2] D.Dubois and H.Prade. Fuzzy sets, probability and measurement. *European J. of Operational Research*, 40:135–154, 1989.

[3] Usama M. Fayyad and R. Uthurusamy. *The Proceedings of the 1st International Conference on Knowledge Discovery and Data Mining.* AAAI Press, Montreal, 1995.

[4] G.J.Klir and Bo Yuan. *Fuzzy Sets and Fuzzy Logic: Theory and Application.* CRC Press, New York, 1995.

[5] Jaiwei Han, Yandong Cai, and Nick Cerone. Data-driven discovery of quantative rules in relational databases. *IEEE Trans. on Knowledge and Data Engineering*, 5(1):29–40, 1993.

[6] Jaiwei Han and Yongjian Fu. Dynamic generation and refinement of concept hierarchies for knowledge discovery in databases. In *AAAI'94 Workshop on Knowledge Discovery in Databases*, pages 157–168, 1994.

[7] J.B.Turksen. Four methods of approximate reasoning with interval-valued fuzzy sets. *International J. of Approximate Reasoning*, 3(2):121–142, 1989.

[8] Deyi Li. Patent number 69272031. China, 1994.

[9] Deyi Li, Xuemei Shi, and Haijun Meng. Membership clouds and cloud generators. *The Research and Development of Computers*, 42(8):32–41, 1995.

[10] P.Smyth U.Fayyad, Piatetsky-Shapiro and R. Uthurusamy. *Advances in Knowledge Discovery and Data Mining.* MIT Press, Cambrige, 1996.

[11] Shouhong Wang. Generating fuzzy membership functions: A monotonic neural network model. *Fuzzy Sets and Systems*, 61(1):71–81, 1994.

[12] L.A. Zadeh. Fuzzy sets. *Information and Control*, 8:338–353, 1965.

[13] L.A. Zadeh. Outline of a new approach to analysis of complex systems and decision processes. *IEEE Trans. Syst. Man. Cybern.*, 3:28–44, 1973.

[14] L.A. Zadeh. The concept of linguistic variable and its application to approximate reasoning. *Information Science*, 8:199–249, 1975.

CLUSTERING LARGE DATA SETS WITH MIXED NUMERIC AND CATEGORICAL VALUES*

ZHEXUE HUANG
CSIRO Mathematical and Information Sciences
GPO Box 664 Canberra ACT 2601, AUSTRALIA
zhexue.huang@cmis.csiro.au

Efficient partitioning of large data sets into homogenous clusters is a fundamental problem in data mining. The standard hierarchical clustering methods provide no solution for this problem due to their computational inefficiency. The *k-means* based methods are promising for their efficiency in processing large data sets. However, their use is often limited to numeric data. In this paper we present a *k-prototypes* algorithm which is based on the *k-means* paradigm but removes the numeric data limitation whilst preserving its efficiency. In the algorithm, objects are clustered against k prototypes. A method is developed to dynamically update the k prototypes in order to maximise the intra cluster similarity of objects. When applied to numeric data the algorithm is identical to the *k-means*. To assist interpretation of clusters we use decision tree induction algorithms to create rules for clusters. These rules, together with other statistics about clusters, can assist data miners to understand and identify interesting clusters.

1 Introduction

Many data mining applications require partitioning of data into homogeneous clusters from which interesting groups may be discovered, such as a group of motor insurance policy holders with a high average claim cost, or a group of clients in a banking database showing a heavy investment in real estate. To perform such analyses at least the following two problems have to be solved; (1) efficient partitioning of a large data set into homogeneous groups or clusters, and (2) effective interpretation of clusters. This paper proposes a solution to the first problem and suggests a solution to the second.

A number of data partitioning methods can be employed for the first problem. When little is known about the distribution of data, clustering methods are often used. However, data mining, distinct from other traditional applications of cluster analysis[1,5], deals with large high dimensional data (thousands or millions of records with tens or hundreds of attributes). This characteristic prohibits many existing clustering algorithms from being used in data mining applications. Another characteristic is that data in data mining often contains both numeric and categorical values. The traditional way to treat categorical attributes as numeric does not always produce meaningful results because many categorical domains are not ordered.

*This Work was supported by the Cooperative Research Centre for Advanced Computational Systems (ACSys) established under the Australian Government's Cooperative Research Centres Program.

Although the standard hierarchical clustering methods can handle data with numeric and categorical values[5,8], the quadratic computational cost makes them unacceptable for clustering large data sets. The *k-means* based methods[12] are efficient for processing large data sets, thus very attractive for data mining. The major handicap for them is that they are often limited to numeric data. The reason is that these algorithms optimise a cost function defined on the Euclidean distance measure between data points and means of clusters[5]. Minimising the cost function by calculating means limits their use to numeric data.

Conceptual clustering algorithms developed in machine learning cluster data with categorical values[6,11,13] and also produce conceptual descriptions of clusters. The latter feature is important to data mining because the conceptual descriptions provide assistance in interpreting clustering results. Unlike statistical clustering methods, these algorithms are based on a search for objects which carry the same or similar concepts. Therefore, their efficiency relies on good search strategies. For problems in data mining, which often involve many concepts and very large object spaces, the concepts based search methods can become a potential handicap for these algorithms to deal with extremely large data sets.

In this paper we present a clustering algorithm to solve data partition problems in data mining. The algorithm is based on the *k-means* paradigm but removes the numeric data only limitation whilst preserving its efficiency. The algorithm clusters objects with numeric and categorical attributes in a way similar to *k-means*. Because objects are clustered against *k prototypes* instead of *k means* of clusters, we call it the *k-prototypes* algorithm. We have developed a method to dynamically update the *k* prototypes in order to maximise the intra cluster similarity of objects. The object similarity measure is derived from both numeric and categorical attributes. When applied to numeric data the algorithm is identical to *k-means*. In testing with real data, this algorithm has demonstrated a capability of partitioning data sets in the range of a hundred thousand records, described by some 20 numeric and categorical attributes, into a hundred clusters in a couple of hours on a SUN Sparc10 workstation.

We also consider conceptual descriptions of clusters. However, in dealing with large data sets we take a different approach. After clustering has been carried out, we fit the classified data into a decision tree induction algorithm[3,15] to create rules for cluster descriptions. These rules, together with some other statistics about clusters, can assist data miners to understand and identify interesting clusters.

The rest of the paper is organised as follows. The next section gives some mathematical preliminaries of the algorithm. In Section 3 we discuss the *k-prototypes* algorithm. In Section 4 we present some simulation results to show how numeric and categorical attributes interact in the process of clustering by the algorithm. We also present some initial performance test results on a large real world data set. In Section 5 we summarise the discussions and point out some directions for our future work.

2 Mathematical Preliminaries

Let $\boldsymbol{X} = \{X_1, X_2, \ldots, X_n\}$ denote a set of n objects and $X_i = [x_{i1}, x_{i2}, \ldots, x_{im}]$ be an object represented by m attribute values. Let k be a positive integer. The objective of clustering $\boldsymbol{X}$ is to find a partition which divides objects in $\boldsymbol{X}$ into k disjoint clusters.

For a given n, the number of possible partitions is definite but extremely large[1]. It is impractical to investigate every partition in order to find a better one for a classification problem. A common solution is to choose a clustering criterion[1,5] to guide the search for a partition. A clustering criterion is called a *cost function* below.

2.1 Cost Function

The widely used cost function is the trace of the within cluster dispersion matrix[5]. One way to define this cost function is

$$E = \sum_{l=1}^{k} \sum_{i=1}^{n} y_{il} d(X_i, Q_l) \tag{2.1}$$

Here, $Q_l = [q_{l1}, q_{l2}, \ldots, q_{lm}]$ is the *representative vector* or *prototype* for cluster l, and y_{il} is an element of a *partition* matrix $Y_{n\text{x}l}$ [9]. d is a similarity measure often defined as the square Euclidean distance.

Y has the following two properties, (1) $0 \le y_{il} \le 1$ and (2) $\sum_{l=1}^{k} y_{il} = 1$. Y is called a *hard partition* if $y_{il} \in \{0,1\}$. Otherwise, it is a *fuzzy partition*[2]. In a hard partition, $y_{il} = 1$ indicates that object X_i is assigned to cluster l by Y. We only consider hard partitions in this paper.

The inner term $E_l = \sum_{i=1}^{n} y_{il} d(X_i, Q_l)$ in Eq. (2.1) is the total cost of assigning $\boldsymbol{X}$ to cluster l, i.e., the total dispersion of objects in cluster l from its prototype Q_l. E_l is minimised if

$$q_{lj} = \frac{1}{n_l} \sum_{i=1}^{n} y_{il} x_{ij} \qquad \text{for } j=1,\ldots,m \tag{2.2}$$

where $n_l = \sum_{i=1}^{n} y_{il}$ is the number of objects in cluster l.

When $\boldsymbol{X}$ has categorical attributes, we can introduce a similarity measure as

$$d(X_i, Q_l) = \sum_{j=1}^{m_r} (x_{ij}^r - q_{lj}^r)^2 + \gamma_l \sum_{j=1}^{m_c} \delta(x_{ij}^c, q_{lj}^c) \tag{2.3}$$

where $\delta(p,q)=0$ for $p=q$ and $\delta(p,q)=1$ for $p \neq q$. x_{ij}^r and q_{lj}^r are values of numeric attributes, whereas x_{ij}^c and q_{lj}^c are values of categorical attributes for object i and the prototype of cluster l. m_r and m_c are the numbers of numeric and categorical attributes. γ_l is a weight for categorical attributes for cluster l.

We can rewrite E_l as

$$\begin{aligned} E_l &= \sum_{i=1}^{n} y_{il} \sum_{j=1}^{m_r} (x_{ij}^r - q_{lj}^r)^2 + \gamma_l \sum_{i=1}^{n} y_{il} \sum_{j=1}^{m_c} \delta(x_{ij}^c, q_{lj}^c) \\ &= E_l^r + E_l^c \end{aligned} \tag{2.4}$$

where E_l^r is the total cost on all numeric attributes of objects in cluster l. E_l^r is minimised if q_{lj}^r is calculated by Eq. (2.2).

Let C_j be the set containing all unique values in the categorical attribute j and $p(c_j \in C_j | l)$ the probability of value c_j occurring in cluster l. E_l^c in Eq. (2.4) can be rewritten as

$$E_l^c = \gamma_l \sum_{j=1}^{m_c} n_l (1 - p(q_{lj}^c \in C_j | l)) \tag{2.5}$$

where n_l is the number of objects in cluster l. The solution to minimise E_l^c is given by the lemma below.

Lemma 1: For a specific cluster l, E_l^c is minimised if and only if $p(q_{lj}^c \in C_j | l) \geq p(c_j \in C_j | l)$ for $q_{lj}^c \neq c_j$ for all categorical attributes.

Finally, we can rewrite E as

$$E = \sum_{l=1}^{k} (E_l^r + E_l^c) = \sum_{l=1}^{k} E_l^r + \sum_{l=1}^{k} E_l^c = E^r + E^c \tag{2.6}$$

Eq. (2.6) is the cost function for clustering a data set with numeric and categorical values. Since both E^r and E^c are non-negative, minimisation of E can be achieved by minimising E^r and E^c, the total costs on numeric and categorical attributes over all clusters. E^r can be minimised by calculating the numeric elements of the k cluster prototypes by Eq. (2.2), whereas E^c can be minimised by selecting the categorical elements of the k cluster prototypes according to Lemma 1. Therefore, Eq. (2.2) and Lemma 1 define a way to choose cluster prototypes to minimise the cost function Eq. (2.6). This is the basis for the *k-prototypes* algorithm to be discussed in Section 3.

2.2 *Similarity Measure*

The cost function Eq. (2.6) is defined on Eq. (2.3), which is a combined similarity measure on both numeric and categorical attributes between objects and cluster prototypes. The similarity measure on numeric attributes is the square Euclidean distance whereas the similarity measure on categorical attributes is the number of mismatches between objects and cluster prototypes. Weight γ_l is introduced to avoid favouring either type of attribute.

The influence of weight γ_l in clustering can be illustrated by Figure 1. Assume the triangles and diamonds represent a set of objects described by a categorical and two numeric attributes. Triangle and diamond represent two values of the categorical attribute whereas numeric attribute values are reflected by locations of the objects. These objects are partitioned into two clusters.

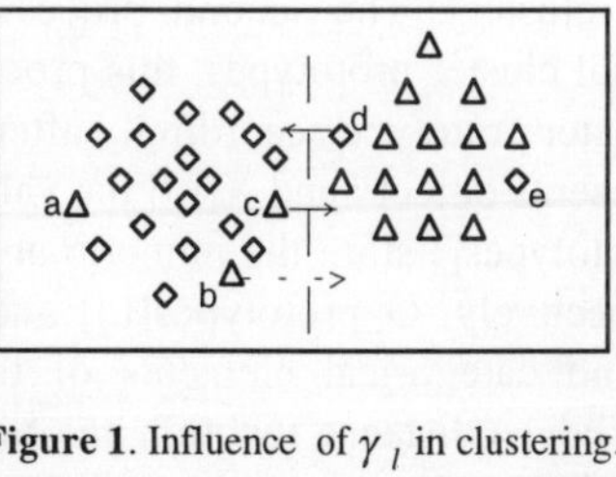

Figure 1. Influence of γ_l in clustering.

If γ_l =0, clustering only depends on numeric attributes, i.e., locations of the objects. The result will be the two clusters separated by the vertical dashed line. If γ_l > 0, then object c may change to the right cluster because it is close to that cluster and its categorical value is the same as that of the majority of objects in that cluster. Similarly, object d may change to the left cluster. However, object a may still stay in the left cluster because it is too far to the right, even though it has a categorical value as same as that of the majority objects in that cluster. Similarly, object e may still be in the right cluster. Object b becomes uncertain, depending on whether γ_l is biased towards numeric or categorical attributes. If γ_l is biased to the categorical attribute, object b may change to the right cluster. Otherwise, it can stay in the left one.

The choice of γ_l is dependent on distributions of numeric attributes. Generally speaking, γ_l is related to σ_l, the average standard deviation of numeric attributes in cluster l. In practice, σ_l can be used as a guidance to determine γ_l. However, since σ_l is unknown before clustering, the overall average standard deviation σ of numeric attributes can be used for all σ_l. In an iterative algorithm, σ_l can be calculated from a preceding clustering result. In Section 4.2 we will present some simulations on γ_l.

3 *k-prototypes* Algorithm

The *k-prototypes* algorithm can be described as follows. (1) Select k initial prototypes from a data set $\boldsymbol{X}$, one for each cluster. (2) Allocate each object in $\boldsymbol{X}$ to a cluster whose prototype is the nearest to it according to Eq. (2.3). Update the prototype of the cluster after each allocation. (3) After all objects have been allocated to a cluster, retest the similarity of objects against the current prototypes. If an object is found such that its nearest prototype belongs to another cluster rather than its current one, reallocate the object to that cluster and update the prototypes of both clusters. (4) Repeat (3) until no object has changed clusters after a full cycle test of $\boldsymbol{X}$.

The algorithm is built upon three processes, *initial prototypes selection*, *initial allocation,* and *re-allocation*. The first process simply randomly selects k objects as the initial prototypes for clusters. The second process is presented in Figure 2. Starting from a set of initial cluster prototypes, this process assigns each object to a cluster and updates the cluster prototype accordingly after each assignment.

In Figure 2, X[i] represents object i and X[i,j] the value of attribute j for object i. O_prototypes[] and C_prototypes[] store the numeric and categorical attribute parts of cluster prototypes respectively. O_prototypes[i,j] and C_prototypes[i,j] are two corresponding numeric and categorical elements of the prototype for cluster i. **Distance**() is a square Euclidean distance function and **Sigma**() is an implementation of function $\delta()$ in Eq. (2.3). Clustership[] and ClusterCount[] record cluster membership of objects and numbers of objects in clusters. SumInCluster[] sums up numeric values of objects in clusters and is used to update numeric attributes of cluster prototypes. FrequencyInCluster[] records frequencies of different values of categorical attributes in clusters. The function **HighestFreq**() is an implementation of Lemma 1 to update categorical attributes of prototypes.

The reallocation process given in Figure 3 is similar to the initial allocation process except that after reallocation of an object, the prototypes for both the previous and current clusters of the object are updated. Variable moves records the number of objects which have changed clusters in the process.

```
FOR i=1 TO NumberOfObjects
    Mindistance=Distance(X[i],O_prototypes[1]) + gamma * Sigma(X[i],C_prototypes[1])
    FOR j=1 TO NumberOfClusters
        distance=Distance(X[i],O_prototypes[j]) + gamma * Sigma(X[i],C_prototypes[j])
        IF (distance<Mindistance)
            Mindistance=distance
            cluster=j
        ENDIF
    ENDFOR
    Clustership[i]=cluster
    ClusterCount[cluster] + 1
    FOR j=1 TO NumberOfNumericAttributes
        SumInCluster[cluster,j] + X[i,j]
        O_prototypes[cluster,j]=SumInCluster[cluster,j]/ClusterCount[cluster]
    ENDFOR
    FOR j=1 TO NumberOfCategoricAttributes
        FrequencyInCluster[cluster,j,X[i,j]] + 1
        C_prototypes[cluster,j]=HighestFreq(FrequencyInCluster,cluster,j)
    ENDFOR
ENDFOR
```

Figure 2. Initial allocation process.

```
moves=0
FOR i=1 TO NumberOfObjects
    ...
    (To find the cluster whose prototype is the nearest to object i.  Same as Figure 2)
    ...
    IF (Clustership[i]<>cluster)
        moves+1
        oldcluster=Clustership[i]
        Clustership[i]=cluster
        ClusterCount[cluster] + 1
        ClusterCount[oldcluster] - 1
        FOR j=1 TO NumberOfNumericAttributes
            SumInCluster[cluster,j] + X[i,j]
            SumInCluster[oldcluster,j] - X[i,j]
            O_prototypes[cluster,j]=SumInCluster[cluster,j]/ClusterCount[cluster]
            O_prototypes[oldcluster,j]=SumInCluster[oldcluster,j]/ClusterCount[oldcluster]
        ENDFOR
        FOR j=1 TO NumberOfCategoricAttributes
            FrequencyInCluster[cluster,j,X[i,j]] + 1
            FrequencyInCluster[oldcluster,j,X[i,j]] - 1
            C_prototypes[cluster,j]=HighestFreq(cluster,j)
            C_prototypes[oldcluster,j]=HighestFreq(oldcluster,j)
        ENDFOR
    ENDIF
ENDFOR
```

Figure 3. Reallocation process.

The algorithm iterates the reallocation process until moves=0, which indicates that the algorithm has stabilised in a local optimum of Eq.(2.6). Figure 4 shows a typical convergence curve of the algorithm, which was obtained from a data set with 75808 records and 20 attributes. The number of clusters is 64.

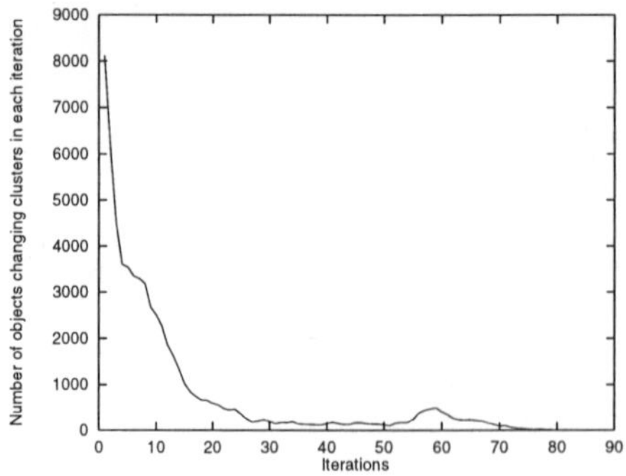

Figure 4. Convergence behaviour of the *k-prototype* algorithm.

We can see that the number of objects changing clusters drops very rapidly in the beginning. Then the dropping speed gradually slows down and becomes nearly unchanged in some stage. It also goes up a little before the number of changes becomes zero. This indicates that iteration of the reallocation process can be terminated at some point when the dropping speed becomes small. This compromise can reduce running time significantly for large data sets.

The computational cost of this algorithm is $O((t+1)kn)$, where n is the number of objects, k the number of clusters and t is the number of iterations of the reallocation process. Usually, $k << n$ and t does not exceed 100 according to our experiments on a large real world data set. Therefore, this algorithm is efficient in clustering large data sets.

Like the *k-means* algorithm, this algorithm also produces local optimal solutions, which are affected by the initial cluster prototypes. To avoid being trapped at a local optimum one can introduce some perturbations in the process. However, it still cannot guarantee a global optimal solution. There are a number of techniques for solving this global optimisation problem, such as simulated annealing[4,10,16] and genetic algorithms[7].

4 Experiments

In this section we present some simulation results of clustering data with mixed numeric and categorical values by the *k-prototypes* algorithm. We also briefly describe an exercise on clustering a real world data set.

4.1 Data Set Construction

In order to simplify illustration we use data records having only three attributes, two numeric and one categorical. These records were generated as follows. We first created two sets of two dimensional points by using methods in [5]. The first set contains 400 points and has one normal distribution (Figure 5a), whereas the second has four normal distributions and contains 300 points (Figure 6a).

We then expanded these points to three dimensions by adding a categorical value to each point (see figures 5b and 6b). For the first data set we deliberately divided it into four parts and assigned to the majority points in each part an identical categorical value and to the rest other categorical values. For instance the majority of points in the left high part in Figure 5b are assigned categorical value C and the rest in this part are assigned A, B or D. All assignments were randomly done. Similar assignments were given to the second point set as well (Figure 6b).

Note that the categorical value of a point does not indicate its class membership. In fact, these points have no classification at all. The categorical values simply represent objects in a third dimension which is not continuous and has no order. We can view this dimension as a set of planes overlaid where the distance between any two planes is 1. Each plane is identified by a unique categorical value. All points are projected to the corresponding planes according to their categorical values.

4.2 Simulations

The main purpose for these simulations was to demonstrate how numeric and categorical attributes interact each other in the process of clustering by the *k-prototypes* algorithm.

Given a set of k cluster prototypes for a data set described in Section 4.1, the rule for assigning an object x to a cluster l is

$$\{x \in l: d(x,q_l) \le d(x,q_v) \wedge l \ne v\} \qquad \text{for } v = 1,\ldots,k$$

Without the third dimension, a point is assigned to a cluster if the prototype of the cluster is nearest to the point. When the third dimension is involved, three situations can happen.

1. A point is assigned to a cluster if the prototype of the cluster is the nearest to the point in the two dimensional numeric space AND the prototype's categorical value of the cluster is same as that of the point.
2. A point may be assigned to a cluster, whose prototype is not the nearest to it in the two dimensional continuous subspace, but the categorical value of majority points in the cluster is same as that of the point.

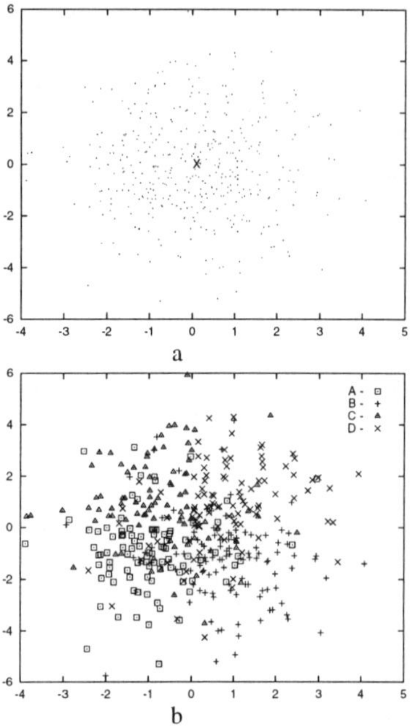

Figure 5.

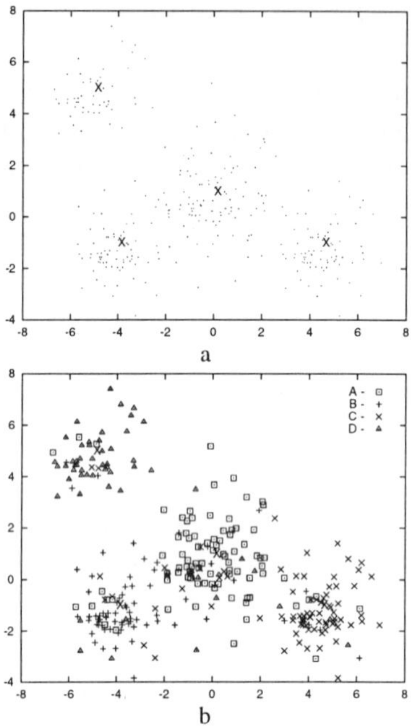

Figure 6.

3. A point may be assigned to a cluster, even though the categorical value of its prototype is different because the distance between the point and the cluster prototype is small enough.

The second situation indicates that the categorical attribute has a strong impact in clustering, whereas the third situation shows a strong impact of numeric attributes.

We have implemented the *k-prototypes* algorithm using a global γ, i.e., the same γ for all clusters. We tested different γ values in clustering the data sets shown in Figure 5b and 6b. A small γ indicates that the clustering process favours the numeric attributes, whereas a large γ means the result is biased towards the categorical attribute.

Figure 7 shows the results of clustering the data set in Figure 5b with three different γ values. When $\gamma = 0$ (Figure 7a), the data is clustered completely on the numeric attributes, equivalent to clustering the data in Figure 5a. It is known that the two dimensional points have only one normal distribution which represents one natural cluster. The clustering process divides the inherent one into four which does not make much sense from classification point of view.

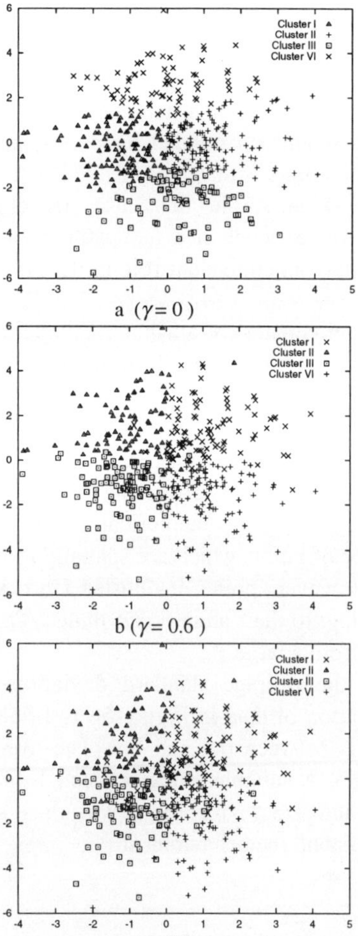

Figure 7.

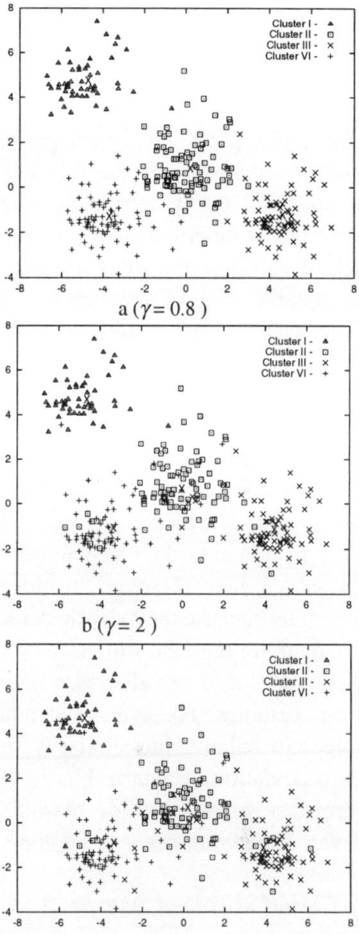

Figure 8.

However, when the third categorical dimension is involved, the inherent distribution is no longer valid in the three dimensional space (see Figure 5b). With some contribution ($\gamma = 0.6$) from the categorical dimension, four new clusters (Figure 7b) were produced which are different from those in Figure 7a. In comparison with Figure 5b, we can find the new clusters represent the four regions, each being dominated by one categorical value. Clustering of the points is dependent on both numeric and categorical values. The points, which are spatially close and have the same categorical values, are clustered together. If a point has a categorical value A but is close the majority of points having categorical value B and far away from the majority points having categorical value A, the point is clustered together with the points, which have categorical value B in majority. In this case, the two numeric values determine the cluster of the point rather than its categorical value. However, if a point having categorical value A and surrounded by points having categorical value B is still not far away from the points with categorical value A, it is clustered with the points with categorical value A. In this case, its cluster membership is determined by its categorical value rather than its spatial location. Therefore, numeric and categorical attributes play an equivalent role in determining cluster memberships of the points.

The result in Figure 7c ($\gamma = 1$) is biased on categorical attribute. Compared to Figure 5b the numeric attributes have played very little role in clustering except for few points.

Figure 8 shows the results of clustering data in Figure 6b. We know the data set has spatially four normal distributions. Figure 8a produced from a small γ clearly recovers the distributions because the clustering is biased towards numeric attributes. Figure 8b shows a medium γ result. In this clustering the categorical attribute has played a significant role. One can see a number of points which are spatially located in cluster VI were clustered in cluster II. However, points in cluster I are very homogenous because they are clustered according to their numeric attributes. This is also evident in Figure 8c which was produced from a large γ.

Selection of a γ value was guided by the average standard deviation σ of numeric attributes. The average standard deviation of data in Figure 5b is 1.658. A suitable γ to balance the similarity measure is between 0.5 and 0.7. The average standard deviation of data in Figure 6b is 3.185. A suitable γ lies between 1 and 2. Therefore, a suitable γ lies between $1/3\,\sigma$ and $2/3\,\sigma$ for these two data sets. However, more work needs to be done to understand the behaviour of γ.

4.3 Clustering a Real Data Set

The algorithm was tested against a real world data set consisting of more than 70,000 records, 9 numeric and 11 categorical attributes. Each record represents a motor insurance policy. The *k-prototypes* algorithm was used to partition the data set into homogenous clusters in order to identify the groups of policy holders which lodged more claims than other groups.

We ran the algorithm on a SUN Sparc10 workstation. Table 1 gives the time performance for partitioning different numbers of policies into 8 clusters. Table 2 shows the time performance for partitioning 30000 policies into different numbers of clusters. The termination condition for these experiments was that no policy changed cluster after a reallocation process. If iteration of the reallocation process was terminated at some point when the number of policies changing clusters in a reallocation process drops very slowly (see Figure 4), running time would be reduced significantly.

Table 1

Records	Time (sec.)
10000	327
30000	824
50000	1267
70000	2051

Table 2

Clusters	Time(sec.)
16	2083
32	5108
64	10740
128	22380

To interpret the clusters, we use a decision tree induction algorithm to derive descriptions of clusters. For example, the description of a cluster in a partition may look like

Age of Policy Holders ≤ 20 **AND**
Sex = Male **AND**
5000 ≤ Insured Amount ≤ 10000

These kinds of descriptions, together with some statistics for clusters such as the number of policies and average claim cost, can assist data miners to understand and identify interesting policy groups.

5 Summary and Future Work

We have presented the *k-prototypes* algorithm to cluster large real world data sets. This algorithm preserves the efficiency of the *k-means* algorithm but removes its numeric data only limitation. We have demonstrated that it is efficient for clustering large data sets with mixed numeric and categorical values. Such data sets often occur in data mining applications.

We have suggested using decision tree induction algorithms to obtain descriptions of clusters. Such descriptions can assist interpretation of clusters and thus aid data miners to understand and identify interesting object groups represented by clusters. We believe that integration of clustering and decision tree induction algorithms can become a useful tool for knowledge discovery in databases.

This work was motivated by the problem of dealing with large mixed data sets, which are common in data mining applications. When the size of a data set exceeds a certain limit, many existing algorithms will be no longer practical. Extremely large data sets in data mining challenge many existing algorithms which are effective for small data sets. We plan to test our algorithm on larger data sets and to pursue a parallel implementation if necessary. This initial work has also opened several research topics we can pursue, such as global optimisation, effective cluster interpretation, and tree-structured clustering[14] for mixed data.

Acknowledgments
The author wants to thank Mr Peter Milne and Drs Glenn Stone, Graham Williams and Phil Kilby for their valuable comments.

References

1. M. R. Anderberg, *Cluster Analysis for Applications*. Academic Press, New York (1973).
2. L. Bobrowski and J. C. Bezdek, *c-Means Clustering with the* l_1 *and* l_∞ *Norms.* IEEE Transactions on Systems, Man and Cybernetics, **21**(3), pp.545-554 (1991).
3. L. Breiman, J. H. Frieman, R. A. Olshen and C. J. Stone, *Classification and Regression Trees.* Wadsworth, Inc. (1984).
4. J. Buhmann and H. Kühnel, *Vector Quantisation with Complexity Costs.* IEEE Transactions on Information Theory, **39**, pp. 1133-1145 (1993).
5. B. Everitt, *Cluster Analysis*. Heinemann Educational Books Ltd. (1974).
6. D. H. Fisher, *Knowledge Acquisition Via Incremental Conceptual Clustering.* Machine Learning, **2**(2), pp.139-172 (1987)
7. D. E. Goldberg, *Genetic Algorithms in Search, Optimisation, and Machine Learning*. Addison-Wesley (1989).
8. J. C. Gower, *A General Coefficient of Similarity and Some of Its Properties.* BioMetrics, 27, pp.857-874 (1971).
9. D. J. Hand, *Discrimination and Classification.* John Wiley & Sons (1981).
10. S. Kirkpatrick, C. D. Gelatt and M. P. Vecchi, *Optimisation by Simulated Annealing*. Science, **220**(4598), pp.671-680 (1983).
11. M. Lebowitz, *Experiments with Incremental Concept Formation.* Machine Learning, **2**(2), pp.103-138 (1987).
12. J. B. MacQueen, *Some Methods for Classification and Analysis of Multivariate Observations.* Proceedings of the 5th Berkeley Symposium on Mathematical Statistics and Probability, pp.281-297 (1967).
13. R. S. Michalski and R. E. Stepp, *Automated Construction of Classifications: Clustering versus Numerical Taxonomy.* IEEE Transactions on Pattern Analysis and Machine Intelligence, **5**(5), pp.396-410 (1983).
14. D. Miller and K. Rose, *A Non-greedy Approach to Tree-Structured Clustering.* Pattern Recognition Letters, **15**, pp. 683-690 (1994).
15. J. R. Quinlan, *C4.5: Programs for Machine Learning*. Morgan Kaufmann Publishers (1993).
16. K. Rose, E. Gurewitz and G. Fox, A *Deterministic Annealing Approach to Clustering*. Pattern Recognition Letters, **11**, pp.589-594 (1990).

Unsupervised Clustering with Mixed Numeric and Nominal Data — A New Similarity Based Agglomerative System[a]

Cen Li and Gautam Biswas
Department of Computer Science
Box 1679, Station B
Vanderbilt University
Nashville, TN 37235, USA.
e-mail: cenli, biswas@vuse.vanderbilt.edu

This paper presents a new Similarity Based Agglomerative Clustering(SBAC) algorithm that works well for data with mixed numeric and nominal features. A similarity measure, proposed by Goodall for biological taxonomy[3], that gives greater weight to uncommon feature-value matches in similarity computations and makes no assumptions of the underlying distributions of the feature-values, is adopted to define the similarity measure between pairs of objects. An agglomerative algorithm is employed to construct a concept tree, and a simple distinctness heuristic is used to extract a partition of the data. The performance of SBAC has been studied on real and artificially generated data sets. Results demonstrate the effectiveness of this algorithm in unsupervised discovery tasks. Comparisons with other schemes illustrate the superior performance of the algorithm.

1 Introduction

Machine learning and statistical analysis techniques form the core of Data mining systems in business, manufacturing, medical, and scientific domains. A number of software packages are being designed to systematize and support the discovery process. When knowledge of the domain is incomplete, conceptual clustering and classification schemes are commonly employed to structure and synthesize knowledge from data.

Most real world data is a combination of numeric and nominal-valued features. It becomes crucial for clustering systems to handle this data effectively. Earlier attempts encoded nominal feature values as numeric integer values and/or discretized numeric feature values, but these methods cause loss of information and difficulty in interpretation.

Recently, systems like AUTOCLASS [1], COBWEB/3 [7], and ECOBWEB [8] have attempted to address this problem. COBWEB-like systems try to generalize criterion functions designed for nominal features to handle numeric features. The primary difficulty in doing this can be attributed to the nature of the criterion functions used. Criterion functions used in symbolic clustering are based on probability distribution functions. For nominal features, probabilities can be approximated by simple counting schemes. Computing and bounding density estimates for numeric features are a much more difficult task. AUTOCLASS uses a fundamental *finite mixture model*, and then derives groupings of objects that locally maximize the posterior probability of individual clusters given the feature distribution assumptions. Experiments on mixed data suggest that numeric feature distributions tend to have a stronger influence on the generated structures. The focus of this paper is on developing an unsupervised clustering system — Similarity Based Agglomerative Clustering(SBAC), which exhibits good performance with mixed numeric and nominal data.

2 The SBAC system

The core of our methodology is a similarity measure from biological taxonomy proposed by Goodall [3]. The measure provides a uniform framework for processing numeric and nominal features, and is coupled with a simple control strategy that agglomeratively constructs a hierarchical concept tree. A distinct partition is extracted by a simple procedure that trades distinctness for parsimony.

2.1 The Similarity Measure

A pair of objects (i, j) is considered more similar to each other than a second pair of objects (l, m) iff the objects i and j exhibit a greater match in feature values that are more uncommon in the population. In other words, uncommon feature values make greater contributions to the overall similarity between two objects.

Given two pairs of objects (i, j) and (l, m), lets assume for nominal feature k, objects i and j have values $(V_i)_k = (V_j)_k$, and objects l and m have values $(V_l)_k = (V_m)_k$, but $(p_i)_k$, the probability of occurrence of $(V_i)_k$ in the population is greater than $(p_l)_k$, the probability of occurrence of $(V_l)_k$ in the same population. Since $(V_i)_k$ is more common than value $(V_l)_k$, we have

$$\left.\begin{array}{l}((V_i)_k = (V_j)_k) \wedge ((V_l)_k = (V_m)_k) \\ ((p_i)_k = (p_j)_k) \geq ((p_l)_k = (p_m)_k)\end{array}\right\} \Longrightarrow (S_{ij})_k \leq (S_{lm})_k, \tag{1}$$

where $(S_{ij})_k$ and $(S_{lm})_k$ represent the similarity contribution from nominal feature k for object pairs (i, j) and (l, m) respectively.

For pairs of numeric feature values, the measure takes into account both the magnitude of the difference between the two values and the uniqueness of the segment enclosed by the two values. The smaller the magnitude of the difference between two values, the less likely it is to pick a value at random that falls in the segment enclosed by the two values, thus the two values are considered more similar. For numeric feature k, given two pairs of objects (i, j) and (l, m):

$$(|(V_i)_k - (V_j)_k| > |(V_l)_k - (V_m)_k|) \Longrightarrow (S_{ij})_k < (S_{lm})_k. \qquad (2)$$

If the magnitude of differences of two pairs of values are equal, then the uniqueness of the segments weights the similarity index. The uniqueness of the segment is computed by summing up the frequency of occurrences (p_t) of all values encompassed by the segment $\sum_{t=(V_i)_k}^{(V_j)_k} p_t$ for object pair (i, j). The less frequent the occurrence of values within a segment, the more unique the segment is, thus the more similar the pair of values associated with the segment:

$$\left.\begin{array}{l} |(V_i)_k - (V_j)_k| = |(V_l)_k - (V_m)_k|) \\ \sum_{t=(V_i)_k}^{(V_j)_k} p_t \;\geq\; \sum_{t=(V_l)_k}^{(V_m)_k} p_t \end{array}\right\} \Longrightarrow (S_{ij})_k \leq (S_{lm})_k. \qquad (3)$$

2.2 Similarity Computation: Nominal Features

For a nominal feature, if the values of a pair of objects are different, then the contribution of this feature to the similarity between the two objects is 0. If the pair of values are identical, then the similarity contribution is a function of the uncommonality of that value within the population. Given two objects i and j, having an identical value for nominal feature k, say $(V_i)_k$, the contribution to the similarity, $(S_{ii})_k$, is defined in terms of the *More Similar Feature Value Set*, i.e., $MSFVS((V_i)_k, (V_i)_k)$. This is the set of all pairs of values for feature k satisfying equation (1). The probability of picking a pair $((V_l)_k, (V_l)_k) \in MSFVS((V_i)_k, (V_i)_k)$ at random is ${(p_l)^2}_k = \frac{(f_l)_k \cdot ((f_l)_k - 1)}{n \cdot (n-1)}$, where $(f_l)_k$ is the frequency of occurrence of value $(V_l)_k$ in the population and n is the total number of objects in the population. Summation of the probabilities of all such pairs gives the dissimilarity value, $(D_{ij})_k$. And the similarity of the pair $((V_i)_k, (V_i)_k)$ is computed as:

$$(S_{ii})_k = 1 - (D_{ii})_k = 1 - \sum_{l \in MSFVS_{((V_i)_k, (V_i)_k)}} {(p_l)_k}^2. \qquad (4)$$

A simple example illustrates this computation. Consider a population of 10 objects, each described by two features, one nominal and one numeric. The feature values of each object are shown in Table 1. As defined above, the similarity value for pairs of nominal feature values that differ is 0, i.e., for feature 1, $S_{(a,b)_1} = S_{(a,c)_1} = S_{(b,c)_1} = 0$. For pairs of identical values, i.e., $S_{(a,a)_1}$, $S_{(b,b)_1}$ and $S_{(c,c)_1}$, we first find the MSFVS for each pair. In this population, values a and b occur less frequently than value c: $f(a) = 3$, $f(b) = 3$, and $f(c) = 4$.

Object Number	Feature 1 (nominal)	Feature 2 (numeric)
1	a	6
2	b	5.5
3	b	7.5
4	a	6
5	c	10.5
6	c	9
7	c	7.5
8	c	9
9	a	7.5
10	b	7.5

Table 1: Sample data set of 10 objects, each described in one nominal feature and one numeric feature

The $MSFVS$ for feature value pair (c, c), $MSFVS(c, c) = \{(a, a), (b, b), (c, c)\}$. Once the MSFVS of the pair is identified, the similarity value for the pair (c, c) is calculated according to equation 4:

$$\begin{aligned} D_{(c,c)_1} &= {p_a}^2 + {p_b}^2 + {p_c}^2 &= \tfrac{3(3-1)}{10(10-1)} + \tfrac{3(3-1)}{10(10-1)} + \tfrac{4(4-1)}{10(10-1)} = 0.267, \\ S_{(c,c)_1} &= 1 - D_{(c,c)_1} &= 0.733. \end{aligned}$$

When computing the similarity between objects 5 and 6, the contribution to the similarity measure from feature 1 is 0.733. On the other hand,

$$\begin{aligned} D_{(a,a)_1} &= {p_a}^2 + {p_b}^2 &= \tfrac{3(3-1)}{10(10-1)} + \tfrac{3(3-1)}{10(10-1)} = 0.133, \\ S_{(a,a)_1} &= 1 - D_{(a,a)_1} &= 0.867. \end{aligned}$$

Therefore, for objects 1 and 4, the contribution to the similarity measure from feature 1 is 0.867 which is greater than that for objects 5 and 8 though both sets have matched feature values.

The computational complexity for determining this value for a feature with m_d observed values is: $O(n + m_d log m_d)$. If $m_d \ll n$, the total number of objects, this reduces to $O(n)$.

2.3 Similarity Computation: Numeric Features

For numeric feature k, to calculate the similarity for a pair of value $((V_i)_k, (V_j)_k)$, first find its *More Similarity Feature Segment Set*, i.e., $MSFSS((V_i)_k, (V_j)_k)$, which includes all pairs of values $((V_l)_k, (V_m)_k)$ satisfying equation (2) or (3). The probability of picking two values from the population, $(V_l)_k$ and $(V_m)_k$,

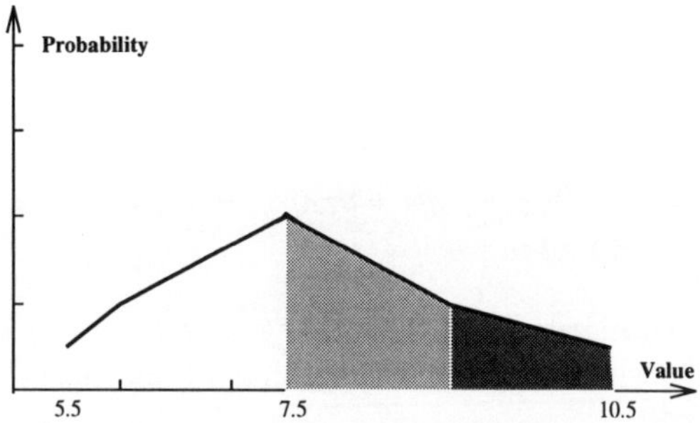

Figure 1: Numeric feature distribution for an example population

where $((V_l)_k, (V_m)_k) \in \text{MSFSS}((V_i)_k, (V_j)_k)$, is

$$\begin{cases} 2(p_l)_k(p_m)_k = \frac{2(f_l)_k(f_m)_k}{n(n-1)}, & (p_l)_k \neq (p_m)_k, \\ (p_l)_k(p_m)_k = \frac{(f_l)_k((f_l)_k-1)}{n(n-1)}, & (p_l)_k = (p_m)_k, \end{cases}$$

where f_l and f_m are the frequencies of occurrence of values $(V_l)_k$ and $(V_m)_k$, respectively, and n is the total number of objects in the population. Summation of the probabilities of all value pairs gives the dissimilarity value, $(D_{ij})_k$. And the similarity of the pair $((V_i)_k, (V_j)_k)$ is computed as:

$$(S_{ij})_k = 1 - (D_{ij})_k = 1 - \sum_{l,m \in \, MSFSS \, ((V_i)_k,(V_j)_k)} 2(p_l)_k(p_m)_k.$$

Using the example in Table 1, we demonstrate next how the similarity measures for numeric features are calculated. The probability distribution of the numeric feature of the sample population is plotted in Figure 1. Consider two pairs of feature values (7.5, 9) and (9, 10.5). Both are 1.5 units apart, but the population encompassed by the two intervals indicated by the light and dark shades, respectively, in Figure 1, it is clear that the area encompassed by frequency distribution for the interval (7.5, 9) is greater than the area encompassed by the frequency distribution for the interval (9, 10.5), therefore, the similarity contribution from feature 2 for the pair (7.5, 9) should be smaller than that of the pair (9, 10.5). The exact similarity values for the two pairs are computed by first identifying the MSFSS for each pair:

$$\begin{aligned} MSFSS(7.5, 9) &= \{(5.5, 5.5), (6, 6), (7.5, 7.5), (9, 9), (10.5, 10.5), \\ &\quad (5.5, 6), (6, 7.5), (7.5, 9), (9, 10.5)\} \\ MSFSS(9, 10.5) &= \{(5.5, 5.5), (6, 6), (7.5, 7.5), (9, 9), (10.5, 10.5), \\ &\quad (5.5, 6), (9, 10.5)\}, \end{aligned}$$

Then we calculate the dissimilarity score for each pair of values as:

$$\begin{aligned} D_{(7.5,9)_2} &= p_{5.5}p_{5.5} + p_6p_6 + p_{7.5}p_{7.5} + p_9p_9 + p_{10.5}p_{10.5} + 2p_{5.5}p_6 \\ &\quad +2p_6p_{7.5} + 2p_{7.5}p_9 + 2p_9p_{10.5} = 0.51, \\ D_{(9,10.5)_2} &= p_{5.5}p_{5.5} + p_6p_6 + p_{7.5}p_{7.5} + p_9p_9 + p_{10.5}p_{10.5} + 2p_{5.5}p_6 \\ &\quad +2p_9p_{10.5} = 0.27. \end{aligned}$$

And finally, the similarity measure for the pair (9, 10.5) is $S_{(9,10.5)_2} = 1 - D_{(9,10.5)_2} = 0.73$, which is greater than that of the pair (7.5, 9), $S_{(7.5,9)_2} = 1 - D_{(7.5,9)_2} = 0.49$.

Note that the similarity contribution from numeric features is a function of both distance and density. As long as a change of scale or a transformation for a numeric feature preserves the order of relative distances between its feature values, the similarity measure for the feature value pairs is invariant. Also, the monotonic nature of the (dis)similarity measures is preserved. For example, $D_{(7.5,9)_2} < D_{(9,11)_2}$ because $|7.5 - 9| < |9 - 11|$ even though the range from 9 to 11 is very sparsely populated in the distribution in Figure 1. On the other hand, if two distances are equal, as in the example shown above, the values at the end points of the interval with the sparser population is considered more similar. Therefore, the metrical properties of the distance measure are retained for numeric features.

The direct implementation of the above calculation takes $O({m_c}^4)$ time complexity for a numeric feature with m_c unique values observed. To speed up the computation, we first find the difference of all pairs of values for a numeric feature and sort the differences in ascending order. An accumulator is then used to accumulate and assign similarity score to pairs of values in the sorted difference list. With this implementation, the time complexity for calculating the similarity score for a numeric feature is cut down to $O(m_c^2 log m_c^2)$. In the worst case, $m_c = n$, where n is the total number of objects, and the above complexity is bounded by $O(n^2 log n^2)$.

2.4 Total Similarity Value

If similarity values from individual features are considered to be individual independent tests of similarity between two objects, then these independent similarity test results can be combined into one aggregate similarity score across all features. One common method of combining probability from different tests make use of the additive properties of χ^2, where the results of the various experiments are expressed as the square of a standard normal deviate. Such a probability may be combined in a simple way using Fisher's χ^2 transformation [2]: $\chi^2 = -2ln(P_i)$. This model works well for data from numeric populations

Calculation Steps	Object Pairs	
	(Obj6, Obj9)	(Obj5, Obj8)
χ_c^2	1.35	2.62
χ_d^2	1.037	3.19
χ^2	2.387	5.81
D	0.66	0.21
S	0.34	0.79

Table 2: The step by step calculation of similarity measure between pairs of objects

and nominal populations, where many different observation values are possible for a feature. However, for nominal features with a few values, empirical results have shown that the transformation causes the mean and standard deviation of the transformed population to deviate significantly from the theoretical mean and standard deviation, thus diminishing the power of the tests [5]. Lancaster suggested, as a remedy, an improved *mean value* χ^2 transformation [5], which aggregates similarity values obtained from all t_d nominal features by:

$$(\chi_d)_{ij}^2 = 2\sum_{k=1}^{t_d}(1 - \frac{(D_{ij})_k ln(D_{ij})_k - (D_{ij})'_k ln(D_{ij})'_k}{(D_{ij})_k - (D_{ij})'_k}), \tag{5}$$

where $(D_{ij})_k$ is the dissimilarity score for nominal feature value pair $((V_i)_k, (V_j)_k)$, $(D_{ij})'_k$ is the next smaller dissimilarity value in the nominal set. χ_d^2 is χ^2 distributed with t_d degrees of freedom. All t_c numeric features can be aggregated using Fisher's χ^2 transformation:

$$(\chi_c)_{ij}^2 = -2\sum_{k=1}^{t_c} ln((D_{ij})_k), \tag{6}$$

where χ_c^2 is also a χ^2 distribution with t_c degrees of freedom.

The addition of two χ^2 distribution is still χ^2, with degree of freedom equal to the sum of the two degrees of freedom. The probability distribution after combining the two types features is χ^2 distributed with $(t_c + t_d)$ degrees of freedom. The significance value can be looked up in standard tables or approximated from the expression:

$$D_{ij} = e^{-\frac{\chi_{ij}^2}{2}} \sum_{k=0}^{(t_d+tc-1)} \frac{(\frac{1}{2}\chi_{ij}^2)^k}{k!},$$

where $\chi_{ij}^2 = (\chi_c)_{ij}^2 + (\chi_d)_{ij}^2$. The overall similarity representing the set of $(t_c + t_d)$ independent similarity measures is $S_{ij} = 1 - D_{ij}$.

Continuing with the sample population of objects given in Table 1, we illustrate the computation for the similarity measure for pairs of objects. We have already shown, for the nominal feature, the dissimilarity measure for object pairs (obj6, obj9) and (obj5, obj8), are $D_{(a,c)_1} = 1$ and $D_{(c,c)_1} = 0.267$, respectively, and for the numeric feature, the similarity measure for the two pairs are $D_{(7.5,9)_2} = 0.51$ and $D_{(9,10.5)_2} = 0.27$, respectively. The similarity measures obtained from individual features are combined to give the overall similarity between pairs of objects. Since there is only one nominal feature and one numeric feature in this example, the summation of t_c and t_d terms in equations 6 and 5 are reduced to single term operations. Results of step by step calculations for χ_d, χ_c, dissimilarity measure and the similarity score for object pairs (obj6, obj9) and (obj5, obj8) are given in Table 2. The overall similarity between object 5 and object 8, 0.79, is higher than that between object 6 and object 9. This is in consistent with the fact that for each individual feature, values between object 5 and object 8 are more similar to each other than those between object 6 and object 9.

2.5 The Control Structure

SBAC's agglomerative, hierarchical clustering algorithm based on the Unweighted Pair Group Method with Arithmetic Average(UPGMA)[4], starts with a dissimilarity matrix D for the set of objects to be clustered. At any step, the clusters that have the minimum pairwise dissimilarity value are merged into a single cluster. Dissimilarity between the new cluster and the other clusters is defined as the average dissimilarity between an old cluster and the component clusters of the new cluster. The end result is a dendrogram (or classification tree) whose leaf nodes are individual objects, and whose root includes all objects.

In the classification tree, each node is associated with a dissimilarity score indicating the dissimilarity level at which its child nodes merge together. From the root of the tree to the leaves, the dissimilarity score along each path monotonically decreases. The decrease of dissimilarity score from a parent node to a child node indicates that the objects in the child node form a more cohesive group than the ones in the parent node. We are interested in clusters that are cohesive yet not fragmented. To achieve this, we traverse the tree top-down along paths in a depth first fashion, cutting off traversal when the difference in dissimilarity value between parent and child node exceeds a threshold value, t. The set of nodes that lie on the frontier of the search define our final groups. In our experiments, we set the threshold value $t = 0.3 * D(root)$, where $D(root)$ is the dissimilarity score associated with the root of the tree.

The overall computational complexity of the SBAC system can be broken down into two parts: (i) generating the dissimilarity matrix for all pairs of objects, and (ii) constructing the hierarchical dendrogram or concept tree. It is well established in literature[4] that the upper bound complexity for part (ii) is $O(n^2)$, where n is the number of objects in the dataset. Also, constructing the similarity matrix for pairs of objects, given the similarity index for individual attributes, is $O(n^2)$. Using the time complexities to compute the individual similarity indices reported earlier, the overall time complexity for generating partitions is $O(n^2 + m_c^2 log m_c^2)$, where m_c is the highest possible number of distinct values observed for a numeric feature. For large data sets, this reduces to $O(n^2)$, where $n \gg m_c$, and for small data sets, it is $O(m_c^2 log m_c^2)$, where $n \ll m_c$.

3 Experimental Studies

Our goal for performing empirical studies with SBAC were two fold: (i) to gain a better understanding of the characteristics of the Goodall similarity measure, and (ii) to compare the performance of SBAC with existing unsupervised discovery systems, such as AUTOCLASS, COBWEB/3, and ECOBWEB. To achieve this, we used two kinds of data (i) artificially generated data, with mixed nominal and numeric features, and (ii) real data sets. Only results from the artificial data sets are reported here. Results for the real data sets appear in Li and Biswas [6].

3.1 Data Description

Each artificial data set had 180 data objects, equally distributed into 3 classes: G_1, G_2, and G_3. Each data point was described with two nominal and two numeric features. A base data set, d0%c0%, was created with no overlap of feature values for the three classes. The nominal feature values for each class are clearly separable and the two numeric features were generated from normal distributions with the means for the three classes three standard-deviations apart from each other.

Six data sets were created by adding non-Gaussian noise to the d0%c0% data through successively mixing up 20%, 40%, and 60% of numeric/nominal feature values from one class with the other two classes.

Another four data sets were created by adding successively higher degree of Gaussian noise to the numeric features in the base data. The Gaussian noise being introduced were normally distributed with $\mu = 0$, and $\sigma = \frac{x}{2}\cdot$ (the standard deviation of the numeric features in the base data). For the four corrupted data sets, $x = 1, 2, 3$, and 4 respectively.

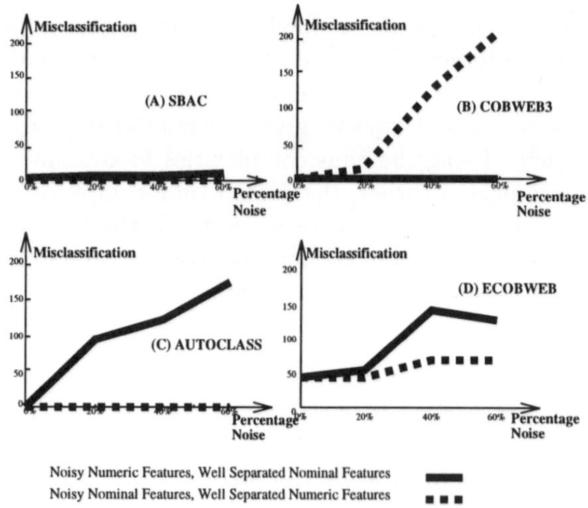

Figure 2: Comparison of partitional structures generated by clustering systems on data with non-Gaussian noise

3.2 Results and Discussion

The cluster structures are further characterized with a *misclassification count* measure. The *misclassification count* measure computes the number of object misclassification in the partitional structures generated by different systems, assuming the partitional structure presented in the base data as the true structure. The smaller this value, the closer the partitional structure is to our true structure.

The *misclassification counts* for partitional structures generated by the four algorithms on data with non-Gaussian noise are plotted in Fig. 2. The solid lines represent the effects of increasing noise added to the numeric features and the dotted lines represented the effects of adding noise to the nominal features. It was observed that AUTOCLASS partitions deteriorated quite drastically as the numeric features were corrupted, while no deterioration were present when the nominal features were corrupted. COBWEB/3 seemed to have the opposite effect. The differences for the two cases were smaller for ECOBWEB, which had a similar trend for numeric and nominal degradation. SBAC's degradation for either case is almost negligible.

Given the way these data sets are generated, SBAC assigns equal similarity scores to the same feature value pairs appearing for each individual feature in each of the seven data sets. When feature values of an object was corrupted by noise(i.e, it took on a value from another class), the contribution of this feature to the similarity computation with other objects belonging to this class decreased significantly, but the other feature contributions remained high. Therefore, the effect of noise was greatly mitigated. This effect is further illustrated in Table 3(A) and 3(B), and the average contribution from the nominal features and the numeric features to the overall similarity measure are compared for pairs of objects from the same class and pairs of objects from different classes. For the data set with well separated numeric features and noisy nominal features, (see Table 3(A)), when comparing the within class and between class object pairs, there is a small difference in average similarity for nominal features. This indicates that the predictability of noisy nominal features is lowered. At the same time, there is a big difference in the within class and between class values for the numeric features. Moreover the contribution to similarity from the contribution features is about 2 times the contribution from the nominal features within a class and about $\frac{1}{2}$ between classes. This big difference indicates that in spite of the noise added, objects from the same class are still more similar to each other than objects from different classes and this is primarily because of the difference in contributions between the uncorrupted versus corrupted features. The overall results for the data set with well separated nominal features and noisy numeric features were just the same, (see Table 3(B)). Here noise reduced the difference between the within and between class similarity values for the numeric features, while maintaining a large difference for the nominal features. However, the differences in contribution were not as distinct, which explain the slightly larger misclassification percentages observed in Figure 2(A).

One possible explanation for the AUTOCLASS results may be that because the numeric data was Gaussian, it provided a closer fit to AUTOCLASS's assumption for the distribution of the prior probability. However, AUTOCLASS assumes a Bernoulli distribution with uniform Dirichlet conjugate prior for the nominal attributes, and this did not quite match the way we generated the nominal data for this experiment. Nevertheless, it is still a little surprising that AUTOCLASS seemed to disregard the distinctive nominal attributes completely in d0%c⋆% cases. Another possible reason for the deterioration of AUTOCLASS's performance to the gradual increase of noise in numeric features is that the noise model assumed by AUTOCLASS is Gaussian. Separate experiments conducted by adding Gaussian noise to the numeric features demonstrated better performance. This is discussed later. Also, when compared to cluster structures generated by the other algorithms, AUTOCLASS tended to construct more groups in the partition structure. This may be attributed to the fact that with the addition of noise, AUTOCLASS found

Similarity Contribution	Object Pairs	
	Same Class	Between Classes
Average χ_c^2	8.44	1.82
Average χ_d^2	4.54	3.72
Average D	0.17	0.69
Average S	0.83	0.31

(A) 40% nominal feature values were corrupted

Similarity Contribution	Object Pairs	
	Same Class	Between Classes
Average χ_c^2	4.66	3.68
Average χ_d^2	7.65	2.20
Average D	0.20	0.67
Average S	0.80	0.33

(B) 40% numeric feature values were corrupted

Table 3: Similarity contribution from nominal and numeric features averaged over all pairs of objects from the same class and all pairs of objects from different classes.

better fit when using a larger number of component distributions. Cheesman and Stutz discuss this issue (*Occam's Razor*[1]) and implement schemes to help prevent AUTOCLASS from overfitting. However, the schemes do not seem to be activated early enough to prevent fragmentation in the partition structures created by AUTOCLASS.

The cluster structure generated by ECOBWEB was not dominated by either well separated nominal attributes or well separated numeric attributes. Despite the fact that ECOBWEB and COBWEB/3 share the same criterion function for nominal attributes, for d0%c⋆% data sets, cluster structures formed by COBWEB/3 are much better than those formed by ECOBWEB. The difference in the partitional structures can be explained by the differences in the implementations of the CU function for numeric features. For COBWEB/3, the $CU_{numeric}$ score depends solely on the standard deviation of the feature distribution for a class. When noise is introduced, the standard-deviations of the "model classes" increase, causing $CU_{numeric}$ to decrease. The higher the level of noise, the less the contribution of $CU_{numeric}$ to the overall CU score. Thus when numeric features were corrupted, the clustering process is mainly based on the $CU_{nominal}$ score which remains high for all d0%c⋆% cases. But for ECOBWEB, its $CU_{numeric}$ score is calculated as the probability of a small interval around the mean value of the feature distribution in a class. When noise is introduced, the mean values of the features are shifted away from those of the "model classes". Depending on the size of the interval defined, the probability calculated around the mean, and thus the $CU_{numeric}$ contribution, can be large enough to make a difference in the overall CU score,

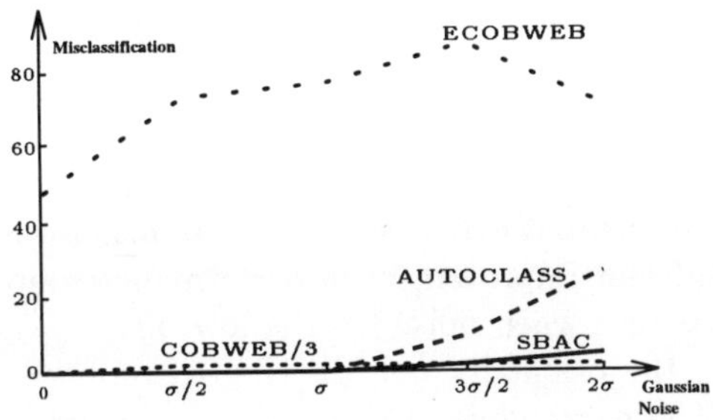

Figure 3: Comparison of partitional structures generated by clustering systems on data with Gaussian noise

which in turn slightly perturbed the class structures that would have been generated by using $CU_{nominal}$ scores alone. It is interesting to observe that the performance of ECOBWEB started to improve after a high level of noise was introduced to the numeric features(60%). A possible explanation for this is when an excessive amount of noise is present, the distribution of numeric features become close to uniform distributions over the entire range. No matter where the estimated mean value is for each of the three classes, the probability of the small interval around each mean is going to be very close. This effectively mitigates the effect of the $CU_{numeric}$ scores on the overall CU measure, causing the clustering system to group objects based mainly on the $CU_{nominal}$ scores.

One the other hand, for d⋆%c0% data, the performance of ECOBWEB is noticeably better than those from COBWEB/3. This is because for COBWEB/3, when compared to the numeric features, nominal features have a greater impact on the CU computation. When nominal features are corrupted, the $CU_{numeric}$ scores may not be big enough to render the corrupted $CU_{nominal}$ scores negligible for the overall CU, especially when the standard deviations of feature distributions in a "true class' exceeds 1. In the case of ECOBWEB, its $CU_{numeric}$ measure is based on the approximation of the true probability of feature distributions in a class. When the approximation is close enough to the real probability, it not only does a better job in capturing the distinct differences in numeric feature values, but also renders the $CU_{nominal}$ scores derived from the corrupted nominal features negligible for the clustering process.

We again used the *misclassification count* on all partitional structures generated from the four clustering systems. The results are plotted in Figure 3. It is observed that the performance of SBAC does not change much from non-Gaussian to Gaussian noise, till the noise levels become very large(2σ). The performance of ECOBWEB with data having Gaussian or non-Gaussian noise follows almost exactly the same pattern: performance degrades as noise levels are increased, but improve slightly when noise levels become too high. Like SBAC and ECOBWEB, there are only minor changes observed for the clusterings generated by COBWEB/3, when Gaussian noise is present. On the other hand, a significant improvement in performance is observed for AUTOCLASS. This is because when noise level is low, i.e., $\sigma_{noise} = \frac{1}{2}\sigma_{feature}$ and $\sigma_{noise} = \sigma_{feature}$, the originally well distributed numeric features were not affected greatly. The parameters of these slightly corrupted normal distributions can still be estimated by AUTOCLASS with sufficient confidence. So, even though the distributions of the nominal features do not satisfy AUTOCLASS's assumption completely, the class structures were preserved by the clustering process. When the noise level was increased for the numeric features, the originally well separated bell shaped distributions for the classes started overlapping, and the parameters estimated by AUTOCLASS for each distribution began deviating from their true values, causing a small number of fragmented groups, therefore, the increase in the misclassification value.

References

1. P. Cheesman and J. Stutz, "Bayesian Classification(AUTOCLASS): Theory and Results", in *Advances in Knowledge Discovery and Data Mining*, U.M. Fayyad, G.P. Shapiro, P. Smythe, and R. Uthurusamy, eds., AAAI/MIT Press, Ch. 6 (1995).
2. R.A. Fisher. *Statistical Methods for Research Workers*, 13th ed. Edinburgh and London: Oliver and Boyd (1963).
3. D.W. Goodall. "A New Similarity Index Based On Probability", in *Biometrics*, 22, pp. 882-907 (1966).
4. A.K. Jain and R.C. Dubes. *Algorithms for clustering data* Prentice Hall, Englewood Cliffs (1988).
5. H.O. Lancaster. "The Combining of Probabilities arising from data in discrete distributions", in *Biometrika*, 36, pp. 370-382 (1949).
6. C. Li and G. Biswas. "Conceptual Clustering with Numeric and Nominal Data – A New Similarity Based System", in review, *IEEE Trans. on Knowledge and Data Engineering* (1996).
7. K. McKusick and K. Thompson. "COBWEB/3: A Portable Implementation," Tech. Rep. FIA-90-6-18-2, NASA Ames Research Center, (1990).
8. Y. Reich. "Building and Improving Design Systems: A Machine Learning Approach". PhD thesis, Dept. of Civil Engineering, Carnegie Mellon University (1991).

INCREMENTAL CONCEPTUAL CLUSTERING IN THE FRAMEWORK OF GALOIS LATTICE

TU BAO HO [a]
Japan Advanced Institute of Science and Technology - Hokuriku
Tatsunokuchi, Ishikawa, 923-12 Japan

Conceptual clustering is a branch of concept learning that aims at discovering conceptual knowledge from data. Like most methods employing the classical view on concepts, method OSHAM allows inducing nonincrementally a concept hierarchy in the framework of Galoi lattice. This paper presents an incremental version of OSHAM for the discovery task in which training instances are presented serially. Experimental results suggest an alternative use of nonincremental and incremental algorithms in order to improve the performance of the discovery process.

1 Introduction

Concept learning methods can be distinguished by the nature of the environment in which learning tasks occur, particularly by the degree of supervision and the manner in which training instances are given. One distinguishes a *supervised* task (when the learner is asked to characterize concepts from a given set of their labelled training instances) and an *unsupervised* task (when the learner is asked to discover concepts from a given set of unlabelled training instances). Also one distinguishes a *nonincremental* task (when all training instances are presented simultaneously) and an *incremental* task (when training instances are presented serially). All of these tasks may occur in realistic situations and have their roles to play in concept learning [8].

Conceptual clustering is a branch of concept learning that relates to concept discovery. Conceptual clustering is often referred to as unsupervised concept learning, and referred to concept formation when the task is incremental. In general, it relates simultaneously to two problems of *hierarchical clustering* (i.e., finding a hierarchy of useful subsets of instances) and *characterization* (i.e., finding an intensional definition for each of these subsets of instances).

Conceptual clustering methods are tied up with the human understanding of concepts and their formation. Among views on concepts in cognitive science which have affected conceptual clustering, the classical, prototype and exemplar ones are widely known and used. In the so-called *classical view*, concepts are represented by pairs of extent and intent (features common to all concept's instances). In the *prototype view* concepts are represented by prototypes that summarize the most common or typical features among the

---

[a] Also with the Institute of Information Technology, TuLiem, Hanoi, Vietnam.

concept's instances. In the *exemplar view* concepts are represented by their individual examples. One may notice that most conceptual clustering methods based on the classical view are nonincremental, e.g., CLUSTER/2 [9], ID3 for decision tree induction [11], while those based on the prototype view on concepts are often incremental [3]. There have been attempts to extend nonincremental methods to incremental ones, e.g., from well-known ID3 to ID4 [12] and ID5 [13].

The unsupervised, nonincremental conceptual clustering method OSHAM[5] employs a variant of the classical view on concepts and carries out a search through the hypothesis space with the Galois lattice structure [14]. OSHAM has been extended to a hybrid system [6] which combines strengths of the three main views on concepts, and associated with a decision procedure combining instance-based reasoning with logical interpretation for exploiting discovered knowledge[7]. This work continues our investigation on the conceptual clustering method OSHAM in which we introduce INCOSHAM, an incremental version of OSHAM. In this paper, we first introduce basic notions of Galois lattice and the essential idea of OSHAM in section 2, then describe INCOSHAM in section 3. An evaluation of INCOSHAM and conclusions are given in sections 4 and 5.

2 Nonincremental Learning in Galois Lattices

Basis of the most widely understanding of a concept in cognitive science and machine learning is the function of collecting individuals into a group with certain common properties. One distinguishes these common properties as the *intent* of the concept that determines its *extent* which are objects accepted as members of the concept. The relationship between intent and extent of concepts is popularized in the machine learning community by the description of the *space of instances* and the *space of hypotheses* [10]. Similarly to the description of instance space and hypothesis space, the notion of concepts under the classical view was mathematically formulated in the theory of formal concept analysis (FCA) by Wille and his colleagues during last fifteen years [14,15]. Formal concept analysis starts with a formal context in which the objects are observed.

Definition 1. A *context* is a triple $(\mathcal{O}, \mathcal{A}, \mathcal{R})$ where $\mathcal{O}$ be a set of objects, $\mathcal{A}$ be a set of attributes and $\mathcal{R}$ be a binary relation between $\mathcal{O}$ and $\mathcal{A}$, i.e., $\mathcal{R} \subseteq \mathcal{O} \times \mathcal{A}$.

For the simplicity, formal concept analysis is always described with Boolean data. However, its notions can be extended for multi-valued data. In general, $(o, a) \in \mathcal{R}$ is understood as "object o has attribute a" in Boolean domains, and can be extended to nominal or discrete numeric domains as "object o has attribute a with some value v". Data from continuous domains need to be discretized into discrete data in order to be used in the framework. The discretization of continuous attributes is out of the scope of this paper and will be described in another work.

Definition 2. Two *derivation operators* $\rho : \wp(\mathcal{A}) \rightarrow \wp(\mathcal{O})$ and $\lambda : \wp(\mathcal{O}) \rightarrow \wp(\mathcal{A})$, where $\wp(\mathcal{O})$ and $\wp(\mathcal{A})$ are the power sets of $\mathcal{O}$ and $\mathcal{A}$, are determined as follows:

$$S \subseteq \mathcal{A}, \quad \rho(S) = \{o \in \mathcal{O} \mid \forall a \in S, (o, a) \in \mathcal{R}\}$$
$$X \subseteq \mathcal{O}, \quad \lambda(X) = \{a \in \mathcal{A} \mid \forall o \in X, (o, a) \in \mathcal{R}\}$$

Definition 3. A *formal concept* C is a pair (X, S) with $X \subseteq \mathcal{O}$, $S \subseteq \mathcal{A}$ satisfying $\rho(S) = X$ and $\lambda(X) = S$. X and S are called the *extent* and the *intent* of C, respectively.

When the extent of a concept C_2 is included in the extent of a concept C_1 we say that C_1 is a *superconcept* of C_2 (C_2 is a *subconcept* of C_1). The basic theorem in FCA [14] show that the set of all possible formal concepts from the context $(\mathcal{O}, \mathcal{A}, \mathcal{R})$, associated with the superconcept-subconcept relation, is a complete lattice [b]. It is called *concept lattice* or *Galois lattice* and denoted by $\mathcal{L}(\mathcal{O}, \mathcal{A}, \mathcal{R})$. Also, FCA shows the natural "duality" between extent (objects) and intent (attributes) in a context, e.g., λ and ρ define a *Galois connection* between $\wp(\mathcal{O})$ and $\wp(\mathcal{A})$. Figure 1 presents a Wille's illustration of a formal context and the corresponding concept lattice $\mathcal{L}(\mathcal{O}, \mathcal{A}, \mathcal{R})$. The formal context is about eight living organisms whose names are heading the rows (with corresponding abbreviations) {Leech (Le), Bream (Br), Frog (Fr), Dog (Dg), Spike-Weed (SW), Bean (Bn), Maize (Mz), Reed e(Rd)}. The living organisms are described by attributes {needs water (nw), lives in water (lw), lives on land (ll), needs chlorophyll (nc), 2 leaf germination (2lg), 1 leaf germination (1lg), is motile (mo), has limbs (lb), suckles young (sk)}. Furthermore, the ○ indicates when an object has an attribute, i.e., which living organism has which attribute. The concept lattice consists of 19 formal concepts $C_1, C_2, ..., C_{19}$ (denoted in the figure by their indexes), for example C_9 = ({Le, Br, Fr}, {nw, lw, mo}).

Definition 4. A *concept hierarchy* $\mathcal{H}$ is a part of the concept lattice $\mathcal{L}$ satisfying the following conditions (1) the root concept $(\mathcal{O}, \lambda(\mathcal{O})) \in \mathcal{H}$; (2) if $C_1 = (X_1, S_1), C_2 = (X_2, S_2) \in \mathcal{H}$ and $X_1 \cap X_2 \neq \varnothing$ then either C_1 is a subconcept of C_2 or C_2 is a subconcept of C_1.

Note that the property $(\{o\}, \lambda(o)) \in \mathcal{H}$ for all $o \in \mathcal{O}$ in the usual definition of the hierarchy structure is not necessarily required here as for the

[b] A lattice $\mathcal{L}$ is complete when each of its subset X has a least upper bound and a greatest lower bound in $\mathcal{L}$.

generalization purpose many concepts at high levels need to be pruned.

objects	abb.	nw	lw	ll	nc	2lg	1lg	mo	lb	sk
Leech	Le	○	○					○		
Bream	Br	○	○					○	○	
Frog	Fr	○	○	○				○	○	
Dog	Dg	○		○				○	○	○
Spike-Weed	SW	○	○		○		○			
Reed	Rd	○	○	○	○		○			
Maize	Mz	○		○	○		○			
Bean	Bn	○		○	○	○				

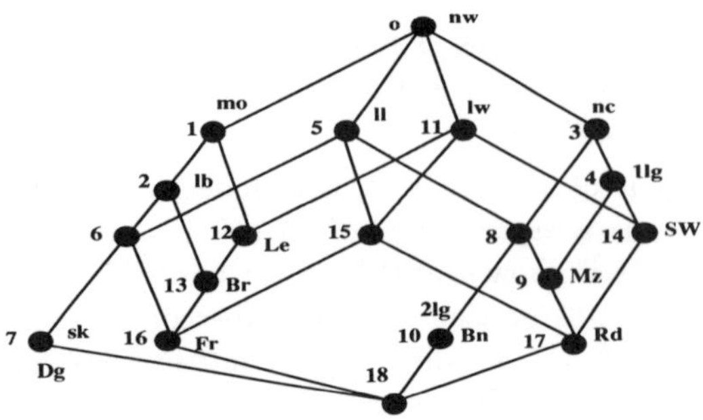

Figure 1: Formal context and concept lattice of living organisms

One can distinguish at least three learning problems in the framework of Galois lattice:

P1. Nonincrementally construct a concept hierarchy: $\mathcal{O} \xrightarrow{\mathcal{L}} \mathcal{H}$
P2. Incrementally update a concept lattice: $\mathcal{L} \cup \{o^*\} \longrightarrow \mathcal{L}^*$
P3. Incrementally update a concept hierarchy: $\mathcal{H} \cup \{o^*\} \xrightarrow{\mathcal{L}^*} \mathcal{H}^*$

where $\mathcal{H}$ is the concept hierarchy to be learned, o^* is an updated instance, $\mathcal{L}^*, \mathcal{H}^*$ are updated lattice and hierarchy when o^* is encountered, $\xrightarrow{\mathcal{L}}$, $\xrightarrow{\mathcal{L}^*}$ show that learning is carried out through the hypothesis space $\mathcal{L}$ or $\mathcal{L}^*$. Algorithm OSHAM [5] is a solution to the problem P1, which was improved from the FCA-based model to a hybrid model by combining its classical view on concepts with the prototype and exemplar views [6]. Recently, some algorithms for the problem P2 have been developed [1,4]. The algorithm INCOSHAM presented in this paper is a solution of the problem P3 inspired by solutions for P1 and P2. The basis of OSHAM is a generate-and-test procedure to split a concept C into subconcepts at a lower level of $\mathcal{H}$. Starting from the root concept with the whole set of training instances, OSHAM extracts the concept hierarchy $\mathcal{H}$ recursively in the top-down direction. The basic idea of algorithm OSHAM is described in Table 1.

Table 1. Basic idea of the algorithm OSHAM

1. While C is still splittable, find a new subconcept of it that corresponds to the hypothesis maximizing a quality function among η hypotheses generated by the following steps
   (a) Find a "good" feature concerning the best cover of C satisfying the minimum intersection condition.
   (b) Find a closed feature subset S containing this feature.
   (c) Form a subconcept with the intent S.
   (d) Evaluate the quality function with the new hypothesized subconcept.
2. If one of the following conditions holds then C is considered as unsplittable
   (a) there exist not any closed proper subset of features.
   (b) the set of unclassified instances of C is too small.
   (c) the set of unclassified instances of C is homogeneous enough.

3 Incremental Inducing Concept Hierarchies

Suppose that o^* is a new undapted instance in database. An efficient solution to the problem P2 for incrementally updating the concept lattice can be obtained by exploiting the fact that in the updated concept lattice, existing concepts are never removed from $\mathcal{L}$ but their extent and intent may be changed, or new concepts may occur with the change of superconcept-subconcept links between concepts. In general, for any subset $X \subseteq \mathcal{O}$, $(X \cup \{o^*\}, \lambda(X) \cap \lambda(\{o^*\}))$ will be added to $\mathcal{L}$ if it is a concept and $\lambda(X) \cap \lambda(\{o^*\})$ is not the intent of any existing concept in $\mathcal{L}$.

Definition 5. *Intersection* between two concepts (X_1, S_1) and (X_2, S_2) in $\mathcal{H}$ is the concept $(\rho(S_1 \cap S_2), S_1 \cap S_2)$.

The following property[1] allows us to find all updated concepts by consider only how o^* relates to existing concepts in $\mathcal{L}$ by the intersection operator.

Proposition 1. *Intersection of* $(\{o^*\}, \lambda(\{o^*\}))$ *with existing concepts in* $\mathcal{L}$ *guarantees to generate all updated concepts.*

When intersecting $(\{o^*\}, \lambda(\{o^*\}))$ with an existing concept $(X, S) \in \mathcal{L}$, basically three cases may happen:

(a) if $S \cap \lambda(\{o^*\}) = \varnothing$ then (X, S) is not changed as they are incomparable.
(b) if $S \cap \lambda(\{o^*\}) = S$ then (X, S) is modified to $(X \cup \{o^*\}, S)$.
(c) if $S \cap \lambda(\{o^*\}) \subsetneq S$ then $(\{o^*\}, \lambda(\{o^*\}))$ relates to a new concept in $\mathcal{L}$ and (X, S) is called a *generator* of the new concept.

The basic theorem[14] and the following property guarantees the unicity of the new concept and shows the way to avoid regenerating new concepts[4].

Proposition 2. *If concept (X, S) is a generator of a new concept (X', S') then (X', S') = inf* $\{(X, S) \in \mathcal{L} \mid S' = S \cap \lambda(\{o^*\})\}$ *and there is no other concepts of the form* (Z, S').

The change from $\mathcal{H}$ to $\mathcal{H}^*$ relates to the change from $\mathcal{L}$ to $\mathcal{L}^*$ when a new instance o^* is encountered and $\mathcal{L}$ can be updated effectively by using only the intersection of existing concepts in $\mathcal{L}$ with $(\{o^*\}, \lambda(\{o^*\})$. From the proposition 2 we note that if (X, S) is a generator of a new concept (X', S') then either (X', S') is a son of some father (least upper bound) of (X, S) (if the intent of that father includes $S \cap \lambda(\{o^*\})$) or the intent of all fathers of (X, S) are incomparable to $S \cap \lambda(\{o^*\})$.

Definition 6. We say that the concept (X, S) *matches* the new instance o^* (also, o^* matches (X, S)) if and only if $S \cap \lambda(\{o^*\}) \subseteq S$.

The main idea of INCOSHAM lies in the fact that instead of extracting $\mathcal{H}$ from the updated concept lattice $\mathcal{L}^*$, INCOSHAM checks only the part of $\mathcal{L}^*$ which concerns with $(\{o^*\}, \lambda(\{o^*\}))$. By the superconcept-subconcept relation of $\mathcal{L}$, if the instance o^* matches a concept it will match all superconcepts of this concepts. This property allows us to consider in each branch of $\mathcal{H}$ only the most specific concept (with the highest level in the branch) that matches o^*.

Note that if o^* matches $C_k = (X_k, S_k)$ but does not match any subconcept $C_{k_i} = (X_{k_i}, S_{k_i})$ of C_k, then when being encountered o^* will change $C_k = (X_k, S_k)$ and its subconcepts. In this case we need to apply OSHAM to C_k in order to reconstruct the subhierarchy under C_k. Starting from the root concept, the incremental algorithm INCOSHAM $(\mathcal{O}, \mathcal{A}, \mathcal{H}, C_k, o^*)$ described briefly in Table 2 is applied recursively to all concepts C_k on $\mathcal{H}$ that match o^*. Two subroutines *Discard* and *Reindex* serve to carry out two basic operators of the updating process. The former cuts off a subhierarchy from $\mathcal{H}$ when its root is a concept to be modified, and the latter reindexes the concept hierarchy after cutting off a subhierarchy so that the remained hierarchy has sequentially indexes, and the root of the discarded subhierarchy becomes the last index in the discarded and reindexed hierarchy.

Proposition 3. *Intersection of* $(\{o^*\}, \lambda(\{o^*\}))$ *with existing concepts in* $\mathcal{H}$ *guarantees to generate all updated concepts in* $\mathcal{H}^*$

Proof. Note that OSHAM extracts $\mathcal{H}$ from $\mathcal{L}$ level by level from the root concept, and at each level it extracts sequentially subconcepts of concepts at the higher level. Each subconcept is formed corresponding to one attribute a^* that covers a maximum number of instances in the extent of its superconcept which are not yet classified according to the quality criterion. When intersecting $(\{o^*\}, \lambda(\{o^*\}))$ with each concept $C_k = (X_k, S_k)$ on $\mathcal{H}$, we are interested only in the case when C_k will be modified or a new node will be added, it means that $(\{o^*\}, \lambda(\{o^*\}))$ matches C_k partially or completely $\lambda(\{o^*\}) \cap S_k \subseteq \lambda(\{o^*\})$. In these situations, o^* is added to the extent of C_k, $X_k = X_k \cup \{o^*\}$, but according to OSHAM, S_k does not change. This remark confirms that the intersection of $(\{o^*\}, \lambda(\{o^*\}))$ with existing concepts in $\mathcal{H}$ guarantees to generate all updated concepts in $\mathcal{H}^*$. ■

Table 2. Algorithm INCOSHAM

Algorithm INCOSHAM $(\mathcal{O}, \mathcal{A}, \mathcal{H}, C_k, o^*)$

Input Concept hierarchy $\mathcal{H}$, concept $C_k = (X_k, S_k)$ that matches o^*.
Top-level INCOSHAM$(\mathcal{O}, \mathcal{A}, \mathcal{H}, root_concept, o^*)$.
Output Updated concept hierarchy $\mathcal{H}^*$.

1. Let $X_k = X_k \cup \{o^*\}$ and modify other components of C_k according to X_k^*.
2. Check all sons C_{k_i} of C_k

   If there exists at least a subconcept C_{k_i} of C_k that matches o^* then

   (a) Apply INCOSHAM $(\mathcal{O}, \mathcal{A}, \mathcal{H}, C_{k_i}, o^*)$ to all C_{k_i} that matches o^*.
   (b) Mark all C_{k_i} that do not match o^* to do not recheck them again.

   elseif there is not any subconcept C_{k_i} that matches o^* then

   (a) Discard the subhierarchy $\mathcal{H}_{C_k}$ with the root is C_k, except C_k.
   (b) Reindex the indexes of nodes in $\mathcal{H} \setminus \mathcal{H}_{C_k}$ so that they are sequential.
   (c) Apply OSHAM $(C_k, \mathcal{H})$ to reconstruct a new subhierarchy $\mathcal{H}_{C_k}$.

---

4 Evaluation of INCOSHAM

This section presents a comparative evaluation between INCOSHAM and OSHAM. They are compared with respect to the following dimensions: learned concept hierarchies, computational cost, and predictive accuracies.

4.1 *Learned concept hierarchies*

Both OSHAM and INCOSHAM extract concept hierarchies from the Galois lattice. Results obtained by applying OSHAM to $\mathcal{O} \cup \{o^*\}$ and INCOSHAM to $\mathcal{H} \cup \{o^*\}$ may be lightly different. This difference is similar to that of results between nonincremental ID3 [11] and its incremental versions ID4 [12] and ID5 [13]. The reason of this difference is when INCOSHAM moves down in $\mathcal{H}$ to modify some subconcept C_{k_i} of C_k, it does not backtrack to recalculate the splitting quality in order to avoid carrying out all operations of OSHAM.

4.2 *Computational time*

In the Galois lattice theory, when constructing a concept lattice from a context, the number of concepts can be exponential in the size of the context, and the complexity of finding concepts is exponential, since the number of concepts may be large. The upper bound of complexity of constructing a concept hierarchy by OSHAM from a given context $(\mathcal{O}, \mathcal{A}, \mathcal{R})$ is $O(|\mathcal{O}| \times |\mathcal{A}|^2 \times |\mathcal{H}|)$. In updating a concept hierarchy by INCOSHAM, when an instance is encountered, only a concept subhierarchy $\mathcal{H}_{C_k}$ with the root (X_k, S_k) will be reconstructed. The complexity of INCOSHAM however is $O(|X_k| \times |\mathcal{A}|^2 \times |\mathcal{H}_{C_k}|)$. As the root of $\mathcal{H}_{C_k}$ is usually at a high level then $|\mathcal{H}| \gg |\mathcal{H}_{C_k}|$, $|\mathcal{O}| \gg |X_k|$.

Suppose that M is the number of training instances which are used to learn a concept hierarchy $\mathcal{H}$ by OSHAM, and N is the number of new updated instances by which one need to modify $\mathcal{H}$. Experimental results in the next subsection 4.4 with different data sets show that the computational time of INCOSHAM is much less then those of OSHAM when N is relatively small, but is much higher when N exceeds some threshold.

4.3 *Predictive accuracy*

There is a less agreement on how to evaluate the predictive accuracy of unsupervised concept learning methods. However, one ultimate goal of learning systems is to use learned knowledge to predict unknown cases. A good way to evaluate unsupervised concept learning is to employ labelled data but hide the label of instances in the whole discovering and matching phases and after that use the instance labels only to estimate the predictive accuracy of the discovered knowledge. We use this method to evaluate INCOSHAM with predicted name of each discovered concept is the most frequently occurring name of instances in its extent. Experimental results carried out in this way show that the predictive accuracy of INCOSHAM is generally similar to that of OSHAM, only in some cases it is lightly lower. This phenomenon occurs as INCOSHAM reuses the local heuristic selection of OSHAM in the search process which may be changed with encountering of new instances. We have evaluate the predictive accuracy of OSHAM by multiple train-and-test experiments (10-fold cross validation). For two data sets described below, the average percentage of successful matched unknown instances of OSHAM is 92.3% for Wisconsin breast cancer, and 93.7% for Congressional voting. OSHAM attains the predictive accuracy of 88.2% and 92.6% for data sets Mushroom and Tic-tac-toe. By using the same experiment conditions, the corresponding predictive accuracy of AUTOCLASS [2] is 96.6%, 91.2%, 86.5%, and 82.3%, respectively [7].

4.4 Experimental results

INCOSHAM is implemented in the X Window, and has been tested and compared with the new version of OSHAM [7] on public data sets from the UC Irvine Repository of Machine Learning. Earlier results from some of them are reported below.

Wisconsin breast cancer: This data set consists of 699 observations of Benign and Malignant cases on 9 symbolic symptoms: Clump Thickness, Uniformity of Cell Size, Uniformity of Cell Shape, Marginal Adhesion, Single Epithelial Cell Size, Bare Nuclei, Bland Chromatin, Normal Nucleoli, Mitoses, each has 10 possible values.

Congressional voting: There are 435 instances in two classes (Democrats and Republicans) represented by 17 attributes in this data set.

Figure 2 gives a comparison of CPU execution time of OSHAM and INCOSHAM on these two data sets by single train-and-test experiments. Figure 2(A) and 2(B) compare the CPU time (sec.) when the number N of updated instances is small (1 and 5) with respect to the increasing numbers M of training instances. Values of M are shown in Figure 2(A) and 2(B). N updated instances are taken randomly from the rest of data sets. These experiments show that the execution time of OSHAM on $M+N$ training instances increases considerably with the increasing numbers M of training instances while the execution time for updating by INCOSHAM the concept hierarchy, generated by these M training instances, with small number N updated instances is relatively low. Figure 2(C) and 2(D) compare the execution time when M is fixed (600 and 400, respectively for Wisconsin breast cancer and Congressional voting data) and N increases smoothly from some small value to values at which execution time of INCOSHAM to update the concept hierarchy, generated by M training instances, becomes higher (and then much higher) than execution time of OSHAM to reconstruct the concept hierarchy from scratch with

$M + N$ training instances. The curves in Figure 2 are not always monotonous or smooth, some of them are rapidly going downwards in 2(B) or upwards in 2(C). This complicated behavior of INCOSHAM can be explained by the fact that if the new updated instance o^* is very different from most training instances it may lead to discard a large subhierarchy $\mathcal{H}_{C_k}$ at a low level and causes an expensive cost for reconstructing the concept hierarchy.

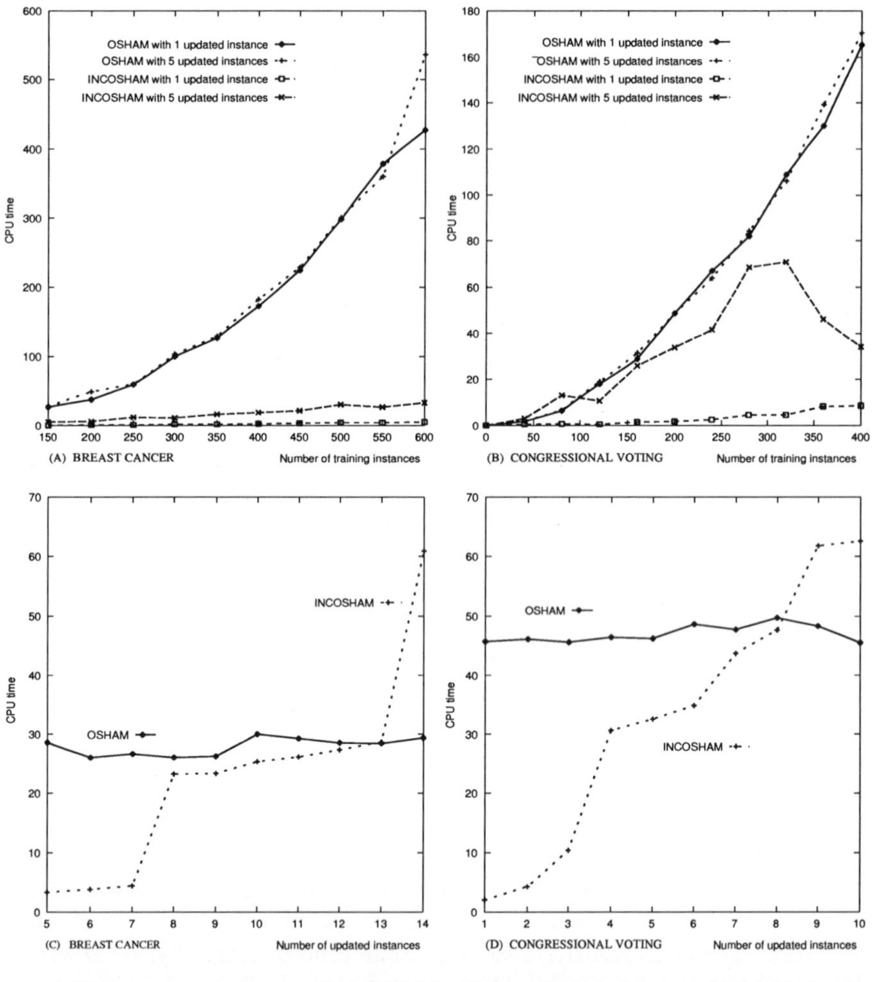

Figure 2. Comparison of OSHAM and INCOSHAM on CPU time

Though INCOSHAM is generally sensitive to the nature of updated instances, experimental results suggest some practical strategy to use alternatively these incremental and nonincremental learning algorithms:

- to use the incremental algorithm to update the concept hierarchy when there is several new updated instances.
- to use the nonincremental algorithm to reconstruct the concept hierarchy when there are a relatively large number of new updated instances.

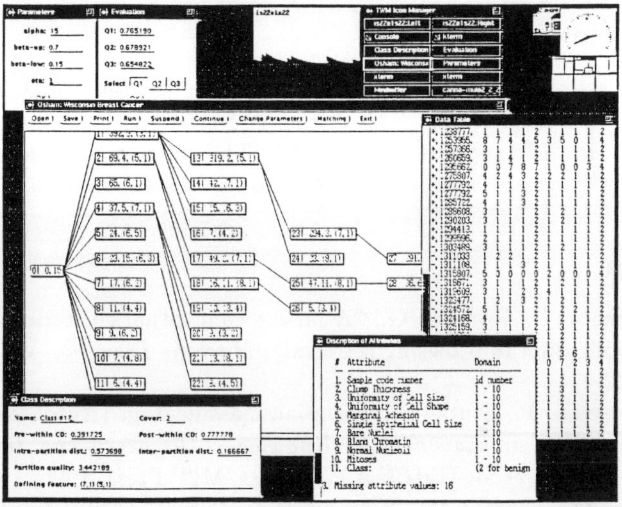

Figure 3. A screen of knowledge discovery system INCOSHAM

5 Concluding Remarks

We have presented INCOSHAM – an incremental algorithm derived from the conceptual learning algorithm OSHAM – that extracts a concept hierarchy from the hypothesis space with the Galois lattice structure. INCOSHAM preserves the nonexhaustive search strategy of OSHAM and exploits only the relevant part of the hypothesis space. The main advantage of OSHAM is the relevant new possible concepts can be obtained by the intersection of the new instance with existing formal concepts without necessarily regenerating the hypothesis space and the concept hierarchy. Experimental results show that both OSHAM and INCOSHAM perform reasonably well on public data sets. We also carried out an experimental comparison of the cost for updating concept hierarchies by OSHAM and INCOSHAM that leads to a general rule of using the alternative algorithms in practice depending on the size of the training set and updated instance set. As our work is under elaboration, it may be possible to improve INCOSHAM in different directions, such as to reduce the difference between results of using OSHAM and INCOSHAM by the processing of exceptional cases and unmatched instances, to extend INCOSHAM into a hybrid system by combining it with some features of probabilistic, exemplar views and the similarity principle of categorization.

Acknowledgments

This work is done by grants from Kokusai Electric Co., Ltd. The author would like to thank Professors M. Kimura (JAIST) and S. Ohsuga (Waseda University) for their support in the work. Thanks also to Takeshi Aoki and Trong Dung Nguyen for their contribution to the implementation of the system.

References

1. Carpineto, C., Romano G., "A lattice conceptual clustering system and its application to browsing retrieval", *Machine Learning*, Vol. 10 (1996), 95–122.
2. Cheeseman, P., Stutz, J., "Bayesian classification (AutoClass): Theory and results", in *Advances in Knowledge Discovery and Data Mining*, U.M. Fayyad et al. (Eds.), AAAI Press/MIT Press, 1996, 153–180.
3. Fisher, D., Pazzani M., "Computer models of concept learning", in D. Fisher et al. (Eds.) *Concept Formation: Knowledge and Experience in Unsupervised Learning*, Morgan Kaufmann 1991, pp. 3-44.
4. Godin, R., Missaoui, R., "An incremental concept formation approach for learning from databases", *Theoretical Computer Science*, 133 (1994), pp. 387–419.
5. Ho, T.B., "An approach to concept formation based on formal concept analysis", *IEICE Trans. Information and Systems*, Vol. E78-D, No. 5, May 1995, 553–559.
6. Ho, T.B., "A hybrid model for concept formation", in *Information Modelling and Knowledge Bases VII*, Jaakkola et al. (Eds.), IOS Publisher, 1996, 22–35.
7. Ho, T.B., "Discovering and Using Knowledge From Unsupervised Data", to appear in *Decision Support Systems*, June 1997.
8. Langley, P., *Elements of Machine Learning*, Morgan Kaufmann, 1996.

9. Michalski R. S., Stepp R. E., Learning from observation: conceptual learning. *Machine Learning: An Artificial Intelligence Approach*, Vol. 1, R. S. Michalski, J. G. Carbonelle, T. M. Michell (Eds.), Morgan Kaufmann, 1983, pp. 331–363.
10. Mitchell, T., "Generalization as search", *Artificial Intelligence*, 18 (1982), pp. 203–226.
11. Quinlan, J. R., "Induction of decision tree", *Machine Learning*, 1 (1986), pp. 81–106.
12. Schlimmer, J.C., Fisher, D., "A case study of incremental concept induction", *Proceedings of the Fifth National Conference on Machine Learning*, 1986, pp. 496–501.
13. Utgoff, P.E., "Incremental induction of decision trees", *Machine Learning*, Vol. 4 (1989), pp. 161–186.
14. Wille, R., "Restructuring lattice theory: an approach based on hierarchies of concepts", in *Ordered Sets*, I. Rival (Ed.), Reidel, 1982, pp. 445-470.
15. Wille, R., "Concept lattice and conceptual knowledge systems", *Computers and Mathematics with Applications*, Vol. 23 (1992), pp. 493–515.

Chapter 2

Classifiers and Classification Techniques

Induction of Fuzzy Classification Trees

I-Jen Chiang Jane Yung-jen Hsu
Department of Computer Science and Information Engineering,
National Taiwan University,
Taipei, Taiwan, 106

The possibilistic tree classifier, ***fuzzy classification trees***, has been introduced to discover the knowledge in large amount of data. Traditional tree classifiers often make a single decision for classifications. A single decision is too overly general for knowledge discovery, especially to some application domains, such as medicine and finance. ***Fuzzy classifications*** have been proposed to solve such a serious problem. Instead of rigidly determining a single class for any given instance, fuzzy classification trees give predictions about the degree of possibility for every class. In order to select the best attribute for each step of the induction task, possibilistic entropy evaluation addressed in this paper is to evaluate the uncertainties in the data. By comparing with decision tree classifier, this paper also shows that the classifier generated in accordance with the concept of fuzzy classifications is a more general model than the traditional tree classifier. The fuzzy classification trees have been applied to some data sets from the UCI repository. Generally speaking from empirical results, the misclassification rates of those data sets are less than C4.5.

1 Introduction

Data mining is inherently an inductive process [1]. The inductive process has been widely used to discover the regularity from a large amount of data. The purpose of induction is to generalize the rules applied not only to the already known data but also to the unseen data as well.

Inductive learning has been used to "*mine*" knowledge from a large amount of data. The knowledge can be used to make prediction. The classification technology is a supervised, inductive learning that is a primary task of data mining. The data are described in terms of attributes, which are categorical or numerical, and associated classes. Classifications are used to discriminate the data according to their classes and generalize them in order to explain the universal world. The classification methods have been widely used in medical and financial applications [2,3].

Traditional tree classifiers classify the data into a single decision. General speaking, it loses to consider all the possibility, which may result in poor predictions. The concept of decision forests [4,5] and the method of soft splitting [6] and kernel smoothing [7] have been proposed to solve such a rigid classifications. Based on the theoretic foundation, the fuzzy classifications have been introduced [8]. Fuzzy classification trees are used to implement it. Data can be softly classified into all possible classes.

Fuzzy classification trees allows multiple prediction to be made, each of which is associated with a degree of possibility. In application domains that involve a large amount of data with uncertainty, such as medical or financial domains, fuzzy classification trees can serve as a useful data mining tool.

This paper will show how the generality of the novel model, fuzzy classification trees, is while comparing with the traditional tree classifiers in section 2. Section 3 will demonstrate the attribute selection measure, possibilistic entropy, for the induction of fuzzy classification trees. Some empirical results will show in section 4, following the conclusion.

2 Fuzzy Classifiers

Fuzzy classification trees and their constructing algorithm were introduced by Hsu and Chiang [8,9]. A fuzzy classification tree is a possibilistic tree classifier, that is a kind of fuzzy classifiers [8]. Fuzzy classifiers will be proved to be more general than traditional decision tree classifiers in this section. Before further identifying the relationship of and the difference between the traditional tree classifier and the possibilistic tree classifier, let us briefly review the definitions of fuzzy classifiers and fuzzy classification trees.

The *fuzzy classifier* **F** can be represented as a vector of functions

$$\langle \wp_1, \wp_2, \ldots, \wp_n \rangle,$$

where $\wp_i$ is a possibility function $\mathcal{X} \to [0,1]$. For any given instance $\mathbf{x}$, the relation $\wp_i(\mathbf{x}) > \wp_j(\mathbf{x})$ indicates that it is more likely for the instance $\mathbf{x}$ to be in class C_i. A fuzzy classifier can be implemented by a *Fuzzy Classification Tree* (FCT).

To facilitate representations, a labeling scheme is used to denote the fuzzy classification tree. Given an *FCT*, each node n in the tree $\mathcal{T}$ is given a label:

$$\text{Label}(n) = \begin{cases} 1 & \text{if } n \text{ is the root;} \\ \text{Label}(n').i & \text{if } n \text{ is the } i\text{th child of node } n'. \end{cases}$$

where . is the concatenation operator.

A sample FCT for two classes C_1 and C_2 is depicted in Figure 1. The symbol N_L denotes the node with label L, and B_L denotes the branch leading into node N_L. Let L be a label of a node in FCT. The possibility function

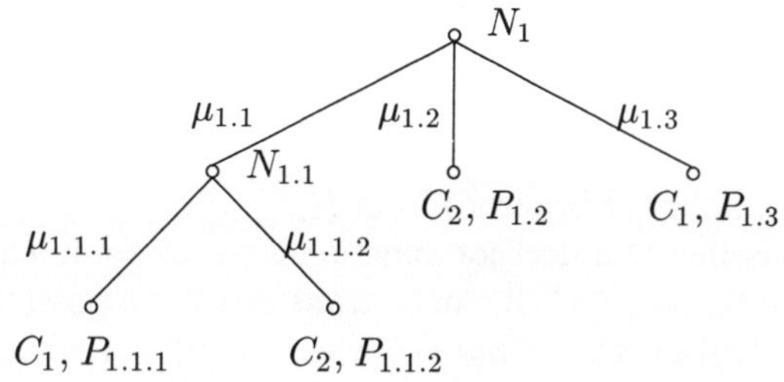

Figure 1: A sample FCT with $\mathcal{C} = \{C_1, C_2\}$

$P_L : \mathcal{X} \rightarrow [0,1]$ is defined by composing the membership functions along the path from the root to node N_L. That is,

$$P_L = \begin{cases} 1 & \text{if } N_L \text{ is the root node;} \\ \\ P_{\hat{L}} \otimes \mu_L & \text{if } N_{\hat{L}} \text{ is the parent of } N_L. \end{cases}$$

The composition operator $\otimes$ is defined in terms of some valid operation for combining two membership functions. A membership function $\mu_{L.i} : \mathcal{X} \rightarrow [0,1]$, defines the degree of possibility that an instance $\mathbf{x} \in \mathcal{X}$ should be propagated down the branch $B_{L.i}$.

The possibilistic tree classifier will be formulated according to the definitions of FCT. Let $\mathcal{X}$ be the instance space, and $\mathcal{C}$ be the set of classes. For a possibilistic tree classifier $\mathbf{F}$, for every instance $\mathbf{x} \in \mathcal{X}$, there exists a possibility $\wp_i(\mathbf{x})$ for each class C_i. Therefore, the possibilistic tree classifiers can be formulated to be the same form as the fuzzy classifiers as

$$\mathbf{F}(\mathbf{x}) = \langle \wp_1(\mathbf{x}), \wp_2(\mathbf{x}), \ldots, \wp_n(\mathbf{x}) \rangle.$$

An FCT is a possibilistic tree classifier, that can be formally defined to be

$$\mathbf{F}(\mathbf{x}) = P_{f_1(\mathbf{x})} \in [0,1]$$

for $C_{f_1(\mathbf{x})}$ where 1 is label of the root of an FCT. The function

$$f_L(\mathbf{x}) = \begin{cases} L.\text{Test}_L(\mathbf{x}) & \text{if } N_{L.\text{Test}_L(\mathbf{x})} \text{ is a terminal node} \\ f_{L.\text{Test}_L(\mathbf{x})}(\mathbf{x}) & \text{otherwise,} \end{cases}$$

where $\text{Test}_L(\mathbf{x})$ is an integer that

$$\text{Test}_L : \mathcal{X} \longrightarrow 2^{b_L}.$$

The value b_L is the number of branches from N_L.

A traditional classifier is a decision function D, such that, $D(\mathbf{x}) = C_i$ for every $\mathbf{x} \in \mathcal{X}$ for some class $C_i \in \mathcal{C}$. It can be transferred to a possibilistic model above as $\mathbf{F}(\mathbf{x}) = \langle \wp_1(\mathbf{x}), \wp_2(\mathbf{x}), \ldots, \wp_n(\mathbf{x}) \rangle$, where $\wp_i(\mathbf{x}) = 1$ when $D(\mathbf{x}) = C_i$ and all the other $\wp_j(\mathbf{x}) = 0$ for $i \neq j$. Class probability trees can also be modeled by this form where $\sum_{i=1}^{n} \wp_i(\mathbf{x}) = 1$. Therefore, $\wp_i(\mathbf{x})$ is the probability that $\mathbf{x}$ is in class C_i. They can be rewritten by the form of FCT above, but the function Test_L is a number between 1 and b_L and $\mathbf{F}(\mathbf{x}) \in \{0, 1\}$. As their characteristics on testing, they are categorized to decision tree classifiers.

Due to that transformation, the relationship of decision tree classifier [10,11,12] which is abbreviated to "DTC" and the possibilistic classifier which is abbreviated to "PC" is clearly identified. In order to distinguish each other, the decision tree classifier is denoted as $\mathbf{F}_D$.

Theorem 1 DTC $\subseteq$ PC.

Proof Assume that DTC $\not\subseteq$ PC, there must exist an instance $\mathbf{x}$ such that $\mathbf{F}_D(\mathbf{x}) = 1$ for class C_i but $\wp_i = 0$ for PC. Suppose that the test at the immediate nodes of the DTC tree is the same as the test at the immediate nodes of the PC trees.

Suppose that there are L and L' which is the value of $f_{L.\text{Test}_L(\mathbf{x})}(\mathbf{x})$ for a decision tree classifier. For an instance in a decision tree classifier, there is only one branch that will be selected for a test Test_L at each nonterminal node N_L. It means that for a possibilistic classifier, the possibility $P_{L'}(\mathbf{x})$ is zero. In the other word, $L' \notin \text{Test}_L(\mathbf{x})$. Since Test_L is the same for DTC and PC, $\text{Test}_L(\mathbf{x})$ can obtain only one solution. This contradicts the assumption that DTC $\not\subseteq$ PC So that DTC $\subseteq$ PC. □

3 Attribute Selection Criteria

Like the decision tree method, one of the important properties of fuzzy classification tree is to identify which attribute is important for classification. According to different position of the attribute in the tree, we can construct many different classification trees. As by Occam's Razor, the simple one can capture more information than the complex one. It is necessary to determine on choosing which attribute from root to leaf will construct a simple tree.

3.1 Properties of Fuzzy Entropy Functions

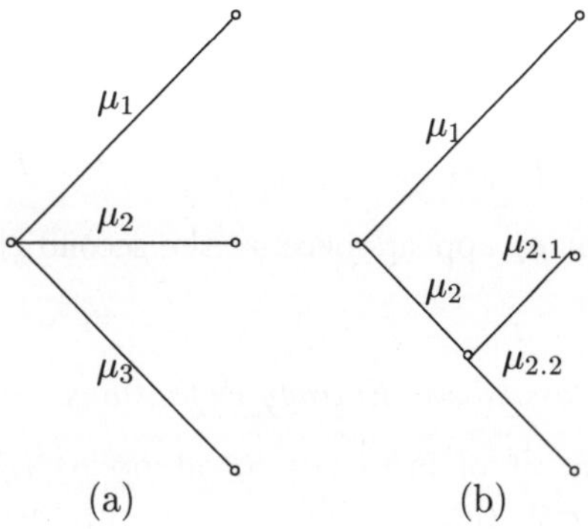

Figure 2: Decomposition of a choice from three possibilities.

According to the original probabilistic entropy defined by Shannon [13] and fuzzy entropy function defined by De. Luca and Termini [14], the information-based measure should satisfy the following criteria. Let The possibility $\wp_i$ for each i define the possibility of an instance, where $\wp_i \in [0,1]$.

[Property 1] Function $H(\wp_1, \wp_2, \ldots, \wp_n)$ should be continuous in $\wp_i$. This property prevents a situation in which a very small change in $\wp_i$ would produce a large (discontinuous) vibration.

[Property 2] Function H must be 0 if and only if all the $\wp_i$ but one are zero. When all but one is possible, there exists no uncertainty in the data.

[Property 3] Function H is the maximum value if and only if the $\wp_i$ are equal because there exists the most uncertainties in the data. That is, no matter what all the $\wp_i$ are, the largest uncertainties happened when all the $\wp_i$ are of the same value.

[Property 4] Function H is a nonnegative valuation on the $\wp_i$.

[Property 5] In order for the purpose that an attribute selection is to reduce the uncertainties in the data, it is necessary that if a choice is broken down into several successive choices, the original H should be no less than the weighted sum of the individual values of H. As illustrated in Figure 2, in (a) we have three possibilities μ_1, μ_2, and μ_3. In (b), on the right, we first choose between two possibilities, μ_1 and μ_2, and if the second occurs make another choice with possibility $\mu_{2.1}$, $\mu_{2.2}$. The final entropy of (b) should be less than or equal to the entropy of (a). That is

$$H(\mu_1, \mu_2, \mu_3) \geq H(\mu_1, \mu_2) + \mu_2 \times H(\mu_{2.1}, \mu_{2.2})$$

The coefficient μ_2 appears because the second choice is made only with possibility μ_2.

3.2 Preliminary Possibilistic Entropy Definitions

Suppose we have a set of instances S_L at node N_L. Assume there are n classes associated with the possibilities of occurrences $\wp_1, \wp_2, \ldots, \wp_n$. Concerning about the measure of how much *choice* is involved in the selection of the instance in S_L or of how uncertain we are of the outcome, we choose the entropy function to evaluate that.

Definition 1 *The entropy for the set of instances S_L at node N_L is defined by*

$$\text{Info}(S_L) = -\sum_{\forall c \in C} \frac{\mathcal{P}_L^c}{\mathcal{P}_L} \times \log_2 \frac{\mathcal{P}_L^c}{\mathcal{P}_L}.$$

where

$$\mathcal{P}_L = \sum_{x \in S_L} P_L(\mathbf{x})$$

is the sum of the possibility value $P_L(\mathbf{x})$ of all instances at node N_L, and

$$\mathcal{P}_L^c = \sum_{\mathbf{x} \in S_L \wedge \text{Class}(\mathbf{x}) = c} P_L(\mathbf{x})$$

is the sum over instances belonging to class c.

The entropy of a set measures the average amount of information needed to identify the class of an instance in the set. It is minimized when the set of instances are homogeneous, and maximized when the set is prefectly balanced among the classes.

A similar measurement can be defined when the set is distributed into b_L subsets, one for each branch based on the test at node N_L. The expected information requirement is the weighted sum over the subsets.

$$\text{Info}_T(S_L) = \sum_{i=1}^{b_L} \frac{\mathcal{P}_{L.i}}{\mathcal{P}_L} \times \text{Info}(S_{L.i}).$$

To asses the "benefits" of a test, we need to consider the increase in entropy. The quality

$$\text{Gain}(\text{Test}_L) = \text{Info}(S_L) - \text{Info}_T(S_L).$$

measures the information gain due to the test Test_L. This gain criterion is used as the basis for attribute selection.

It is easy to see that $\text{Info}(S_L)$ satisfies the first four properties. The remaining question is whether it satisfies the last property.

Theorem 2 *Let $\otimes$ be the* fuzzy t-norm *operator. If $\sum_{i=1}^{b_L} \mu_L(\mathbf{x}) \le 1$ for every $\mathbf{x} \in S_L$. Definition 1 satisfies the fifth property of entropy. That is*

$$\text{Info}(S_L) \ge \sum_{i=1}^{b_L} \frac{\mathcal{P}_{L.i}}{\mathcal{P}_L} \text{Info}(S_{L.i})$$

Proof   Let α be the maximal membership value for all membership functions. Let us derive from the right-hand-side of the inequality

$$\begin{aligned}
& \sum_{i=1}^{b_L} \tfrac{\mathcal{P}_{L.i}}{\mathcal{P}_L} \text{Info}(S_{L.i}) \\
= \quad & -\sum_{i=1}^{b_L} \tfrac{\mathcal{P}_{L.i}}{\mathcal{P}_L} \sum_{c \in C} \tfrac{\mathcal{P}_{L.i}^c}{\mathcal{P}_{L.}} \log_2 \tfrac{\mathcal{P}_{L.i}^c}{\mathcal{P}_{L.i}} \\
= \quad & -\sum_{i=1}^{b_L} \tfrac{\mathcal{P}_{L.i}}{\mathcal{P}_L} \sum_{c \in C} \tfrac{\mathcal{P}_L^c \otimes \mu_{L.i}}{\mathcal{P}_L \otimes \mu_{L.i}} \log_2 \tfrac{\mathcal{P}_L^c \otimes \mu_{L.i}}{\mathcal{P}_L \otimes \mu_{L.i}} \\
\le \quad & -\sum_{c \in C} \tfrac{\mathcal{P}_L^c \otimes \alpha}{\mathcal{P}_L \otimes \alpha} \log_2 \tfrac{\mathcal{P}_L^c \otimes \alpha}{\mathcal{P}_L \otimes \alpha} \\
& (\sum_l \mu_l(\mathbf{x}) \le 1 \text{ and } \alpha \ge \mu_l(\mathbf{x}), \forall l, \mathbf{x}) \\
\le \quad & -\sum_{c \in C} \tfrac{\mathcal{P}_L^c}{\mathcal{P}_L} \log_2 \tfrac{\mathcal{P}_L^c}{\mathcal{P}_L} \\
& (\sum_{c \in C} \mathcal{P}_L^c \le \mathcal{P}_L) \\
= \quad & \text{Info}(S_L).
\end{aligned}$$

□

3.3 Possibilistic Conditional Entropy

Density estimates can give valuable indication of data distribution features as skewness and multimodality in the data. Many methods [15,16,7] have been proposed to explore and present the data. Basically, these methods can be thought as clustering methods. The data can be partitioned into a lot of clusters that can be modeled by density functions. In this thesis, the fuzzy clustering methods can partition the data into several clusters. The membership function is used to model the data distribution.

Let c_j for each j be a cluster of S_L in node N_L of a fuzzy classification tree and c_{ij} be the jth cluster of S_L in class C_i of a fuzzy classification tree. As shown in Figure 3, the dotted line denotes the joint possibility of the instances

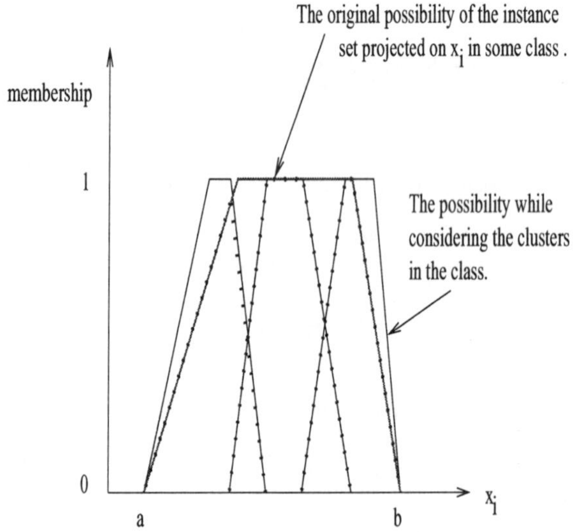

Figure 3: The possibility function of S_L projected on an attribute by considering its clusters of a class.

in class C_i while considering the clusters in C_i. The possibility $\mathcal{P}_L^{c_j}$ be the sum of possibility $P_L(\mathbf{x})$ for all $\mathbf{x}$ in node N_L of cluster c_j. The set of instances in S_L which are also in cluster c_j with membership value greater than zero is denoted to be $S_L^{c_j}$. Different with the cluster possibility, the possibility $\mathcal{P}_L^{C_i}$ for class C_i defines the class possibility seen before, and $S_L^{C_i}$ is the set of instances in S_L and also in C_i with membership value greater than zero. According to the entropy definition in fuzzy classification trees, let c_{ij} be the jth cluster of class C_i.

The possibilistic entropy should not consider only the class but also need to deliberate the clusters in a class. Referring to the Shannon's conditional entropy definitions, we define the joint and conditional possibilistic entropy as follows.

Definition 2 *Given the set S_L of instances in N_L, let $P_L^{c_{ij}}$ represent the possibility function of joint event in which* $\mathbf{x}$ *is in class C_i and* $\mathbf{x}$ *is in cluster c_j. Then for each* $\mathbf{x}$, *the possibility $P_L^{c_{ij}}(\mathbf{x}) = \min\left(P_L^{C_i}(\mathbf{x}), P_L^{c_j}(\mathbf{x})\right)$. The joint possibility is under the constraints of $P_L^{C_i}(\mathbf{x}) = \sum_{\forall j} P_L^{c_{ij}}(\mathbf{x})$ and $P_L^{c_j}(\mathbf{x}) = \sum_{\forall i} P_L^{c_{ij}}(\mathbf{x})$.*

Let $S_L^{c_{ij}}$ be the set of instances both in class C_i and in cluster c_{ij}. The set $S_L^{c_{ij}}$ can be thought as a joint event of $S_L^{C_i}$ and $S_L^{c_j}$.

Definition 3 *The entropy of the joint event is*

$$\text{Info}(S_L^{c_{ij}}) = -\frac{\mathcal{P}_L^{c_{ij}}}{\mathcal{P}_L} \log_2 \frac{\mathcal{P}_L^{c_{ij}}}{\mathcal{P}_L}.$$

Theorem 3 *The joint entropy is always less than or equal to the sum of individual entropy considered only the class or the cluster. That is,*

$$\sum_{i,j} \text{Info}(S_L^{c_{ij}}) \leq \sum_{i,j} \text{Info}(S_L^{C_i}) + \sum_{i,j} \text{Info}(S_L^{c_i}).$$

Proof According to the possibility theorem [17,18], $1 \geq P_L^{C_i}(\mathbf{x})$ and $1 \geq P_L^{c_j}(\mathbf{x})$ for all $\mathbf{x}$. Since

$$1 \geq P_L^{c_{ij}}(\mathbf{x}) = \min\left(P_L^{C_i}(\mathbf{x}), P_L^{c_j}(\mathbf{x})\right)$$

and

$$\min\left(P_L^{C_i}(\mathbf{x}), P_L^{c_j}(\mathbf{x})\right) \geq P_L^{C_i}(\mathbf{x}) \cdot P_L^{c_j}(\mathbf{x}),$$

as well as

$$1 \geq P_L^{c_{ij}}(\mathbf{x}) \geq P_L^{C_i}(\mathbf{x}) \cdot P_L^{c_j}(\mathbf{x}).$$

Therefore,

$$\mathcal{P}_L^{c_{ij}} \geq \mathcal{P}_L^{C_i} \cdot \mathcal{P}_L^{c_j}.$$

The function $\log_2$ is monotonous and $\log_2 x \geq 0$ for all $x \geq 1$ and $\mathcal{P}_L \geq \mathcal{P}_L^{c_{ij}} \geq \mathcal{P}_L^{C_i} \cdot \mathcal{P}_L^{c_j} \geq 0$, and because that

$$\sum_{i,j} \text{Info}(S_L^{C_i}) = -\sum_{i} \frac{\mathcal{P}_L^{C_i}}{\mathcal{P}_L} \log_2 \frac{\mathcal{P}_L^{C_i}}{\mathcal{P}_L} = -\sum_{i,j} \frac{\mathcal{P}_L^{c_{ij}}}{\mathcal{P}_L} \log_2 \sum_{j} \frac{\mathcal{P}_L^{c_{ij}}}{\mathcal{P}_L},$$

and

$$\sum_{i,j} \text{Info}(S_L^{c_j}) = -\sum_{i} \frac{\mathcal{P}_L^{c_i}}{\mathcal{P}_L} \log_2 \frac{\mathcal{P}_L^{c_i}}{\mathcal{P}_L} = -\sum_{i,j} \frac{\mathcal{P}_L^{c_{ij}}}{\mathcal{P}_L} \log_2 \sum_{i} \frac{\mathcal{P}_L^{c_{ij}}}{\mathcal{P}_L},$$

so the sum of the entropy of $S_L^{C_i}$ and $S_L^{c_i}$ is

$$\begin{aligned}\sum_{i,j}(\text{Info}(S_L^{C_i}) + \text{Info}(S_L^{c_j})) &= -\Big(\sum_{i,j}\frac{\mathcal{P}_L^{c_{ij}}}{\mathcal{P}_L}\log_2\sum_j\frac{\mathcal{P}_L^{c_{ij}}}{\mathcal{P}_L} + \sum_{i,j}\frac{\mathcal{P}_L^{c_{ij}}}{\mathcal{P}_L}\log_2\sum_i\frac{\mathcal{P}_L^{c_{ij}}}{\mathcal{P}_L}\Big)\\ &= -\sum_{i,j}\frac{\mathcal{P}_L^{c_{ij}}}{\mathcal{P}_L}\log_2\frac{\Big(\sum_j \mathcal{P}_L^{c_{ij}}\cdot\sum_i \mathcal{P}_L^{c_{ij}}\Big)}{(\mathcal{P}_L)^2}\\ &= -\sum_{i,j}\frac{\mathcal{P}_L^{c_{ij}}}{\mathcal{P}_L}\log_2\frac{\mathcal{P}_L^{C_i}\cdot\mathcal{P}_L^{c_j}}{(\mathcal{P}_L)^2}.\end{aligned}$$

Therefore,

$$\sum_{i,j}(\text{Info}(S_L^{C_i}) + \text{Info}(S_L^{c_j})) - \sum_{i,j}\text{Info}(S_L^{c_{ij}}) \geq 0$$

Hence,

$$\sum_{i,j}\text{Info}(S_L^{c_{ij}}) \leq \sum_{i,j}\text{Info}(S_L^{C_i}) + \sum_{i,j}\text{Info}(S_L^{c_i}).$$

□

The joint event $S_L^{c_{ij}}$ denotes the set of instances both in class C_i and cluster c_j with membership greater than zero in node N_L. It can be thought as the jth cluster c_{ij} in class C_i, and versus. The possibilistic conditional entropy can be defined as follows.

Definition 4 *The* possibilistic conditional entropy, $\text{Info}^{C_i}(S_L^{c_{ij}})$, *of* $S_L^{c_{ij}}$ *as the average of the entropy of* c_j *for each class* C_i*, weighted sum according to the possibility of getting the particular class* C_i*.*

$$\text{Info}_i(S_L^{c_{ij}}) = -\sum_{i,j}\frac{\mathcal{P}_L^{c_{ij}}}{\mathcal{P}_L}\log_2\hat{\wp}_i(j).$$

It measures how uncertain we are of $S_L^{c_{ij}}$ *on the average when we know* C_i*. Class* C_i *and the cluster* c_j *are not necessary independent. For any particular value* C_i *it can be assumed there is a conditional possibility* $\hat{\wp}_i(j)$ *that has the value* c_j*. This is given by*

$$\hat{\wp}_i(j) = \frac{\mathcal{P}_L^{c_{ij}}}{\sum_i \mathcal{P}_L^{c_{ij}}}.$$

Substitute the value of $\hat{\wp}_i(j)$ we obtain

$$\begin{aligned}\text{Info}_i(S_L^{c_{ij}}) &= -\sum_{i,j} \frac{\mathcal{P}_L^{c_{ij}}}{\mathcal{P}_L} \log_2 \frac{\mathcal{P}_L^{c_{ij}}}{\mathcal{P}_L} + \sum_{i,j} \frac{\mathcal{P}_L^{c_{ij}}}{\mathcal{P}_L} log_2 \frac{\sum_j \mathcal{P}_L^{c_{ij}}}{\mathcal{P}_L} \\ &= \text{Info}(S_L^{c_{ij}}) - \text{Info}(S_L^{C_i})\end{aligned}$$

The entropy of the joint events C_i, c_j is the entropy of C_i plus the entropy of c_j when C_i is known.

Because

$$\text{Info}(S_L^{C_i}) + \text{Info}(S_L^{c_j}) \geq \text{Info}(S_L^{c_{ij}}) = \text{Info}(S_L^{C_i}) + \text{Info}^{C_i}(S_L^{c_{ij}}),$$

hence

$$\text{Info}(S_L^{c_j}) \geq \text{Info}^{C_i}(S_L^{c_{ij}}).$$

The entropy of c_j is never increased by the knowledge of C_i.

Definition 5 *The* possibilistic conditional entropy *can be rewritten as*

$$\text{Info}_i(S_L^{c_{ij}}) = -\frac{\mathcal{P}_L^{c_{ij}}}{\mathcal{P}_L} \log_2 \frac{\mathcal{P}_L^{c_{ij}}}{\mathcal{P}_L}.$$

So the corrected entropy function is as follows.

Definition 6 *Let c_{ij} denote the jth cluster in class C_i. The* entropy *function,* Disorder, *of an FCT from node N_L is*

$$\text{Info}(S_L) = -\sum_{\forall C_i \in C} \sum_{\forall c_{ij}} \frac{\mathcal{P}_L^{c_{ij}}}{\mathcal{P}_L} \times \log_2 \frac{\mathcal{P}_L^{c_{ij}}}{\mathcal{P}_L}.$$

4 Empirical Results

We have tested our algorithm on five data sets from the UCI repository (ftp://ftp.ics.uci.edu/machine-learning-databases).

Glass This is sample data set including 214 instances in determining whether the glass was a type of "float" glass or not for criminological investigation. Seven classes with 9 numerical attributes with missing data.

Monks' Problem The three Monks' problems are a collection of three binary classification problems over a six-attribute discrete domain. The classes is either 0 or 1. 6 categorical value attributes, no missing value. There are noisy data in *monk1* and *monk2.*

Ionosphere This data set is a binary classification task. The radar data was collected by a system in Goose Bay, Labrador. This system consists of a phased array of 16 high-frequency antennas with a total transmitted power on the order of 6.4 kilowatts. The targets were free electrons in the ionosphere. "Good" radar returns are those showing evidence of some type of structure in the ionosphere. "Bad" returns are those that do not; their signals pass through the ionosphere. There are 351 instances with all 34 numerical attributes, no missing value.

The result of comparing the accuracy of FCT with C4.5 on these problems is shown in Table 3. Note the tree that we use to compare is without pruning.

Table 3: Average accuracy between C4.5 and FCT over the golf, monks, and ionosphere problems.

	Glass	Monk1	Monk2	Monk3	Ionosphere
C4.5	$94.4 \pm 3.2\%$	76.6%	65.3%	92.6%	96.5%
FCT	$95.8 \pm 2.7\%$	86.5%	73.4%	93.2%	96.2%

The glass data set was tested according to the F-test under the confident level of 95%.

The clustering method determines the performance of FCT. The clustering method used for classifications is fuzzy c-partition algorithm. It full satisfies the criteria of possibilistic entropy. As the result on the *ionosphere* problem, the accuracy of FCT is lower than the accuracy of C4.5. Since the values of all the attributes are distributed in $[-1, 1]$, the size of the clusters has an effect on the accuracy of FCT. To improve the clustering method is one of our further objectives.

5 Conclusion

The paper introduces a novel model, *fuzzy classifier*, and the implementing method, *fuzzy classification tree*, classifications. Fuzzy classifications generalize the consideration of traditional single decision classifications. A theoretic proof has shown that the decision-tree-based classifier is a special case of the fuzzy classifier in this paper. It can "softly" consider the instance belonging to different classes without losing any generality.

This paper extends the definition of the original Shannon's entropy to the possibilistic model and gives the possibilistic interpretation. The possibilistic entropy evaluation can full satisfy the criteria of information entropy. Based on the possibilistic entropy, the goodness of split has been properly defined and the fuzzy operators are also restricted.

According to empirical results, under the best clustering deliberation, the accuracy rates of those benchmark tests of FCTs are better than the accuracy rates of C4.5. The best clustering consideration means that the data are made the most proper partition according to the data distribution for each attribute. According to the clustering, the lowest entropy of each attribute can be obtained. Then the most proper attribute which has the lowest possibilistic conditional entropy in all can be selected for classifications. The testing result of the glass data set is formally under the consideration of F-test at the confident level of 95%. Using five-fold cross validation testing, we will see that the accuracy rate of FCT is better than C4.5.

1. B. Kero, L. Russell, and S. Tsur. An overview of database mining techniques. Technical report, Argonne National Laboratory, 1995.
2. G. Landeweerd, T. Timmers, E. Gersema, M. Bins, and M. Halic. Binary tree versus single level tree classification of white blood cells. *Pattern Recognition*, 16:571–577, 1983.
3. J. R. Quinlan. Decision trees and decision making. *IEEE Transactions on Systems, Man, and Cybernetics*, 20:339–346, 1990.
4. W. Buntine. Operations for learning with graphical models. *Journal of Artificial Intelligence Research*, 2:159–225, 1994.
5. R. Rymon. An SE-tree based characterization of the induction problem. In *Proceedings of the Tenth International Conference on Machine Learning*, pages 268–275, Amherst, MA, 1993.
6. M. I. Jordan and R. A. Jacobs. Supervised learning and divide-and-conquer: A statistical approach. In *Proceedings of the Ninth International Conference on Machine Learning*, pages 159–166, Aberdeen, Scotland, 1992.
7. P. Smyth, A. Gray, and U. M. Fayyad. Retrofitting decision tree classifiers using kernel density estimation. Technical report, Jet Propulsion Laboratory, California Institute of Technology, Pasadena, CA.
8. J. Y. Hsu and I. Chiang. Fuzzy classification trees. In *Proceedings of the Ninth International Symposium on Artificial Intelligence*, pages 431–438, Cancun, Mexico, 1996.
9. I. Chiang and J. Hsu. Integration of fuzzy classifiers with decision trees. In *Proceedings of Asian Fuzzy Systems Symposium*, Kenting, Taiwan, 1996.
10. X. Li and R. C. Dubes. Tree classifier design with a permutation statistics. *Pattern Recognition*, 19:229–235, 1984.
11. J. R. Quinlan. Induction of decision trees. *Machine Learning*, 1:81–106, 1986.
12. J. Schuermann and W. Doster. A decision theoretic approach to hierarchical classifier design. *Pattern Recognition*, 17(3):359–369, 1984.

13. C. E. Shannon. A mathematical theory of communication. *The Bell System Technical Journal*, 27:379–423, 623–656, 1948.
14. A. De Luca and S. Termini. A definition of a nonprobabilistic entropy in the setting of fuzzy sets theory. *Information and Control*, 20:301–312, 1976.
15. S. K. Murthy. *On Growing Better Decision Trees from Data.* PhD dissertation, The Johns Hopkins University, Baltimore, Maryland, 1995.
16. B. W. Silverman. *Density Estimation for Statistics and Data Analysis.* Chapman and Hall, London, UK, 1986.
17. G. J. Klir and B. Yuan. *Fuzzy Sets and Fuzzy Logic.* Prentice-Hall, Englewood Cliffs, NJ, 1995.
18. H. J. Zimmermann. *Fuzzy Set Theory and Its Applications, Second Edition.* Kluwer Academic, Boston, MA, 1991.

A TUNING AID FOR DISCRETIZATION IN RULE INDUCTION

M. POSTEMA, X. WU, T. MENZIES
Department of Software Development, Monash University, 900 Dandenong Rd, Melbourne, Vic 3145, AUSTRALIA

This paper examines where a tuning aid can be useful to help discretization of numerical attributes in rule induction, and subsequently improve deduction of induction results. Different discretization methods use different strategies to set up the borders for continuous attributes. They mostly incorporate class supervision to define the discretization borders. The tuning aid we present uses an unsupervised method to define the intervals at induction time. We then supervise the learning process, by comparing the performance in terms of predictive accuracy with the information gain based discretization methods implemented in HCV (Version 2.0) and C4.5.

1 Introduction

In the context of rule induction and decision tree construction, dealing with a continuous attribute means discretization of the numerical attribute into a number of intervals. The discretized intervals can be treated in a similar way to nominal values during induction and deduction. The essential aspect of discretization is to find the right places to set up interval borders. In supervised discretization methods, such as the information gain based methods implemented in C4.5 [9] and HCV (Version 2.0) [11], the class information of examples in a training set is used. In unsupervised (or class-blind) discretization methods, such as equal-width discretization and equal-frequency discretization [2], training examples are grouped into intervals without taking into account the respective classes of the training examples. Discretization can be performed at induction time (such as in C4.5) or before induction takes place (see [3] and [7]).

Among various discretization methods, the information gain based methods have been widely used and cited [3,12]. C4.5 provides only binary discretization at induction time based on an information gain approach for real-valued attributes. In HCV (Version 2.0), an information gain based method is the default discretization method for processing numerical attributes before induction takes place. In this paper, we present an unsupervised tuning aid, based on domain distribution, for discretization of real-valued attributes. The method has been incorporated into HCV (Version 2.0) as a counterpart to the information gain method, and we compare its performance with the information gain method also implemented in HCV (Version 2.0). The results of C4.5 with its binary discretization method are also included for comparison, although this inclusion might not be relevant because C4.5 and HCV (Version 2.0) have different induction strategies.

The rest of this paper is organized as follows. Section 2 outlines HCV (Version 2.0) and the information gain heuristic, Section 3 discusses the fine tuning design, Section 4 details the experiments, and we follow this with results and finally a conclusion.

2 HCV (Version 2.0) and the Information Gain Heuristic

2.1 HCV (Version 2.0)

The HCV algorithm [10] is a representative of the extension matrix based family of attribute-based induction algorithms, originating with J.R. Hong's AE1 [6]. By dividing the positive examples (PE) of a specific concept in a given example set into intersecting groups and adopting a set of strategies to find a heuristic conjunctive rule in each group which covers all the group's positive examples and none of the negative examples (NE), HCV can find a rule in the form of variable-valued logic for the concept in low-order polynomial time. If there exists at least one conjunctive rule in a given training example set for PE against NE, the rule produced by HCV must be a conjunctive one. The rules in variable-valued logic generated by HCV have been shown [11] empirically to be more compact than the decision trees or their equivalent decision rules produced by the ID3 algorithm (the best-known induction algorithm to date) and its successors (e.g., C4.5) in terms of the numbers of conjunctive rules and conjunctions.

The HCV (Version 2.0) software is a C++ implementation of the HCV algorithm. In this implementation, HCV can work with noisy and real-valued domains as well as nominal and noise-free databases. It also provides a set of deduction facilities for the user to test the accuracy of the produced rules on test examples. The detailed description of the software is included in [11].

In addition to a set of discretization facilities, such as the information gain heuristic outlined in the next section, HCV (Version 2.0) permits the user to specify their own discretization of real-valued attributes by providing a set of intervals in the structure file, which specifies the attributes (with their order and value domains) and classes used in the data files. This is a very useful way for integrating domain specific information. The tuning aid designed in Section 3 will start with this facility.

2.2 The Information Gain Heuristic for Discretization

When the examples in a training set have taken values of $x_1, ..., x_n$ in ascending order on a continuous attribute, we can use the information gain heuristic adopted in ID3 [8] to find a most informative border to split the value domain of the continuous attribute. Fayyad and Irani [4] have shown that the maximum information gain by the heuristic is always achieved at a cut point (say, the mid-point) between the values taken by two examples of different classes.

The information gain heuristic is adopted in HCV (Version 2.0) in the following way. Each $x = (x_i + x_{i+1})/2$ $(i = 1, ..., n-1)$ is a possible cut point if x_i and x_{i+1} have been taken by examples of different classes in the training set. Use the information gain heuristic to check each of the possible cut points and find the best split point. Run the same process on the left and right halves of the splitting to split them further. The number of intervals produced this way may be very large if the attribute is not very informative. Catlett [1] has proposed some criteria to stop the recursive splitting which have been adopted in HCV (Version 2.0):

- Stop if the information gain on all cut points is the same,
- Stop if the number of examples to split is less than a certain number (*e.g.* fourteen in HCV (Version 2.0)), and
- Limit the number of intervals to be produced to a certain number (*e.g.* eight in HCV (Version 2.0)).

In C4.5 [9], the information gain approach is revised in the following ways. Firstly, each of the possible cut points is not the midpoint between the two nearest values, but rather the greatest value in the entire training set that does not exceed the midpoint. This ensures that all border values occur in the training data. Each border value in this case is not necessarily the same as the lower of the two neighbouring values since all training examples are examined for the selection. Secondly, C4.5 adopts the information gain ratio rather than the information gain heuristic. Finally, C4.5 does binarization of continuous attributes, which means only one interval border is found for each continuous attribute at each decision node.

3 A Fine Tuning Aid to HCV (Version 2.0)

3.1 Related Work

The tuning aid that we present in Section 3.2 is similar to *Adaptive Quantizers* discussed in Dougherty [3]. The Adaptive Quantizers method begins with a binary equal width partitioning of the continuous feature. Induction is performed and tested for predictive accuracy. The interval with the lowest predictive accuracy is split into two equal width partitions. The induction and evaluation processes are then repeated until some performance criteria is met. This method appears to overcome some of the limitations of unsupervised discretization, but comes with a high computational cost. This is due to numerous runs of the rule induction process. The method also assumes that a high level of accuracy can be achieved.

The minimal entropy heuristic [1,3] uses class information entropy of candidate partitions to select the intervals.

The method we present uses some of the above mentioned algorithms slightly differently. Based on the HCV (Version 2.0) facility for user-specified intervals (see Section 2.1), the tuning aid method for discretization is designed in Section 3.2.

3.2 Fine Tuning Design

We use an unsupervised learning method that firstly partitions the continuous attribute into ten equal width intervals. We then find three intervals based on the data, not the class distribution. These intervals are then incorporated into the induction algorithm. If the performance decreases (compared to the default) we don't do any further processing. Whilst the computational cost increases (refer Section 4.2), this is marginal when compared to the improvement of results. The hypothesis and tuning aid are presented in Sections 3.2.1 and 3.2.2 respectively.

Hypothesis

Initial experiments were devised based on the attribute information available in the dictionary files. As is standard with data sets from the University of California at Irvine Repository of Machine Learning Databases and Domain Theories, a dictionary file specifies the attributes (with their order and value domains) and classes used in the training and test data. From here a hypothesis was formed that the overall data distribution could be analyzed to determine intervals in the *low, average* and *high* range. This was facilitated by plotting a histogram of the data in the training files into ten equal intervals. These intervals were then analyzed to find the following three intervals:

- *Low* which contained approximately 25% of the data
- *Average* which contained approximately 50% of the data

- *High* which contained the remaining data

Since it is not possible to use this method when a large percentage (say 70%) of the data lies at either extremes of the range of values, a second method is introduced which includes overlapping class intervals. For example, if class 1 has values ranging 0-100 and class 2 has values ranging 85-150, the intervals used are 0-100 and 85-150. This method had limited use and success.

Tuning Aid

1. Run the HCV (Version 2.0) software on a database to obtain baseline results. The database should consist of at least one continuous attribute.

2. Select a continuous attribute in the database.

3. Check the overall data distribution on the selected attribute.

4. Divide the continuous attribute into the following three intervals

   - low (approximately 25% of the data)
   - average (approximately 50% of the data)
   - high (approximately 25% of the data)

   If the above fails attempt to determine overlapping class intervals (as mentioned in Section 3.2.1).

5. If intervals were found in step 4, run the HCV (Version 2.0) software with these intervals and obtain results, else go to step 7.

6. If the results are improved or no worse than the baseline ones, keep them, else discard these intervals.

7. If no more continuous attributes, STOP.

8. Select another continuous attribute.

9. Go to step 3.

The second method discussed in Section 3.2.1 and Step 4 above deals with domains with some degree of fuzziness. For example, we could classify someone who is 170cm in height as 'Normal Height' or 'Tall Height' depending on our outlook. Instead of discretizing the domain into fixed intervals, some sort of curve could be applied to give a fuzzy border. Thus a value could belong to more than one interval at the same time. Results can be classified in terms

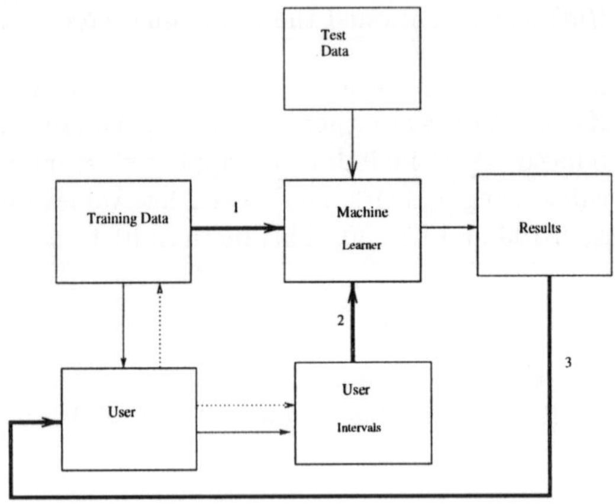

Figure 1: The Machine Learning Cycle

of degrees of membership in each interval. Discretizing a continuous domain in this way is termed *fuzzy matching*[13]. Alternatively, the number of intervals and their values could also be modified, which is the principle used in fuzzy expert systems. This above method combines probabilistic analysis (refer to Step 4) and fuzzy logic.

The method based on the information in the dictionary file and the data in the training files can be related to the probability surveys between domain experts when designing a fuzzy expert system[5]. A summary of the tuning aid method can be included into the machine learner as shown by Figure 1, where the user can specify the intervals from the training examples. Following the heavy arrowed lines, we can see:

1. Training and test data are fed into the machine learner as a baseline.

2. The user specifies intervals, feeds these into the machine learner and runs the process again.

3. The deduction of induction results on test data are then compared to determine which method gave the best results.

The dotted lines indicate the user decision.

Table 1: Success Analysis of Results

Domain	*Success Analysis*
Wine	⊕ ⊖ ⊕ ⊕ ⊕ ⊕ ⊖ ⊖ ⊖
Bupa	⊕ ⊕ ⊖ ⊖ ⊖ ⊖
Labor Neg	⊕ ⊕ ⊖ ⊖ ⊖ ⊖
Swiss 5	⊕ ⊖ ⊖ ⊖
Cleveland 2	⊕
Cleveland 5	⊙
Va 5	⊕
Va 2	⊖
Crx	⊕
Imports 85	⊙ ⊙ ⊖ ⊙ ⊖ ⊖ ⊖ ⊕ ⊙ ⊖ ⊖ ⊕ ⊖ ⊖
Pima	⊖ ⊖ ⊖ ⊖ ⊖ ⊕
Glass (without ID)	⊖ ⊖ ⊖ ⊖ ⊖ ⊖

Legend

⊙ indicates same accuracy (intervals were included in subsequent experiments).

⊖ indicates decreased accuracy (subsequently discarded).

⊕ indicates improved result.

4 Experiments

The experiments were performed with data sets from the University of California at Irvine Repository of Machine Learning Databases and Domain Theories. The inputs for the machine learners include the *dictionary, training* and *testing* files, which describe the attributes, and include training and testing examples respectively.

4.1 Baseline

The experimental results can be compared to those obtained by Wu et al. [14]. The best results in terms of predictive accuracy for each problem is given in *bold* in Table 2.

4.2 Results

Table 1 analyses the success of using the data distribution method defined in Section 3.2 to specify the intervals in continuous domains. One interesting observation is that the probabilistic method is actually a search for attributes that can be discretized usefully. In the twelve data sets, 16 of the 55 continuous

Table 2: Summary and Comparison of Results

	Accuracy (%)		
Domain	**C4.5**	**HCV (Ver2.0)**	**HCV (Tuned)**
Bupa	**73.7**	57.6	65.3
Cleveland 5	47.3	**56.0**	**56.0**
Cleveland 2	68.4	78.0	**82.4**
Crx	79.5	82.5	**85.0**
Imports 85	64.4	62.7	**66.1**
Labor Neg	**82.4**	76.5	**82.4**
Pima	**75.1**	73.9	**75.1**
Swiss 5	31.2	28.1	**34.4**
Va 5	26.8	26.8	**32.4**
Va 2	66.7	**78.9**	70.4
Wine	90.4	90.4	**98.1**
Glass (without ID)	64.6	**72.3**	69.2

attributes experimented with give improved results, 34 give worse results and 5 make no difference.

The induction algorithm is run $N+1$ times where N represents the number of continuous attributes, thereby increasing the computational cost by N times.

The experiments including the probabilistic method are recorded as HCV (Tuned) in Table 2. The overall success in terms of accuracy is high if we consider that results from HCV (Tuned) have the highest accuracy on 7 out of the 12 data sets tested, and matched C4.5 in another two.

5 Conclusion

The success of fuzzy expert systems in the area of domain specific controllers has been one of the stimulations for further research work in improving machine learning results. This paper has presented a tuning aid method, which combines probability analysis and fuzzy logic, for discretization of continuous attributes, and has compared its results with the information gain based discretization methods implemented in HCV (Version 2.0) and C4.5 on various problem domains. Experimental results have shown that the tuning aid method has given the highest accuracy on 7 out of the 12 data sets tested, with equal results in two other data sets. Based on the analysis of fuzzy expert systems, future work will include optimizing the number of intervals and incorporating the tuning aid into other machine learners, such as C4.5.

References

1. J. Catlett. On Changing Continuous Attributes into Ordered Discrete Attributes. *Proceedings of the 1991 European Working Session on Learning*, 1991.
2. D. Chiu, A. Wong and B. Cheung. Information Discovery through Hierarchical Maximum Entropy Discretization and Synthesis. In Piatetsky-Shapiro, G., and W.J. Frowley, editors, *Knowledge Discovery in Databases*. MIT Press, 1991.
3. J. Dougherty, R. Kohavi and M. Sahami. Supervised and Unsupervised Discretization of Continuous Features. *Proceedings of the 12th International Conference on Machine Learning*, 194–202, 1995.
4. U.M. Fayyad and K.B. Irani. On the Handling of Continuous-Valued Attributes in Decision Tree Generation. *Machine Learning*, **8**(1992), 87–102.
5. L.O. Hall and A. Kandel. The Evolution of Expert Systems. In F. Aminzadeh and M. Jamshidi, editors, *Soft Computing: Fuzzy Logic, Neural Networks, and Distributed Artificial Intelligence*. Prentice Hall, New Jersey USA, 1994.
6. J.R. Hong. AE1: An Extension Matrix Approximate Method for the General Covering Problem. *International Journal of Computer and Information Sciences*, **4**(1985): 421–437.
7. B. Pfahringer. Compression-Based Discretization of Continuous Attributes, *Proceedings of the 12th International Conference on Machine Learning*, 456–463, 1995.
8. J.R. Quinlan. Induction of Decision Trees. *Machine Learning*, **1**(1986), 81–106.
9. J.R. Quinlan. *C4.5: Programs for Machine Learning*. Morgan Kaufmann Publishers, 1993.
10. X. Wu. The HCV Induction Algorithm. In S.C. Kwasny and J.F. Buck, editors, *Proceedings of the 21st ACM Computer Science Conference*, 168–175. ACM Press, USA, 1993.
11. X. Wu. *Knowledge Acquisition from Databases*. Ablex, USA, 1995.
12. X. Wu. A Bayesian Discretizer for Real-Valued Attributes. *The Computer Journal*, **39**(1996).
13. X. Wu and P. Måhlén. Fuzzy Interpretation of Induction Results. *Proc. of the 1995 International Conference on Knowledge Discovery and Data Mining (KDD-95)*, Montreal, Canada, August 20-21, 1995, 325–330.
14. X. Wu, J. Krisár, and P. Måhlén. Noise Handling with Extension Matrices. *International Journal of Artificial Intelligence Tools*, **5**(1996), 81–97.

CONSTRUCTING CONJUNCTIONS USING SYSTEMATIC SEARCH ON DECISION TREES

Z. ZHENG
School of Computing and Mathematics
Deakin University, Geelong, Victoria 3217, Australia
(zijian@deakin.edu.au)

This paper discusses a dynamic path-based mathod for constructing conjunctions as new attributes for decision tree learning. It searches for conditions (attribute-value pairs) from paths to form new attributes. CAT, a constructive decision tree learning algorithm, which adopts this dynamic path-based method is described. It employs the hypothesis-driven strategy for constructing new attributes, and uses conjunction and negation (implicitly) as its constructive operators. Compared with other hypothesis-driven constructive decision tree learning algorithms such as algorithms of the FRINGE family, the new idea of CAT is that it carries out systematic search with pruning over each path of a tree to select conditions for generating a conjunction. Therefore, in CAT, conditions for constructing new attributes are decided dynamically during search. Empirically investigation in a set of artificial and real-world domains shows that CAT can improve the performance of selective decision tree learning in terms of both higher prediction accuracy and lower theory complexity. In addition, it shows some performance advantages over the constructive decision tree learning algorithms that use a fixed path-based method and a fixed rule-based method to construct conjunctions as new attributes.

1 Introduction

Machine learning, especially supervised learning, plays an important role in KDD. Constructive induction has been studied as a means to improve the quality of learned theories. New attributes are constructed from primitive attributes that are used to describe examples. The former are expected to be more appropriate than the latter for representing theories to be learned. People have explored fixed path-based and fixed rule-based approaches to constructing new binary attributes for decision tree learning [2,7,20]. The number and positions of conditions for generating a new attribute in a path of a tree or a rule are predecided (fixed) in these algorithms. It has been shown that the number and locations of conditions in a path of a tree or a rule which are used to form a conjunction affect the performance of this type of constructive induction algorithm [2,20].

This paper presents a method of constructing new attributes by performing a search over a path of a tree. It can find relevant conditions to form the best conjunction that can be created from the path in terms of an attribute evaluation function. It does not need to predecide the number and positions of conditions for generating new attributes. The conditions in a path used to construct a new attribute are selected dynamically. The number of conditions used to generate a new attribute is also decided dynamically. Therefore, this approach is referred to as the dynamic path-based approach.

A systematic search method with pruning [16] is employed. It considers all possible combinations of conditions in a path and is efficient in practice as some parts of the search space are eliminated during search. This method is due to Webb's work on rule learning [16].

2 The CAT Algorithm

Like the FRINGE family of algorithms [2,7] and the CI algorithms [20], CAT is also a hypothesis-driven constructive induction algorithm for learning multivariate trees. It constructs new binary attributes by carrying out systematic search over previously learned decision trees. Its constructive operators are conjunction and negation (implicitly).

2.1 Control Structure of CAT

CAT creates new attributes from paths of a tree. It iterates a tree learning process (using C4.5) and a new attribute construction process. The whole process consists of two stages.

In each iteration of the first stage, CAT learns a raw tree and a pruned tree based on relevant or important primitive attributes identified in the previous iteration. It constructs new attributes from the raw tree. CAT then builds two other pruned trees and identifies relevant or important primitive attributes. One pruned tree is based on both primitive and new attributes, while the other is based only on new attributes. Those primitive attributes that occur (directly or through new attributes) in the better one of these two trees are considered to be relevant or important, and are transferred to the next iteration. During this stage, new attributes contain only primitive attributes. After a stopping criterion is satisfied, CAT chooses the best tree among all the pruned trees that have been built. The relevant primitive attributes used in the iteration where the best tree occurs are used as the primitive attributes for the second stage.

In each iteration of the second stage, CAT builds a raw tree and a pruned tree based on existing attributes including both primitive attributes and previously created new attributes. New attributes are constructed from the raw tree, and are used for building decision trees in subsequent iterations. They may consist of both primitive and new attributes. Finally, CAT selects the best pruned tree from the two stages as its output.

CAT uses an MDL-inspired heuristic function as its tree evaluation function[22]. The function is similar to the coding cost function used by Quinlan and Rivest[8], but exceptions of a tree on the training set are replaced by the more pessimistically estimated exceptions of the tree[9]. In addition, new attributes are encoded[22]. In the current implementation, CAT adopts the following stopping criterion:

- No new attribute can be constructed, or
- No better pruned tree has been built in five consecutive iterations,[a] or
- A given maximum iteration number is reached.[b]

2.2 *Systematic Search with Pruning for Constructing Conjunctions*

Here, the class labeled by the leaf of a path is referred to as the positive class and all other classes are referred to as the negative class. All problems are temporarily transformed into binary class problems when constructing new attributes.[c]

Systematic search with pruning has the same outcome as exhaustive search, but it does not examine every state of the search space although it considers all the states. Some portions of the space can be eliminated as search progresses. To do this, all the states are organized into a tree structure such that every state can be visited once and only once by traversing the tree. In addition, the evaluation function should be able to tell whether or not a better state could be found by searching the subtrees of a node.

For the purpose of searching for the best conjunction of conditions from a path in terms of an evaluation function, the search space consists of all possible conjunctions that can be constructed from the path. Since the order of conditions of a conjunction does not matter, a search tree can be generated as follows. Its root is an empty conjunction that contains no conditions and is always true. Each possible direct specialization of a node that is derived from the node by adding one condition forms a child. All the children of a node are created in some order such that, when generating their subtrees, each child does not use the conditions that are most recently added into those children that are created before it. This makes sure that each conjunction occurs once and only once in the search tree. One simple way to order the children of

[a]Five consecutive iterations without producing better pruned trees are allowed to avoid a local optimum tree. The arbitrary number "five" is just a default option setting of the algorithm.

[b]The default value is 20.

[c]When building and evaluating decision trees after new attributes have been constructed, the learning problems are still the original ones with original classes.

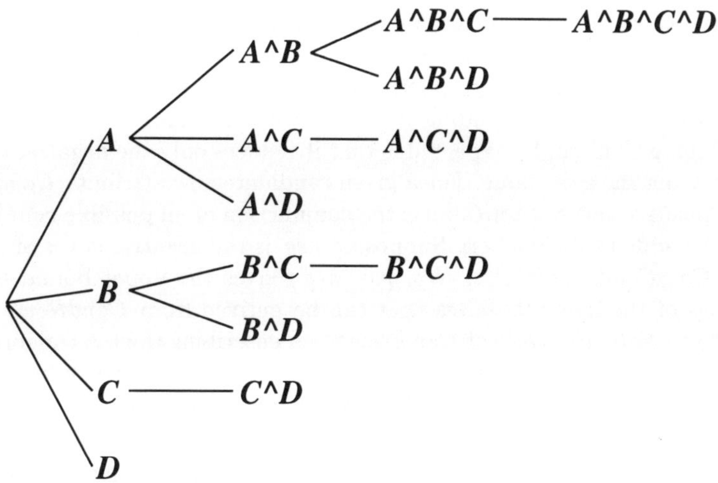

Figure 1: A search tree for constructing conjunctions from conditions A, B, C, and D

a node is using the sequence of the conditions, given that the attributes and their values are ordered when used to describe data. A condition that can be added to a conjunction must have a higher order than existing conditions of the conjunction. For example, given four conditions and their order as: A, B, C, and D, Figure 1 shows a search tree. However, following the idea of OPUS [16], CAT uses an information-based evaluation function (different from that of OPUS) to order the children of a node when generating them. The objective is to increase the size of the regions that can be pruned.

The new attribute evaluation function used by CAT for carrying out systematic search is information gain. It satisfies the requirement for performing systematic search with pruning. In addition, its disadvantage of favoring attributes with more different values [9] does not show up here since all new attributes are binary.

Supposing a conjunction covers *pos* out of *Pos* positive examples and *neg* out of *Neg* negative examples in a training set, it is not difficult to prove that $gain(Pos, Neg, pos, neg)$ defined as in equation 1 is monotonic with respect to either *pos* or *neg* when $\frac{pos}{Pos} > \frac{neg}{Neg}$. The function $gain(Pos, Neg, pos, neg)$ decreases when *pos* decreases and increases when *neg* decreases under the condition $\frac{pos}{Pos} > \frac{neg}{Neg}$, which is a reasonable restriction because a conjunction, as a candidate new attribute, is expected to cover (relatively) more positive examples than negative examples. The examples covered by a conjunction are referred to as the *cover* of the conjunction. The positive examples and the negative examples in the cover are referred to as the *positive cover* and the *negative cover* of the conjunction respectively. Adding conditions to a conjunction usually reduces its cover including positive cover, or negative cover, or both. The best thing that can be expected is that it reduces only the negative cover, thus increasing the gain value. For a given candidate new attribute *CandNew*, *pos* is its positive cover. *ConjCond* is the conjunction of all possible conditions that can be added to *CandNew*. Supposing *neg'* is the negative cover of (*CandNew* $\wedge$ *ConjCond*), *gain*(*Pos*, *Neg*, *pos*, *neg'*) gives the upper bound of the gain values of the new attributes that can be derived from *CandNew*.[d] It is referred to as *Potential-Gain* of *CandNew* when describing the CAT algorithm. If it is not higher than the gain value of the current best new attribute, further searching on the subtree rooted at *CandNew* is not necessary.

$$gain(Pos, Neg, pos, neg) = info(Pos, Neg) - (\frac{pos + neg}{Pos + Neg} \times info(pos, neg) + \frac{Pos - pos + Neg - neg}{Pos + Neg} \times info(Pos - pos, Neg - neg)), \quad (1)$$

$$info(p,n) = -\frac{p}{p+n} \times \log_2(\frac{p}{p+n}) - \frac{n}{p+n} \times \log_2(\frac{n}{p+n}) \quad (2)$$

Figure 2 details the method of systematic search with pruning used by CAT.[e] The data structure for a candidate new attribute, *Cand*, contains three parts: *Cand.Cs*: its conditions, *Cand.PCs*: a set of potential conditions that can be added to *Cand* when extending it, and *Cand.LastC*: the condition that is most recently added to *Cand*. Given a path consisting of conditions and its labeled class as well as the entire training set, the algorithm systematically searches through all possible conjunctions that can be generated from the path. To do so, it gradually extends an empty conjunction to create candidate new attributes by adding one possible condition of the path each time. Some parts of the search space are pruned during search.

The algorithm starts from a candidate new attribute with no conditions (always true) in it. Its potential condition set contains all conditions of the path. It is used as the initial best new attribute, *Best*, and the only initial member of the set of candidate new attributes, *Candidates*. When there are still some candidates worth extending, the one most likely leading to the best new attribute is first chosen to extend. This is done by inspecting *Candidates* to see whether it contains at least one candidate with a higher potential gain

[d] Adding *ConjCond* to *CandNew* reduces only its negative cover.
[e] Some ideas are from OPUS, which is used to learn unordered rules [16].

```
Systematic-Search-Pruning(Path, D_training)
  INPUT: Path: all conditions in the path and its labeled class,
         D_training: training set.
  OUTPUT: a conjunction as a new attribute.

  Best.Cs := true
  Best.PCs := {all conditions in Path}
  Candidates := {Best}
  WHILE (Candidates has at least one candidate whose
         Potential-Gain() > Gain(Best.Cs)) DO
  {  Remove the candidate that maximizes Potential-Gain() from
       Candidates and assign it to Cand
     TempCandidates := { }
     FOR each condition Cond in Cand.PCs
     {  New.Cs := Cand.Cs ∧ Cond
        New.LastC := Cond
        IF ((RelPosCover(New.Cs) > RelNegCover(New.Cs)) ∧
            (Gain(New.Cs) > Gain(Best.Cs)))
        THEN Best := New
        IF ((Potential-Gain(New.Cs, Cand.PCs − Cond)
              > Gain(Best.Cs)) ∧
            (not Cannot-Improve(Cand.Cs, New.Cs, Cand.PCs − Cond))
        THEN Add New to TempCandidates
        ELSE Remove Cond from Cand.PCs
     }
     FOR each candidate New in TempCandidates
         in ascending order wrt. Potential-Gain()
     {  Remove New.LastC from Cand.PCs
        New.PCs := Cand.PCs
        IF (Potential-Gain(New.Cs, New.PCs) > Gain(Best.Cs))
        THEN Add New to Candidates
     }
  }
  RETURN Best.Cs
```

Figure 2: Systematic search with pruning for constructing a new attribute from a path value than the gain value of the current best new attribute. If so, the candidate, *Cand*, with the highest potential gain value is removed from *Candidates*. The algorithm extends *Cand* to create specialized candidates by adding each of its potential conditions in turn. Each extended new attribute is examined to see whether it can be the current best new attribute and whether it is worth further exploring. If an extended new attribute, *New*, has a higher gain value than *Best* and covers relatively more positive examples than negative examples, it becomes the current best new attribute. If *New*'s potential gain value is higher than the gain value of *Best* and the gain value of every new attribute that can be derived from *Cand* but without considering the condition *New.LastC*, it is added to a temporary set of candidate new attributes, *TempCandidates*. Function "Cannot-Improve(*Cand.Cs*, *New.Cs*, *Cand.PCs* − *Cond*)" returns true if "Potential-Gain(*Cand.Cs*, *Cand.PCs* − *Cond*) ≥ Potential-Gain(*New.Cs*, *Cand.PCs* − *Cond*)", where *New.Cs* is derived by adding *Cond* to *Cand.Cs*. This means that any extension of *New.Cs* is worse than, or as good as, some extensions of *Cand.Cs* without considering *Cond*.

After every potential condition in *Cand.PCs* is examined, the algorithm generates children of the node *Cand* in the search tree using candidate new attributes that are worth further extending. It examines each candidate, *New*, in *TempCandidates* in ascending order with respect to potential gain. The condition *New.LastC* is removed from *Cand.PCs*, and the resulting conditions form the set of potential conditions for *New*. If *New* has a higher potential gain value than the gain value of *Best*, it is added to *Candidates* for further extending later; otherwise, it is pruned from further exploring as it cannot lead to a better new attribute. Note that the potential conditions of any child of *Cand* do not contain conditions being most recently added to the children of *Cand* that are generated earlier. Finally, when *Candidates* contains no candidate new attribute that is worth further extending, *Best* contains the best new attribute. It is worth mentioning that functions "Gain()", "Potential-Gain()", "Cannot-Improve()", "RelPosCover()", and "RelNegCover()" need $D_{training}$ and the class labeled by the path to compute their values, but here they are omitted for the sake of simplicity.

The worst case time complexity of the "Systematic-Search-Pruning" algorithm is exponential on the size of a path,[f] but it is quite efficient in practice when solving learning problems. The reason is that considerable portions of search spaces are eliminated. For example, in the Nettalk(Stress) domain, when constructing new attributes from the first tree, the search space contains 41728.6 states on an average of the ten trials, while only 5033.8 states are really examined. More than 87.9% of the search space is pruned. It is even

[f] It is linear in the size of a training set.

better in the Cleveland Heart Disease domain. The search space contains, on average, 93563.3 states when constructing new attributes from the first tree, while only 732.3 states are really examined. More than 99.2% of the search space is pruned.

3 Experiments

This section uses experiments to evaluate the CAT algorithm by comparing its prediction accuracy and theory complexity with those of the C4.5 [9], SFRINGE [22], and CI3 [22] algorithms in a set of artificial and real-world domains. The theory complexity [21] is the modified tree size. It is the sum of the sizes of all the nodes of the tree rather than the number of decision nodes or all the nodes of the tree. The size of a leaf is 1. The size of a decision node is 1 for a univariate tree, and is the number of attribute-value pairs, or conditions, in the test of the node for a multivariate tree.

3.1 Experimental Domains and Methods

Fourteen artificial (logical) domains are from Pagallo's PhD. thesis [6]. We adopt the same experimental method used by Pagallo [6], including the sizes of training and test sets. For each experiment, a training set and a test set are independently drawn from the uniform distribution. Experiments are repeated ten times in each of these domains.

Besides the fourteen artificial domains, three Monks domains and ten real-world domains from the UCI repository of machine learning databases [4] are used. The ten real-world domains consist of five medical domains (Cleveland Heart Disease, Hepatitis, Liver Disorders, Pima Indians Diabetes, Wisconsin Breast Cancer), one molecular biology domain (Promoters), three linguistics domains (Nettalk(Phoneme), Nettalk(Stress), Nettalk(Letter)), and one game domain (Tic-Tac-Toe). On the three Nettalk domains, we use the 1000 most common English words containing 5438 letters. For each real-world domain, a 10-fold cross-validation is conducted on the entire data set and all algorithms are run on the same partitions. For each Monks domain, one trial is carried out using the fixed training and test sets because they are provided by the problem designers [15].

To compare the accuracies of two algorithms, a two-tailed block-based pairwise t-test is conducted.[g] A difference is considered as significant if the significance level is above 95%. In tables summarizing accuracies, boldface

[g] An instance-based pairwise sign-test is used on each Monks domain since only one trial is conducted.

font indicates that an algorithm is significantly better than C4.5, while italic font indicates that an algorithm is significantly worse than C4.5.

3.2 Experimental results

Table 1 shows the prediction accuracies and theory complexities of C4.5, SFRINGE, CI3, and CAT in the artificial, the Monks, and the real-world domains. We first compare CAT with C4.5. The table shows that CAT obtains significantly more accurate trees than C4.5 in all the artificial and Monks domains, except for the MX6 domain in which both C4.5 and CAT have a 100% accuracy. In twelve out of these seventeen domains, CAT builds much simpler trees than C4.5.[h] In all the ten real-world domains, CAT has higher accuracies than C4.5. Five accuracy improvements are significant. In terms of theory complexity, trees generated by CAT are less complex than those built by C4.5 in seven domains and are more complex than those built by C4.5 in the other three domains.

These results illustrate that CAT can improve the performance of C4.5 in terms of higher prediction accuracy as well as lower theory complexity. Now, let us consider the comparison of CAT with SFRINGE and CI3.

In the artificial domains as shown in Table 1, the accuracies of SFRINGE, CI3, and CAT are quite similar. CAT generates significantly more accurate trees than SFRINGE in one domain (Maj13) which is indicated by "$\ominus$", while SFRINGE learns significantly more accurate trees than CAT also in one domain (Parity5) labeled by "$\oplus$". No other accuracy difference between CAT and SFRINGE or CI3 in these domains is significant. The theory complexities of CAT are lower than those of SFRINGE in six out of the fourteen domains, and are higher than those of SFRINGE in the other eight domains. Compared with CI3, CAT achieves lower theory complexities in half of the fourteen domains, and obtains higher theory complexities in the other half of the domains.

As shown in Table 1, CAT obtains the highest prediction accuracies in all the three Monks domains among these four learning algorithms. In the Monks2 and Monks3 domains, CAT is significantly more accurate than both SFRINGE and CI3. This is indicated using "$\ominus$" in the table. In the Monks1 and Monks3 domains, CAT learns smaller trees than SFRINGE and CI3. Monks2 is an exactly M-of-N concept. Conjunctions are not appropriate new attributes for this domain, so the SFRINGE, CI3, and CAT algorithms cannot learn a really good decision tree, whatever new attribute construction methods are

---

[h] In the DNF4 domain, CAT learns a very complex tree in one of the ten trials because it creates some poor new attributes. This results in CAT having a large theory complexity in this domain. In the Parity5 domain, CAT also constructs some large new attributes, thus building trees with high complexity.

Table 1: Results of C4.5, SFRINGE, CI3, and CAT

Domain	Accuracy(%)				Complexity			
	C4.5	SFRINGE	CI3	CAT	C4.5	SFRINGE	CI3	CAT
DNF1	87.2	**97.1**	**100.0**	**99.4**	263.0	125.3	60.7	69.1
DNF2	90.7	**99.6**	**99.9**	**99.2**	202.0	45.5	70.6	47.5
DNF3	93.8	**99.5**	**99.9**	**99.4**	101.8	37.9	43.4	45.2
DNF4	74.0	**100.0**	**100.0**	**99.2**	525.0	48.2	43.7	2480.0
CNF1	86.9	**96.5**	**100.0**	**99.4**	271.2	140.6	55.3	61.2
CNF2	90.6	**99.3**	**99.5**	**99.2**	192.8	36.0	62.3	34.0
CNF3	93.3	**99.7**	**99.7**	**99.3**	94.4	39.9	50.8	30.5
CNF4	72.9	**99.4**	**100.0**	**99.1**	532.8	71.6	44.0	98.5
MX6	100.0	100.0	100.0	100.0	48.6	15.8	15.4	14.0
MX11	97.2	**100.0**	**100.0**	**100.0**	168.6	55.1	76.1	34.0
Parity4	67.5	**100.0**	**100.0**	**99.8**	238.4	38.4	47.6	42.9
Parity5	52.2	**⊕87.3**	**74.7**	**65.6**	1339.4	445.2	351.3	2022.9
Maj11	82.9	**92.7**	**92.8**	**92.5**	461.6	725.1	1076.7	1538.9
Maj13	76.3	**⊖82.7**	**86.5**	**85.7**	527.4	692.6	1496.7	916.5
Monks1	75.7	**100.0**	**100.0**	**100.0**	18.0	11.0	12.0	9.0
Monks2	65.0	⊖64.1	⊖67.1	**75.9**	31.0	13.0	22.0	73.0
Monks3	97.2	⊖97.2	⊖95.8	**100.0**	12.0	14.0	12.0	6.0
Heart Disease	73.3	75.9	75.5	75.9	49.8	45.6	20.5	81.1
Hepatitis	78.2	80.0	**82.7**	**82.0**	13.6	10.8	14.0	12.2
Liver Disorders	62.1	64.9	63.4	67.0	79.4	75.4	44.3	152.7
Diabetes	71.5	71.5	73.7	73.0	128.8	128.8	25.3	64.5
Breast Cancer	94.8	95.4	96.0	95.0	20.6	14.9	14.1	28.3
Promoters	76.3	78.1	**82.9**	**86.9**	22.6	14.0	11.8	11.9
Phoneme	81.1	**83.7**	**82.4**	**83.5**	2339.2	1176.7	1615.9	876.1
Stress	82.7	**⊖85.8**	**⊖86.2**	**88.0**	2077.3	858.6	812.9	372.4
Letter	73.7	**⊕77.8**	*⊖66.8*	74.6	3394.9	1821.5	1172.5	762.0
Tic-Tac-Toe	84.7	**97.6**	**98.4**	**98.3**	128.5	69.3	31.9	26.0

used.[i] The results in the Monks domains illustrate the performance advantage of CAT over SFRINGE and CI3 in terms of higher prediction accuracy.

In the ten real-world domains, as far as prediction accuracy is concerned, CAT is better than SFRINGE in six domains, the same in one domain, and worse in the other three domains. Among the accuracy differences between CAT and SFRINGE, only in the Nettalk(Stress) domain is CAT significantly better than SFRINGE, and only in the Nettalk(Letter) domain is CAT significantly worse than SFRINGE. In terms of theory complexity, CAT is better than SFRINGE in six domains, and worse in the other four domains.

Compared with CI3, CAT obtains higher accuracies in six domains, and

[i] It is similar in the parity and majority domains.

lower accuracies in the other four domains. Only in the Nettalk(Stress) and Nettalk(Letter) domains does CAT achieve significantly higher accuracies than CI3. The theory complexities of CAT are lower than those of CI3 in five domains, and are higher than those of CI3 in the other five domains.

In summary, the performance of CAT is, on average, slightly better than SFRINGE and CI3 in terms of prediction accuracy in the set of domains tested. Compared with SFRINGE, CAT is significantly more accurate in four domains and is significantly less accurate in two domains. CAT is significantly more accurate than CI3 in four domains. In terms of theory complexity, CAT is less complex in fourteen domains and is more complex in thirteen domains than both SFRINGE and CI3.

4 Discussion

The new attribute search space for CAT is a superset of that for CI3 and SFRINGE. However, our experimental results show that CAT cannot achieve the higher of the accuracies obtained by CI3 and SFRINGE in quite a few domains tested, although the accuracy differences are not large. One reason might be that information gain is used as the heuristic function to evaluate new attributes. Good new attributes cannot always be selected even if they are examined. On the other hand, this can be explained as the oversearching phenomenon [10].

5 Related Work

As far as constructing new attributes for decision tree learning is concerned, related work includes the FRINGE family of algorithms such as FRINGE, DUAL FRINGE, SYMMETRIC FRINGE [6,7], SYMFRINGE, DCFRINGE [19], and SFRINGE [22], the CITRE algorithm [2,3], the CI algorithms [20,22], the LFC algorithm [11], the ID2-of-3 algorithm [5], the LMDT algorithm [1], and the XofN algorithm [21].

As far as systematic search is concerned, the closest related work is OPUS [16]. It carries out systematic search with pruning over the space of all possible disjuncts at the inner level of a covering rule learning algorithm. The method of systematic search with pruning used in CAT is very similar to that in OPUS. The main difference is that CAT uses information gain as the evaluation function, while OPUS employs the Laplace function [16]. In addition, CAT searches for a conjunction as a new attribute for learning a decision tree, whereas OPUS searches for a conjunction as a rule for learning a set of unordered rules. Rymon [12,13] uses systematic search with pruning to learn SE-trees, a type of tree structure containing rules that predict classes using attributes. Schlimmer [14] adopts systematic search with pruning for inducing determinations that identify which factors influence others. Webb [17,18] further explores the systematic search in a more general way. In addition, Webb [18] proposes a few new pruning rules for systematic search.

6 Conclusions and Future Work

This paper has investigated a dynamic path-based approach to constructing new attributes for decision tree learning. For each path of a tree, a conjunction is generated by searching over the path. A systematic search method with pruning has been explored. The advantage of this approach is that the number and locations of conditions for creating a conjunction are decided dynamically. Irrelevant conditions should be filtered out from new attributes. In the current implementation of CAT, systematic search with exclusive pruning is used. Inclusive pruning [18] may further reduce execution time. The principal idea of the dynamic path-based method is to generate conjunctions by carrying out search over every path of a tree instead of employing the fixed strategy to create new attributes by using conditions from predefined positions of each path. Alternative search methods such as simple and less expensive greedy search are worth exploring, especially considering the oversearching phenomenon [10].

The experiments found that the dynamic path-based method can significantly improve the performance of decision tree learning in most of the domains studied in terms of both higher prediction accuracy and lower theory complexity. In no case does CAT reduce the accuracy of C4.5. Comparison with SFRINGE and CI3 reveals that the dynamic path-based method performs, on average, slightly better than the fixed path-based method and the fixed rule-based method in the artificial and real-world domains tested.

Acknowledgements

The research reported here was done when the author was in the University of Sydney. It was partially supported by an ARC grant (to Ross Quinlan) and by a research agreement with Digital Equipment Corporation. The paper is composed in Deakin University. The author appreciates the advice and suggestions Ross Quinlan has given. Ross Quinlan predicted that constructing conjunctions by searching over paths of a tree should be better than or at least as good as creating conjunctions from production rules for decision tree learning. This initiated the idea of this paper. Mike Cameron-Jones, Kai Ming Ting, and Alen Varšek gave many helpful suggestions. Many thanks to Ross Quinlan for providing C4.5, and to Geoff Webb for his useful comments and helping me to obtain a better understanding of some details of systematic search with pruning. P.M. Murphy and D. Aha are gratefully acknowledged for creating and managing the UCI Repository of machine learning databases.

References

1. C.E. Brodley and P.E. Utgoff, Multivariate versus univariate decision trees. COINS Technical Report 92-8, Department of Computer Science, University of Massachusetts, Amherst, MA (1992).
2. C.J. Matheus, *Feature Construction: an Analytic Framework and an Application to Decision Trees,* Ph.D. Thesis, Department of Computer Science, University of Illinois at Urbana-Champaign, Urbana, IL (1989).
3. C.J. Matheus and L.A. Rendell, Constructive induction on decision trees. *Proceedings of the Eleventh International Joint Conference on Artificial Intelligence*, San Mateo, CA: Morgan Kaufmann, 645-650 (1989).
4. P.M. Murphy and D.W. Aha, *UCI repository of machine learning databases* [Machine-readable data repository]. Department of Information and Computer Science, University of California, Irvine, CA, Available by anonymous ftp at ics.uci.edu in the pub/machine-learning-databases directory (1995).
5. P.M. Murphy and M.J. Pazzani, ID2-of-3: constructive induction of M-of-N concepts for discriminators in decision trees. *Proceedings of the Eighth International Workshop on Machine Learning*, San Mateo, CA: Morgan Kaufmann, 183-187 (1991).
6. G. Pagallo, *Adaptive Decision Tree Algorithms for Learning from Examples,* Ph.D. Thesis, University of California at Santa Cruz, Santa Cruz, CA (1990).
7. G. Pagallo and D. Haussler, Boolean feature discovery in empirical learning. *Machine Learning*, **5**, 71-100 (1990).
8. J.R. Quinlan and R.L. Rivest, Inferring decision trees using the minimum description length principle. *Information and Computation*, **80**, 227-248 (1989).
9. J.R. Quinlan, *C4.5: Programs for Machine Learning*, San Mateo, CA: Morgan Kaufmann (1993).
10. J.R. Quinlan and R.M. Cameron-Jones, Oversearching and layered search in empirical learning. *Proceedings of the Fourteenth International Joint Conference on Artificial Intelligence*, San Mateo, CA: Morgan Kaufmann, 1019-1024 (1995).
11. H. Ragavan and L. Rendell, Lookahead feature construction for learning hard concepts. *Proceedings of the Tenth International Conference on Machine Learning*, San Mateo, CA: Morgan Kaufmann, 252-259 (1993).

12. R. Rymon, Search through systematic set enumeration. *Proceedings of the Third International Conference on Principles of Knowledge Representation and Reasoning*, Cambridge MA: MIT Press, 539-550 (1992).
13. R. Rymon, An SE-tree based characterization of the induction problem. *Proceedings of the Tenth International Conference on Machine Learning*, San Mateo, CA: Morgan Kaufmann, 268-275 (1993).
14. J.C. Schlimmer, Efficiently inducing determinations: a complete and systematic search algorithm that uses optimal pruning. *Proceedings of the Tenth International Conference on Machine Learning*, San Mateo, CA: Morgan Kaufmann, 284-290 (1993).
15. S.B. Thrun, J. Bala, E. Bloedorn, I. Bratko, B. Cestnik, J. Cheng, K. De Jong, S. Džeroski, S.E. Fahlman, D. Fisher, R. Hamann, K. Kaufman, S. Keller, I. Kononenko, J. Kreuziger, R.S. Michalski, T. Mitchell, P. Pachowicz, Y. Reich, H. Vafaie, W. Van de Welde, W. Wenzel, J. Wnek, and J. Zhang, The MONK's problems - a performance comparison of different learning algorithms. Technical Report CMU-CD-91-197, Department of Computer Science, Carnegie Mellon University, Pittsburgh, PA (1991).
16. G.I. Webb, Systematic search for categorical attribute-value data-driven machine learning. *Proceedings of the Sixth Australian Joint Conference on Artificial Intelligence*, Singapore: World Scientific, 342-347 (1993).
17. G.I. Webb, OPUS: an efficient admissible algorithm for unordered search. *Journal of Artificial Intelligence Research*, **3**, 431-465 (1995).
18. G.I. Webb, Inclusive pruning: a new class of pruning rule for unordered search and its application to classification learning. *Proceedings of the Nineteenth Australian Computer Science Conference*, Australian Computer Science Communications, **18**, 1-10 (1996).
19. D. Yang, L. Rendell, and G. Blix, A scheme for feature construction and a comparison of empirical methods. *Proceedings of the Twelfth International Joint Conference on Artificial Intelligence*, San Mateo, CA: Morgan Kaufmann, 699-704 (1991).
20. Z. Zheng, Constructing conjunctive tests for decision trees. *Proceedings of the Fifth Australian Joint Conference on Artificial Intelligence*, Singapore: World Scientific, 355-360 (1992).
21. Z. Zheng, Constructing nominal X-of-N attributes. *Proceedings of the Fourteenth International Joint Conference on Artificial Intelligence*, San Mateo, CA: Morgan Kaufmann, 1064-1070 (1995).
22. Z. Zheng, *Constructing New Attributes for Decision Tree Learning*, Ph.D. Thesis, Basser Department of Computer Science, The University of Sydney (1996).

Improved Nearest Neighbour Classification Performance by Discretisation and Weighting

W.Z. LIU

Department of Information Science, University of Portsmouth, Locksway Road, Milton, Portsmouth, Hants PO4 8JF, UK

A.P. WHITE

School of Mathematics and Statistics, University of Birmingham, Birmingham B15 2TT, UK

One of the problems with conventional nearest neighbour classification algorithms is that attributes are all given the same weighting in the distance computations which form the basis of the technique. A new approach is described, in which continuous attributes are first discretised using a method which was originally developed for tree-based classification algorithms. Distances between value pairs on each of these discrete variables are then derived, using an association-based approach. The resulting metric reflects attribute importance. A simulation experiment shows that the use of this metric in nearest neighbour classification leads to improved performance over the traditional approach.

1 Introduction

The fundamental problem of learning how to classify objects has been approached from different perspectives, by those researching in areas of artificial intelligence, machine learning, mathematical statistics and other fields. One classification technique which has the appeal of conceptual simplicity is the nearest neighbour algorithm. In its simplest form, this involves storing a set of training cases (each consisting of a class membership indicator and a vector of attribute values) and classifying each new case (of unknown class membership) simply by predicting its class membership to be the same as that of its nearest neighbour in the training set. More generally, the k-nearest neighbour algorithm operates in the same sort of way, except that the k nearest neighbours to the case undergoing classification are used to form estimates of the probability of class membership of the various classes.

2 The Attribute Weighting Problem

For continuous attributes on an interval scale of measurement [1], distances between cases are usually computed as Euclidean distances, D_2, in the attribute space, where:

$$D_2 = \sqrt{\sum_{i=1}^{N} d_i^2}$$

where N is the number of attributes and d_i is the value difference of the two instances on the ith attribute. However, other distance metrics such as the Manhattan distance, D_1, may be preferred for some applications, where:

$$D_1 = \sum_{i=1}^{N} d_i$$

Before computing these distances, it is usual to rescale each attribute by dividing it by its standard deviation. This puts all the attributes on a sort of common scale of magnitude and prevents those which originally had large variances from dominating the distance computation.

However, there is a problem working with this conventional approach, arising from the fact that these distances are calculated from all the attributes weighted equally, without regard for their relative importance in discriminating between the classes. In statistical terms, the technique really involves conditioning on *all* the available attributes, including those which have no value at all in the discrimination (if the application includes such variables). Recently, Liu and White [2] made a comparison between nearest neighbour and tree-based classification techniques and showed that the nearest neighbour method can suffer from overfitting which, in turn, renders sub-optimal performances in domains where the number of variables is large or the variables are of unequal importance in discriminating between the classes. It is not difficult to see that the worst situation would be when many attributes are present and some of these attributes are irrelevant to the discrimination task. In order to overcome this problem, attributes really need to be *weighted* (either explicitly or implicitly) in the calculation of the overall distance between two cases.

3 Association-based Distance Metrics

3.1 Background

The proposed solution to the problem has its origin in two ideas. The first of these comes from the Value Difference Metric (VDM), proposed by Stanfill and Waltz [3] and described by Liu [4]. This was actually introduced to replace the simple 'overlap' metric (Hamming distance), for measuring the distance between values of symbolic features (categorical attributes). This measure is useful and important because it introduces attribute weights, implicitly, into the distance metric. Unfortunately, in a domain when numeric-valued attributes are involved, the VDM cannot be used directly, simply because numeric attributes have too many possible values and some values in *new* cases may not even exist in the training set. One naive way of solving this problem would be to discretise numeric-valued attributes by dividing them into equal intervals, and then to use the VDM as the distance metric on these discretised attributes.

However, this approach to discretising the attributes is arbitrary and consequently sub-optimal. Fortunately, it is possible to do better than this. The second idea involves using the same sort of approach to discretising attributes as is used in tree-based approaches to classification, when they are applied to continuous attributes [5, 6, 7]. The benefits of doing this are that the attributes are discretised at those places where it is optimal to do so. Briefly, this involves splitting each attribute at a point between each pair of adjacent values and cross-tabulating the derived binary variable against the indicator variable for class. An appropriate statistic (such as χ^2) is then applied to the table and used as a measure of goodness-of-split. The attribute is then discretised at that point which maximises the value of the goodness-of-split measure over the various possible cutting points. This procedure is then applied recursively to both sub-ranges of the original attribute, subject to a stopping rule which is usually specified in terms of a threshold value of the goodness-of-split measure. Further details are given in the references cited earlier.

The result of this part of the process is that continuous attributes which are important in discriminating between classes are split at one or more points in their range, into two or more sub-ranges. The points at which the splitting is done are those where there is a high rate of change in the relative frequencies of the classes. For any attribute which has been subjected to this splitting process, a derived discrete variable is produced, simply by attributing consecutive integer values to consecutive sub-ranges of the original attribute. Thus, an attribute which is split just once will give rise to a derived binary variable, an attribute which is split at two points will yield a ternary variable, and so on. It is worth noting that an attribute which is not split at any point in its range does not yield a derived variable at all and hence this process also functions as a mechanism for filtering out attributes which have little or no power to discriminate between the classes. Thus, the final result of the discretisation process is a set of discrete variables that represents the important aspects of the discrimination power of a possibly larger set of continuous attributes.

3.2 The Value Distance Metric

Having described the discretisation process, it is now necessary to return to the value distance metric, in order to explain how it works. The essence of the problem is that, for a discrete attribute with, say, m possible values, it is first of all necessary to define a distance metric such that the distance between any two possible values on this variable reflects the difference in relative class frequencies between these values. In other words, the greater the difference in the relative class frequencies between two values of the same attribute, the greater the distance between the two values is assumed to be.

Let us assume a problem domain with v classes C_1, C_2, ..., C_v and N symbolic attributes A_1, A_2, ..., A_N. Let us also assume that attribute A_i (i = 1, 2, ..., N) has m different values. From the cases in the training set, a contingency table, representing the cross-classification of class and attribute A_i can be constructed, as shown in Table 3.2. In this table, n_{ij} (i = 1, 2, ..., v; j = 1, 2, ..., m) represent the frequency counts of cases with class C_i and attribute value a_j; and hence:

Table 1: A contingency table representing a cross-tabulation of class and attribute A_i.

	a_1	a_2		a_m	
C_1	n_{11}	n_{12}	...	n_{1m}	n_{1*}
C_2	n_{21}	n_{22}	...	n_{2m}	n_{2*}
⋮	⋮	⋮	...	⋮	⋮
C_v	n_{v1}	n_{v2}	...	n_{vm}	n_{v*}
	n_{*1}	n_{*2}	...	n_{*m}	n_{**}

$$n_{i*} = \sum_{j=1}^{m} n_{ij}$$

$$n_{*j} = \sum_{i=1}^{v} n_{ij}$$

$$n_{**} = \sum_{i=1}^{v} \sum_{j=1}^{m} n_{ij}$$

In the VDM, the distance d between any two values a_i, a_j is defined as:

$$d(a_i, a_j) = \sum_{k=1}^{v} \left| \frac{n_{ki}}{n_{*i}} - \frac{n_{kj}}{n_{*j}} \right| \tag{1}$$

Using this definition, a matrix of value differences for each attribute in the training set can be computed. Equation 1 defines a geometric distance [8], because it has the following properties

- $d(a, b) \geq 0,\ a \neq b$
- $d(a, b) = d(b, a)$
- $d(a, a) = 0$
- $d(a, b) + d(b, c) \geq d(a, c)$

The total distance D between two cases is given by:

$$D(X, Y) = \sum_{i=1}^{N} d(x_i, y_i) \tag{2}$$

where X and Y represent the two cases, x_i and y_i denote values of the ith attribute for X and Y and where there are N features (attributes) in the problem domain. The idea behind the VDM is that distances defined as in Equation 2 can then be used in *any* domain in which the attributes have a relatively small number of discrete values, whether those values are ordered or not.

3.3 General Association Metrics

Another way of looking at the VDM is as a measure of association between class and attribute. To be more precise, in the case of attributes having more than two different values, the VDM might be better described as a measure of association between class and an *attribute value pair*, because the measure is applied to only two values of an attribute at any given time. Thus, the VDM could be seen either as a measure of association or as a distance metric. The basis of the equivalence between these two ways of looking at the VDM can be explained quite easily. To keep matters simple, let us consider the simplest possible situation of two classes and a binary attribute. If the attribute is a powerful discriminator between the classes, then this is reflected in a value of high magnitude for the association between class and attribute. If we look at the same problem in terms of a distance metric, then a measure such as the VDM uses the distance between the attribute values to express the same idea. The greater the distance between the values, the better the attribute is as a discriminator between the classes.

Thus the VDM could be regarded as a measure of association and may be compared with other measures of association. These could be used in the same sort of pairwise application as the VDM, in order to derive a matrix of values for associations between class on the one hand and all possible pairs of attribute values on the other. Perhaps the most common measure of association used in computer science is transmitted information, H_T (also known as information gain). This is defined elsewhere [9]. In the context of a general discrimination task, this measure is best interpreted as the information about class membership which is conveyed by attribute value. However, it can quite easily be applied to a *particular pair* of attribute values, in the same way as the VDM. In such a situation, the value of H_T should be regarded as the information about class membership which is conveyed by that pair of attribute values.

Work in progress by the current authors suggests that the VDM is biased in favour of attributes with unequal attribute values. Therefore, the use of another measure such as H_T might be preferable. If this is done, then the information about class membership, conveyed by a particular pair of values on a given discrete variable is used as the distance between those values on the dimension defined by the variable concerned. The total distance between two cases is taken as the sum of such distances, over all such variables, in the same way as for the VDM (Equation 2).

4 A Simulation Experiment

4.1 Introduction

Simulation experiments can be a useful way of testing hypotheses concerning classification algorithms and have been used successfully for this purpose in the past [2, 10]. They have two principal advantages. Firstly, the datasets can be generated specifically to possess the particular features that are important for a given investigation. Secondly, they are more amenable to statistical verification.

Given a dataset with a substantial number of continuous attributes, of which only some are important in discriminating between the classes, a conventional nearest neighbour algorithm would be expected to perform sub-optimally because of over-fitting. The intention here is to test the hypothesis that a modified nearest neighbour approach, using an association-based distance metric operating on discretised attributes (as outlined earlier in the paper) would provide superior classification performance.

4.2 Method

A Monte Carlo simulation experiment was designed in which two different nearest neighbour techniques were tested and compared. One was the conventional nearest neighbour method, using Euclidean distance operating on continuous attributes. The other (experimental) technique involved discretising each attribute using χ^2, as described in Section 3.1. A cutoff value of 6.64 was applied to terminate the splitting process. (This value is actually the 99th percentage point of the cumulative distribution function for chi-square with one degree of freedom). An additional constraint was employed to prevent splits leading to fewer than six cases in either of the resulting divisions from being performed. The discrete variables derived from this process were then used to construct distances, by using H_T as described in Section 3.3.

100 different datasets were generated. Each dataset consisted of 400 cases. Each case contained a binary class variable (using values 1 or 2) and 40 continuous independent variables (attributes). The class variable was generated so as to have exactly 200 cases of each class. Two different types of independent variable were employed. One type (termed *signal* variables) incorporated information about class membership. The other type (*noise* variables) were produced so as to contain no information about class. All the noise variables were generated as samples from the standard normal distribution (i.e., a normal distribution with zero mean and unit standard deviation), using a random number generator. Signal variables were derived from noise variables by the simple method of adding half the class variable. (This would result in an expected difference of 0.5 in the mean scores on a signal variable between the two classes). This ensured that the signal variable contained information about class membership. Five signal variables were employed in the experiment and 35 noise variables. Before use, all the variables were re-standardised, so as to have a standard deviation of unity.

Nine different values of values for k, the number of nearest neighbours, were tested. The values of k employed were all the odd numbers from 1 to 17 inclusive. Even-numbered values of k were avoided because of possible difficulties arising from ties [11].

A two-way repeated measures experimental design [12] was employed, in which the dataset was the basic unit of replication. Thus each of the experimental factors (method and number of nearest neighbours) were varied within each dataset, i.e., each dataset was subjected to 18 separate analyses. The number of correct classifications for each dataset under each condition was recorded.

4.3 Results and Discussion

Table 4.3 shows the results of the experiment, in terms of mean classification performance for each experimental condition. The overall classification performance was better for the experimental method (63.23% correct) than for the conventional one (58.96% correct). The difference was highly significant under the appropriate F test ($F = 114.03$; $df = 1, 99$; $p < 0.001$). This strongly supports the idea that the new approach can offer superior performance, at least for certain datasets.

Table 2: Classification performance for each condition in the simulation experiment. Each entry is a mean, taken over 100 datasets and expressed as the percentage of cases classified correctly.

	Conventional	Experimental
1-NN	55.15	60.53
3-NN	56.71	62.15
5-NN	58.11	63.05
7-NN	58.79	63.46
9-NN	59.24	63.65
11-NN	60.09	63.93
13-NN	60.55	63.94
15-NN	60.82	64.17
17-NN	61.17	64.23

The effect of k, the number of nearest neighbours, was also found to be highly significant ($F = 188.15$; $df = 8, 792$; $p < 0.001$). For both methods, classification performance improved monotonically as k was increased, throughout the range studied although, for each method, performance seems to be tending towards an asymptote. This was probably due to the values of k being too small for this particular task. This is in some ways equivalent to having terminal node frequencies too small in a tree-based classification task, which also reduces classification accuracy [13].

There is also a significant interaction between the method used and the number of nearest neighbours, such that the performance of the new technique improved less rapidly than that of the conventional approach, as k was increased ($F = 13.87$; $df = 8, 792$; $p < 0.001$). From the results obtained, it is difficult to say whether the classification performance for larger values of k would continue to show a difference between the two methods for larger values of k, or not. All that can be said at present is that, for 17 nearest neighbours (the largest value of k studied), there was still a significant difference on a matched-pairs t test between the two methods ($t = 6.98; df = 99; p < 0.001$). Work on this and other aspects of the performance evaluation is continuing.

5 Conclusions

This new approach to nearest neighbour discriminant analysis seems able to overcome some of the problems with the conventional approach. The use of an association-based distance metric means that the distance attributed to the difference between two values of an attribute is a reflection of the importance that that particular value difference has in discriminating between the classes in the problem. In other words, the nature of the metric itself ensures that attributes (or rather their derived discrete counterparts) are accorded appropriate weightings. The weightings are implicit in the metric.

As mentioned elsewhere (Liu, to appear), the use of any association-based metric is obviously appropriate for dealing (directly) with categorical attributes. When combined with the discretisation approach for continuous attributes described here, the result is a flexible technique that seems potentially capable of coping with a mixture of attribute types within a nearest neighbour framework.

References

1. S.S. Stevens, On the theory of scales of measurement, *Science*, **103**, 677–680 (1946).
2. W.Z. Liu and A.P. White, A comparison of nearest neighbour and tree-based discriminant analysis, *Journal of Statistical and Computational Simulation*, **53**, 41–50 (1995).
3. C. Stanfill and D. Waltz, Towards memory-based reasoning, *Communications of the ACM*, **29 (12)**, 1213–1228 (1986).
4. W.Z. Liu, An integrated approach for multiple attribute types in nearest neighbour classification, *Knowledge Engineering Review* (to appear).
5. J. Catlett, On changing continuous attributes into ordered discrete attributes, In Y. Kodratoff (Ed.), *Proceedings of the European Working Session on Learning* (1991).
6. W.Z. Liu and A.P. White, A review of inductive learning, In *Research and Development in Expert Systems* VIII, edited by I.M. Graham and R.W. Milne, pp. 112–126 (Cambridge University Press, 1991).
7. A.P. White and W.Z. Liu, Probabilistic induction by dynamic path generation for continuous attributes, In *Research and Development in Expert Systems* VII, edited by T.R. Addis and R.M. Muir, pp. 285–296 (Cambridge University Press, 1990).

8. S. Cost and S. Salzberg, A weighted nearest neighbour algorithm for learning with symbolic features, *Machine Learning*, **10**, 57–78 (1993).
9. A.P. White and W.Z. Liu, Bias in information-based measures in decision tree induction, *Machine Learning*, **15**, 321–329 (1994).
10. W.Z. Liu and A.P. White, The importance of attribute selection measures in decision tree induction, *Machine Learning*, **15**, 25–41 (1994).
11. A.P. White, Cross-validation of nearest-neighbour discriminant analysis — a warning to SAS users, *Journal of Statistical Computation and Simulation*, **49**, 129–140 (1994).
12. G. Keppel, *Design and analysis: a researcher's handbook* (Englewood Cliffs, N.J: Prentice-Inc, 1946).
13. L. Breiman *et al*, *Classification and Regression Trees* (Wadsworth, 1984).

ANALYSIS OF MACHINE LEARNING CLASSIFIERS FOR SOIL SALINITY

Peter W. EKLUND
Department of Computer Science, The University of Adelaide
Adelaide 5005, Australia

Stephen D. KIRKBY
Key Centre for Social Applications of Geographical Information Systems
The University of Adelaide, Adelaide 5005, Australia

In physical geography data collection is usually labor intensive and expensive to conduct. Data models of the environment should be constructed using the minimum data but maintain relevance and detail. This paper shows how machine learning classifier techniques can be used to help determine the minimum amount of data required in physical geographic models. Two case studies are considered that report the use of machine learning classifiers to obtain minimum sample sizes for ground-based data surveys in environmental domains. One such learning algorithm, the inductive learning program C4.5 was used to verify that a high performance classifier, better than 95% classification accuracy on unseen data, can be constructed using 235 sample points in the case-study area. We compare this result to the magnitude of sample sizes required for similar classification performance using back-propagation neural networks and instance-based learning. We examine the reasons and implications for these variations with reference to the domain.

1 Introduction

Physical geographers and environmental scientists construct data models of the environment that are spatially referenced. These data are either collected from expensive ground-surveys or remotely sensed. Although remotely sensed data has come down in price, it can rarely be used solely for land management applications and is often augmented by coarser field survey data. One difficulty using field surveys is they are sometimes destructive, for example measuring depth to ground water requires a drill hole to be sunk. Such data collection is always labor intensive and expensive to conduct. To minimize overheads (and environmental damage), data models of the environment should be constructed using the minimum field-surveyed data but maintain relevance and detail. This paper shows how machine learning classifier techniques can be used to determine the minimum amount of data required for use in a physical geographic model. This paper extends on the other work in knowledge discovery in spatial domains[12,13,4,5]. A complete and unabridged version will be reported in Eklund *et al*[6].

The paper firstly describes the data used in the case-study and an explanation of its purpose for sustainable environmental land management. It then describes the experimental starting point as a knowledge acquisition exercise using inductive learning. This leads us to comparatively examine inductive learning classifiers against other machine learning (ML) techniques. In particular we compare classifiers constructed using Instance-based Learning (IBL) and Backpropogation neural networks. Our objective is to minimize the size of the training set while maximising classification accuracy against a synthetic ground-truth. The result are learning curves, a plot of the number of training points against classification accuracy for each of the ML classifiers. The plots reveal the best performing ML technique for this domain. We hypothesis that this method can be generalized and similar experiments repeated in different domains to isolate the most appropriate ML technique.

1.1 Background

The data used for this study was collected for an environmental assessment in a physical geography case-study involving soil salinity[8]. The data is spatial consisting of 302 × 402 data cells representing an area of 10 × 12 km 200 km NNW of the city of Adelaide in the mid-north of South Australia. Data was collected for the study at various times since 1990 and includes map layers soil type, geology, slope, elevation, ground water depth, drainage lines, cadastral (property ownership), roads, spot heights, contours and a LandSat5 TM, 7 band scene, collected May 1990 [a]. Additionally, soil and geology layers were digitized by the South Australian Department of Agriculture who also collected the depth to ground-water data layer from wells sunk in the area — such wells use monitoring equipment called piezometers. Each cell in the spatial database is described by the schema illustrated in Table 1. Each attribute represents a layer in the database and can be rendered as a 2D map. These maps can be overlayed in the usual way. TMBAND1—TMBAND7 are digital spectral ranges for seven LandSat5 TM bands. Table 1 shows the range of values for a given attribute and whether the attribute is a continuous real value or an enumerated type such as *Soil* and *Geology*.

This model and accompanying data are input to a rule-base system used for decision support for soil salinity management [8,9]. The task is to determine the *salinity class* for each cell. For example, a high potential for saline discharge (HPD) — a potential high concentration of salt in the soil — are coloured areas of a map classed as HPD. These individual pixels can be rendered a particular

[a] This is the optimal time of year to assess the relative health of vegetation in this part of the world since plant life experiences a so called *spring flush* with a clear "healthy vegetation" signature through LandSat5 TMBANDs 3 and 4.

Table 1: Schemata for the study database.

Attribute name	Data type	Value range
Ground water	continuous	1–14
Elevation	continuous	1–6
Slope	continuous	1–7
Geology	discrete 8	$\{1, 2, \cdots, 8\}$
Soil	discrete 13	$\{1, 2, \cdots, 13\}$
TMBAND1	continuous	64–159
TMBAND2	continuous	24–90
TMBAND3	continuous	22–145
TMBAND4	continuous	28–190
TMBAND5	continuous	16–233
TMBAND6	continuous	125–154
TMBAND7	continuous	4–145

colour and displayed as a map. The map reveals those spatial regions with a high concentration of salt in the soil according to some classification criteria formulated by an expert (further described in Kirkby[8,9]). Some example rules are shown in Figure 2. Sixteen rules of this type are defined for six classes of soil salinity given in Table 2. Rules are defined for each class of salinity and each pixel assigned a different map color. The rules forward chain over the data to derive a total salinity map illustrated in Figure 1.

Table 2: Rules are defined for each of the six salinity classes.

Class Description	Class
Existing discharge (ED)	1
High potential discharge (HPD)	2
Low potential discharge (LPD)	3
Low potential recharge (LPR)	4
Medium potential recharge (MPR)	5
High potential recharge (HPR)	6

2 Experiments

Three experiments structure our results. In the first, classified spatial data is passed to an inductive learning program. The program's task is to reconstruct the rule-base. In this way, synthesized rules can be used to improve classification speed — performance is an issue due to the volume of data involved with each classification run. The second experiment predicts the effect of a

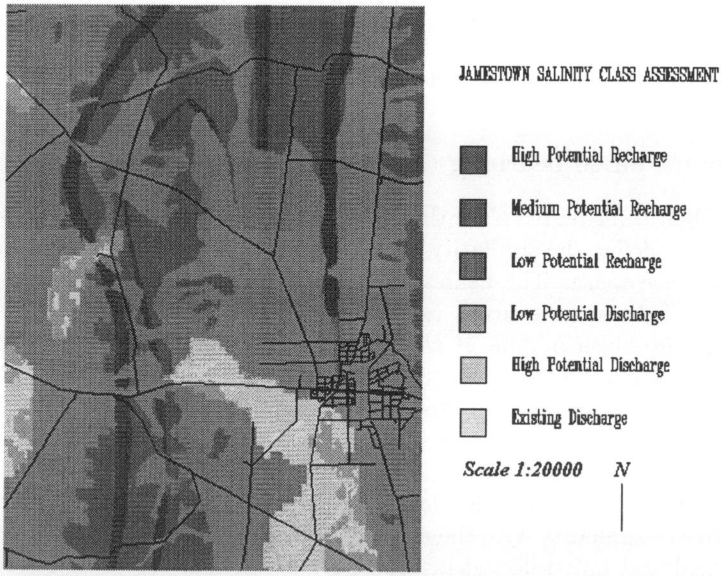

Figure 1: A portion of the total salinity map, each salinity class is rendered a different color.

new data layer called EM31 on the classification result [4]. Thirdly, we compare the classification viability of different machine learning algorithms. Does one technique produce a better classifier than another and how can we maximize classifier performance and yet minimize the quantity of training data?

A key justification of the experiment lies in the perception of the rule-base classification as a synthetic ground truth from which to measure classifier performance. This is motivated in two ways: (i) data acquisition and collection at each cell position is a physical impossibility, e.g. installing piezometers for every cell is destructive; (ii) because the classification rules are heuristic, classes such as "potential discharge" and "potential recharge" do not directly measure current environmental damage but rather its "potential" to occur over time. The classification map shown in Figure 1 is therefore a predictor rather than a literal interpretation of salt affectedness. Although this suggests no way of measuring the rule-base system output against an objective ground truth, it is possible to measure the heuristic classification against a ground truth map and Kirkby [8] reports a high correlation between the rule-base salinity map and a small quantity of ground based truth data — better than 80%.

Each learning technique we examine measures the scale of the training data required for a high correlation to the synthetic ground truth. There is therefore a natural bias towards C4.5[10] given the rule-base is symbolic and the output from C4.5 is likewise — this issue is further discussed below in the *Methodological Results* section below.

3 Instance-based Learning (IBL)

All IBL algorithms derive from the well-known *nearest neighbor* pattern classifier[3]. They define the similarity of two instances as their Euclidean distance in the instance space. The nearest neighbor method classifies an instance as a member of the same concept as its most similar instance[1,2]. Several IBL algorithms are given in Aha *et al*[1,7,2]. These include the IB1 and IB2 algorithms; and also a multi-pass instance learning (MPIL) algorithm[11]. The IB1 algorithm is the simplest instance-based learning algorithm. It is equivalent to the nearest neighbor algorithm, except it normalizes the attribute ranges and has the capability to deal with missing values. The IB2 algorithm is identical to IB1 except it saves only misclassified instances. The algorithm displays a high degree of similarity with the condensed nearest neighbor algorithm[3] since it saves and uses only selected instances for prediction. By being selective in the instances it saves, its storage requirements are significantly less than those of IB1 especially when instances are adequately separated in feature space.

On the other hand, IB2 appears to be more sensitive to noise than IB1. The multi-pass instance learning (MPIL) algorithm allows multiple passes over the complete set of instances, as opposed to a single pass in the IB1 and IB2 algorithms. An instance is represented by features, where a feature represents a continuous or discrete attribute value. Associated with every instance is a neighborhood (spanned by the instance) that can be either a sphere (MPIL1) or a k-dimensional box (MPIL2 algorithm). The details of these two algorithms are given in Romaniuk[11]. The purpose of "neighborhood" is to define a degree of similarity between instances defining the same concept. Storage efficiencies can be achieved by: (i) appropriately defining the neighborhood for every instance; and (ii) removing instances in the defined neighborhood of another instance. Instances associated with different concepts define valid neighborhoods. A neighborhood is valid if instances enclosed within it describe the same concept as the instance that spans the neighborhood[11].

All supervised learning classifiers involve training and testing but IB1 stores all its training data and does not involve any training phase. For IB2, MPIL1 and MPIL2, training involves storing prototypical cases that summarize training data. All four IBL algorithms have the same testing phase. Each test case is scanned and the algorithm selects the most similar case from its attributes. If classes of the test and selected case are identical, the classification is correct.

4 Backpropagation

We implement back-propagation in C. Discrete attributes are encoded using a set of binary input units — one for each value. For example, *geology* (from Table 1) has eight input units or attribute values. If an instance has a geology '5', then the fifth input unit for geology is set to 1.0 and the other seven are set to 0. Each continuous attribute is modeled by one input unit and scaled between 0 and 1. Output units correspond uniquely to classes, one unit for each class. The network was tested with several hidden units and one and two hidden layers. Optimal results are obtained with 10 hidden units and one hidden layer. Extending the model to two hidden layers had no effect on classification performance. Therefore, for the salinity data, 31 input, 10 hidden and 6 output units were employed. The network was tested with various learning rates (0.05, 0.1, 0.5, 1) and momentum (0.0, 0.1, 0.5, 0.9). Of these, a 0.05 learning rate and a momentum value of 0.9 gave best classification results against test data.

5 Knowledge Discovery with C4.5

An important aspect of this research is to confirm that the C4.5 output corresponds to the logic of the domain expert. C4.5 derived rules were shown to the domain experts. They were asked to identify spurious rules. Initially, experts were puzzled by the combination of C4.5 rules shown in Figure 2 believing they represent an illogical combination.

```
Rule 1:    ground_water <= 3
           slope <= 3
           tmband3 <= 39
           soil in {12, 13, 3, 5, 7}
           slope <= 3
           tmband4 <= 100
           -> class 2

Rule 14:   elevation <= 2
           ground_water <= 3
           slope <= 3
           soil in {12, 13, 3, 5, 7}
           tmband3 > 58
           -> class 2

Rule16:    elevation <= 2
           ground_water <= 3
           slope <= 3
           soil in {12, 13, 3, 5, 7}
           tmband4 > 100
           -> class 2
```

Figure 2: Conflict and inconsistency in inductive rules suggest a split HPD class.

Stressed vegetation expected for HPD (class 2) is consistent with, and satisfied by, rule 14 (High spectral response in TMBAND 3). However, rules 1 and 16 cover vegetation experiencing flush growth, note the conditionals, TMBAND 3 low spectral response and TMBAND 4 high spectral response. Rules 1 and 16 are inconsistent with HPD (class 2) as the healthy vegetation implies a high ground-water table with low salt content. The rules in Figure 2 suggest two proper subclasses of HPD. The original HPD class was split: HPD_f, indicating healthy vegetation and HPD_s — indicating stressed vegetation. These two HPD classes better explain potential discharge for stressed/unstressed vegetation.

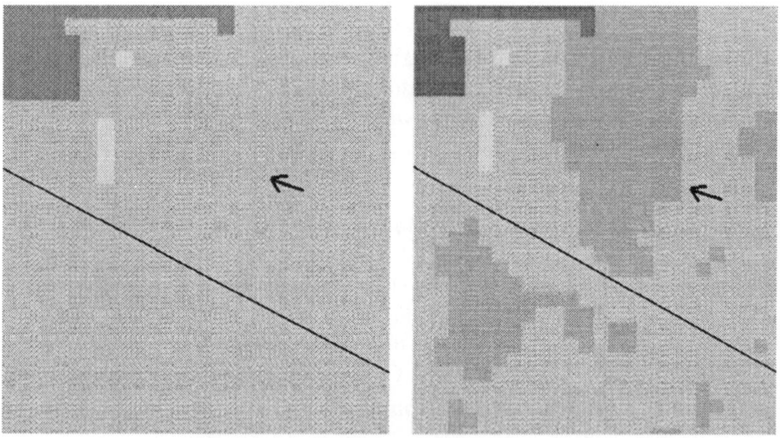

Figure 3: The classification indicating new HPD_f class within class 2 (darker to the right).

C4.5 precipitated this discovery which was later verified by a visit to the case-study area. HPD_f classes in the map correspond to areas where stormwater contouring and engineering works had taken place. This provides clear and independent evidence that such water management is having a positive effect on saline discharge, ie. salts being flushed from the groundwater table enabling vegetation to take advantage of the good water source. Importantly, the HPD_f class only occurred within the vicinity of the engineering and contouring works. The domain discovery is therefore in terms of conditioning the classification criteria.

6 Experimental Description

The three classifiers (C4.5, IBL and Backpropagation) were tested in two domains: the salinity spatial database and the same data augmented with an EM31 data coverage. The EM31 augmented database is similar to that of salinity database described in Table 1, with the addition of two continuous electromagnetic attributes. These values determine soil conductivity and are expected to have some influence in determining salinity. The EM31 data consists of 14 attribute values and a class. Each domain was partitioned into training and test sets.

Table 3: Performance accuracy and storage requirements of IBL algorithms.

Performance on salinity data			
algorithm	**training**	**test**	**storage**
IB1	100%	89%	100%
IB2	89.2%	85.6%	13.88%
MPIL1	100%	89%	12.5%
MPIL2	100%	95.8%	9.9 %
Performance on EM31 data			
algorithm	**training**	**test**	**storage**
IB1	100%	60.1%	100%
IB2	56.3%	56.9%	19.7%
MPIL1	100%	85.2%	18.5%
MPIL2	100%	84.9%	19.2 %

The first set of results compare the performance accuracy of the four IBL algorithms. Performance is split in three parts: (i) performance on training set only; (ii) performance on the unseen test set; and (iii) storage requirements for the different approaches. For storage, IB1 is used as a base case — it stores all training instances. For the other IBL derived algorithms we reduce statistical fluctuations by averaging results over five different training and testing sets produced by randomly placing two-thirds of the examples for each category in the training set and the others in a corresponding test set.

Table 3 gives insight into the performance of the four learning algorithms on salinity and EM31 domains. The training and test set size is 800 and 500 respectively for both salinity and EM31 domains. Comparing IBL classifiers, the most striking result is the performance of MPIL1 and MPIL2 over IB1. MPIL1 and MPIL2 achieved perfect results on the training set and a high accuracy on the test set. However, they require only a small fraction of the storage. MPIL1 achieves the highest accuracy for the EM31 data while MPIL2 outperforms other classifiers for salinity data.

Table 4 lists the results achieved by the back-propagation classifier for the two activation functions: sigmoid and hyperbolic tangent. The number of hidden units was varied from 0 (one layer only) to 20. The results are given for the two data for 0, 5, 10 and 15 hidden units. For both domains, the network gives best results with 10 hidden units using sigmoid as its activation function. No improvement was observed by increasing the number of hidden units through the range of 10—20 nor by introducing a second hidden layer.

Table 4: Performance Accuracy of Backpropagation.

Activation function vs accuracy				
#hidden units	**sigmoid**		**hyperbolic**	
	Salinity	EM31	Salinity	EM31
0	92.6%	82.4%	91%	80.1%
5	96.9%	78.5%	94.7%	77.8%
10	97.6.4%	91.5%	97.1%	88.2%
15	95.3%	90.6%	94.8%	85%

Training consists of consecutive forward and backward passes. This process is repeated until a satisfactory generalization performance is obtained and the weights assigned. Testing consists of forward passing an input pattern and assigned to the class whose output unit has the highest value. Again, in order to reduce statistical fluctuations, each backpropagation run uses a different random seed number for the initial network weights.

Table 5: Performance Accuracy of C4.5.

	Accuracy of C4.5		
Domain	**Decision tree**	**Pruned**	**Rules**
salinity	99.4%	99.8%	99.8%
EM31	94%	96%	95.5%

The training phase for inductive learning involves generation of the decision tree and classify the test data using the tree. Inductive learning achieved 99.8% and 96% (after pruning the decision tree) accuracy on salinity and EM31 data respectively. Results are shown in Table 5.

7 Learning Curves

The graph in Figure 4 shows the learning curves of the three techniques for salinity classification. From the plots in Figure 4 we conclude that C4.5 produces a classification accuracy better than 95%, even for a small training set of 235 instances. To achieve the same accuracy using backpropagation more than 500 training instances are required and more than 700 training instances for MPIL2. Figure 4 also suggests backpropagation and MPIL2 perform well for large training sets but their performance degrades markedly for smaller training sets.

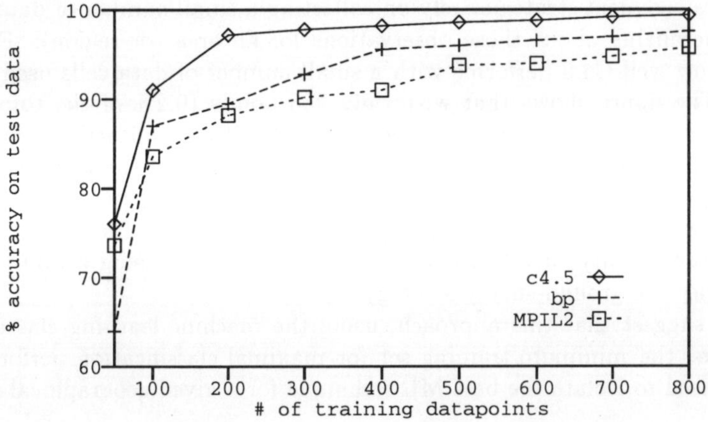

Figure 4: Accuracy as a function of number of data cells in learning set.

7.1 Analysis of Results

There are several reasons why C4.5 outperforms both backpropagation and MPIL2. Firstly, the domain itself favors the symbolic attribute-value treatment. Certain attributes in salinity class discrimination are more significant than others, e.g. ground-water depth is <u>the</u> prime discriminator for saline discharge. High ground-water depth is an obvious indicator of potential discharge[b]. Likewise, LandSat5 TMBAND3 directly indicates vegetation in stress, another important saline indicator. In domains where attributes have a more uniform influence on classification, the performance of backpropagation and MPIL2 will be significantly improved.

Secondly, the ground truth data has been synthesized using a symbolic classifier. These classifiers precisely resemble the output vocabulary of C4.5. This biases results in favor of C4.5. For these reasons, no conclusions can

[b]Salt affected water close to the Earth's surface characterizes discharge. Salt affected or not, water close to the surface belongs to the HPD class.

be drawn about the performance of the instance-based, neural and inductive learning algorithms in general from this study. However, on the basis of results in this domain, C4.5 emerges with the most effective classifier on the smallest training set against the synthesized ground truth.

7.2 Methodological Results

Land management strategies rely on collecting a small number of data points and generalizing about those observations for an area (or region). Figure 4 shows how well C4.5 performs with a small number of data cells used as test data. The figure shows that with only 235 points (0.2% of the total data) — chosen randomly as training data — gives 95.7% classification accuracy on the entire 121,404 element database. With 0.5% (618) of the total data cells, drawn randomly from the data, 99% classification accuracy is observed. This suggests inductive learning, used to classify small parcels of land, can be used to scale up salinity classification studies to other areas using a minimal cost data collection ground-survey strategy.

We suggest that this approach, using the machine learning classifiers to determine the minimum training set for maximal classification performance, can be used to isolate the best ML technique for a given geographical survey.

8 Conclusion

The inductive learning program C4.5 [10] is used to verify that an acceptable classifier can be constructed using only 235 sample points from the study area, a classifier with better than 95% classification accuracy is considered acceptable in this domain. We compare this result to the magnitude of sample sizes required for back-propagation neural networks and instance-based learning and examine reasons for this result. This method, of comparing the classification accuracy on unseen data for varying training set sizes, gives us a way of choosing the "best" ML classifier for the geographical survey task and a means of suggesting the minimum number of field survey sites required as test data. The method has particular merit in physical geography where data collection via ground surveys are expensive and time consuming and the number of points from which to be able to build a sufficient classifier are generally unknown.

Acknowledgments

This research was supported by the Australian Research Council and The University of Adelaide. Thanks to Peter Deer from the Defence Science Technology

Organisation (DSTO) for his comments on earlier drafts.

References

1. D.W. Aha and D. Kibler, "Noise-tolerant instance-based learning algorithms", *Proceedings of the Eleventh International Joint Conference on Artificial Intelligence*, pp. 794–799, Morgan Kaufmann, (1989).
2. D.W. Aha, D. Kibler and M. K. Albert, "Instance-based learning algorithms", *Machine Learning*, **6**, (1), 37–66, (1991).
3. T.M. Cover and P.E. Hart, "Nearest neighbor pattern classification", *IEEE Transactions on Information Theory*, **13**, 21–27, (1967).
4. P. W. Eklund and S.D. Kirkby and A. Salim. "A Framework for Incremental Knowledge-base Update from Additional Data Coverages", *7th Australiasian Conference on Remote Sensing*, pp. 364–377, (1994).
5. P.W. Eklund, S.D. Kirkby, "Machine Learning Classifier Performance as an Indicator for Data Acquisition Regimes in Geographical Field Surveys", *Australian and New Zealand Conference on Intelligent Information Systems*, ANZIIS-95, pp. 45–50, Perth, (1995).
6. P.W. Eklund, S.D. Kirkby and A. Salim, "Inductive Machine Learning and Soil Salinity Analysis", *International Journal of GIS* — in press (1997).
7. D. Kibler, D.W. Aha and M. Albert, *Instance-based prediction of real valued attributes, Computational Intelligence*, **5**, 51–57, (1989).
8. S. D. Kirkby, *Managing Dryland Salinisation with an Integrated GIS/ES*, PhD Thesis, Department of Geography, The University of Adelaide (1994).
9. S. D. Kirkby, "Integrating a GIS and Expert System to Identify and Manage Dryland Salinity", *Journal of Applied Geography*, **16** (4), 289–303, (1996).
10. J. R. Quinlan, *C4.5 Programs for Machine Learning*, Morgan Kaufmann, (1993).
11. S.G. Romaniuk, *Multi-Pass Instance Based Learning*, Department of Information System and Computer Science, Technical Report TRH3/93, National University of Singapore, (1993).
12. G. J. Williams, *Inducing and Combining Decision Structures for Expert Systems*, PhD Thesis, Department of Computer Science, The Australian National University (1990).
13. K. Zhang and J. Giardino, "Expert System based knowledge extraction from GIS", *International Geoscience and Remote Sensing Symposium IGARSS* pp. 319–321, IEEE press, (1992).

KNOWLEDGE DISCOVERY FROM NUMERICAL DATA

C. MORITA, H. TSUKIMOTO
Systems & Software Engineering Laboratory,
Research & Development Center, Toshiba Corporation.
70, Yanagi-cho, Saiwai-ku, Kawasaki 210, Japan.

Since many real data consist of numerical data, the discovery of understandable propositions from numerical data is important, and can be regarded as inductive learning with continuous classes. One of the authors previously presented an algorithm for discovering understandable propositions from numerical data. The algorithm consists of normalization, multiple regression analysis and the approximation of multilinear functions by continuous Boolean functions. Continuous Boolean functions are included in the space of multilinear functions. The space of multilinear functions can be corresponded to the space of probability distributions using the principle of indifference. The distance between two probability distributions is described by Kullback-Leibler (KL) information. Thus, the distance between multilinear functions and continuous Boolean functions is described using KL information. Therefore multilinear functions can be approximated to continuous Boolean functions. However, since the approximation algorithm is exponential in computational complexity, it can hardly be applied to real databases. This paper presents a polynomial approximation algorithm and applies the algorithm to ***bodyfat*** data to discover understandable propositions.

1 Introduction

This paper describes knowledge discovery from numerical data. The following table shows an example of numerical data. In Table 1, $x_i (i = 1, \ldots, 9)$ are

Table 1: An example of numerical data

x_1	x_2	$\cdots$	x_9	x_{10}
780	1280	$\cdots$	456	845
562	1300	$\cdots$	425	910

independent variables and x_{10} is a dependent variable, that is, x_{10} is represented as the function of $x_i (i = 1, \ldots, 9)$. If x_{10} is discrete, the problem is a classification. Therefore, the discovery of understandable propositions from numerical data can be regarded as inductive learning with continuous classes.

Inductive learning in AI can be applied to classification problems with discrete classes, but cannot be applied to problems with continuous classes. For example, C4.5 does not work well for the classification problem with continuous classes [5].

On the other hand, statistical methods have been developed for numerical data. But most statistical models obtained by statistical methods are mathematical expressions and difficult to understand without interpretation by a statistician. Thus, we present an algorithm for knowledge discovery from numerical data.

The outline of the algorithm is as follows:

1. The numerical data are normalized to [0,1].

2. Multiple regression analysis is performed.

3. The multilinear function obtained by step 2 is approximated to a continuous Boolean function using KL information.

The algorithm is based on the space of multilinear functions presented by one of the authors [7]. For example, the multilinear function of 2 variables is $axy + bx + cy + d$, where a, b, c, d are real. When the domain is {0,1}, the space of multilinear functions is the linear space spanned by the atoms of Boolean algebra. The functions obtained from Boolean functions by extending the domain from $\{0, 1\}$ to [0,1] are called continuous Boolean functions. For example, xy and $1 - y(= \overline{y})$ are continuous Boolean functions, where $x, y \in [0, 1]$. x stands for a direct proportion and $\bar{x}$ stands for an "inverse" proportion. In the case of [0,1] domain, the space of multilinear functions can be made into the linear space spanned by functions corresponding to the atoms of Boolean algebra.

The space of multilinear functions can be corresponded to the space of probability distributions using the principle of indifference. The distance between two probability distributions is described by Kullback-Leibler (KL) information. Therefore multilinear functions can be approximated to continuous Boolean functions. The distance for the approximation is described using KL information in probability distributions. Thus, the approximation algorithm finds a probability distribution corresponding to a continuous Boolean function that minimizes KL information.

The space of multilinear functions is briefly given in Section 2. Approximating multilinear functions is explained in Section 3. The experiment is described in Section 4.

2 The space of multilinear functions

Definition 1 *Definition of multilinear functions.*

Multilinear functions of n variables are as follows:

$$\sum_{i=1}^{2^n} a_i x_1^{e_1} \cdots x_n^{e_n},$$

where a_i is real, x_i is variable, and e_i is 0 or 1.

For example, multilinear functions of 2 variables are as follows:

$$axy + bx + cy + d.$$

In this paper, for simplification, $\sum$ stands for $\sum_{i=1}^{2^n}$, and n stands for the number of variables.

Theorem 2 *The space of multilinear functions ($\{0,1\}^n \to \mathbf{R}$) is the linear space spanned by the atoms of Boolean algebra.*

Proof can be found in reference [9].

In the case of [0,1] domain, the space of multilinear functions can be made into the linear space. While, in the case of {0,1} domain, the space is spanned by the atoms of Boolean algebra, in the case of [0,1] domain, the space is spanned by the corresponding functions[6].

Definition 3 *Definition of τ.*

Let $f(x)$ be a real polynomial function. Consider the following formula:

$$f(x) = p(x)(x - x^2) + q(x),$$

where $q(x) = ax + b$, where a and b are real, that is, $q(x)$ is the remainder.

τ_x is defined as follows:

$$\tau_x : f(x) \to q(x).$$

The above definition implies the following property:

$$\tau_x(x^k) = x.$$

where k is any natural number. In the case of n variables, τ is defined as follows:

$$\tau = \prod_{i=1}^{n} \tau_{x_i}.$$

For example, $\tau(x^2y^3 + y + 1) = xy + y + 1$.

Definition 4 *Definition of logical operations.*
Logical operations are defined as follows:

$$\begin{aligned} AND(\wedge) &: \tau(fg), \\ OR(\vee) &: \tau(f+g-fg), \\ NOT(\neg) &: \tau(1-f). \end{aligned}$$

Theorem 5 *The functions obtained from Boolean functions by extending the domain from $\{0,1\}$ to $[0,1]$ can satisfy all axioms of classical logic with the logical operations defined above.*

Proof can be found in reference [8].

Therefore, in this paper, the functions obtained from Boolean functions by extending the domain from $\{0,1\}$ to [0,1] are called continuous Boolean functions. For example, xy and $1-y(=\overline{y})$ are continuous Boolean functions, where $x, y \in [0,1]$. x stands for a direct proportion and $\bar{x}$ stands for an "inverse" proportion.

The functions corresponding to the atoms in the case of {0,1} domain are as follows:

$$\phi_i = \prod_{j=1}^{n} e(x_j) \ (i = 1, \ldots, 2^n), \text{where } e(x_j) = 1 - x_j \text{ or } x_j.$$

It is easily understood that these functions are the expansion of atoms in Boolean algebra of Boolean functions. For example, in the case of 2 variables, the functions are as follows:

$$xy,\ x(1-y),\ (1-x)y,\ (1-x)(1-y).$$

Since multilinear functions can be represented as vectors, multilinear functions are also described as (f_i), (g_i), ... , where f_i and g_i stand for the components. The vector representations are called logical vectors and the vector representations of continuous Boolean functions are called Boolean vectors. Hereinafter, the domain is [0,1].

3 Approximating multilinear functions by continuous Boolean functions

KL information, that is, the distance of probability distributions[1,10], can be introduced to the space of multilinear functions. Since KL information is the distance between probability distributions, multilinear functions (logical vectors) must be transformed to the corresponding probability distributions. In this section, first, KL information is explained, second, transforming logical vectors to probability distributions is described, and finally, an algorithm is explained.

3.1 KL information

Kullback-Leibler (KL) information is used as a criterion for the distance between probability distributions. In discrete probability distributions, let

$$\boldsymbol{p} = \{p_1, p_2, \cdots, p_m\}$$

be a true probability distribution, and let

$$\boldsymbol{q} = \{q_1, q_2, \cdots, q_m\}$$

be a model, then KL information $I(\boldsymbol{p}; \boldsymbol{q})$ is as follows:

$$I(\boldsymbol{p}; \boldsymbol{q}) = E[\log \frac{\boldsymbol{p}}{\boldsymbol{q}}] = \sum_{i=1}^{m} p_i \log \frac{p_i}{q_i},$$

where $E[\cdot]$ means the expectation. The less $I(\boldsymbol{p}; \boldsymbol{q})$ is, the nearer the model $\boldsymbol{q}$ is.

3.2 Transforming logical vectors to probability distributions

In this subsection, probability distributions are called probability vectors. The principle of indifference states that, when we have no information, the probability distribution is uniform [3]. Using this principle, logical vector (1, 1) corresponds to probability distribution $(1/2, 1/2)$, because logical vector (1, 1) means $x + \overline{x}(= 1)$, which is a tautology. Similarly, the following correspondences between logical vectors and probability vectors are obtained:

$$\begin{array}{lccc} \text{2 variables} & (1,1,1,1) & \Leftrightarrow & (1/4,1/4,1/4,1/4), \\ n \text{ variables} & (1,\ldots,1) & \Leftrightarrow & (1/(2^n),\ldots,1/(2^n)). \end{array}$$

The following correspondences are obtained in the same manner:

$$\begin{array}{lccc} x \text{ of 1 variable} & (1,0) & \Leftrightarrow & (1,0), \\ x \text{ of 2 variables} & (1,1,0,0) & \Leftrightarrow & (1/2,1/2,0,0). \end{array}$$

Theorem 6 *Using the principle of indifference, the following correspondence is obtained.*

Let (f_i) stand for a logical vector and let (p_i) stand for the probability vector corresponding to (f_i). Suppose m components of (f_i) are 1.

$$p_i = \begin{cases} 1/m \ (f_i = 1), \\ \quad 0 \ (f_i = 0). \end{cases}$$

Proof has been shown above.

Logical vectors and the corresponding probability vectors are the same in direction and differ in norm. The above discussion holds for Boolean vectors. Hereinafter, the above correspondence will be used for non-Boolean vectors. Therefore, the transformation formula below from logical vectors to probability vectors is obtained.

Theorem 7 *Let $\boldsymbol{f}(=(f_i))$ be a logical vector. The corresponding probability vector $\mathbf{p}(=(p_i))$ is as follows:*

$$p_i = \frac{f_i}{\sum f_i}.$$

Proof The direction of the corresponding probability vector is the same as that of a logical vector. Therefore, the probability vector $\boldsymbol{p}$ is

$$\boldsymbol{p} = k\boldsymbol{f},$$

where k is real. Since $\sum p_i = 1$, k is obtained as follows:

$$k = \frac{1}{\sum f_i}. \quad \square$$

3.3 An approximation algorithm

A logical vector can be transformed to a probability distribution, and, using KL information, the probability distribution corresponding to the nearest Boolean vector in terms of KL information can be obtained.

Let $\boldsymbol{f}(=(f_i))$ be a multilinear function and let $\boldsymbol{p}(=(p_i))$ be the probability distribution corresponding to the multilinear function. Let $\boldsymbol{q}(=(q_i))$ be the probability distribution corresponding to a continuous Boolean function $\boldsymbol{g}(=(g_i))$. The nearest (q_i) satisfies the following formula:

$$\sum p_i \log p_i - \sum p_i \log q_i \to \min \tag{1}$$

Because the first term in the above formula is constant, it can be deleted. Therefore, the above formula can be transformed as follows:

$$\begin{aligned} &-\textstyle\sum p_i \log q_i \\ &= -(p_1 \log q_1 + p_2 \log q_2 + \cdots + p_{2^n} \log q_{2^n}) \to \min \end{aligned} \tag{2}$$

Since (q_i) corresponds to a continuous Boolean function, $q_i = 0$ or $1/m$. In this case, we can find (q_i) satisfying formula (2) from among the following probability distributions,

$$(\frac{1}{m}, \ldots, \frac{1}{m}, 0, \ldots, 0).$$

The proof is omitted due to space limitations.

Now we can sort (p_i) satisfying

$$p_1 \geq p_2 \geq \cdots \geq p_{2^n}.$$

Since $q_i = 0$ or $1/m$, we have the following formula:

$$q_1 = \cdots = q_m = \frac{1}{m}, \quad q_{m+1} = \cdots = q_{2^n} = 0.$$

Therefore, formula (2) is transformed to the following formula:

$$\begin{aligned}(2) &= -(p_1 + \cdots + p_m)\log \tfrac{1}{m} - (p_{m+1} + \cdots + p_{2^n})\log \epsilon \\ &= (p_1 + \cdots + p_m)\log m + (p_{m+1} + \cdots + p_{2^n})\log \tfrac{1}{\epsilon}, \rightarrow \min\end{aligned} \tag{3}$$

where ϵ is a small positive number. Since log0 cannot be calculated, 0 is replaced by a small positive number.

By substituting $p_i = f_i / \sum f_i$ (Theorem 7), the following formula is obtained:

$$\begin{aligned}(3) &= \tfrac{1}{\sum f_i}(f_1 + \cdots + f_m)\log m + \tfrac{1}{\sum f_i}(f_{m+1} + \cdots + f_{2^n})\log \tfrac{1}{\epsilon} \\ &= \tfrac{1}{\sum f_i}((f_1 + \cdots + f_m)\log m + (f_{m+1} + \cdots + f_{2^n})\log \tfrac{1}{\epsilon}) \rightarrow \min \\ &\Leftrightarrow (f_1 + \cdots + f_m)\log m + (f_{m+1} + \cdots + f_{2^n})\log \tfrac{1}{\epsilon} \rightarrow \min\end{aligned} \tag{4}$$

Since $\sum q_i = 1$ and $\epsilon(> 0)$ is used for 0, $1/m$ must be modified to x such that $mx + (2^n - m)\epsilon = 1$.

$$x = \frac{1 - (2^n - m)\epsilon}{m}$$

The following formula is obtained:

$$(4) = (f_1 + \cdots + f_m)\log \frac{m}{1 - (2^n - m)\epsilon} + (f_{m+1} + \cdots + f_{2^n})\log \frac{1}{\epsilon} \rightarrow \min \tag{5}$$

However, since the number of f_i is 2^n, when n is big, the above formula cannot be calculated. Therefore, we sort a_i to satisfy the following formula:

$$|a_1| \geq |a_2| \geq \cdots \geq |a_n|,$$

and we use a_i up to a certain number, that is, we neglect small a_i. We find m such that it satisfies the formula (5). We can also know the threshold, that is, f_m corresponding to the m. In the following experiments, a_is are used up to a_{20}.

We can obtain the nearest $\boldsymbol{q}(=(1/m,\ldots,1/m,0,\ldots,0))$, and we can also obtain the nearest continuous Boolean function $\boldsymbol{g}(=(1,\ldots,1,0,\ldots,0))$ corresponding to $\boldsymbol{q}$. From Theorem 6, the following formula is obtained:

$$g_i = \begin{cases} 1 \ (g_i \geq f_m), \\ 0 \ (g_i < f_m). \end{cases}$$

As can be seen from the above formula, f_m is a threshold.

The above approximation algorithm is exponential in computational complexity, and therefore the above approximation algorithm is not realistic when variables are many. A polynomial approximation algorithm is presented.

3.4 The condition that x_i exists in the continuous Boolean function after approximation.

A polynomial approximation algorithm is presented when the function is linear. Hereinafter, multilinear functions are limited to linear functions.

Let a linear function be

$$p_1x_1 + \cdots + p_nx_n + p_{n+1},$$

and let the orthonormal expansion be

$$a_1x_1\cdots x_n + a_2x_1\cdots\overline{x_n} + \cdots + a_{2^n}\overline{x_1}\cdots\overline{x_n}.$$

Theorem 8 *a_i's are as follows:*

$$\begin{aligned} a_1 &= p_1 + \cdots + p_n + p_{n+1}, \\ &\cdots \\ a_{2^{n-1}} &= p_1 + p_{n+1}, \\ a_{2^{n-1}+1} &= p_2 + p_3 + \cdots + p_n + p_{n+1}, \\ &\cdots \\ a_{2^n-1} &= p_n + p_{n+1}, \\ a_{2^n} &= p_{n+1}. \end{aligned}$$

Proof a_1 can be obtained by substituting $x_1 = \cdots = x_n = 1$ in the following formula.

$$p_1x_1 + \cdots + p_nx_n + p_{n+1} = a_1x_1\cdots x_n + a_2x_1\cdots\overline{x_n} + \cdots + a_{2^n}\overline{x_1}\cdots\overline{x_n}$$

The other coefficients can be obtained in a similar manner. □

Theorem 9 *The condition that* $x_{i_1} \cdots x_{i_k} \overline{x}_{i_{k+1}} \cdots \overline{x}_{i_l}$ *exists in the continuous Boolean function after approximation is as follows:*

$$\sum_{i_1}^{i_k} p_{i_j} + p_{n+1} + \sum_{1 \le j \le n, j \ne i_1, \ldots, i_l, p_j < 0} p_j \ge a,$$

where a *is a threshold.*

Proof Consider the existence condition of x_1 in the continuous Boolean function after approximation. (For simplification, this condition is called the existence condition). Because $x_1 = x_1x_2 \cdots x_n \vee x_1x_2 \cdots \overline{x_n} \vee \cdots \vee x_1\overline{x_2} \cdots \overline{x_n}$, the existence of x_1 equals the existence of the following terms:

$$x_1x_2 \cdots x_n, \quad x_1x_2 \cdots \overline{x_n}, \ldots, x_1\overline{x_2} \cdots \overline{x_n}$$

The existence of the above terms means that all coefficients of these terms $a_1, a_2, \ldots, a_{2^n-1}$ are greater than or equal to a. That is,

$$\text{Min}\{a_i\} \ge a (1 \le i \le 2^{n-1}),$$

Because a_i's $(1 \le i \le 2^{n-1})$ are

$$\begin{aligned} a_1 &= p_1 + \cdots + p_n + p_{n+1}, \\ &\cdots \\ a_{2^n-1} &= p_1 + p_{n+1}, \end{aligned}$$

each $a_i (1 \le i \le 2^{n-1})$ contains p_1. If each p_j is non-negative, $a_{2^n-1} (= p_1 + p_{n+1})$ is the minimum because the other a_i's contain other p_j's, and therefore the other a_i's are greater than or equal to $a_{2^n-1} (= p_1 + p_{n+1})$. Generally, since each p_j is not necessarily non-negative, the Mina_i is a_i which contains all negative p_j. That is,

$$\text{Min} a_i = p_1 + p_{n+1} + \sum_{1 \le j \le n, j \ne 1, p_j < 0} p_j,$$

which necessarily exists in $a_i (1 \le i \le 2^{n-1})$, because $a_i (1 \le i \le 2^{n-1})$ is

$$p_1 + p_{n+1} + (\text{arbitrary sum of} p_j (2 \le j \le n)).$$

From the above arguments, the existence condition of x_1, Min$a_i \ge a$, is as follows:

$$p_1 + p_{n+1} + \sum_{1 \le j \le n, j \ne 1, p_j < 0} p_j \ge a.$$

Since $p_1x_1 + \cdots + p_nx_n + p_{n+1}$ is symmetric for x_i, the above formula holds for other variables; that is, the existence condition of x_i is

$$p_i + p_{n+1} + \sum_{1\le j\le n, j\ne i, p_j<0} p_j \ge a.$$

Similar discussions hold for $\overline{x}_i$, and therefore we have the following formula:

$$p_{n+1} + \sum_{1\le j\le n, j\ne i, p_j<0} p_j \ge a.$$

Similar discussions hold for higher order terms $x_{i_1}\cdots x_{i_k}\overline{x}_{i_{k+1}}\cdots\overline{x}_{i_l}$, and therefore we have the following formula:

$$\sum_{i_1}^{i_k} p_{i_j} + p_{n+1} + \sum_{1\le j\le n, j\ne i_1,\ldots,i_l, p_j<0} p_j \ge a. \square$$

3.5 Generation of DNF formulas

The approximation algorithm generates terms using the above formula from the lowest order up to a certain order. A DNF formula can be generated by taking the disjunction of the terms generated by the above formula. A term whose existence has been confirmed does not need to be re-checked in higher order terms. For example, if the existence of x is confirmed, then it also implies the existence of $xy, xz, \ldots$, because $x = x \vee xy \vee xz$; hence, it is unnecessary to check the existence of $xy, xz, \ldots$. As can be seen from the above discussion, the generation method of DNF formulas includes reductions such as $xy \vee xz = x$. Let

$$f = 0.65x_1 + 0.23x_2 + 0.15x_3 + 0.20x_4 + 0.02x_5$$

be the linear function. Let the threshold be a 0.5. The existence condition of $x_{i_1}\cdots x_{i_k}$ is

$$\sum_{i_1}^{i_k} p_{i_j} + p_{n+1} + \sum_{1\le j\le n, j\ne i_1,\ldots,i_l, p_j<0} p_j \ge 0.5.$$

In this case, each p_i is positive and there is no constant term p_{n+1}; therefore the above formula can be simplified to

$$\sum_{i_1}^{i_k} p_{i_j} \ge 0.5.$$

For x_i, the existence condition is $p_i \geq 0.5$. For $i = 1, 2, 3, 4, 5$, $p_1 \geq 0.5$, and therefore x_1 exists. For $x_i x_j$, the existence condition is $p_i + p_j \geq 0.5$. For $i, j = 2, 3, 4, 5$, $p_i + p_j < 0.5$, and therefore no $x_i x_j$ exists. For $x_i x_j x_k$, the existence condition is $p_i + p_j + p_k \geq 0.5$. For $i, j, k = 2, 3, 4, 5$, $p_2 + p_3 + p_4 \geq 0.5$, and therefore $x_2 x_3 x_4$ exists. Because higher order terms cannot be generated from x_5, the algorithm stops. Therefore, x_1 and $x_2 x_3 x_4$ exist and the DNF formula is the disjunction of these terms, that is,

$$x_1 \vee x_2 x_3 x_4.$$

The computational complexity of generating the mth order terms is a polynomial of $\binom{n}{m}$, that is, a polynomial of n. Thus, the computational complexity of generating up to the kth order terms is $\sum_{m=1}^{m=k} \binom{n}{m}$, which is a polynomial of n. Therefore, the computational complexity of generating DNF formulas from the linear functions is a polynomial of n.

When the domain is $\{0, 1\}$, Linial showed the following theorem[4]:

> *Assume that the probability distribution is the uniform distribution.*
>
> $$\sum_{|S|>k} \hat{f}(S)^2 \leq 2M 2^{-k^{1/2}/20},$$
>
> *where f is a continuous Boolean function, S is a term, $|S|$ is the order of S, k is any integer, $\hat{f}(S)$ denotes the Fourier Transform of f at S and M is the circuit's size of the function.*

The above formula shows the high order terms have little power; that is, low order terms are informative. Therefore, a good approximation can be obtained by generating terms up to a certain order. When the domain is [0,1], a similar theorem holds, which will be presented in another paper.

4 An experiment

We present an experiment using *bodyfat* data in this section.

4.1 Data

This data is in StatLib in CMU. *bodyfat* consists of the percentages of body fat and various body circumference measurements for 199 men. The class (dependent variable) is the percentage of body fat, which is shown by density determined from underwater weighing. 13 numerical attributes(independent variables) are as follows.

Age, Weight, Height, Neck circumference, Chest circumference, Abdomen circumference, Hip circumference, Thigh circumference, Knee circumference, Ankle circumference, Biceps (extended) circumference, Forearm circumference, Wrist circumference.

4.2 Procedures

The procedures of the experiment are as follows.

1. Normalize data to [0,1].
   Let a stand for the maximum data and let b stand for the minimum data.
   $$y = \frac{x-b}{a-b},$$
   where x is a given data and y is the normalized data.

2. Execute multiple regression analysis.
   A linear function is obtained by the usual multiple regression analysis.

3. Re-normalize data.
   Components of a logical vector must be non-negative, because a probability vector (distribution) is created by a logical vector (refer to Theorem 7). Therefore class values are normalized again so that components of a logical vector are non-negative.

4. Approximate a linear function by a continuous Boolean function.
   A continuous Boolean function is obtained by the approximation using the algorithm in the preceding section.

4.3 Results

A continuous Boolean function follows:

$$\overline{\texttt{Abdomen circumference}} \vee (\overline{\texttt{Weight}} \wedge \texttt{Wrist circumference}).$$

It means "If his Abdomen circumference is small, or his Weight is small and his Wrist circumference is large, then his density is large". We have discovered that even if wrist circumference is thick, he is not fat.

Numerical data are transformed to discrete data in order to evaluate a continuous Boolean function, because continuous Boolean functions are shown by words such as "small" or "large". In this paper, data are discretized into three values ("False", "Undefined","True") by the following method.

Let r be a percentage of True and False. Let x be a given data. The transformation is as follows:

$$0 \leq x < \frac{r}{100} \rightarrow \text{False}$$

$$\frac{r}{100} \leq x < \frac{100-r}{100} \rightarrow \text{Undefined}$$

$$\frac{100-r}{100} \leq x \leq 1 \rightarrow \text{True}$$

"False" and "True" correspond to small and large, respectively.

Table 2 shows the truth table of the three-valued calculus of Lukasiewicz [2]. In this paper, r is 15. The accuracy of the continuous Boolean function is 80%. Thus we have obtained a good continuous Boolean function.

Table 2: Truth table of three-valued logic

∧(and)	T	U	F	∨(or)	T	U	F		¬ (not)
T	T	U	F	T	T	T	T	T	F
U	U	U	F	U	T	U	U	U	U
F	F	F	F	F	T	U	F	F	T

The polynomial approximation algorithm is presented in section 3.4 and 3.5. In this experiment, the polynomial approximation algorithm stops in a low order, because higher order terms cannot be generated. Therefore, the computational complexity of the experiment is small.

4.4 Remarks

Some readers may think that the propositions obtained by the algorithm in this paper can also be obtained by the following method:

1. Discretize continuous data to {0,1} using a threshold, for example, if the data is greater than 0.5, the discretized data is 1 and otherwise the discretized data is 0.

2. Obtain a proposition using some inductive learning algorithm from the discretized data.

However, the above method does not work well [7]. The propositions obtained by the algorithm in this paper cannot be obtained by the above method.

Linear functions are used as regression functions in this paper. If linear functions do not work well as regression functions, multilinear functions of a higher order — for example, in the case of two variables, a second order multilinear function can be represented as $axy + bx + cy + d$ — should be used for multiple regression analysis.

5 Conclusions

This paper has presented an algorithm for knowledge discovery from numerical data using KL information and the principle of indifference. The algorithm can find continuous Boolean functions from multilinear functions. The computational complexity is polynomial. We have experimentally confirmed good performance of our algorithm. The application of the algorithm to real large data and the improvement of the method for approximating multilinear functions to continuous Boolean functions will be included in future work.

References

1. S. Amari, *Differential-Geometrical Methods in Statistics* (Springer-Verlag, 1985).
2. L. Bolc and P. Borowik, *Many-Valued Logics 1* (Springer-Verlag, 1992).
3. J. M. Keynes, *A Treatise on Probability* (Macmillan, London, 1921).
4. N. Linial, Y. Mansour and N. Nisan, Constant depth circuits, Fourier Transform, and Learnability, *Journal of the ACM*, Vol.40, No.3, pp.607-620, (1993).
5. J. R. Quinlan, *Programs for Machine Learning*, Morgan Kaufmann, (1993).
6. H. Tsukimoto and C. Morita, The discovery of propositions in noisy data, *Machine Intelligence 13*, pp.143-167, Oxford University Press, (1994).
7. H. Tsukimoto, The discovery of logical propositions in numerical data, *AAAI'94 Workshop on Knowledge Discovery in Databases*, pp.205-216, (1994).
8. H. Tsukimoto, On continuously valued logical functions satisfying all axioms of classical logic, *Systems and Computers in Japan* Vol.25, No.12, pp.33-41, SCRIPTA TECHNICA, INC., (1994).
9. H. Tsukimoto and C. Morita, Efficient algorithms for inductive learning-An application of multi-linear functions to inductive learning, *Machine Intelligence 14*, pp.427-449, Oxford University Press, (1996) .
10. S. S. Wilks, *Mathematical Statistics*, John Wiley & Sons, (1962).

DISCOVERING INTERESTING MISSING PATTERNS

BING LIU, WYNNE HSU, LAI-FUN MUN
Department of Information Systems and Computer Science
National University of Singapore, Lower Kent Ridge Road,
Singapore 119260, Republic of Singapore
{liub, whsu, munlaifu}@iscs.nus.sg

HING-YAN LEE
Information Technology Institute, 11 Science Park Road, Singapore Science Park II,
Singapore 117685, Republic of Singapore
hingyan@iti.gov.sg

One of the important issues in data mining is the subjective "interestingness" problem. It has been shown that in many situations a huge number of patterns can be discovered from a database. Most of these patterns are actually useless or uninteresting to the user, and they tend to overwhelm the user. Past research has proposed two main measures of subjective interestingness: unexpectedness and actionability. These measures, however, only help the user identify interesting discovered patterns. In this paper, we show that missing patterns (absence of certain patterns) are interesting too. An approach for finding interesting missing patterns is proposed. This technique is an extension to our previous work, which studies the subjective interestingness problem based on the concepts of user's expectations and fuzzy set theory. In that study, the discovered patterns are ranked in different ways according to their degrees of interestingness to the user. In this paper, we present the proposed extension for finding interesting missing patterns.

1 Introduction

In data mining, techniques are constantly being developed and improved for discovering various types of patterns in databases. While these techniques were shown to be useful in numerous applications, new problems have also emerged. One major problem is that, in practice, it is all too easy to discover a huge number of patterns in a database [10, 8, 12]. Most of these patterns are actually redundant or uninteresting to the user. But due to the sheer number of the patterns, it is very difficult for the user to scan through all the discovered patterns and to identify those patterns that are of interest to him/her. Hence, techniques are needed to rank the discovered patterns according to their degrees of interestingness to the user.

Past research has identified a number of "interestingness" measures. They include: coverage, strength, support, statistical significance, simplicity, unexpectedness, actionability, etc. [8, 11, 1, 9, 12, etc.]. The first five measures are the so-called objective measures [12]. They can be handled easily with techniques that do not require the user knowledge. The last two measures are called the subjective measures [12]. They are defined as follows:

- *Unexpectedness*: Patterns are interesting if they are unexpected or previously unknown to the user.
- *Actionability*: Patterns are interesting if the user can do something with them to his/her advantage.

So far, the study of interestingness issues focuses primarily on the discovered patterns, i.e., identifying those discovered patterns that are unexpected and/or actionable [9, 12, 5, 6]. In this paper, we show that there is another class of interesting information that we might be able to deduce. This class of interesting information is the so-called missing patterns (the absence of certain patterns). Let us illustrate what a missing pattern is with an example. A particular service organization keeps a database of its customers (which consists of *large, medium*, and *small* companies). To improve its services to its customers, the organization performs a data mining session. The outcome of the session consists of a set of discovered patterns of which two are listed below:

Pattern 1. **If** Compy_Size = *large* **then** Service = *service1*

Pattern 2. **If** Compy_Size = *small* **then** Service = *service1*

Pattern 1 says that if the company size is large it uses the service *service1*. Pattern 2 says that if the company size is small, then it also uses *service1*. Immediately we begin to wonder what happens to those companies whose size is *medium*? Why aren't they using *service1*? The realization of this information may lead this particular service organization to probe into the possibilities of modifying *service1* or of doing more promotion to the *medium* size companies in order to attract them to use the service. In other words, the pattern:

If Compy_Size = *medium* **then** Service = *service1*

is missing and it is actionable and/or unexpected. Like the discovered patterns, not all missing patterns are interesting. In general, the number of missing patterns is huge because any attribute-value combination that is not in the set of discovered patterns can be considered a missing pattern. Clearly, it is not useful to list all the missing patterns to the user. Instead, only the subset of interesting missing patterns should be given. So, how can we identify the interesting missing patterns? We believe our proposed technique provides a partial solution. The proposed technique is an extension of our previous research [5, 6]. In that research, a technique, based on the concept of user expectations (i.e., user's previous knowledge or hypotheses about the database) and fuzzy set theory, is used to identify unexpected patterns. The user is first asked to supply a set of expected patterns. This set of expected patterns is then used in a fuzzy matching algorithm to analyze and rank the discovered patterns. Based on the ranking, we can determine how well a discovered pattern conforms to the user's expectations or how different it is from the user's expectation. With some extensions to the algorithm, we are able to help the user find unexpected missing patterns. This extension is the focus of this paper.

2 Problem Definition

As mentioned in the introduction, the number of missing patterns are typically huge (and possibly infinite). We denote the set of possible missing patterns as B. There is only a subset I of them that are of interest to the user, i.e., $I \subseteq B$. Obviously, I is subjective because it is specific to the particular user. A missing pattern becomes interesting if it is unexpected and/or it is useful to the user. Following the measures of interestingness of the discovered patterns, we say that interesting missing patterns are also of two types as well: unexpected and actionable missing patterns.

Unexpected missing patterns: these are the patterns that the user expects to find in the database, but are not found, neither are their contradictory patterns.

Actionable missing patterns: these are the patterns that are not found in the database, but their absence made them actionable.

Note that there is an important distinction between a missing pattern and an unexpected pattern. For instance, in the previous example, the user expects companies of all sizes to use *service1*. Suppose the following patterns are present in the set of discovered patterns:

Pattern 1. **If** Compy_Size = *large* **then** Service = *service1*

Pattern 2. **If** Compy_Size = *small* **then** Service = *service1*

Pattern 3 **If** Compy_Size = *medium* **then** Service = *not_service1*.

Even though

MissPattern1 **If** Compy_Size = *medium* **then** Service = *service1*

is not in the discovered set, we do not say that MissPattern1 is a missing pattern since its contradictory pattern (Pattern 3) is present. In general, missing patterns arise due to the incompleteness of the databases. For example, if the service organization does not record which customers do not use their service, this omission implies that it is impossible to discover Pattern 3. Hence, we can then conclude that MissPattern1 is indeed a missing pattern.

In the above example, the attribute *Compy_Size* takes discrete values. What happens when an attribute takes on continuous values? The situation is similar. For example, if the user expects the following pattern to be true:

If A1 $\geq$ 5 **then** C = Yes, where domain(A1) = [0, 80].

Suppose this expectation is indeed true. However, it may be the case that when C = *Yes*, *A1* only ranges from 5-10 and 35-80 in the database. We can thus conclude that

If A1 > 10, A1 < 35 **then** C = Yes

is a missing pattern. As the number of conditions in the expected pattern increases, the discovery of missing patterns gets more and more complicated. The details of the algorithm is presented in Section 3 and 4.

It should be noted that if a missing pattern is what the user expects, then it is not interesting. For instance, suppose the user knows beforehand that *medium* size companies do not use their *service1* due to certain restrictions, then informing the user of this fact is not interesting, unless the user wishes to confirm his/her knowledge. However, if the user expects the *medium* size companies to use their *service1*, and there is no such pattern generated from the database, then reporting this missing pattern becomes important and useful.

So the key here is that: in order to find interesting missing patterns, the system must know what the user expects in the first place. This expectation can be specified in the form of expected patterns. In this paper, we focus on a particular type of patterns that takes the following form:

If $P_1, P_2, P_3, \ldots, P_n$ **then** C (or $P_1, P_2, P_3, \ldots, P_n \rightarrow C$)

where "," means "and", and P_i is a condition of the form,

attr OP value,

where *attr* is an attribute name in the database, and *value* is a possible value for the attribute *attr* and $OP \in \{=, \neq, <, >, \leq, \geq\}$ is the operator. C is the consequent, which has the format of,

attr = *value*.

This format is commonly used to represent classification patterns and association patterns.

3 Overview of the Proposed Technique

In this section, we present a high-level view of the proposed technique. It consists of two main steps:

1. The user is asked to provide a set of patterns E that he/she expects to find in the database D, and also an optional number, T_j, denoting the expected number of tuples in the database that should satisfy (or support) each $E_j \in E$ (both the conditional and the conclusion parts). The user-expected patterns are regarded as fuzzy patterns. A fuzzy pattern has the same syntax as the original pattern, but its attribute values must be described using fuzzy linguistic variables [13]. See the definition below.
2. The system goes through the database D (1) to compute the correctness of each expected pattern $E_j \in E$, (2) to count the actual number of tuples that satisfy (or

support) E_j, and (3) to discover missing patterns with respect to each E_j by consulting the database tuples.

An important issue here is the representation of the expected patterns. Using fuzzy set theory is a natural choice because human knowledge, hypotheses or intuitive feelings are typically fuzzy. Let us review the definition of a fuzzy linguistic variable [13].

Definition: A fuzzy linguistic variable is a quintuple $(x, T(x), U, G, \tilde{M})$ in which x is the name of the variable; $T(x)$ is the term set of x; that is, the set of names of linguistic values of x, with each value being a fuzzy variable denoted generally by x and ranging over a universe of discourse U; G is a syntactic rule for generating the name, X, of values of x; and M is a semantic rule for associating with each value X its meaning, $\tilde{M}(X)$ which is a fuzzy subset of U. A particular X is called a *term*.

For example, if *speed* is interpreted as a linguistic variable with $U = [1,140]$, then its term set *T*(*speed*) could be

$$T(speed) = \{slow, moderate, fast, ...\}.$$

$\tilde{M}(X)$ gives a meaning to each term. For example, $\tilde{M}(slow)$ may be defined as follows:

$$\tilde{M}(slow) = \{(u, \mu_{slow}(u)) \mid u \in [1, 140]\},$$

where $$\mu_{slow}(u) = \begin{cases} 1 & u \in [1,30] \\ -\dfrac{1}{30}u + 2 & u \in (30,60] \\ 0 & u \in (60,140] \end{cases}$$

$\mu_{slow}(u)$ denotes the degree of membership of u in term *slow*.

4 Detailed Computation in the Proposed Technique

After discussing the basic idea of the proposed technique, we now present the detailed computations in Step 2.

4.1 Computing the correctness of the expected pattern E_j

Naturally, when the user provides an expected pattern $E_j \in E$, he/she wishes to know whether the pattern is correct or not. To obtain this correctness value, the system needs to check against the database to see how true E_j is. Since E_j is regarded as a fuzzy pattern, matching E_j with each tuple in the database is also fuzzy. It returns a value in the range [0, 1]. Thus, to consider a match to be satisfactory, a cutoff value needs to be used.

Let *cutoff* be a value in the range (0, 1] denoting the minimal degree that a data tuple $D_k \in D$ must match (or satisfy) the conditional or conclusion part of $E_j \in E$. The value of *cutoff* is specified by the user. Let $|A_j|$ be the number of attributes mentioned in the conditional part of E_j. We denote $V_{a,k,j}$ as the match value of the *a*th conditional proposition of E_j with D_k, and $Z_{k,j}$ as the match value of the conclusion of E_j with D_k. We then define

$$M_{cond}^{k,j} = \min(V_{1,k,j}, V_{2,k,j}, \ldots, V_{|Aj|,k,j})$$

to be the degree of condition match of D_k and E_j (or the degree that D_k satisfies the conditions of E_j) and similarly, we define $M_{concl}^{k,j}$ (= $Z_{k,j}$) to be the degree of match of the conclusion. The detailed computation of $V_{a,k,j}$ and $Z_{k,j}$ is discussed below. The *correctness* of E_j, $Corr_j$, is hence computed as follows:

$$Corr_j = \frac{\text{Total number of tuples with } M_{cond}^{k,j} \geq cutoff \text{ and } M_{concl}^{k,j} \geq cutoff}{\text{Total number of tuples with } M_{cond}^{k,j} \geq cutoff}$$

4.2 Computing $V_{a,k,j}$ and $Z_{k,j}$

To compute $V_{a,k,j}$ and $Z_{k,j}$, we need to consider both the attribute values and the operators in E_j. In addition, the attribute value types (discrete or continuous) are also important. Since the computations of $V_{a,k,j}$ and $Z_{k,j}$ are the same, it suffices to just consider $V_{a,k,j}$.

4.2.1 Matching of discrete attribute values

In this case, the semantic rule for each term (X) used in describing the expected pattern is defined over the universe (or domain) of the discrete attribute. We denote U as the set of possible values for the attribute. For each $u \in U$, the user needs to input the membership value of u in X, denoted as $\mu_X(u)$. For example, the user gives the following pattern:

If *Grade* = *poor* **then** *Class* = *reject*

Here, *poor* is a fuzzy term. Assume the universe of the discrete attribute *Grade* = $\{A, B, C, D, F\}$. The user may specify that *poor* grade means,

$\{(F, 1), (D, 0.8), (C, 0.2)\}$,

where the left coordinate is an element in the universe of *Grade*, and the right coordinate is the degree of membership of that element in the fuzzy set *poor*, e.g., $\mu_{poor}(D) = 0.8$. It is assumed that all the other attribute values not mentioned in the set have the degree of membership 0.

As mentioned, when evaluating $V_{a,k,j}$, both the fuzzy set of the attribute value description and the operator used play an important role. In the discrete case, the valid operators are "=" and "≠". Suppose the conditional proposition to be matched in E_j is:

attr Opu X,

where *attr* is an attribute name, *Opu* belongs to the set {=, ≠}, and *X* is the term. Assume *S* is the value of the attribute *attr* in the data tuple D_k. Two cases result:

Case 1. *Opu* = "=": $V_{a,k,j} = \mu_X(S)$.

Case 2. *Opu* = "≠": $V_{a,k,j} = \mu_{\neg X}(S)$.

4.2.2 Matching of continuous attribute values

When an attribute takes continuous values, the semantic rule for the term (*X*) takes on the form of a continuous function. To simplify the user's task of specifying the shape of this function, we assume the function has a curve of the form as shown in Figure 1. Thus, the user merely needs to provide the values for *a*, *b*, *c*, and *d*.

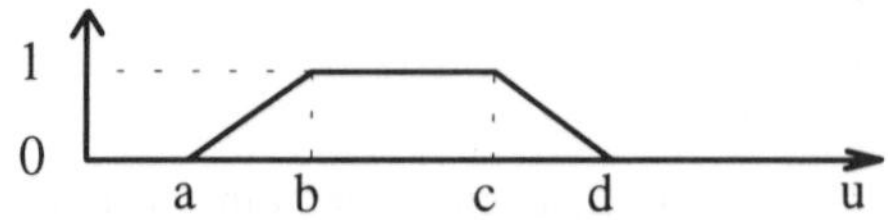

Figure 1. Membership function

For example, the user gives the pattern:

If *Age* = *young* **then** *Class* = *accept*

Here, *young* is a term for the variable *Age* whose domain is [0, 80]. Thus, *young* may be described with $a = 15$, $b = 20$, $c = 30$, and $d = 35$.

In the continuous case, the range of values that the operator can take is expanded to {=, ≠, >, <, ≥, ≤, ≤≤, <<}. "≤≤" is used to represent a range like this: $X_1 \leq attr \leq X_2$, and "<<" is used to represent: $X_1 < attr < X_2$. With this expansion, the total number of possible cases to be considered is 8. The computation of $V_{a,k,j}$ here is quite similar to that in the discrete attribute case. Due to space limitation, we will not discuss them here.

4.3 Discovering unexpected missing patterns

After computing the correctness of the expected pattern E_j, we now present the technique for discovering unexpected missing patterns. By definition, a missing pattern is one that the user expects to find but is missing.

Definition: A unexpected missing pattern with respect to $E_j \in E$ is a pattern that should cover some tuples that satisfy both the conditional and conclusion parts of E_j, but those tuples are absent in the database.

The algorithm for identifying such missing patterns is presented below.

```
1   Initialize PatternNo_j, CondNo_j to 0 for 1 ≤ j ≤ |E|;
2   For each expected pattern, E_j Do
3     For each condition attr_i op value in E_j Do
4         Divide the value range of the condition into a number of small buckets
5     Endfor
6   Endfor;
7   For each tuple, D_k, in the database Do
8     For each expected pattern, E_j of the form PE_j → CE_j Do
9       Compute M^{k,j}_{cond}, and M^{k,j}_{concl};
10      If M^{k,j}_{cond} ≥ cutoff Then
11        Increment CondNo_j;   /* no. of tuples that satisfy PE_j */
12        If M^{k,j}_{concl} ≥ cutoff Then
13          Increment PatternNo_j;  /* no. of tuples that satisfy both PE_j and CE_j */
14          For each condition attr_i op value Do
15              Increment the count_{i,j,l} of bucket l where the value of attr_i
                        in the tuple D_k falls in;
16          Endfor;
17        Endif;
18      Endif;
19    Endfor;
20  Endfor;
21  For each expected pattern E_j Do  Corr_j = PatternNo_j / CondNo_j ; Endfor;
22  For each expected pattern, E_j Do
23    For each attr_i in the conditional part of E_j Do
24        Group the buckets for attr_i into value ranges according to whether they are
              filled or not;
25        For each attr_i's value range R Do
26            If R is a unfilled range Then output a missing pattern Endif;
27        Endfor;
28    Endfor;
29  Endfor
```

We use an example to illustrate how to the algorithm works. Assume an expected pattern E_j be

If A1 > 3, A2 > 7 **Then** C = Yes.

Note that we do not use fuzzy terms for the values 3 and 7 for easy explanation (a crisp pattern is just a special case of a fuzzy pattern). Assume the maximal value of A1 is 13 and the maximal value of A2 is 17.

- The algorithm consists of 4 main steps:

Step 1 (line 2-6): Divide the value range of each condition of E_j into a number of small buckets. For discrete value attribute, each relevant value forms a bucket. In our example, the value ranges of A1 > 3 and A2 > 7 are divided into many small equal size buckets as shown in Figure 2. In our implementation, we set the default number of buckets to 20 (or less, if the value range is small). The user is also allowed to specify a different number of buckets.

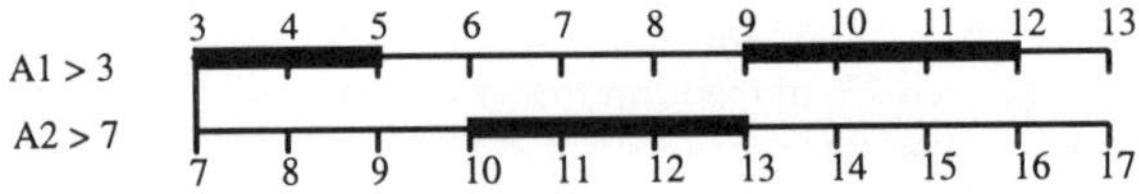

Figure 2. An example

Step 2 (line 7-20): Count the number of tuples that fall in each bucket for each conditional attribute of E_j. Note that each bucket has an associated counter, $count_{i,j,l}$, which is initialized to 0 in the beginning.

Step 3 (line 21): Compute the correctness of E_j.

Step 4 (line 22-29): Group the buckets for each $attr_i$ in the conditional part of E_j into ranges of two types, *filled* and *unfilled* (line 24). A *filled* range is made up of a number of consecutive filled buckets. A bucket is considered *filled* if it satisfies the following formula:

$$count_{i,j,l} \geq e \times \frac{EN}{\text{The total number of buckets}}$$

where EN is T_j if the user provides the expected number of tuples, otherwise it is the total number of tuples in the databse that satisfy (or support) E_j, and e is the *cutoff coefficient* (the default value is 0.3). Those buckets that do not satisfy the condition are said to be *unfilled*. In our example, $A1$ is grouped into four value ranges, 3-5, 5-9, 9-12, and 12-13 with the dark lines representing the *filled* ranges (see Figure 2). For each *unfilled* range (line 26), we generate a missing pattern of the form:

If <unfilled_range>, <other_conditions_of_ P_{E_j} > **Then** C_{E_j}

Thus, in our example, the following missing patterns will be produced.

If $5 < A1 \leq 9$, $A2 > 7$ **Then** C = Yes

If $A1 > 3$, $7 < A2 \leq 10$ **Then** C = Yes

If $A1 > 3$, $13 < A2 \leq 17$ **Then** C = Yes

Note that there is no missing pattern for A1 > 12 because we assume that a *unfilled* range must be formed by more than two consecutive buckets before a missing pattern will be generated.

At this point, we note that our proposed method for generating missing patterns is, in fact, not complete. For instance, instead of merely generating the missing patterns corresponding to each *unfilled* range, we can record the mapping relationships between the buckets of *A1* and the buckets of *A2* (see Figure 3). Then, more accurate description of the missing patterns can be generated. For example, the following missing pattern can be generated:

If $3 < A1 \leq 5, (7 < A2 \leq 10 \text{ or } 12 < A2 \leq 17)$ **Then** C = Yes

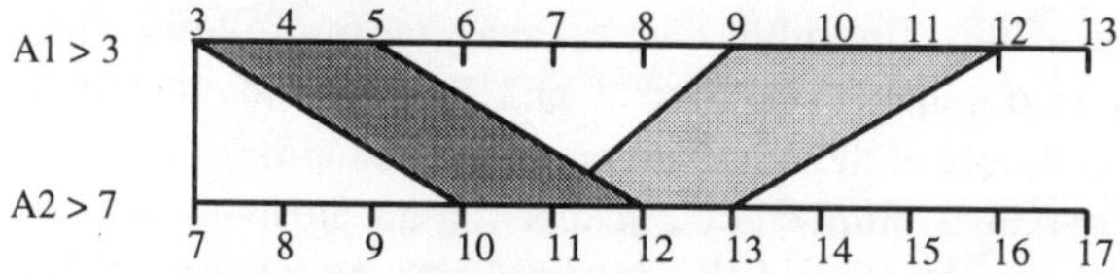

Figure 3. A more complex situation

The drawback of this later approach is that: (1) it can potentially produce a large number of complex missing patterns that serves little useful purpose except to confuse the user, (2) the data structure required to store the mapping information increases exponentially with the number of conditions in E_j. In view of these two drawbacks, we decide to implement the first approach with the objective of alerting the user without overwhelming him/her. Our system will be used as a starting point to identify interesting missing patterns. To further analyze such missing patterns, data visualization tools such as WinViz [4] can be used.

- $PatternNo_j$ also serves to inform the user whether the number of tuples that satisfy E_j exceeds the expected number T_j. If the number is smaller than T_j, then we can conclude that E_j itself is, in fact, a missing pattern.
- Though we strive to make a distinction between a missing pattern and an unexpected pattern in Section 2, for practical implementation, we find that such distinction is difficult to achieve without domain knowledge. For example, suppose the user expects that companies of all sizes use their *service1*. The set of discovered patterns are:

  Pattern 1. **If** Compy_Size = *large* **Then** Service = *service1*

  Pattern 2. **If** Compy_Size = *small* **Then** Service = *service1*

  Pattern 3. **If** Compy_Size = *medium* **Then** Service = *service2*

  Then the pattern

  MissPattern 1 **If** Compy_Size = *medium* **Then** Service = *service1*,

  is not a missing pattern if Pattern 3 and MissPattern 1 are mutually exclusive. Instead, Pattern 3 should be reported as an unexpected pattern. If, however, no such relationship exists between them, then MissPattern 1 will be reported as a missing pattern. In other words, to correctly recognize a pattern as a missing pattern, the system needs to know whether a value has some relationship with other values. This involves asking the user to supply the necessary information. To simplify the task for the user, we have decided to report a pattern as missing pattern regardless of whether an unexpected pattern exists or not. This is reasonable because it may only give a bit of redundant information, and it does not create any confusion.

- Complexity of this algorithm can be analyzed as follows: the computational complexity is dominated by Step 2 and Step 4. Step 1 and 3 requires little computation time. Let the maximal number of conditions of an expected pattern be N, the maximal number of buckets for an attribute be L, the number of expected patterns be $|E|$ and the database size be $|D|$. Line 9 takes $O(N)$ time. Line 15 takes $O(1)$ time. Thus, the time complexity of Step 2 is $O(|E||D|N)$. The time complexity of Step 4 is $O(|E|NSL)$.

5 An Illustration

We use the credit screening database created by Chiharu Sano in UCI machine learning repository to illustrate the discovery of unexpected missing patterns. This database has 10 attributes and two conclusion classes *Yes* and *No* representing whether credit has been granted. The database contains 125 cases or tuples. The meanings of the attributes appeared below are self-explanatory. The user-expected patterns are given below:

- **User-expected patterns**

Expected pattern 1:	IF YR_Work >= Few	{a = 2, b = 3, c = 4, d = 5}
	THEN Granted = YES	{(Yes, 1), (No, 0)}
Expected pattern 2:	IF Bought = Any	{(bike, 1), (car, 1), (furniture, 1), (jewel, 1), (medinstru, 1), (pc, 1), (stereo, 1)}
	Jobless = NO	{(No, 1), (Yes, 0)}
	THEN Granted = YES	{(Yes, 1), (No, 0)}

No expected number of tuples that satisfy (or support) either expected patterns is specified by the user.

The running results are reported below (0.6 is used as the *cutoff* match value):

- **Correctness (or accuracy) of the expected patterns**

Expected Pattern 1:	Correctness: 90.0%	Coverage Of Condition: 70 cases
		Coverage Of Pattern: 63 cases
Expected Pattern 2:	Correctness: 74.8%	Coverage Of Condition: 111 cases
		Coverage Of Pattern: 83 cases

From the indicated *correctness*, we can see that the two patterns are quite accurate, which means that the user's knowledge is quite correct.

- **Missing patterns**

Missing patterns for expected pattern 1

Missing Pattern 1: If 21 < YR_Work <= 24 Then Granted = YES
System's Estimated Expected Support = 6.3 tuples
Observed Support = 0 tuples

Missing Pattern 2: If 30 < YR_Work <= 33 Then Granted = YES
System's Estimated Expected Support = 6.3 tuples
Observed Support = 0 tuples

From these two missing patterns we see that no people whose year of work (which is a continuous attribute) is in the range (21, 24] or (30, 33] was granted a loan. This is rather unexpected and the user may be very interested to know why that is the case.

Missing patterns for expected pattern 2

Missing Pattern 1: If Bought = bike, Jobless = NO Then Granted = YES
System's Estimated Expected Support = 11.9 tuples
Observed Support = 3 tuples

This missing pattern also shows something unexpected because the user expects that as long as the person has a job and bought something, he/she should be granted a loan. However, this is not the situation. In fact, the missing pattern indicates that the database contain very few tuples of a person who has a job and bought a bike, and was granted a loan.

From this example, we see that the absence of certain patterns can serve to alert the user and prompt the user to perform some actions so as to improve the missing pattern situation.

6 Related Work

Subjective interestingness has long been identified as an important problem in data mining. Current research on subjective interestingness focuses on identifying interesting discovered patterns, i.e., unexpected discovered patterns and actionable discovered patterns. To the best of our knowledge, there is no reported work on helping user discover interesting missing patterns.

[9] studied the issue of subjective interestingness in the context of a health care application. The system (called KEFIR) analyzes the health care information to uncover interesting deviations (from the norms) or "key findings". A domain expert system is built to identify findings that are actionable and the actions to be taken.

KEFIR does not identify interesting missing patterns. The KEFIR approach is also application specific. Our system is domain independent.

[12] proposes to use probabilistic beliefs and belief revision as the framework for describing subjective interestingness. Specifically, a belief system is used for defining unexpectedness. However, this work also does not deal with missing patterns.

In [5], [6] and [7], we reported two fuzzy matching techniques to perform post-analysis of the discovered patterns in order to help the user identify unexpected patterns. This work attempts to extend the method in [6] such that interesting missing patterns may also be identified.

7 Conclusion

This paper points out that in some situations, missing patterns may be interesting to the user. A technique is proposed to help the user find some unexpected missing patterns. This method is characterized by asking the user to provide his/her expectations or existing knowledge. The system then uses a simple algorithm to find the unexpected missing patterns. The proposed technique is domain and application independent. In our future work, we plan to integrate this technique with a data visualization system so that the missing patterns can be displayed graphically to make them easier for the user to understand.

Acknowledgments

We thank Gui-Jun Yang for implementing part of the system. This project is funded by Singapore National Science and Technology Board.

References

1 W. J. Frawely, G. Piatesky-Shapiro, C. J. Matheus. Knowledge discovery in databases: an overview. In G. Piatetsky-Shapiro and W.J Frawley (eds), *Knowledge Discovery in Databases*, AAAI/MIT Press, 1991, 1-27.
2 J. Han, Y. Cai, and N. Cercone. Data driven discovery of quantitative rules in relational database. *IEEE Trans. Knowl. & Data Eng.* 5, 1993, 29-40.
3 W. Klosgen. Problems for knowledge discovery in databases and their treatment in the statistics interpreter explora. *International Journal of Intelligent Systems*, 7(7), 1992, 649-673.
4 H.Y Lee, H.L Ong and L.H Quek, Exploiting visualization in knowledge discovery, *KDD-95*, 1995.
5 B. Liu and W. Hsu. Post-analysis of learned rules. *AAAI-96*, 1996, 828-834.
6 B. Liu, W. Hsu, H. Y Lee and L.F. Mun. Tuple-level analysis of learned rules. *DISCS Technical Report*, National University of Singapore, 1996.

7 B. Liu, W. Hsu, L.F. Mun and H. Y Lee. Finding interesting patterns using user expectations. *Technical Report TRA7/96*, Department of Information Systems and Computer Science, National University of Singapore, 1996.

8 J. A. Major, J. J. Mangano. Selecting among rules induced from a hurricane database. *Proceedings of AAAI Workshop on Knowledge Discovery in Databases*, 1993, 30-31.

9 G. Piatesky-Shapiro and C. J Matheus. The interestingness of deviations. *Proceedings of AAAI Workshop on Knowledge Discovery in Databases*, 1994, 25-36.

10 G. Piatetsky-Shapiro, C. Matheus, P. Smyth, and R. Uthurusamy. KDD-93: progress and challenges ... *AI magazine*, Fall, 1994, 77-87.

11 J. Ross Quinlan. *C4.5: program for machine learning*. Morgan Kaufmann, 1992.

12 A. Silberschatz and A. Tuzhilin. On subjective measures of interestingness in knowledge discovery. *KDD-95*, 1995, 275-281.

13 H. -J. Zimmermann. *Fuzzy set theory and its applications*. Kluwer Academic Publishers, 1991.

Incremental Learning of Probabilistic Rules from Clinical Databases based on Rough Set Theory

Shusaku Tsumoto and Hiroshi Tanaka
Department of Information Medicine, Medical Research Institute,
Tokyo Medical and Dental University
1-5-45 Yushima, Bunkyo-ku Tokyo 113 Japan
E-mail tsumoto.com@mri.tmd.ac.jp, tanaka@cim.tmd.ac.jp

There have been several symbolic inductive learning methods such as induction of decision trees and rule induction methods. These methods are applied to discover meaningful knowledge from large databases, and their usefulness is in some aspects ensured. However, most of the approaches induces rules from all the data in databases, and cannot induce incrementally when new samples are derived. Thus, we have to apply rule induction methods to the databases when such new samples are given, which causes the computational complexity to be expensive even if the complexity is n^2. Extending concepts of rule induction methods based on rough set theory, we introduce a new approach to knowledge acquistion, which induces probabilistic rules incrementally, called PRIMEROSE-INC (Probabilistic Rule Induction Method based on Rough Sets for Incremental Learning Methods). This method first uses coverage rather than accuracy, to search for the candidates of rules, and secondly uses accuracy to select from the candidates. This system is evaluated by clinical databases on headache and meningitis. The results show that PRIMEROSE-INC induces the same rules as those induced by PRIMEROSE, which extracts rules from all the datasets, but that the former method requires much computational resources than the latter approach.

1 Introduction

There have been proposed several symbolic inductive learning methods, such as induction of decision trees[1,2,7], and AQ family[3,4,5]. These methods are applied to discover meaningful knowledge from large databases, and their usefulness is in some aspects ensured. However, most of the approaches induces rules from all the data in databases, and cannot induce incrementally when new samples are derived. Thus, we have to apply rule induction methods again to the databases when such new samples are given, which causes the computational complexity to be expensive even if the complexity is n^2.

Thus, it is important to develop incremental learning systems in order to manage large databases[10,13]. However, most of the previously introduced learning systems have the following two problems: first, those systems do not outperform ordinary learning systems, such as AQ15 [5], C4.5 [8] and CN2 [3]. Secondly, those incremental learning systems mainly induce deterministic rules. Therefore, it is indispensable to develop incremental learning systems which induce probabilistic rules to solve the above two problems.

Extending concepts of rule induction methods based on rough set theory, we introduce a new approach to knowledge acquistion, which induces probabilistic rules incrementally, called PRIMEROSE-INC (Probabilistic Rule Induction Method based on Rough Sets for Incremental Learning Methods).

Although the non-incremental rule induction method PRIMEROSE [12], which extracts rules from all the data in database uses apparent accuracy to search for probabilistic rules, PRIMEROSE-INC first uses coverage, to search for the candidates of rules, and secondly uses accuracy to select from the candidates.

This system is evaluated by two clinical databases: databases on meningoencephalitis and databases on headache with respect to the following four points: accuracy of classification, the number of generated rules, spatial computational complexity, and temporal computational complexity. The results show that PRIMEROSE-INC induces the same rules as those induced by PRIMEROSE, but that the former method requires much computational resources than the latter approach.

The paper is organized as follows: in Section 2, we make a brief description about rough set theory and the definition of probabilistic rules based on this theory. Section 3 discusses problems in incremental learning of probabilistic rules. Then, Section 4 presents an induction algorithm for incremental learning. Section 5 gives experimental results. Section 6 we discuss the problems of our work and related work, and finally, Section 7 concludes our paper.

2 Rough Sets and Probabilistic Rules

2.1 Rough Set Theory

Rough set theory clarifies set-theoretic characteristics of the classes over combinatorial patterns of the attributes, which are precisely discussed by Pawlak [6,15]. This theory can be used to acquire some sets of attributes for classification and can also evaluate how precisely the attributes of database are able to classify data.

Let us illustrate the main concepts of rough sets which are needed for our formulation. Table 1 is a small example of database which collects the patients who complained of headache. First, let us consider how an attribute "loc" classify the headache patients' set of the table. The set whose value of the attribute "loc" is equal to "who" is {1,2,4,5}, which shows that the 1st, 2nd, 4th, 5th case (In the following, the numbers in a set are used to represent each record number). This set means that we cannot classify {1,2,4,5} further solely by

Table 1: An Example of Database

No.	loc	nat	his	nau	class
1	who	per	per	no	m.c.h.
2	who	per	per	no	m.c.h.
3	lat	thr	per	no	migraine
4	who	thr	per	yes	migraine
5	who	per	per	no	psycho

NOTATIONS. loc: location, nat: nature
his: history, nau: nausea, who: whole
lat: lateral, per: persistent, thr: throbbing,
m.c.h.: muscle contraction headache,
migraine: classic migraine,
psycho: psychogenic headache

using the constraint $R = [loc = who]$. This set is defined as the indiscernible set over the relation R and described as follows: $[x]_R = \{1, 2, 4, 5\}$. In this set, {1,2} suffer from muscle contraction headache("m.c.h."), {4} from classical migraine("migraine"), and {5} from psycho("psycho"). Hence we need other additional attributes to discriminate between "m.c.h.", "migraine", and "psycho". Using this concept, we can evaluate the classification power of each attribute. For example, "nat=thr" is specific to the case of classic migraine ("migraine"). We can also extend this indiscernible relation to multivariate cases, such as $[x]_{[loc=who]\wedge[nau=no]} = \{1, 2\}$ and $[x]_{[loc=who]\vee[nat=no]} = \{1, 2, 4, 5\}$, where $\wedge$ and $\vee$ denote "and" and "or" respectively. In the framework of rough set theory, the set {1,2} is called *strictly definable* by the former conjunction, and also called *roughly definable* by the latter disjunctive formula. Therefore, the classification of training samples D can be viewed as a search for the best set $[x]_R$ which is supported by the relation R. In this way, we can define the characteristics of classification in the set-theoretic framework. For example, accuracy and coverage, or true positive rate can be defined as:

$$\alpha_R(D) = \frac{|[x]_R \cap D|}{|[x]_R|}, \text{ and } \kappa_R(D) = \frac{|[x]_R \cap D|}{|D|},$$

where $|A|$ denotes the cardinality of a set A, $\alpha_R(D)$ denotes an accuracy of R as to classification of D, and $\kappa_R(D)$ denotes a coverage, or a true positive rate of R to D, respectively. For example, when R and D are set to $[nau = yes]$ and $[class = migraine]$, $\alpha_R(D) = 1/1 = 1.0$ and $\kappa_R(D) = 1/2 = 0.50$.

It is notable that $\alpha_R(D)$ measures the degree of the sufficiency of a proposition, $R \to D$, and that $\kappa_R(D)$ measures the degree of its necessity. For example, if $\alpha_R(D)$ is equal to 1.0, then $R \to D$ is true. On the other hand, if $\kappa_R(D)$ is equal to 1.0, then $D \to R$ is true. Thus, if both measures are 1.0, then $R \leftrightarrow D$.

For further information on rough set theory, readers could refer to [6,15,16].

2.2 Probabilistic Rules

The simplest probabilistic model is that which only uses classification rules which have high accuracy and high coverage.[a] This model is applicable when rules of high accuracy can be derived. Such rules can be defined as:

$$R \overset{\alpha,\kappa}{\to} d \quad \text{s.t.} \quad R = \vee_i R_i = \vee \wedge_j [a_j = v_k],$$
$$\alpha_{R_i}(D) > \delta_\alpha \text{ and } \kappa_{R_i}(D) > \delta_\kappa,$$

where δ_α and δ_κ denote given thresholds for accuracy and coverage, respectively. For the above example shown in Table 1, probabilistic rules for m.c.h. are given as follows:

$$[loc = who]\&[nau = no] \quad \to m.c.h. \quad \alpha = 2/3 = 0.67,\ \kappa = 1.0,$$
$$[nat = per] \quad \to m.c.h. \quad \alpha = 2/3 = 0.67,\ \kappa = 1.0,$$

where δ_α and δ_κ are set to 0.5 and 0.3, respectively.

It is notable that this rule is a kind of probabilistic proposition with two statistical measures, which is one kind of an extension of Ziarko's variable precision model(VPRS)[16].[b]

2.3 Formal Definition of Probabilistic Rules

The above probabilistic rules are defined formally in terms of rough set theory. First, a combination of attribute-value pairs, which is corresponding to a complex in AQ terminology[4], is denoted by an equivalence relation R_f, which is defined as follows.

Definition 1 (Equivalence Relation) *Let U be a universe, and V be a set of values. A total function f from U to V is called an assignment function of an attribute. Then, we introduce an equivalence relation R_f such that for any $u, v \in U$, uR_fv iff $f(u) = f(v)$.*

---

[a] In this model, we assume that accuracy is dominant over coverage.

[b] In VPRS model, the two kinds of precision of accuracy is given, and the probabilistic proposition with accuracy and two precision conserves the characteristics of the ordinary proposition. Thus, our model is to introduce the probabilistic proposition not only with accuracy, but also with coverage.

For example, $[loc = who]\&[nat = per]$ will be one equivalence relation, denoted by $R_f = [loc = who]\&[nat = per]$. Then, a probabilistic rule is defined as:

Definition 2 (Probabilistic Rules) *Let R_f be an equivalence relation specified by some assignment function f, D denote a set whose elements belong to a class d, or positive examples in all training samples (the universe), U. Finally, let $|D|$ denote the cardinality of D. A probabilistic rule of D is defined as a quadruple, $< R_f \stackrel{\alpha,\kappa}{\rightarrow} d, \alpha_{R_f}(D), \kappa_{R_f}(D) >$, where $R_f \stackrel{\alpha,\kappa}{\rightarrow} d$ satisfies the following conditions:* [c]

$$(1) \qquad [x]_{R_f} \bigcap D \neq \phi,$$

$$(2) \qquad \alpha_{R_f}(D) = \frac{|[x]_{R_f} \bigcap D)|}{|[x]_{R_f}|},$$

$$(3) \qquad \kappa_{R_f}(D) = \frac{|[x]_{R_f} \bigcap D)|}{|D|}.$$

□

3 Problems in Incremental Induction of Probabilistic Rules

The most important problem in incremental learning is that it does not always induce the same rules as those induced by ordinary learning systems[d], although an applied domain is deterministic. Furthermore, since induced results are strongly dependent on the former training samples, the tendency of overfitting is larger than the ordinary learning systems.

The most important factor of this tendency is that the revision of rules is based on the formerly induced rules, which is the best way to suppress the exhaustive use of computational resources. However, when induction of the same rules as ordinary learning methods is required, computational resources will be needed, because all the candidates of rules should be considered.

Thus, for each step, computational space for deletion of candidates and addition of candidates should be needed, which causes the computational speed of incremental learning to be slow. Moreover, in case when probabilistic rules should be induced, the situation becomes much severer, since the candidates for probabilistic rules become much larger than those for deterministic rules.

For the above example, no deterministic rule can be derived from Table 1. Then, when an additional example is given as shown in Section 4 (the 6th

[c]It is notable that this rule is a kind of probabilistic proposition with two statistical measures, which is one kind of an extension of Ziarko's variable precision model(VPRS) [16].

[d]Here, ordinary learning systems denote methods that induce all rules by using all the samples.

example), $[loc = lat]\&[nau = yes] \rightarrow m.c.h.$ will be calculated. However, in the case of probabilistic rules, two rule will be derived under the condition that $\delta_\alpha = 0.5$ and $\delta_\kappa = 0.3$, as shown in Section 3. If these thresholds are not used, induced probabilistic rules becomes much larger. Thus, there is a trade-off between the performance of incremental learning methods and its computational complexity.

In our approach, we first focus on the performance of incremental learning methods, that is, we introduce a method which induces the same rules as those derived by ordinary learning methods. Then, we estimate the effect of this induction on computational complexity.

4 An Algorithm for Incremental Learning

In order to provide the same classificatory power to incremental learning methods as ordinary learning algorithms, we introduce an incremental learning method PRIMEROSE-INC (Probabilistic Rule Induction Method based on Rough Sets for Incremental Learning Methods). PRIMEROSE-INC first measures the statistical characteristics of coverage of elementary attribute-value pairs, which corresponds to selectors. Then, it measures the statistical characteristics of accuracy of the whole pattern of attribute-value pairs observed in a dataset.

In this algorithm, we use the following characteristic of coverage.

Proposition 1 (Monotonicity of Coverage) *Let R_j denote an attribute-value pair, which is a conjunction of R_i and $[a_{i+1} = v_j]$. Then,*

$$\kappa_{R_j}(D) \leq \kappa_{R_i}(D).$$

Proof.
Since $[x]_{R_j} \subseteq [x]_{R_i}$ holds, $\kappa_{R_j}(D) = \frac{|[x]_{R_j} \cap D|}{|D|} \leq \frac{|[x]_{R_i} \cap D|}{|D|} = \kappa_{R_i}(D).$ □

Furthermore, in rule induction methods, R_j is selected to satisfy $\alpha_{R_j}(D) > \alpha_{R_i}(D)$. Therefore, it is sufficient to check the behavior of coverage of elementary attribute-value pairs in order to estimate the characteristics of induced rules, while it is necessary to check the behavior of accuracy of elementary attribute-value pairs and accuracy of patterns observed in the databases in order to estimate the characteristics of induced rules.

Algorithm

From these consideration, the selection algorithm is defined as follows, where the following four lists are used. $List_1$ and $List_2$ stores an elementary relation which decrease and increase its coverage, respectively, when a new training sample is given. $List_a$ is a list of probabilistic rules which satisfy the condition on the thresholds of accuracy and coverage. Finally, $List_r$ stores a list of probabilistic rules which do not satisfy the above condition.

1. Revise the coverage and an accuracy of each elementary attribute value pair $[a_i = v_j]$ by using a new additional sample S_k.

2. For each pair $r_{ij} = [a_i = v_j]$, if $\kappa_{r_{ij}}$ decreases, then store it into $List_1$. Else, store it into $List_2$.

3. For each member r_{ij} in $List_1$, Search for a rule in $List_a$ whose condition R includes r_{ij} and which satisfies $\alpha_R > \delta_\alpha$ and $\kappa_R > \delta_\kappa$. Remove it from $List_a$ and Store it into $List_r$.

4. For each member r_{ij} in $List_2$, Search for a rule in $List_r$ whose condition R includes r_{ij}. If it satisfies $\alpha_R > \delta_\alpha$ and $\kappa_R > \delta_\kappa$, then Remove it from $List_r$ and Store it into $List_a$. Else, search for a rule which satisfies the above condition by using rule induction methods. [e]

5. For other rules in $List_r$, revise accuracy and coverage. If a rule does not satisfy $\alpha_R > \delta_\alpha$ and $\kappa_R > \delta_\kappa$, then Remove it from $List_r$ and Store it into $List_a$.

For example, let us consider a case when the following new sample is provided after probabilistic rules are induced from Table 1: [f]

No.	loc	nat	his	nau	class
6	lat	thr	per	no	m.c.h.

The initial condition of this system derived by Table 1 is summarized into Table 2, and $List_a$ and $List_r$ for m.c.h. are given as follows: $List_a = \{[loc = who]\&[nau = no], [nat = per]\}$, and $List_r = \{[loc = who], [loc = lat], [nat = thr], [his = per], [nau = yes], [nau = no]\}$. Then, the first procedure revises accuracy and coverage for all the elementary relations (Table 3). Since the coverages of $[loc = lat]$, $[nat = thr]$, and $[nau = yes]$ become larger than 0.3, they are included in $List_2$. In the same way, $[loc = who]$, $[nat = per]$, and $[nau = no]$ are included in $List_1$.

Next, the second procedure revises two measures for all the rules in $List_a$ whose conditional parts include a member of $List_1$. Then, the formerly induced probabilistic rules are revised into:

---

[e] That is, it makes a conjunction of attribute-value pairs and checks whether this conjunction satisfies $\alpha_R > \delta_\alpha$ and $\kappa_R > \delta_\kappa$.

[f] In this example, δ_α and δ_κ are again set to 0.5 and 0.3, respectively.

Table 2: Accuracy and Coverage of Elementary Relations (m.c.h.)

Relation	Accuracy	Coverage
$[loc = who]$	0.5	1.0
$[loc = lat]$	0.0	0.0
$[nat = per]$	0.67	1.0
$[nat = thr]$	0.0	0.0
$[his = per]$	0.4	1.0
$[nau = yes]$	0.0	0.0
$[nau = no]$	0.5	1.0

Table 3: Revised Accuracy and Coverage of Elementary Relations (m.c.h.)

Relation	Accuracy	Coverage
$[loc = who]$	0.5	**0.67**
$[loc = lat]$	**0.5**	**0.33**
$[nat = per]$	0.67	**0.67**
$[nat = thr]$	**0.33**	**0.33**
$[his = per]$	**0.5**	1.0
$[nau = yes]$	**0.5**	**0.33**
$[nau = no]$	0.4	**0.67**

$$[loc = who]\&[nau = no] \quad \rightarrow m.c.h. \quad \alpha = 0.67, \kappa = 0.67,$$
$$[nat = per] \quad \rightarrow m.c.h. \quad \alpha = 0.67, \kappa = 0.67,$$

and none of them are not removed from $List_a$. Then, the third procedure revises two measures for all the rules in $List_r$ whose conditional parts include a member of $List_2$. Then, the following probabilistic rule satisfies $\alpha > 0.5$ and $\kappa > 0.3$:

$$[loc = lat]\&[nau = yes] \quad \rightarrow m.c.h. \quad \alpha = 1.0, \kappa = 0.33,$$

and is stored into $List_a$. Finally, $List_a$ and $List_r$ for m.c.h. are calculated as follows:

$$\begin{aligned} List_a &= \{[loc = who]\&[nau = no], [nat = per]\&[nau = no], \\ &\qquad [loc = lat]\&[nau = yes]\}, \\ List_r &= \{[loc = who], [loc = lat], [nat = per], [nat = thr], [his = per], \\ &\qquad [nau = yes], [nau = no]\}. \end{aligned}$$

Table 4: Information about Databases

Domain	Samples	Classes	Attributes
headache	1477	10	20
meningitis	198	3	25

Table 5: Experimental Results: Accuracy and Number of Rules (Headache)

Method	Accuracy	No. of Rules
PRIMEROSE-INC	$89.5 \pm 5.4\%$	67.3 ± 3.0
PRIMEROSE	$89.5 \pm 5.4\%$	67.3 ± 3.0
PRIMEROSE0	$76.1 \pm 1.7\%$	15.9 ± 4.1
C4.5	$85.8 \pm 2.4\%$	16.3 ± 2.1
CN2	$87.0 \pm 3.9\%$	19.2 ± 1.7
AQ15	$86.2 \pm 2.6\%$	31.2 ± 2.1

5 Experimental Results

PRIMEROSE-INC [g] is applied to headache and meningitis, whose precise information is given in Table 4, and compared with PRIMEROSE [12], its deterministic version PRIMEROSE0 [h], C4.5, CN2 and AQ15. The experiments are performed by the following three procedures. First, these samples are randomly splits into pseudo-training samples and pseudo-test samples. Second, by using the pseudo-training samples, PRIMEROSE-INC, PRIMEROSE, and PRIMEROSE0 induces rules and the statistical measures [i]. Third, the induced results are tested by the pseudo-test samples. These procedures are repeated for 100 times and average each accuracy and the estimators for accuracy of diagnosis over 100 trials.

Table 5 and 5 give the comparison between PRIMEROSE-INC and other rule induction methods with respect to the averaged classification accuracy and the number of induced rules. These results show that PRIMEROSE-INC attains the same performance of PRIMEROSE, which is the best performance in those rule induction systems.

Table 5 and 5 give the comparison between PRIMEROSE-INC and other rule induction methods with respect to the code area, CPU time for total rule induction, and culmative CPU time, which denotes how much time is totally

[g] The program is implemented by using SWI-prolog [11] on Sparc Station 20.

[h] This version is given by setting δ_α to 1.0 and δ_κ to 0.0.

[i] The thresholds δ_α and δ_κ is set to 0.75 and 0.5, respectively in these experiments.

Table 6: Experimental Results: Accuracy and Number of Rules (Meningitis)

Method	Accuracy	No. of Rules
PRIMEROSE-INC	$81.5 \pm 3.2\%$	52.3 ± 1.4
PRIMEROSE	$81.5 \pm 3.2\%$	52.3 ± 1.4
PRIMEROSE0	$72.1 \pm 2.7\%$	12.9 ± 2.1
C4.5	$74.0 \pm 2.1\%$	11.9 ± 3.7
CN2	$75.0 \pm 3.9\%$	33.1 ± 4.1
AQ15	$80.7 \pm 2.7\%$	32.5 ± 2.3

Table 7: Experimental Results: Spatial and Temporal Complexity (Headache)

Method	Code-Area			CPU time(sec)			Cul-CPU time(sec)		
PRIMEROSE-INC	18241	±	219	4027	±	61	4027	±	61
PRIMEROSE	1210	±	98	721	±	31	107403	±	219
PRIMEROSE0	910	±	12	324	±	25	50192	±	108
C4.5		–		914	±	31	79198	±	193
CN2		–		1024	±	22	118197	±	211
AQ15		–		1042	±	31	120192	±	108

DEFINITION. Cul-CPU time: Culumative CPU time

needed to rerun the rule induction methods from scratch when a new sample is added. These results show that PRIMEROSE-INC overperforms all the other non-incremental learning methods, although they need much larger memory space for running.

6 Related Work

6.1 Comparison with PRIMEROSE

As shown in Section 5, PRIMEROSE-INC needs much larger computational resources than PRIMEROSE. Thus, when all the information about attributes and classes in databases are fixed, PRIMEROSE outperforms PRIMEROSE-INC. However, one of the advantages of PRIMEROSE-INC over the non-incremental learning methods is culumative CPU time. If the training samples grows larger, culumative CPU time of non-incremental learning methods will grow larger, that is, the temporal complexity totally increases higher.

Another advantage is that in many practical applications, knowledge about attributes and classes is growing, and several attributes may be provided in

Table 8: Experimental Results: Spatial and Temporal Complexity (Meningitis)

Method	Code-Area			CPU time(sec)			Cul-CPU time(sec)		
PRIMEROSE-INC	1241	±	34	1902	±	710	1902	±	710
PRIMEROSE	210	±	14	992	±	191	16269	±	508
PRIMEROSE0	119	±	12	202	±	215	1011	±	614
C4.5		–		579	±	1.0	11862	±	707
CN2		–		600	±	1.4	11117	±	504
AQ15		–		621	±	2.1	12117	±	299

DEFINITION. Cul-CPU time: Culumative CPU time

Table 9: Decision Matrix for m.c.h.

U	3	4	5
1	$(l=w),(n=p)$	$(n=p),(n_a=n)$	ϕ
2	$(l=w),(n=p)$	$(n=p),(n_a=n)$	ϕ

NOTATIONS: l=w: loc=who, n=p: nat=per, $n_a = n$: nau=no.

the future. This effect will degrade the performance of non-incremental learning methods. Thus, incremental learning methods is powerful and robust in these dynamical situations, since change of databases is required for ordinary learning methods.

6.2 Decision Matrix

Shan and Ziarko introduce decision matrix method, which is based on an indiscernible matrix introduced by Skowron and Rauser [9], in order to make incremental learning methods efficient [10,16].

Their approach is simple, but very powerful. For the above example shown in Table 1, the decision matrix for m.c.h. is given as Table 9, where the rows denote positive examples of m.c.h., the columns denote negative examples of m.c.h., and each matrix element a_{ij} shows the differences in attribute-value pairs between ith sample and jth sample. Also, ϕ denotes that all the attribute-value pairs in two samples are the same. Shan and Ziarko discuss induction of deterministic rules in their original paper, but it is easy to extend it into probabilistic domain. In Table 9, the appearance of ϕ shows that decision rules for m.c.h. should be probabilistic. Since the first and the second row have the same pattern, {1,2,5} have the same pattern of attribute-value pairs, whose

Table 10: Decision Matrix with Additional Sample

U	3	4	5
1	$(l = w), (n = p)$	$(n = p), (n_a = n)$	ϕ
2	$(l = w), (n = p)$	$(n = p), (n_a = n)$	ϕ
6	$(na = y)$	$(l = l)$	$(l = l), (n = t), (n_a = y)$

NOTATIONS: l=w: loc=who, l=l: loc=lat, n=p: nat=per, n=t: nat=thr, $n_a = y/n$: nau=yes/no

accuracy is equal to 2/3=0.67.

Furthermore, rules are obtained as: $([loc = who] \vee [nat = per]) \wedge ([nat = per] \vee [nau = no]) \rightarrow m.c.h.$, which are exactly the same as shown in Section 3.

When a new example is given, it will be added to a row when it is a positive example, and a column when a negative example. Then, again, new matrix elements will be calculated. For the above example, the new decision matrix will be obtained as in Table 10.

Then, from the last row, the third rule $[loc = lat] \wedge [nau = yes] \rightarrow m.c.h.$ is obtained.

The main difference between our method and decision matrix is that the latter approach is based on apparent accuracy, rather than coverage. While the same results are obtained in the above simple example, the former approach is sensitive to the change of coverage and the latter is to the change of accuracy. Thus, if we need rules of high accuracy, decision matrix technique is very powerful. However, when an applied domain is not so stable, calculation of rules is not so easier. Furthermore, in such an application area, a rule of high accuracy supports only a small case, which suggests that this rule is overfitted to the training samples. Thus, in this domain, coverage should be dominant over accuracy in order to suppress the tendency of overfitting, although rules of high coverage are weaker than rules of high accuracy in general[j].

However, original decision matrix technique does not incorporate such calculation of coverage. Thus, it needs to include such calculation mechanism when we extend it into the usage of both statistical measures.

[j] This suggests that there is a trade-off between accuracy and coverage. As shown in the definition, the difference between accuracy and coverage is only their denominators: $[x]_R$ and D. Although it is difficult to discuss the differences in the behavior between accuracy and coverage, accuracy is inversely proportional to coverage in many domains. The closer examination of accuracy and coverage will be our future work.

7 Conclusion

Extending concepts of rule induction methods based on rough set theory, we introduce a new approach to knowledge acquistion, which induces probabilistic rules incrementally, called PRIMEROSE-INC. This method first uses coverage to search for the candidates of rules, rather than apparent accuracy and secondly uses accuracy to select from the candidates.

This incremental rule induction system is evaluated on two kinds of clinical databases: databases on meningoencephalitis and databases on headache. The experimental results show that the introduced system induces the same rules as those induced by PRIMEROSE, but that the former method requires much computational resources than the latter approach.

References

1. Breiman, L., Freidman, J., Olshen, R., and Stone, C. (1984). *Classification And Regression Trees.* Belmont, CA: Wadsworth International Group.
2. Cestnik, B., Kononenko, I., Bratko, I. (1987). Assistant 86: A knowledge elicitation tool for sophisticated users. *Proceedings of the Second European Working Session on Learning*, pp.31-45, Sigma Press.
3. Clark, P., Niblett, T. (1989). The CN2 Induction Algorithm. *Machine Learning*, **3**,261-283.
4. Michalski, R. S. (1983). A Theory and Methodology of Machine Learning. Michalski, R.S., Carbonell, J.G. and Mitchell, T.M., *Machine Learning - An Artificial Intelligence Approach.* Morgan Kaufmann, Palo Alto, CA.
5. Michalski, R. S., Mozetic, I., Hong, J., and Lavrac, N. (1986). The Multi-Purpose Incremental Learning System AQ15 and its Testing Application to Three Medical Domains. *Proceedings of the fifth National Conference on Artificial Intelligence*, 1041-1045, AAAI Press, Palo Alto, CA.
6. Pawlak, Z. (1991). *Rough Sets.* Kluwer Academic Publishers, Dordrecht.
7. Quinlan, J. R. (1986). Induction of decision trees. *Machine Learning*, **1**, 81-106.
8. Quinlan, J.R. (1993). *C4.5 - Programs for Machine Learning*, Morgan Kaufmann, CA.
9. Skowron, A. and Rauser, C.M. The Discerniblity Matrix and Functions in Information Systems, in: Slowinski, R.(ed) *Intelligent Decision Support. Handbook of Application and Advances of the Rough Set Theory*, Kluwer Academic Publishers, 1992, Dordrecht, pp.331-362.

10. Shan, N. and Ziarko, W. Data-Based Acquisition and Incremental Modification of Classfication Rules. *Computational Intelligence*, **11**, 357-370, 1995.
11. SWI-Prolog Version 2.0.9 Manual, University of Amsterdam, 1995.
12. Tsumoto, S. and Tanaka, H. PRIMEROSE: Probabilistic Rule Induction Method based on Rough Sets and Resampling Methods. *Computational Intelligence*, **11**, 389-405, 1995.
13. Utgoff, P.E. (1989) Incremental Learning of Decision Trees. *Machine Learning*, **4**, 161-186.
14. Walker, M. G. and Olshen, R. A. (1992). Probability Estimation for Biomedical Classification Problems. *Proceedings of the sixteenth Symposium on Computer Applications on Medical Care*, McGrawHill, New York.
15. Ziarko, W. (1991). The Discovery, Analysis, and Representation of Data Dependencies in Databases. in: Shapiro, G. P. and Frawley, W. J. (eds), *Knowledge Discovery in Databases*, AAAI press, Palo Alto, CA, pp.195-209.
16. Ziarko, W. (1993). Variable Precision Rough Set Model. *Journal of Computer and System Sciences*, **46**, 39-59.

Chapter 3

Concept Learning and Rule Discovery

DISCOVERY OF FIRST PRINCIPLE BASED ON DATA-DRIVEN REASONING

T. WASHIO, H. MOTODA
Institute of Scientific and Industrial Research, Osaka University
8-1 Mihogaoka, Ibaraki, Osaka, 567, JAPAN
e-mail: {washio, motoda}@isir1.sanken.osaka-u.ac.jp

We propose a novel approach to automatically discover formulae of first principles from the measurement data. We try to use the knowledge of the target relation as little as possible, so that it can be applied to various domains which are not limited to physics problem. In spite of its data-driven feature, the formulae obtained by our approach are ensured to represent sound first principles. The basic idea is the combined use of deductive scale type-based reasoning and data-driven reasoning. This approach may provide a basis to discover qualitative first principles of ambiguous domains such as biology, psychology, economics and social science.

1 Introduction

One of the early work to automatically discover formulae of physical first principles is a method called dimensional analysis that was based on the product theorem [2], [1].

Product Theorem *Assuming absolute significance of relative magnitudes of physical quantities, the function f relating a secondary quantity to the appropriate primary quantities, $x, y, ...$ has the form: $f = Cx^a y^b z^c ....$, where $C, a, b, c, ...$ are constants.*

There is another important theorem that is called Buckingham Π-theorem [3], [1].

Buckingham Π-theorem *If $\phi(x, y, ...) = 0$ is a complete equation, then the solution can be written in the form $F(\Pi_1, \Pi_2, ..., \Pi_{n-r}) = 0$, where n is the number of arguments of ϕ, and r is the basic number of dimensions in $x, y, ...$. For all i, Π_i is a dimensionless number.*

Basic dimensions are such dimensions as length $[L]$, mass $[M]$ and time $[T]$, scaling quantities independently of other dimensions in the given ϕ. This theorem can be used together with the product theorem to obtain the oscillation period $t[T]$ of a simple pendulum from its stick length $l[L]$, gravity acceleration $g[LT^{-2}]$ and deviation angle θ [no dimension] (see Fig.1.). We can find two dimensionless quantities $\Pi_1 = t(g/l)^{1/2}$ and $\Pi_2 = \theta$, and derive the basic formula of the solution as $F(\Pi_1, \Pi_2) = F(t(g/l)^{1/2}, \theta) = 0$ based on the theorem. Using these dimensional analysis techniques, Bhaskar and Nigam introduced a concept "*regime*" which is a formula $\rho_i(\Pi_i, x, y, ...) = 0$ defining a dimensionless

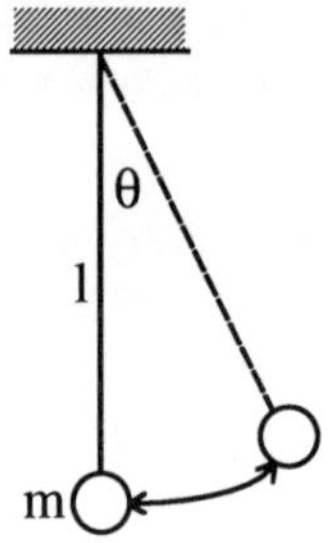

Figure 1: A simple pendulum

quantity Π_i^1. In the above example, $t(g/l)^{1/2}$ and θ are the regimes. Further, they defined an "*ensemble*" which is a set of regimes contained in a complete equation $F(\Pi_1, \Pi_2, ..., \Pi_{n-r}) = 0$. In the current example, $F(t(g/l)^{1/2}, \theta) = 0$ is the ensemble. A regime refers to a decomposable subprocess. An ensemble stands for a complete physical process in the system. The dimensional analysis utilizes the physical insights into the objective system that is described by the unit dimension of each quantity. Another method to automatically derive physical formulae is symmetry-based approach which was proposed by Ishida[5]. He applied the principle of symmetry to physical domains. The system he developed heuristically searches for the invariant physical formula under a given set of isomorphic mappings. In the example of the simple pendulum, we can apply further constrains of symmetry such as phase translatory symmetry and mirror symmetry of the time on the form $F(t(g/l)^{1/2}, \theta) = 0$. A formula satisfying these symmetries is $\theta = \sin(t(g/l)^{1/2})$. As is evident, this method also has to utilize the explicit knowledge of physical characteristics of the object in terms of symmetry.

In contrast with these methods that are grounded on physical knowledge, a challenge has been made by Langley and Zytkow to discover the formulae of the first principles that govern the objective system [7]. They used a data-driven approach and developed BACON that discovers formulae by using heuristic search algorithm. The objects in various domains can be modeled because it does not use any a priori knowledge of the objects. However, the heuristics in the search algorithm have no firm theoretical bases, and the search is limited to enumerating only polynomial and meromorphic formulae. Accordingly, the set of the solutions obtained is not ensured to be sound and complete.

All the previous approaches employ the following assumptions.

Assumption 1 *The relation among quantities under consideration is represented by a complete equation.*

Though Bhaskar and Nigam demonstrated the applicability of their dimension-based method to the systems consisting of multiple complete equations, the specification of a set of quantities is required for each complete equation in the framework, and thus this assumption must be maintained[1]. Their dimension-based approach also requires the following assumptions.

Assumption 2 *The type of scales of physical quantities is limited to ratio scale.*

Assumption 3 *Given a regime $\rho_i(\Pi_i, x, y, ...) = 0$, either one of the following conditions holds.*

i) It is a unique regime of a complete equation.

ii) For each quantity x in ρ_i, any other regimes do not contain x, or any other regimes are related in such a way that x does not change Π_i from outside of ρ_i.

The assumption 2 is the restatement of the assumption in the product theorem, *i.e.*, the absolute significance of relative magnitudes of physical quantities. Although the quantities of the ratio scale are quite common in various domains, there is another scale type of quantities called as "*interval scale*" which is also widely encountered as explained later. The assumption 3 was recently pointed out by Kalagnanam and Henrion[6]. The data-driven approach of BACON assumes the following environment of data measurement.

Assumption 4 *The measurements on the relation in any subset of quantities in a complete equation can be made while holding the other variables constant under an experimental environment, and the measured data can be sequentially used to reason the formula relating the variables.*

The objective of this paper is to propose a new approach to automatically discover formulae of first principles. Our approach lies in between the deductive approaches as represented by dimension-based and symmetry-based reasoning and the empirical approaches as represented by BACON. The following theoretical aspects removing the limitations of assumptions 2 and 3 are newly introduced in this paper.

i) The sound relations among quantities of ratio and interval scales within a regime are characterized, and the product theorem is extended to reflect the relations.

ii) The structure of dimension is characterized for both ratio and interval scale quantities, and the Buckingham Π-theorem is extended for the structure.

iii) The condition that each regime contains a set of quantities that are mutually exclusive in an ensemble is characterized (*i.e.*, the condition that a set of regimes forms a partition of the quantities), and an algorithm to identify such regimes is proposed.

The other two assumptions remain the same in our approach at present. On these grounds, our approach can derive a sound set of solutions of the formulae for each regime similarly to the dimension-based approach while still maintaining the advantage of the data-driven approach like BACON, *i.e.*, it does not require a priori insights into the objective system but only data that can be obtained by measurements. Thus, it can be applied to various domains and is not limited to physics.

2 Basic Principle of Scale Type-Based Reasoning

Since after Helmholtz originated a research field of "*measurement theory*" [4], many literatures have been published on that topic in the 20th century. Stevens defined the measurement process as "*the assignment of numerals to object or events according to rules*" [10]. He claimed that different kinds of scales and different kinds of measurement are leaded, if numerals can be assigned under different rules. Two of the scale categories he defined are reproduced in Table 1. The interval scale and the ratio scale are the majorities of quantities in physical, psychological, economical and sociological domains. Examples of the interval scale quantities are temperature in Celsius and Fahrenheit, energy, entropy, time (not time interval), and sound tone (proportional to the order of white keys of a piano). The zero point level of their scales are not absolute, and are changeable by human's definitions. Examples of the ratio scale quantities are physical mass, absolute temperature, pressure, time interval, frequency, and currency value. Each has an absolute zero point, and the ratio of two different values x_1/x_2 is invariant against their unit change. The scale is different from the dimension. The scale just represents the definition of the measurement rule. Another point we should clarify is that dimensionless quantities are the quantities of "*absolute scale*" having the group structure of $x' = x$ named as "*Identical group*". Any unit conversion is not admissible within this group structure, because any change of units is not defined for absolute scale quantities.

Luce claimed that the basic formula of the functional relation between any two quantities can be determined by the scale features of these two quantities, if the quantities are not coupled through any dimensionless quantities[8]. Suppose x and y are both ratio scale quantities, and y is defined by x through a continuous functional relation $y = u(x)$. Suppose the form of $u(x)$ is logarithmic, *i.e.*, $y = \log x$. We can multiply a positive constant k to x, *i.e.*, a change of unit, without violating the group structure of the ratio scale quantity x shown in Table 1. However, this leads $u(kx) = \log k + \log x$, and this fact causes the shift of the origin of y by $\log k$, and violates the group structure of y which is the ratio scale quantity. Hence, the functional relation from x to

Table 1: Scale types

Scale	Basic·Empirical Operations	Mathematical Group Structure
Interval	Determination of equality of intervals or differences	Generic linear group $x' = kx + c$
Ratio	Determination of equality of ratios	Similarity group $x' = kx$

x: quantity in original unit dimension,
x': a quantity in converted unit dimension.

y must not be logarithmic. As the admissible transformations of x and y in their group structures are $x' = kx$ and $y' = Ky$ respectively, the relation of $y = u(x)$ becomes as $y' = u(x') \leftrightarrow Ky = u(kx)$. The factor K of the changed unit of y may depend on k, but it shall not depend upon x, so we denote it by $K(k)$. Consequently, we obtain the following constraints on the continuous function $u(x)$.

$$u(kx) = K(k)u(x),$$

where $k > 0$ and $K(k) > 0$, as these are the factors of the changed units. The constraints for the different combinations of the scale types are summarized on the fourth column in Table 2 [8]. Luce derived each solution of $u(x)$ under the condition of $x \geq 0$ and $u(x) \geq 0$. We extended his theorems to cover the negative values of x and $u(x)$, and the result is summarized on the last column in Table2. Because of the space limitation, we omit the proof for the results. For the detail, see the reference [11, 12].

The impossibility of the definition of a ratio scale from an interval scale in Table2 is because the ratio scale involves the information of an absolute origin, but the interval scale does not. Luce gave some examples of the equations in Table2[8]. The quantities entering into Coulomb's law, Ohm's law and Newton's gravitation law are all ratio scales, and the formula of each law is a power function which follows the formula of Eq.1 in the table. We see examples of Eqs.2.1 and 2.2 for laws associated with energy and entropy. The total energy U of a body having a constant mass m and moving at velocity v is $U = mv^2/2 + P$, where P is the potential energy. If the temperature of a perfect gas is constant, then the entropy E of the gas as a function of the pressure p is of the form $E = -R \log p + E'$, where R and E' are Boltzmann's constant and a reference value of entropy respectively. In psychophysics, Fechner's law states that the sound tone s of human sensing (proportional to the order of white keys of a piano) is proportional to the logarithm of the sound frequency f, *i.e.*, $s = \alpha \log f + \beta$, where s is an interval scale, and f is a ratio scale. As

Table 2: Constraints and thier possible equations satisfying the scale characteristics

No.	Scale Types Independent variable	Dependent (Defined) variable	Constraints	Admissible Relations
1	ratio	ratio	$u(kx) = K(k)u(x)$	$u(x) = \alpha_*\|x\|^{\beta}$
2.1	ratio	interval	$u(kx) = K(k)u(x) + C(k)$	$u(x) = \alpha_*\|x\|^{\beta} + \delta$
2.2				$u(x) = \alpha \log\|x\| + \beta_*$
3	interval	ratio	$u(kx + c) = K(k, c)u(x)$	impossible
4	interval	interval	$u(kx + c) = K(k, c)u(x) + C(k, c)$	$u(x) = \alpha_*\|x\| + \beta$

1) $k > 0, K(k) > 0, K(k, c) > 0, *c$ and C can be any real numbers.
2) The notations α_*, β_* are α_+, β_+ for $x \geq 0$ and α_-, β_- for $x < 0$, respectively.

an example of Eq.4, there is the relation $x = vt + x_0$ for a particle moving at its constant velocity v, where x is the position at the present time t and x_0 is the initial position x.

Finally, the following important consequence should be indicated.

Theorem 1 *An absolute scale quantity can have functional relations of any continuous formulae with other absolute scale quantities.*

As an absolute scale quantity, i.e., a dimensionless quantity, does not have any dimensional unit, any mathematical constraint associated with unit conversion is not applied to $u(x)$. An example of such relation is the behavior solution of the simple pendulum of Fig.1 which is $\theta = \sin(t(g/l)^{1/2})$. The triangular function sin which does not belong to Table 2 can hold, because θ and $t(g/l)^{1/2}$ are dimensionless, *i.e.*, absolute scale.

3 Theory and Method to Derive Possible Equations of First Principles

3.1 Scale Type-Based Reasoning within a Regime

This subsection describes the theory and the method of scale type-based reasoning which uses a priori knowledge of quantity scales (not the knowledge of physics) to derive the formula of ρ_i for a given regime. The product theorem is extended to include interval scale quantities.

Theorem 2 *Given a set of quantities $Q = \{x_1, x_2, ..., x_m\}$ forming a regime where some quantities are interval scales and the others ratio scales, the relation $f = 0$ among $x_1, x_2, ..., x_m$, has either one of the two forms.*

$$f(x_1, x_2, ..., x_m) = (\prod_{x_i \in R} |x_i|^{a_i})(\sum_{x_j \in I_1} b_{*j}|x_j| + c_{*1}) + \sum_{x_k \in I_2} b_k|x_k| + c_2 = 0 \quad (i)$$

$$f(x_1, x_2, ..., x_m) = \sum_{x_i \in R} a_i \log|x_i| + \sum_{x_j \in I} b_j|x_j| + c_* = 0 \quad (ii)$$

Here, R is a set of quantities of ratio scale in Q, and I is a set of all quantities of interval scale in Q. Also, I_1 and I_2 are any partition of I where $I_1 + I_2 = I$.

Theorem 3 *If $R = \phi$, i.e., $I = Q$, in Theorem 2 then the relation $f = 0$ among $x_1, ..., x_m$ has the following form.*

$$f(x_1, x_2, ..., x_m) = \sum_{x_j \in I} b_j|x_j| + c_*$$

Because of the space limitation, the proofs of theorems 2 and 3 are omitted. For the detail, see the reference[11], [12]. The principle of the extension is a certain symmetry that the relations given in Table 2 must hold for each pair of quantities in a regime. For example, if we look at the relation on any pair of x and $y(= u(x))$ in R while regarding the rest of quantities as constants, both *Eq.(i)* and *(ii)* in theorem 2 reduce to the relation of $y = u(x) = \alpha_*|x|^\beta$ which is the first relation in Table 2. Thus, both formulae are the extention of the product theorem. Furthermore, if we look at the relation on any pair of x in R and $y(= u(x))$ in I, both formulae reduce to the relations 2.1 and 2.2 in the table. The similar discussion holds for the relation on a pair of two interval scale quantities. Accordingly, these theorems are the generic relation among ratio and interval scale quantities.

Now, we consider to derive the candidates of formula $f = 0$ of a given regime ρ, where the set of quantities except dimensionless Π in ρ is $Q = \{x_1, ..., x_m\}$. The following algorithm based on the product theorem and the above theorems 2 and 3 derives the candidates.

Algorithm 1

(Step 1) $Q = \{x_1, ..., x_m\}$, $S = \phi$. Let R be a set of all quantities of ratio scale in Q. Let I be a set of all quantities of interval scale in Q.

(Step 2) If $I = \phi$ {

Based on the product theorem, push the following to S.

$f(x_1, x_2, ..., x_m) = \prod_{x_i \in R} |x_i|^{a_i} + c_* = 0.$ }

else if $R = \phi$ {

Push the relation of theorem 3 to S.}

else {

Enumerate candidate relations of (i) in theorem 2 for all binary partitions $\{I_1, I_2\}$ of I, and push those candidates to S. Push the relation of (ii) in theorem 2 to S.}

The candidates are rested in the list S. The result of S is sound, since the soundness is ensured by the product theorem, the theorems 2 and 3. The complexity of this algorithm is low except the enumeration of all binary partitions $\{I_1, I_2\}$ of I, where the complexity is $O(2^{|I|})$. The exchange of I_1 and I_2 essentially gives an equivalent relation, as it is easily understood by the form of the original relation (i) of the theorem 2. Therefore, the complexity reduces to $O(2^{|I|-1})$. In any case, it is not very problematic, because the size of a regime is generally quite limited.

We implemented this algorithm by using a commercial formula-processing package MATLAB[9]. This algorithm have been tested by various physical laws. The following is an example of the ideal gas equation which forms a unique regime. A regime involving four quantities of pressure p, volume v, mass m and temperature t is given, thus $Q = \{p, v, m, t\}$. The quantities p, v and m are ratio scales, while only t is an interval scale unless it is absolute temperature. We assumed the positive sign of p, v and m in advance, hence the solutions for their negative values were omitted. The algorithm figured out the two candidate relations. The first one comes from (i) of theorem 2:

$$0 = c_1 p^{a_1} v^{a_2} m^{a_3} + b_1 t + c_2,$$

and the second one comes from (ii) of theorem 2:

$$0 = a_1 \log p + a_2 \log v + a_3 \log m + b_1 * t + c.$$

From these, the following candidates were obtained.

$$p^{a_1} v^{a_2} = m^{-a_3}(-\frac{b_1 t + c_2}{c_1}).$$

$$p^{a_1} v^{a_2} = m^{-a_3} \exp(-b_1 t - c).$$

The former solution reflects the right formula of the ideal gas equation, when the temperature is not absolute one. Once the candidate formulae of a regime are determined, the correct formula and the values of its coefficients must be specified in data-driven manner.

3.2 Data-Driven Reasoning on Ensemble

Before proposing the data-driven reasoning on an ensemble, the definition of dimension, regime, ensemble and the consequence of Buckingham Π-theorem need to be re-examined. Within the conventional view, a basic dimension, D, of a quantity is defined by a basic unit, U, of the quantity, i.e., the basic dimension is represented as D(U). The value of a measured quantity is represented by the number of units equivalent to the amount of the quantity. For example, if the mass of an object is equal to the mass of seven basic units where each mass unit is named as $1kg$, then the mass of the object is said to be $7kg$. When we use another basic unit such as $1g$, then the measured value of the same object will be 1000 times larger. This definition is valid only for basic quantities of ratio scale. Basic quantities of interval scale has a bit more complex structure of dimensions. A basic unit and a ***basic origin*** are required to determine the value of temperature in Celsius. These unit and origin are different for temperature in Fahrenheit. Consequently, we need to extend the notion of a basic dimension as D(U, O) where O stands for a basic origin. In case of a basic quantity of ratio scale, O is constrained to be 0, while O can take an arbitrarily value for a basic quantity of interval scale.

Based on the above discussion, the notion of the structure of a general dimension consisting of multiple basic dimensions is also extended. For example, let us consider the total energy of a particle. The particle having a certain temperature is moving at a certain height in a certain velocity. Thus, its total energy E_t is:

$$E_t = E_h + E_p + E_m,$$

where E_h, E_p and E_m are contained heat energy, potential energy and kinematic energy respectively. Every energy has an identical unit of $[M][L]^2[T]^{-2}$ where $[M], [L]$ and $[T]$ are basic units of mass, length and time. On the other hand, E_h, E_p and E_m are interval scale, since E_h is defined by temperature measured on a reference temperature point $[T_o]$, E_p by a reference height level $[H_o]$ and E_m by the kinematic energy of a reference coordinate $[E_o]$. Every energy component has its own reference point, i.e. the basic origin. Because E_t is the summation of E_h, E_p and E_m, the dependency of the value of E_t to these basic origins has a linear form of $mc[T_o] + mg[H_o] + [E_o]$ where m is the mass of this particle, c the specific heat coefficient and g the gravitational acceleration. Accordingly, the structure of the dimension of E_t is represented as $D([M][L]^2[T]^{-2}, mc[T_o]+mg[H_o]+[E_o])$. The structure of a general dimension can be represented as $D(U_1^{\alpha_1}U_2^{\alpha_2}\cdots, \beta_1 O_1 + \beta_2 O_2 + \cdots)$ where $U_1, U_2, \cdots$ are basic units, and $O_1, O_2, \cdots$ are basic origins. This is because the relation among origins follows the theorem 3, while the relation among units follows the product theorem.

This extended structure of the dimension requires to extend the Buckingham Π-theorem as follows.

Theorem 4 (Extended Buckingham Π-theorem) *If $\phi(x, y, ...) = 0$ is a complete equation, then the solution can be written in the form $F(\Pi_1, \Pi_2, ..., \Pi_{n-r-s}) = 0$, where n is the number of arguments of ϕ, and r and s are the number of basic units and that of basic origins of the dimensions in $x, y, ...$. For all i, Π_i is a dimensionless number.*

The basic background of the original Buckingham Π-theorem is the fact that the intrinsic degree of freedom of n ratio scale quantities of $x, y, ...$ is $n - r$, because the values of r quantities are determined by the specification of r basic units in the measurement. As an interval scale quantity has an extra factor, i.e., basic origin, beside the basic unit, the values of $r + s$ quantities are determined by the specification of the measurement, and the intrinsic degree of freedom reduces to $n - r - s$. This theorem ensures that we can remove the limitation of the assumption 2.

Another important subject is to overcome the limitation of the assumption 3 that was pointed out by Kalagnanam and Henrion[6]. The process of identifying the formula of each regime $\rho_i(\Pi_i, x, y, ...) = 0$ is basically to find a relation among a subset of quantities in a complete equation while holding the condition that must hold outside of $\rho_i = 0$ constant as stated in the assumption 4. If the assumption 3 does not hold, this operation is impossible because of the dependency among multiple regimes. This difficulty can be removed by introducing an idea of *pseudo-regime.*

Definition of pseudo-regime

A pseudo-regime is a subsystem, where the relation among quantities follows one of the product theorem, theorem 2 and 3, of a given complete equation.

Consider the example of convection heat transfer given by Kalagnanam et al. [6] The heat transfer from a fluid to a pipe wall takes place through convection when a fluid is forced through a pipe. A complete equation for this phenomenon under the turbulent flow is known as follows.

$$\Pi_1 = 0.023{\Pi_2}^{0.8}{\Pi_3}^{0.4},$$

where $\Pi_1 = \frac{hd}{k}, \Pi_2 = \frac{dv\rho}{\mu}$ and $\Pi_3 = \frac{c\mu}{k}$. Here, h is the convection heat transfer coefficient dependent to the other quantities, d and v are diameter of pipe and velocity of stream, and μ, ρ, c and k are the material quantities of the fluid, *i.e.*, viscosity, density, specific heat and thermal conductivity respectively. The number of quantities and that of the basic dimensions are $n = 7, r = 4$ and

$s = 0$ respectively. Hence, three $(n - r - s = 3)$ regimes exist in this ensemble, and Π_1, Π_2 and Π_3 are called as Nusselt's, Reynold's and Prandtl's numbers in the thermal hydraulics domain. This example violates the assumption 3, because d, μ and k appear in multiple regimes. However, this equation is regarded as a unique pseudo-regime, because it can be rewritten to follow the product theorem as:

$$\frac{k^{0.6}v^{0.8}\rho^{0.8}c^{0.4}}{hd^{0.2}\mu^{0.4}} - \frac{1}{0.023} = 0.$$

Accordingly, the data-driven search of a pseudo-regime can discover this formula without facing the difficulty pointed out by Kalagnanam and Henrion. In addition, these regimes can be decomposed into:

$$\Pi'_1 = d, \quad \Pi'_2 = k, \quad \Pi'_3 = \mu, \quad \Pi'_4 = \frac{h\Pi'_1}{\Pi'_2}, \quad \Pi'_5 = \frac{\Pi'_1 v\rho}{\Pi'_3} \quad \text{and} \quad \Pi'_6 = \frac{c\Pi'_3}{\Pi'_2}.$$

Because these pseudo-regimes are mutually independent, the data-driven discovery of these pseudo-regimes is also possible. Consequently, the following theorem can be stated.

Theorem 5 *Given a complete equation $\phi(x_1, x_2, ...x_n) = 0$, its decomposition into pseudo-regimes always exists where*

$$F(\Pi_1, \Pi_2, ..., \Pi_k) = 0 \quad \textit{and} \quad \{\rho'_i(\Pi_i, x_{1_i}, x_{2_i}, ...x_{m_i}) = 0 | i = 1, ..., k\}.$$

Here $\{Q_i | Q_i = \{x_{1_i}, x_{2_i}, ...x_{m_i}\}, i = 1, ..., k\}$ is a partition of entire quantity set $Q = \{x_1, x_2, ...x_n\}$.

The quantity Π of a quasi-regime may not be dimensionless, since a quasi-regime does not have to consist of quantities that cancel out every dimensions. Therefore, the following assumption must hold.

Assumption 5 *The measurement for the data of the entire complete equation must follow a consistent unit system.*

Otherwise, the formulae of the ensemble may become invalid, since it is not invariant to the change of dimensions.

The algorithm to discover an ensemble and a set of quasi-regimes involves a stage to identify quasi-regimes, a stage to determine the arguments Πs of the ensemble and a stage to determine the formula of the ensemble. The following algorithm to discover the formula of a complete equation from the given data has been constructed.

Algorithm 2

(Step 1) $E = \{x_1, x_2, ...x_n\}$, $LE = \phi$ and $k = 1$.

(Step 2) Repeat until k becomes equal to n. {
    Repeat for every partition Γ_i of E where $|\Gamma_i| = k$. {
        Repeat for every $Q_{i_j} \in \Gamma_i (j = 1, ..., k)$. {
            Apply the algorithm 1 to Q_{i_j} to identify a quasi-regime. Test each solution in S through the least square fitting to the measured data under some sets of values of quantities in $(E - Q_{i_j})$. If some solutions are accepted, substitute them to a list LQ_{i_j}.}
        If every $LQ_{i_j} \neq \phi$, let a list $L\Gamma_i = \{LQ_{i_j} | Q_{i_j} \in \Gamma_i, j = 1, ..., k\}$.
        Push $L\Gamma_i$ to LE.}
    If $LE \neq \phi$, go to (Step 3), else $k = k + 1$.}
(Step 3) Repeat for every $L\Gamma_i$ in LE. {
    Repeat for every LQ_{i_j} in $L\Gamma_i (j = 1, ..., k)$. {
        Repeat for every solution of a quasi-regime, s_{i_j}, in LQ_{i_j}. {
            Determine an argument quantity $\Pi(s_{i_j})$ based on the coefficients of s_{i_j} evaluated through the least square fitting to the measured data.}}}
(Step 4) Repeat for every $L\Gamma_i$ in LE. {
    Take Cartesian products $LP_i = LQ_{i_1} \times LQ_{i_2} \times \cdots \times LQ_{i_k}$ in $L\Gamma_i$.
    Repeat for every $\{s_{i_1}, s_{i_2}, ..., s_{i_k}\} \in LP_i$. {
        Determine the formula $F(\Pi(s_{i_1}), \Pi(s_{i_2}), ..., \Pi(s_{i_k})) = 0$.}}

More concrete contents of this algorithm are demonstrated through an example of Black's specific heat law. This relates the initial temperatures of two substances T_1 and T_2 with their temperature T_f after they have been combined. This law has the formula of $T_f = (w_1M_1/(w_1M_1 + w_2M_2))T_1 + (w_2M_2/(w_1M_1 + w_2M_2))T_2$ where M_1 and M_2 are the masses of the two substances, and w_1 and w_2 are their specific heat coefficients. The conditions of $M_1 = 0.5M_2$ and $w_1 = w_2$ are applied in our example. In (Step 1), the set of measured quantities E is set as $\{T_f, T_1, T_2, M_1, M_2\}$. (Step 2) is the process to enumerate all partitions of E where each subset of E is interpreted as a quasi-regime. The goodness of the least square fitting of each candidate solution derived by the algorithm 1 is checked through the F-test which is a statistical hypothesis test to judge if the measured data follows the solution. If a parameter is close enough to an integer value, then the parameter is forced to be the integer, because the parameter having an integer value is quite common in various domains. Every partition Γ_i, where all of its subsets are judged to be quasi-regimes, is searched in an ascending order of the cardinal number k of the partition. Once such partitions are found at the level of the certain cardinal number, (Step 2) is finished at that level to obtain the solutions of the ensembles involving the least number of quasi-regimes. This criterion decreases the ambiguity of the formula of the ensemble by reducing the number of the absolute scale quantities in it. In the current example, only the partition of $\{\{T_f, T_1, T_2\}, \{M_1, M_2\}\}$ is accepted at the least cardinal number, $k = 2$. All quantities in the former quasi-regime are of interval scale, and those in the latter are of ratio scale, and thus the formula of these quasi-regimes are enumerated as:

$$T_f = b_1 T_1 + b_2 T_2 + c_1, \qquad M_1^{a_1} M_2^{a_2} + c_1 = 0.$$

Notice that the number of quantities n is 5 while $r = 2$ and $s = 1$ since temperature is interval scale and mass ratio scale. Therefore, the number of regime must be $n - r - s = 2$ according to the extended Buckingham Π-theorem which is consistent with the above result. Their more specific formulae are identified through the data fitting as follows.

$$T_f = b_1 T_1 + b_2 T_2, \qquad M_1 M_2^{-1} + c_1 = 0.$$

(Step 3) defines an argument Π for each quasi-regime. The definition can be made in various ways. In our approach, a parameter in a quasi-regime, which varies by the influence from the other quasi-regimes, is chosen to be a Π, and the other variable parameters in the quasi-regime are evaluated in terms of the Π. In the current example, both of b_1 and b_2 in the former quasi-regime are observed to be variable depending on the values of M_1 and M_2. Accordingly, many data of $\{b_1, b_2\}$ are evaluated through fitting to the measured data of T_f, T_1 and T_2 under various values of M_1 and M_2. Then, b_1 is chosen to be the Π_1 of the quasi-regime, and various formulae of $f(\Pi_1)$ are tested for b_2 through the F-test of the least square fitting to the data of $\{b_1, b_2\}$. The class of $f(\Pi_1)$ is limited to polynomial and meromorphic formulae in our current study. The following is the most simple formula accepted in the test.

$$b_1 = \Pi_1, \qquad b_2 = 1 - \Pi_1.$$

For the latter quasi-regime, c_1 is uniquely chosen to be the Π_2. (Step 4) searches the relation of each ensemble found in the preceding steps. In the example under consideration, first, many data of $\{\Pi_1, \Pi_2\}$ are obtained by applying various combinations of values of $\{T_f, T_1, T_2, M_1, M_2\}$. Then various formulae of $F(\Pi_1, \Pi_2) = 0$ are tested for the ensemble while limiting the class of F to polynomial and meromorphic formulae. The most simple formula accepted is as follows.

$$\Pi_1 \Pi_2 - \Pi_1 - \Pi_2 = 0.$$

By combining above formulae, the familiar equation of the Black's specific heat law under the condition of $w_1 = w_2$ is obtained.

$$T_f = \frac{M_1}{M_1 + M_2} T_1 + \frac{M_2}{M_1 + M_2} T_2.$$

4 Conclusion

In this paper we have proposed a new method that enables us to automatically discover formulae of first principles. Our approach lies in between the deductive approaches and the empirical data-driven approaches. The major characteristics of our approach are summarized as follows.

i) The sound solutions of basic formulae of law equations within a regime are provided by using only the knowledge of quantity scales.
ii) An ensemble and its quasi-regimes in the objective system are identified from the experimental data without any strong limitations.
iii) The applicability is not limited to well-defined domains because the method does not require a priori knowledge except the knowledge of quantity scales.

The scale type-based reasoning may provide a basis to discover qualitative models of ambiguous domains such as biology, psychology, economics and social science.

References

1. Bhaskar R. and Nigam A. *Artificial Intelligece*, **45**, 73–111 (1990).
2. Bridgman P.W. *Dimensional Analysis.* Yale University Press, New Haven, CT (1922).
3. Buckingham E. *Phys. rev.*, **IV**, 4, 345–376 (1914).
4. Helmholtz H.V. *Numbering and Measuring from Epistemological Viewpoint.* Philosophische Aufsatze (1887).
5. Ishida Y. *Working Papers of Nith International Workshop on Qualitative Reasoning*, pp.84–93 (1995).
6. Kalagnanam J., Henrion M. and Subrahmanian E. *Computational Intelligence*, **10**, 2, 117–133 (1994).
7. Langley P. and Zytkow J.M. *Artificial Intelligece*, **40**, 283–312 (1989).
8. Luce R.D. *The Psychological Review*, **66**, 2, 81–95 (1959).
9. The MathWoks MATLAB User's Guide Version 4.0 (1992).
10. Stevens S.S. *Science*, **103**, 2684, 677–680 (1946).
11. Washio T. and Motoda H. *AAAI Technical Report WS-96-01: Tenth Int. Workshop on Qualitative Reasoning*, pp.255-264 (1996).
12. Washio T. and Motoda H. *Working Papers of PKAW'96: The 1996 Pacific Rim Knowledge Aquisition Workshop*, pp.130-149 (1996).

Generalization Based on the Connectionist Networks Representation of a Generalization Distribution Table

Ning Zhong, Shinichi Fujitsu
Dept. of Computer Science and Systems Engineering
Faculty of Engineering, Yamaguchi University
Tokiwa-Dai 2557, Ube 755, Japan
E-mail: {zhong,fuji}@ai.csse.yamaguchi-u.ac.jp

Setsuo Ohsuga
Department of Information and Computer Science
School of Science and Engineering, Waseda University
3-4-1 Okubo Shinjuku-Ku, Tokyo 169, Japan

This paper proposes a new approach for mining rules from databases. We first define a Generalization Distribution Table (GDT) as a hypothesis search space for generalization, and then describe that the GDT can be represented by connectionist networks. Furthermore, we discuss a rule mining process based on the connectionist networks representation. The main features of this approach are that not only the uncertainty of a rule including the prediction of possible instances can be explicitly represented in the strength of the rule, but also noisy data and data change can be handled effectively, biases can be flexibly selected for search control, and *if-then* rules can be discovered in an evolutionary, parallel-distributed cooperative mode.

1 Introduction

Mining *if-then* rules from databases can be viewed as a process of generalization in a hypothesis search space. This idea is based on this view of *generalization as search* proposed by Mitchell in his development of *version space* for concept learning as a symbolic approach [7,8]. In version space, the learning task is to search a hypothesis space, subject to constrains imposed by the training instances, to determine plausible generalizations. Version space is a typical bottom-up, incremental approach for learning concepts and rules, in which learning a concept is possible not only when instances are input simultaneously but also when they are given one by one. Although version space as a landmark work has led to some success and provides a good background for our research, some issues on real-world applications such as

- How can rules be learned in the environment with noise and incompleteness?
- How can unseen instances be predicted and the uncertainty of a rule including the prediction be represented explicitly?

- How can biases can be selected and/or altered dynamically for search control?
- How can rules be mined from very large, complex databases?

are still the ones to which no satisfactory solution has been found.

On the other hand, *back propagation* proposed by Rumelhart et al as a connectionist approach has proven to be a powerful and general technique for machine learning [10]. However, it also has disadvantages such as

- Without the ability to explain its decisions, it is hard to be confident in the reliability of a network that addresses a real-world problem. Although it learns, it does not provide us with a theory about what it has learned - it is simple black boxes that give answers but provide no clear idea as to how they arrived at these answers [13];
- Background knowledge is rather difficult to be incorporated to the back propagation networks;
- The training time needed for the back propagation networks to obtain a satisfied result is usually long. This is because learning in the back propagation networks is basically based on multiple passes over the training data set.

The disadvantages lead to that it have been thought not well suited for mining *if-then* rules from databases.

This paper proposes a new approach for mining rules from databases, in which a variant of transition matrix in stochastic process named Generalization Distribution Table (GDT) is used as a hypothesis search space for generalization. Furthermore, by representing the GDT as connectionist networks, *if-then* rules can be discovered in an evolutionary, parallel-distributed cooperative mode. The theoretical basis and principles of our methodology have been discussed in our paper [14]. This paper focuses on some basic concepts of our methodology, the connectionist networks representation of the GDT and a rule mining process based on the connectionist networks representation. We will describe that the issues and disadvantages of both version space and back propagation stated above can be solved/overcame systematically in the approach proposed in this paper.

2 Generalization Distribution Table for KDD

We define that a Generalization Distribution Table (GDT) for knowledge discovery and data mining (KDD) consists of three components: the *possible instances*, the *possible generalizations* for instances and the *probabilistic relationships* between the possible instances and the possible cases of generalization. Thus, the basic process of hypothesis generation is that of generalizing the observed instances by searching the GDT.

Definition 2.1 The possible instances.

We say that the *possible instances*, which are denoted in columns in a GDT, are all possible combinations of attribute values, and the number of the possible instances is

$$\prod_{i=1}^{m} n_i, \tag{1}$$

where m is the number of attributes, n is the number of different data values in each attribute. □

Definition 2.2 The possible generalizations for instances.

We say that the *possible generalizations* for instances, which are denoted in rows in a GDT, are all possible cases of generalization for all possible instances, and the number of the possible generalizations is

$$\prod_{i=1}^{m}(n_i + 1) - (\prod_{i=1}^{m} n_i) - 1. \tag{2}$$

□

Definition 2.3 The probabilistic relationships between the possible instances and the possible cases of generalization.

We say that the *probabilistic relationships* between the possible instances and the possible cases of generalization, which are denoted in the elements t_{ij} in a GDT, are the probabilistic distribution for describing the strength of the relationship between every possible instance and every possible generalization. □

Table 1 is an example of the GDT for KDD, in which three attributes, A, B, C, from a sample database as shown in Table 2 and

$A \in \{a_0, a1\}$, $B \in \{b_0, b1, b2\}$, $C \in \{c_0, c1\}$,

are used as *condition* attributes (e.g., the real meaning of these attributes can be respectively assigned as *Weather, Temperature, Humidity* in a weather forecast database, or *Temperature, Cough, Headache* in a medical diagnosis database) for creating the GDT as the possible instances. Thus, the number of the possible instances for this example is $2 \times 3 \times 2 = 12$. Although the attribute D in Table 2 is not used for creating a GDT, it is used in Eq.(7), which will be described in Sections 4 and 5, as a *decision* attribute for classification (e.g.,

Table 1: A Generalization Distribution Table for a sample database

	a0b0c0	a0b0c1	a0b1c0	a0b1c1	a0b2c0	a0b2c1	a1b0c0	...	a1b2c1
*b0c0	1/2						1/2		
*b0c1		1/2						...	
*b1c0			1/2					...	
*b1c1				1/2				...	
*b2c0					1/2			...	
*b2c1						1/2		...	1/2
a0*c0	1/3		1/3		1/3			...	
a0*c1		1/3		1/3		1/3		...	
a1*c0							1/3	...	
a1*c1								...	1/3
a0b0*	1/2	1/2						...	
a0b1*			1/2	1/2				...	
a0b2*					1/2	1/2		...	
a1b0*							1/2	...	
a1b1*								...	
a1b2*								...	1/2
**c0	1/6		1/6		1/6		1/6	...	
**c1		1/6		1/6		1/6		...	1/6
b0	1/4	1/4					1/4	...	
b1			1/4	1/4				...	
b2					1/4	1/4		...	1/4
a0**	1/6	1/6	1/6	1/6	1/6	1/6		...	
a1**							1/6	...	1/6

the real meaning of the decision attribute can be assigned as *Wind* or *Flu* corresponding to the one of the assigned condition attributes).

Furthermore, "$*$" in Table 1, which specifies a wild card, denotes the generalization for instances. For example, the generalization $*b_0c_1$ for the instance $a_0b_0c_1$ means the attribute A is unimportant for describing a concept. And the number of the possible generalizations is $3 \times 4 \times 3 - 12 - 1 = 23$.

Finally, the probability distribution, which describes the probabilistic relationships between the possible instances and the possible cases of generalization as shown in Table 1, is equiprobable[a], because we do not consider to use background knowledge for it, currently.

Definition 2.4 Levels of generalization.

Let all possible cases of generalization for instances in the GDT be divided into different levels according to the number of "$*$" in every possible case of generalization, and the different levels are called *levels of generalization.* □

For example, all the possible cases of generalization shown in Table 1 are divided into two levels of generalization, that is,

$$Level_1 \in \{*b_0c_0, *b_0c_1, \ldots, a_1b_2*\}$$
$$Level_2 \in \{**c_0, **c_1, \ldots, a_1 * *\}.$$

Thus, we can see that any generalization in a lower level is properly contained by one or more possible cases of generalization in an upper level. As default, our

[a]In the GDT shown in Table 1, the elements that are not displayed are all zero.

Table 2: A sample database

No	A	B	C	D
1	a0	b0	c1	y
2	a0	b1	c1	y
3	a0	b0	c1	y
4	a1	b1	c0	n
5	a0	b0	c1	n
6	a0	b2	c1	y

approach prefers more general hypotheses in an upper level of generalization to more specific ones in a lower level of generalization. However, we can alter the bias into preferring more specific hypotheses to more general ones by using a meta control.

Definition 2.5 Contradictory rules.

We say that *contradictory rules* are the ones that have the conjunction of same conditions that the rules must satisfy, but describe different concepts with nearly same strength. □

For example, the rules, which are discovered from a database on *weather forecast*,

$$Weather(clear) \wedge Humidity(low) \rightarrow Wind(yes) \text{ with } P = 0.25$$

and

$$Weather(clear) \wedge Humidity(low) \rightarrow Wind(no) \text{ with } P = 0.25,$$

are contradictory rules because they have same conditions $Weather(clear) \wedge Humidity(low)$ and describe different concepts $Wind(yes)$ and $Wind(no)$ with same strength $P = 0.25$.

3 Representing the GDT by Connectionist Networks

A GDT can be represented by connectionist networks for mining rules in an evolutionary, parallel-distributed cooperative mode. Figure 1 shows a representation of connectionist networks for our purpose. We can see that the connectionist networks consist of three layers: input unit layer, hidden unit layer and output unit layer.

Definition 3.1 Three kinds of units.

A unit that receives instances from a database is called an *input unit*, and the number of the input units corresponds to the number of condition attributes. A unit that receives a result of learning in a hidden unit, which is

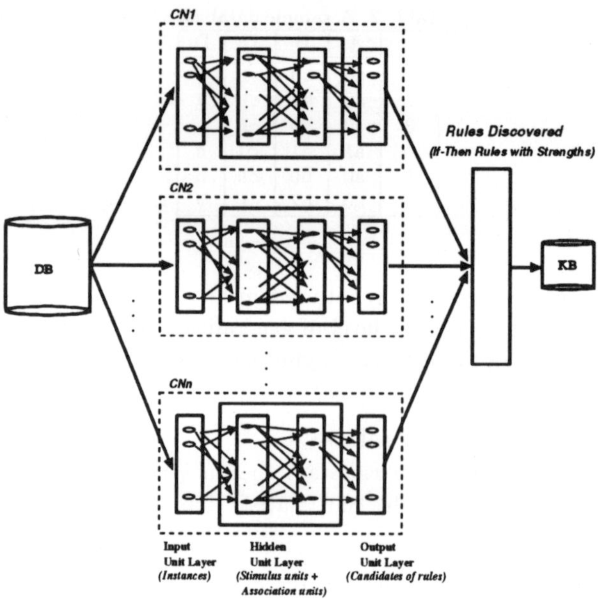

Figure 1: A representation of connectionist networks for KDD

used as one of the rule candidates discovered, is called an *output unit.* A unit that is neither input nor output unit is called a *hidden unit.* □

Let the hidden unit layer be further divided into *stimulus units* and *association units.* The stimulus units are used for representing the possible instances like the columns in a GDT, and the association units are used for representing the possible generalizations in a same level of generalizations for instances like the rows of representing some level of generalizations in a GDT. Furthermore, there is a link between a stimulus unit and an association unit if the association unit represents a possible generalization for a possible instance representing in the stimulus unit. Moreover, the probabilistic relationship between the possible instances and the possible cases of generalization is denoted in the weight of the link, and the initial weights are equiprobable like the t_{ij} in a GDT.

Definition 3.2 The excitatory link vs. the inhibitory link.

We say a link between a stimulus unit and an association unit is an *excitatory link* if the link is connected to a unit that was stimulated by an instance. We say a link between a stimulus unit and an association unit is an *inhibitory*

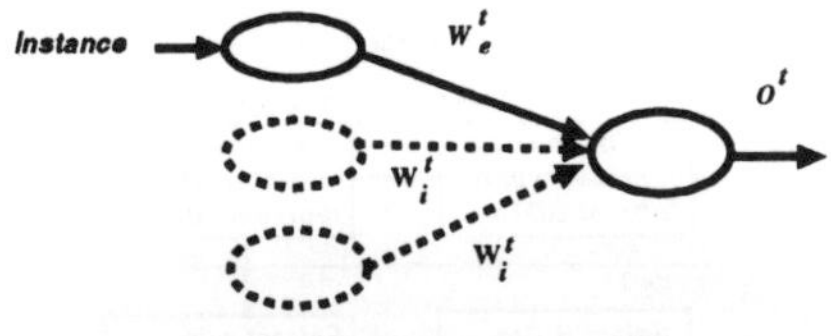

Figure 2: The relationship between stimulus units and an association unit with different links

link if the link is connected to a unit that was not stimulated by an instance in the input unit layer.

Let W_e^t be the weight of the excitatory link and W_i^t be the weight of the inhibitory link at time t. □

Figure 2 shows the relationship between stimulus units and an association unit with different links. Here we would like to stress that

- In the representation, a connectionist network is only used for representing the possible generalizations for the possible instances in some level of generalization. Hence, we need to create n connectionist networks if there are n levels of generalization as shown in Figure 1. Thus, the number of connectionist networks that should be created, N_{cns}, is

$$N_{cns} = N_{attrs} - 2, \tag{3}$$

where N_{attrs} is the number of attributes in a database. The merit of the approach is obvious, that is, the rule candidates can be generated in parallel. For example, we need to use two connectionist networks for the sample database shown in Table 2.

- Since a GDT can be decomposed into several sub-GDTs by using different attributes (i.e., the different sub-sets of attributes are used for creating a set of GDTs), these sub-GDTs can be represented by different connectionist networks for handling large, complex databases in a distributed cooperative mode.

- Since the creation of the connectionist networks is based on the GDTs, the meaning of every unit in the networks can be explained clearly. Thus, not only the trained results in the connectionist networks are explicitly represented in the form of *if-then* rule with *strength*, but background knowledge can also be used for dynamically revising and changing the connectionist networks representation in the rule mining process. Hence,

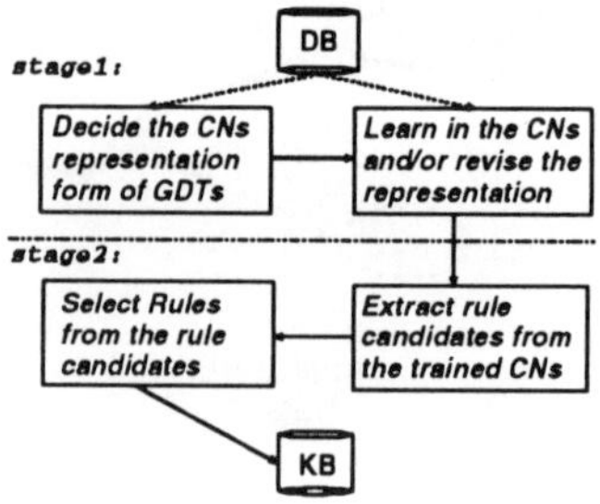

Figure 3: Block diagram of the basic process of rule mining

the connectionist networks are called *knowledge-oriented connectionist networks.*

- The connectionist networks do not need to be explicitly created in advance. They can be embodied in the search algorithm, and we only need to record the weights and the units stimulated by instances. In fact, the instances collected, in many real-world databases, are generally a small part of all possible instances. Hence, the real size of the connectionist networks is much smaller than the size of the corresponded GDT.

4 The Basic Process of Mining Rules from a Database

We have developed an effective method for incremental rule mining based on the connectionist networks stated in Section 3. One good feature of our approach is that every instance in a database is only searched once, and if the data in a database are changed (added, deleted or updated), then we only need to modify the connectionist networks and the discovered rules related the changed data, but the database is not searched again. That is, unlike the back propagation networks, our approach does not need multiple passes over the training data set. We argue this is a very important feature for mining rules from very large databases. Figure 3 gives an overall view of the basic process of mining rules from databases. We can see that the process is divided into two main stages.

The *first* stage is that of deciding the form of the connectionist networks representation and revising the weights by learning in every connectionist network in parallel. The main steps are as follows:

*step*1 : Suppose the set of instances that can be input, which is stored in a database, $\mathbf{I} = \{I_1, I_2, \ldots, I_n\}$, is given. Before learning (i.e., time $t = 0$), all of units and links are in inhibitory state and

$$W_i^t = \frac{1}{N_{il}^t}, (t = 0), \tag{4}$$

where N_{il}^t is the number of the inhibitory links for an association unit.

step2 : Put an instance, which is picked up from $\mathbf{I}$, in the input unit layer and $t = t + 1$. As the result of this operation, the units corresponding to the instance in the hidden unit layer are stimulated.

step3 : Update the values of W_e^t and W_i^t in Eqs. (5) and (6) respectively.

$$W_e^t = \frac{1 + \alpha N_{ins-new}^t}{N_{il}^t + N_{el}^t + \alpha N_{ins-rel}^t}, (t > 0), \tag{5}$$

$$W_i^t = \frac{1 - \sum W_e^t}{N_{il}^t}, (t > 0), \tag{6}$$

where N_{el}^t is the number of the excitatory links for an association unit in time t, $N_{ins-rel}^t$ is the number of all instances that were putted in the input unit layer and that are related to some case of generalization in time t, $N_{ins-new}^t$ is the number of instances that are the same as the new putted instance in time t, and α is a constant of representing the learning rate for controlling the speed of approaching 1 of W_e^t.

step4 : If there are still the instances that are not processed, then go to *step2*. Otherwise, start the *second* stage of the process.

The *second* stage of the rule mining process is that of generating rules based on the result learned in the *first* stage. The main steps are as follows:

step1 : Extract the rule candidates from the excitatory association units and compute the strengths of the rules, O_c^t, in Eq.(7). Then put them in the output unit layer.

$$O_c^t = (\sum W_e^t) \times \frac{N_{ins-class}^t}{N_{ins-rel}^t}. \tag{7}$$

Where $N_{ins-class}^t$ is the number of instances relating to some case of generalization and belonging to a class in time t.

step2 : Select *if-then* rules from the rule candidates generated in *step1* by heuristic search.

A heuristic search method for selecting rules can be divided into three operations:

- Adjust the threshold value to distinguish contradictory rules and noise dynamically.

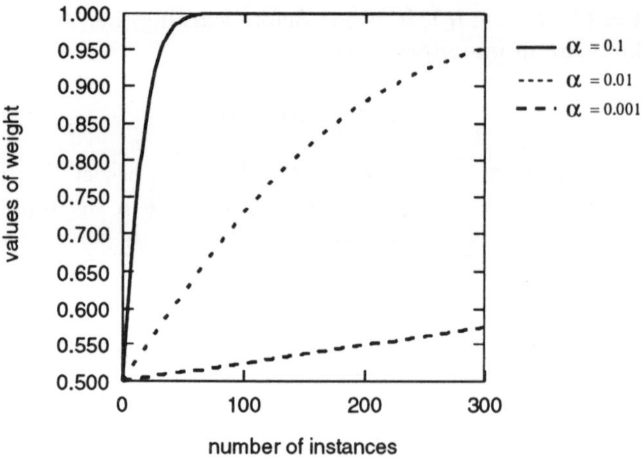

Figure 4: Controlling the learning rate by adjusting α

- Delete the contradictory rules and the rules with weaker strength in every level of generalization in parallel.

- Delete the redundant rules between different levels.

Here, we would like to further explain Eqs.(5) and (6). The explanation for Eq.(7) will be described in Section 5. Eqs.(5) and (6) can be considered a variant of the *Hebbian* learning rule [3]. The basic ideas can be summarized as follows:

- If an instance is observed, then the weight that represents the probabilistic relationship between this observed instance and its possible generalizations should be strengthened in Eq.(5), and the more same instances are observed, the more the weight is strengthened. In contrast, the weight that represents the probabilistic relationship between the unobserved possible instances and their possible generalizations should be weakened in Eq.(6).

- α in Eq.(5) is a constant of representing the learning rate. In our applications, we may need, in some cases, a smoother speed of approaching 1 by giving a lower value of α, and in other cases, a higher value of α is given for speed up. In other words, α is a bias for controlling the search and rule mining. Figure 4 gives an example of describing how to control

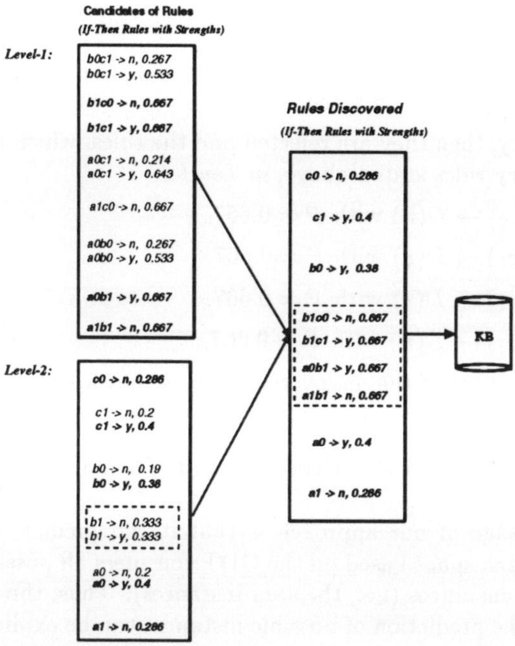

Figure 5: Rules discovered from a sample database

the learning rate by adjusting α. For simplicity, in the rest of the paper, we assume that the value of $\alpha = 1$.

- If we do not consider that data change (e.g., the data in a database are added, deleted or updated) may cause the modification of the connectionist networks representation, Eqs.(5) and (6) can be represented in an iterative form. However, the iteration relationship between W^t and W^{t-1} will not hold if the connectionist networks are modified dynamically along with data change. Hence, Eqs.(5) and (6) are used in our system.

Figure 5 gives a result of discovering rules from the sample database shown in Table 2 by using the method stated above. It includes the rule candidates extracted from the connectionist networks and *if-then* rules selected from the candidates. In this example, we prefer more general rules. Thus, we first consider to select the rules from *Level-2* of the rule candidates. Due to the rules in *Level-2*,

$B(b_1) \rightarrow D(n)$ with $P = 0.333$

and

$B(b_1) \rightarrow D(y)$ with $P = 0.333$,

are contradictory, then they are rejected and the rules, which are contained by the contradictory rules stated above, in *Level-1*,

$B(b_1) \wedge C(c_0) \rightarrow D(n)$ with $P = 0.667$,

$B(b_1) \wedge B(c_1) \rightarrow D(y)$ with $P = 0.667$,

$A(a_0) \wedge B(b_1) \rightarrow D(y)$ with $P = 0.667$,

$A(a_1) \wedge B(b_1) \rightarrow D(n)$ with $P = 0.667$,

are selected as a part of the discovered rules as shown in Figure 5.

5 Rule Strength and the Prediction of Unseen Instances

Another advantage of our approach is that it can predict unseen instances because the search space based on the GDT considers all possible combination of the observed instances (i.e., the seen instances). Thus, the uncertainty of a rule including the prediction of possible instances can be explicitly represented in the strength P.

We can see that Eq.(7), which is used for defining the strength of a rule, can be divided into two parts. The first part is

$$\sum W_e^t$$

which is used for describing the strength of a rule and including the prediction for unseen instances. For instance, based on the result of learning by using the method stated in Section 4, the rule

$r_{1.1} : A(a_0) \wedge B(b_1) \rightarrow D(y)$ with $P = 0.667$

can be acquired by generalizing the instance, $a_0b_1c_1$. The reason why the strength of the rule is 0.667 is that we only observed one of two kinds of possible instances, which can be generalized into $A(a_0) \wedge B(b_1)$, in the database shown in Table 2. In other words, we did not observe another kind of possible instance, $a_0b_1c_0$, in this database. Thus, based on the learning method stated in Section 4, we first revise the weights relating the generalization, $A(a_0) \wedge B(b_1)$, into 0.667 and 0.333 in Eqs.(5) and (6) respectively, and then get the strength of the rule in the first part of Eq.(7). Furthermore, if the instance, $a_0b_1c_0$, is added in the database shown in Table 2, then we can revise the weights into 0.5 in Eqs.(5) and (6) again, and then increase the strength of the rule to 1 in the first part of Eq.(7).

We argue that the prediction for the unseen instances is an important function for mining rules from real-world databases. In most cases, the set of instances collected in a database represents a part of all possible instances. This is reasonable, because we expect to learn rules without first collecting every possible instance (like physicians to learn how to diagnose diseases without first having seen every possible patient) [12]. However, it also means that the learning task is ill-posed, because for previous inductive approaches, without some other source of constraint, there is no way to know the instances of describing a concept that has never before been observed. Our approach based on the Generalization Distribution Table provides a possibility for predicting the unseen instances and for explicitly representing the strength of a rule including the prediction. In other words, our approach tries to find definitions of concepts that generalize to new instances, rather than ad hoc definitions of concepts that only apply to the instances observed during learning.

The second part of Eq.(7) is

$$\frac{N^t_{ins-class}}{N^t_{ins-rel}}.$$

This part is available for representing the strength of a rule only when the rule is acquired from the instances with noise. It shows the quality of classification, that is, how many same instances as conditions that the rules must satisfy can be classified into same class. The question is whether the ratio denoted in the second part of Eq.(7) is either too far from 1 or near to 0.5 if the classification is limited in two classes for convenience to explain. Thus, we can distinguish the following three cases on handling noisy data:

- If the ratio is 1 then there is not noisy data, that is, all same instances as conditions that the rules must satisfy can be classified into same class. In this case, the second part of Eq.(7) is not used for describing the strength of a rule.

- If the ratio is near to 0.5 then the rules are contradictory and/or the attributes now available are insufficient for describing some concepts. That is, we may guess there is a *hidden attribute* that is not collected for describing the concepts.

- If the ratio is neither 1 nor near to 0.5 then we conclude there are noisy data in current database for the classification.

We would like to use the example of describing Eq.(7) again. If we only observed one of two kinds of possible instances, which can be generalized into

$A(a_0) \wedge B(b_1)$, in the database shown in Table 2, and we know its classification is y, then we can acquire the rule $r_{1.1}$. In other words, in this time, we did not observe another kind of possible instance, $a_0b_1c_0$, in the database shown in Table 2 and we also do not know that its classification is either y or n. However, if the instance $a_0b_1c_1$ is added in the database shown in Table 2 and its classification is y, then we can first revise the weights in Eqs.(5) and (6), and then increase the strength of the rule to 1 in Eq.(7). In contrast, if the classification of the new added instance is n, then the strength of the rule $r_{1.1}$ is revised into 0.5 and a new rule candidate,

$$r_{1.2} : A(a_0) \wedge B(b_1) \rightarrow D(n) \text{ with } P = 0.5,$$

is generated. This means both of the rules $r_{1.1}$ and $r_{1.2}$ must be deleted because they are contradictory.

On the other hand, if 40 same instances $a_1b_0c_1$ are added, and only one of them is classified into n, other 39 instances are classified into y, then the following rules,

$$r_{2.1} : B(b_0) \rightarrow D(y) \text{ with } P = 0.976$$

and

$$r_{2.2} : B(b_0) \rightarrow D(n) \text{ with } P = 0.024.$$

can be generated by the method stated in Section 4. We can see that the second part of Eq.(7) is used for describing the strengths of the rules $r_{2.1}$ and $r_{2.2}$ because the rules are generated by generalizing the instances $a_1b_0c_1$ with different classification. In this case, we infer that the instance $a_1b_0c_1$ with classification n is a noisy data because the strength of $r_{2.2}$ is much smaller than $r_{2.1}$. Thus, $r_{2.2}$ is deleted.

6 Concluding Remarks

In this paper, we presented a new methodology of rule mining based on the connectionist networks representation of a Generalization Distribution Table (GDT). We discussed basic concepts of our methodology, the connectionist networks representation of the GDT and a rule mining process based on the connectionist networks representation. Main features of our methodology can be summarized as follows:

- It is basically an incremental, bottom-up learning approach, but it also has some advantages belonging to top-down fashion;
- It can predict unseen instances and represent explicitly the uncertainty of a rule including the prediction of possible instances in the strength of the rule;

- It can effectively handle noisy data and data change;
- It can flexibly select biases for search control;
- It can use background knowledge for dynamically revising and changing the connectionist networks representation of the GDT in the rule mining process;
- It can discover *if-then* rules in an evolutionary, parallel-distributed cooperative mode.

That is, we described that the issues and disadvantages of both version space and back propagation stated in Section 1 can be solved/overcame systematically in the methodology proposed in this paper.

Our ultimate aim of the research project is to create a hybrid intelligent model and system for KDD, in which the typical methods of symbolic reasoning such as deduction, induction and abduction can be cooperatively used by taking the GDTs, transition matrixes in stochastic process, and their connectionist networks representation as the mediums. That is, the work that we are doing takes but one step toward a hybrid intelligent model and system for knowledge discovery and data mining.

References

1. U.M. Fayyad et al. (eds.) *Advances in Knowledge Discovery and Data Mining*, AAAI Press (1996).
2. D.F. Gordon and M. DesJardins *Evaluation and Selection of Biases in Machine Learning*, Machine Learning **20**, (1995) 5-22.
3. D.O. Hebb *The Organization of Behavior*, Wiley (1949).
4. G.E. Hinton *Connectionist Learning Procedures*, Artificial Intelligence **40**, (1989) 185-234.
5. H. Hirsh *Generalizing Version Spaces*, Machine Learning **17**, (1994) 5-46.
6. R.S. Michalski, J.G. Carbonell, and T.M. Mitchell *Machine Learning - An Artificial Intelligence Approach*, Morgan Kaufmann Publishers (1983, 1986, 1990).
7. T.M. Mitchell *Version Spaces: A Candidate Elimination Approach to Rule Learning.* Proc. 5th Int. Joint Conf. Artificial Intelligence (1977) 305-310.
8. T.M. Mitchell *Generalization as Search.* Artificial Intelligence **18**, (1982) 203-226.
9. S. Ohsuga *Symbol Processing by Non-Symbol Processor.* Proc. 4th Pacific Rim Inter. Conf. on Artificial Intelligence (PRICAI'96) (1996).
10. D.E. Rumelhart, G.E. Hinton and R.J. Williams *Learning Internal Representations by Back-Propagation Errors.* Nature **323**, (1986) 533-536.
11. G. Piatetsky-Shapiro and W.J. Frawley (eds.) *Knowledge Discovery in Databases.* AAAI Press and The MIT Press (1991).
12. J.W. Shavlik and T.G. Dietterich (eds.) *Readings in Machine Learning.* Moran Kaufmann Publishers (1990).
13. G.G. Towell and J.W. Shavlik *Extracting Refined Rules from Kowledge-Based Neural Networks.* Machine Learning **13**, (1993) 71-101.
14. N. Zhong and S. Ohsuga *Using Generalizations Distribution Tables as a Hypotheses Search Space for Generalization.* Proc. 4th International Workshop on Rough Sets, Fuzzy Sets, and Machine Discovery (RSFD-96) (1996) 396-403.

SEARCHING MULTIPLE DATABASES FOR INTERESTING COMPLEXES

JUN YAO and HUAN LIU
Department of Information Systems and Computer Science
National University of Singapore
Kent Ridge, Singapore 119260
{yaojun, liuh}@iscs.nus.sg

When many databases are available for knowledge discovery, one pressing problem is which databases have interesting knowledge. To solve this problem, users can pose a query when investigating databases and search for interesting information. In order to find interesting information and avoid unnecessary search in irrelevant databases, interestingness measures and efficient search methods are needed. In this paper, we propose a method based on a statistical measure by which some relevant databases can be detected. Knowledge, in the form of complexes, can be extracted which contains potentially interesting information. Users can identify importance and relevance of each database according to extracted knowledge. A heuristic function is applied to make the search more efficient. The extension of this method is also discussed.

1 Introduction

Large sized database, diverse relations of data and many sources from which data is collected are obstacles for users to find useful knowledge. Information among databases is not always useful for particular applications because of data redundancy and irrelevance, so efficiently inferring useful knowledge from the multiple databases is important for users. When many databases are available for knowledge discovery, one pressing issue is which databases have interesting knowledge for a particular application. To solve the problem, the process of knowledge discovery could be incorporated with a user's intentions or interests. Posing a query is one way of embedding a user's intents and interests in the process of knowledge discovery. Some methods of posing queries for knowledge discovery are proposed [1 2 3 4]. A user's interest, intuition or prior knowledge can be conveyed by means of such queries. In the case of multiple databases, problems arise: how to efficiently search for interesting knowledge in many databases by posing queries.

In this paper, we propose an approach to search for interesting knowledge in multiple databases according to a user's query. This process can be viewed as retrieval of interesting information from many databases. There are different kinds of ways to pose queries, we don't discuss how queries are made in detail, we only regard a query as a constrain which specifies a subset in all data. We focus on what interesting knowledge about this subset can be derived. A query, in our discussion, is the conditional part of a rule, the knowledge derived from multiple databases is the conclusion part of a rule, called *complexes*. These complexes should represent special or interesting knowledge in the data. A conclusion part or complex can be a conjunction of several attribute values (high order complex) as well as a single attribute value (low order complex). A large number of combinations of attribute values prohibits efficient search of high order complexes in many databases. A heuristic function is presented here to enable potentially interesting complexes to be found in relevant databases and avoid unnecessary search of high order complexes in irrelevant databases.

2 Notion of interestingness

Knowledge Discovery in Databases (KDD) targets at finding useful knowledge from large real world databases. Mining valuable knowledge is an important issue in KDD. The measurement of knowledge's value is usually determined by a user's specific application needs. *Interestingness* is usually taken as an overall measure in KDD. There is a lot of literature [5, 6, 7, 8] about the interestingness issue. The definition of interestingness mainly includes: validity, novelty, usefulness and ease of understanding [5]. These factors reflect a user's requirements on the whole.

In many situations, although discovered knowledge is highly understandable, valid and consistent with data, it is useless because it tells us nothing but common phenomena in the data. Besides the validity of knowledge, users are more concerned about what surprising variations are in data. Hence, our interestingness measure essentially is a statistical measure or so-called discrepancy measure [9], by which users can detect the deviations that indicate some outcomes in the subset covered by a query differing from those in the whole dataset. Deviation is a powerful and simple way of identifying interesting knowledge in data [7], because it indicates how the distribution of the observed events in certain subset differs from a reference level. The expected value according to the whole data (the average value) or normative value according to prior knowledge can be chosen as the reference level. We choose the expected value as our reference level. By detecting deviations in many database, users obtain complexes derived from multiple databases at the end of discovery process, each with a significance value by which users can also analyse and identify the relevance and importance of certain databases for their particular applications.

A production rule, a comprehensible representation of knowledge, is in the form as:

$$\text{IF} \quad Q \quad \text{THEN} \quad R$$

in which the right-hand side R is a *complex* rather than a class label in our discussion. Both Q and R are conjunctions of *selectors* that are in the form of: *attr* OP *value*. *attr* is the name of an attribute in a database, *value* is the possible values of an attribute *attr* and OP $\in (=, <, >, \leq, \geq)$ is an operator. We call Q the condition part and R the conclusion part.

As the condition part of a rule is specified by users, the task of our algorithm is to search for complexes, i.e., the conclusion parts that satisfy our criteria. In order to identify valid and novel complexes in data, we define the measure of significance for a complex as:

$$S = P(R|Q) log \frac{P(R|Q)}{P(R)} \qquad (1)$$

where P(R) is the probability of the event R occurring in a database and $P(R|Q)$ is the conditional probability of R occurring in the case of Q occurring.

The value of $P(R|Q)/P(R)$ shows the degree of the deviation between the probability of the event R occurring under the condition Q and the probability of R occurring in the whole database. If the nearer $P(R|Q)/P(R)$ is 1, i.e., the nearer S is 0, the closer the distribution of R in Q conforms to that of R in the whole database and the less novelty of the event R given Q; The larger $P(R|Q)/P(R)$ (i.e. $P(R|Q)/P(R) \gg 1$) is, the more likely the event R has a genuine correlation with Q; When $P(R|Q)/P(R) < 1$, the value of $\log P(R|Q)/P(R)$ is negative. The nearer $P(R|Q)/P(R)$ is 0, the more likely the two events R and Q are exclusive. In this paper, the complex which value $0 \leq P(R|Q)/P(R) < 1$ is discarded, we focus on the events related to Q. $P(R|Q)$ is used as the weight. Thus trivial outcomes in databases have low significance values.

$P(R|Q)$ also represents the accuracy or validity of a rule. The lower bound value (a threshold) can be determined by a user. A complex is rejected if its accuracy value is below the threshold. When the search begins, the conclusion part is an empty complex (a conjunction of zero selector). During the search, this part is specialized by intersections of the selectors. If the accuracy value of a specialized complex does not pass the lower bound, then the search on this node is pruned.

The similar significance measure is adopted in CN2 [10] called *likelihood ratio statistic* [9]. The significance values in our method and in CN2 both reflect the degree of the correlation between a complex and a class (in CN2) or a complex and the condition part of a query (in our method). The difference lies in that the significance value in our method is used to identify the novelty or unexpectness of a complex covered by a query at certain specified accuracy; the significance value in CN2 is used to evaluate the reliability of a complex classifying a class with high accuracy, i.e., high accuracy on classifying training data is not just due to chance.

3 Algorithm

Algorithm: Finding Interesting Complexes in Multiple Databases
Input: The condition part of a rule (A query)
  Databases $D_1, .., D_n$
Output: A set of Complexes with *significance* values
define: $Complexlist_i$ is a set of complexes found in D_i
define: $Selectors_i$ is the set of all possible selectors covered by the query in D_i
Main procedure:
  For each D_i
    If D_i has the same domain as one in the query
      Then call **function**(search for complexes in D_i)
      $Complexlist_i$=a set complexes found in D_i
    Else next database
function(search for complexes in D_i)
{ For each $Selectors_i$ calculate accuracy P and significance S
  Choose the selectors that have high significance values as *star*
  (The accuracy values of selected selectors should exceed the threshold)
  (The significance values of the selectors in *star* > 0)
  (The number of the selectors in *star* $\leq$user-defined maximum number)
 Do while any new complexes are added to *star*
  Let *newstar* be the set $\{x \wedge y | x \in$ the new complexes in *star*, y$\in Selectors_i\}$
  If the complexes in *newstar* can't satisfy the criteria
    Then remove the complexes out of *newstar*
  Add *newstar* to *star*
  Remove the least significant complex from *star* until
  The number of the complexes in *star* $\leq$user-defined maximum number
 return $Complexlist_i$ = *star*}

Figure 1: The algorithm of knowledge discovery

In our discussion, the search space in one database consists of all possible combinations of the selectors in a database. Assuming a database has n attributes besides the attributes whose names are the same as those in a query and each attribute of the examples covered by a query has m possible values, the number of possible combinations of the selectors is $(m+1)^n - 1$. When the number of attributes and the number of attribute values become large, heuristic functions are needed for efficient search. Our algorithm only searches a part of the search space of a database and tries to find potentially novel complexes. When there are no more complexes found in a database, we stop the search of this database. The algorithm is presented in Figure 1, which mainly consists of three steps as follows:

1. At the beginning, we enumerate all possible selectors in the database, then choose the most promising selectors as the initial complexes to form the *star* according to our accuracy and significance criteria. The number of the complexes (N_{max}) in the star is defined by a user and the significance values of the selected complexes must be larger than zero. So the search strategy of the algorithm is actually a beam search with the width of N_{max}.

2. Implementing combinations of the selectors is to intersect the complexes in current star with the set of all possible selectors. The new complexes generated by intersection form the *newstar*. "Good" complexes in the newstar should be selected and added to the star for replacing those not so "good" complexes compared with the new complexes. In this case, using the criteria of the step 1 to evaluate the complexes is insufficient, because intersecting the selector (or complex) of high significance value with the selector of low significance value could yields a complex of high significance. Low significance selectors usually couldn't improve the significance of a complex.

   We call the components of an intersection *predecessors* and the result of an intersection a *descendant*. If the accuracy values of predecessors and a descendant are the same, it is obvious that the significance value of the descendant is not less than those of the predecessors according to our significance definition. In order to eliminate the selectors that don't improve the significance of complexes, we define the *significance gain* to evaluate the novelty of a new complex. The complex which significance value satisfies the following inequality and its accuracy value passes the threshold is selected.

$$S_{new} - S_{max} > S_{min}$$

   Where S_{new} means the significance of a new complex;
   S_{max}=Max(the significance values of the predecessors of a new complex);

S_{min} is the significance value of the complex (C_{min}) which has the least value in the old star.

The measure of the significance gain actually evaluates the degree of improvement of the descendant's novelty in respect to the predecessors'. If the significance gain value of a new complex is larger than the significance value of C_{min}, this means the combination of a complex with a selector is more novel than the complex C_{min}.

3. Sort the new complexes and the complexes in the star according to the values of significance and choose the high ranking complexes, the number of the complexes in the star $\leq$user-defined number N_{max}. Repeat step 2 until no more complexes can be found, the search in a database is finished. At the end of a search in a database, we get a set of rules which orders are sorted according to descending significance value. If no complexes of a database satisfy the criteria at step 1, that means the database is irrelevant to the user's interests and we stop searching this database. Hence this method searches many databases efficiently.

4 Case study

In this section, we will illustrate how the algorithm works in two small databases. These databases are about people's diet habits, we suppose they are obtained from different sources. A user can find some complexes that he is interested by the way of posing a query to retrieve these databases. For example, when a user wants to know some diet habits about Chinese people, i.e., particularity of Chinese diet habits or difference from people of other countries. A query, in the form of "If nationality=Chinese Then ?", is presented. In this experiment, we specify the threshold value as 65%, the maximum number of complexes in the star as 3.

In Table 1 the query covers six examples, all possible selectors about Chinese and the significance values (S) and accuracy values (P) are:
(1)main food=rice; S=0.737; P=100%
(2)regular eating times=3; S=0; P=100%
(3)favorite drink=tea; S=0.697; P=83.33%
(4)favorite drink=cola; S=-0.113; P=16.67%
(5)vegetarian=yes; S=-0.044; P=16.67%
(6)vegetarian=no; S=0.049; P=83.33%

According to the criteria of the algorithm ($S > 0$ and $P \geq 65\%$), selectors (1),(3),(6) are selected as the initial complexes in the star. The minimum

Table 1: Diet habit I

ID	Nationality	main food	regular eating times	drink	vegetarian
950351	Chinese	rice	3	tea	no
950301	Chinese	rice	3	tea	no
950282	Chinese	rice	3	tea	no
940112	Chinese	rice	3	tea	yes
940226	Chinese	rice	3	cola	no
950578	Chinese	rice	3	tea	no
950122	American	bread	3	cola	no
940227	American	rice	3	cola	yes
940121	American	bread	3	tea	no
950612	American	bread	3	coffee	no
940109	Indian	bread	3	tea	no
950123	Indian	rice	3	cola	no
950348	Indian	bread	3	coffee	no
940247	Indian	rice	3	coffee	no
950312	Indian	bread	3	coffee	yes

Table 2: Diet habit II

ID	Nationality	alcohol	on diet	between-meal	favorite non-veg
1122	Chinese	never	no	sometimes	pork
1078	Chinese	never	no	seldom	pork
1690	Chinese	sometimes	no	seldom	chicken
1432	Chinese	often	no	often	chicken
1364	Chinese	sometimes	no	sometimes	beef
1574	Chinese	sometimes	no	sometimes	egg
2345	American	never	no	seldom	beef
2434	American	often	no	sometimes	beef
2566	American	sometimes	no	sometimes	chicken
2567	American	sometimes	no	often	pork
3545	Indian	often	no	sometimes	fish
3256	Indian	sometimes	no	seldom	pork
3854	Indian	never	no	sometimes	chicken
3976	Indian	sometimes	no	sometimes	fish
3431	Indian	never	no	sometimes	beef

significance value of the complexes in the star is 0.049. After intersecting of (1),(3),(6) with other selectors respectively, we get the new complexes that pass the threshold value as:

$(1)\wedge(2)$; S=0.737; P=100%; $S_{gain} = 0.737 - 0.737 < 0.049$;
$(1)\wedge(3)$; S=1.102; P=83.33%; $S_{gain} = 1.102 - 0.737 > 0.049$;
$(1)\wedge(6)$; S=0.697; P=83.33%; $S_{gain} = 0.697 - 0.737 < 0.049$;
$(2)\wedge(3)$; S=0.697; P=83.33%; $S_{gain} = 0.697 - 0.697 < 0.049$;
$(2)\wedge(6)$; S=0.049; P=83.33%; $S_{gain} = 0.049 - 0.049 < 0.049$;
$(3)\wedge(6)$; S=0.491; P=66.67%; $S_{gain} = 0.491 - 0.697 < 0.049$;

From the complexes above, only the complex $(1)\wedge(3)$ satisfies the criterion of the significance gain, then add this complex to the star and remove the complex (6) whose significance value is the least one. Because no complex satisfies the criteria after intersecting of the new complex in the star with the selectors again, the search in Table 1 stops. As the result, we obtain three rules:

1.If a person is Chinese Then his main food is rice and favorite drink is tea. S=1.102; P=83.33%
2.If a person is Chinese Then his main food is rice. S=0.737; P=100%
3.If a person is Chinese Then his favorite drink is tea. S=0.697; P=83.33%

From Table 1, the novelty of complexes means the particularity of diet habits, the first rule with the highest significance value most clearly shows the particularity of diet habit of Chinese people.

In Table 2, the selectors covered by the query and their significance and accuracy values are as follows:

drink alcohol=never; S=0; P=33.33%;
drink alcohol=sometimes; S=0.05; P=50%;
drink alcohol=often; S=0.044; P=16.67%;
on diet=no; S=0; P=100%;
take between-meal=sometimes; S=-0.131; P=50%;
take between-meal=seldom; S=0.107; P=33.33%;
take between-meal=often; S=0.054; P=16.67%;
favorite non-veg food=pork; S=0.107; P=33.33%;
favorite non-veg food=chicken; S=0.107; P=33.33%;
favorite non-veg food=beef; S=-0.113; P=16.67%;
favorite non-veg food=egg; S=0.22; P=16.67%;

In Table 2, there is only one selector's accuracy value pass the threshold (whether on diet=no), but its significance value is zero. So no complex satisfies the criteria at the first step, the search in this table stops. From the two tables, we can intuitively find that there exist some regularities of diet habits among people of different nationality in Table 1, while no particular in Table 2.

5 Related work

Several methods of knowledge discovery in multiple databases have been proposed [1,2]. In the paper [1], database techniques are used for knowledge discovery in multiple databases. When a query q (a SQL-like query in the form of: Select $attribute_i$,..; From $Database_k$,... ; Where $attribute_j = m$,...) is posed, a new table is joined according to a user's intents. The attributes in the Where clause are called *reference attributes*. The attributes in the Select clause are called *target classes*. The new table is decomposed in terms of target classes. The reference attributes are used to check whether the *decomposed table* preserves *characterizations*. A new rule discovered from the table is satisfied by all *positive examples*. If the new table is not decomposed because all the values of the target attribute are the same in the table, this means the table preserves all the reference attribute values. A rule, in the form of "If q Then *target attribute*=value", is obtained. In this method, the derived rule reflects the relation of databases.

Another knowledge discovery method was introduced [2]. The main idea of this research is to apply knowledge discovered from one database to enhance the process of knowledge discovery in other databases. This work includes the incorporation of the *primary key* and the *foreign keys*. The primary key is designated by database designers and uniquely identifies each record in the database. The foreign key occurs in other databases and has a domain equivalent to that of the primary key. The primary key and the foreign key serve as the links across the databases. A rule generated from the database with the primary key is in the form of "If Q Then R". Assuming the examples covered by the condition part Q in the database with the primary key are $\{E_1, E_2, ..E_i\}$. Through the links of the primary key and the foreign key, mapping these examples to another database, we get $\{E'_1, E'_2, ..E'_i\}$. If $\{E'_1, E'_2, ..E'_i\}$ satisfy *knowledge association coefficient* criterion (KAC) given by a user on a *target class*.. A new rule is obtained.

For example, in a database with a foreign key, if all examples $\{E'_1, E'_2...E'_i\}$ and only these examples belong to a *target class*: R′=value. By *deductive generalization*, a new rule (If Q then R′=value) is obtained. The KAC is defined as follows:

$$KAC = coverage \times specificity$$

in which *coverage* is the percentage of the examples in the target class which are covered by Q (i.e. $P(Q|R')$, and *specificity* is the percentage of the examples covered by Q and belonging to the target class R′ (i.e. $P(R'|Q)$).

At the example above, both coverage and specificity values are 100%. This method is actually equivalent to posing queries according to existing rules (i.e.

the condition part of the rule), which specifies the subset of the data in the next database by the links of the primary key and the foreign key, and finding the new conclusion parts satisfying the KAC criterion.

The earlier works have some limitations for employing them in practical applications:

1. The two criteria (KAC [2] and whether a decomposed table preserves the characterization [1]) both have bias toward the complexes that fall in a target class as far as possible, in other words they only consider the distributions of complexes in target classes rather than distributions of complexes both in target classes and in all data. Those complexes that do not satisfy the criterion perfectly but still reflect some special attribute value distributions among data may be overlooked.

2. The ability of the two methods to handle noise is not desirable, especially the first method is sensitive to data with even little noise.

3. The *target class* in above two methods is only a single attribute value, but in many situations, combinations of these attribute values often imply some useful information.

Our approach of defining the significance of a complex is capable of finding not only the single selector complexes with a high specificity value but also those potentially interesting complexes with relatively low specificity values and the complexes composed of several selectors. The calculation of a complex's significance value is based on the whole dataset, noisy data does not have large effect on calculation.

In the case study, we consider the simple situation that the databases have the same domain as that of the query. The algorithm can be extended to the situation in which databases have the links by the primary key and the foreign key. This method can make use of the relations among different databases for knowledge discovery.

A user can also pose a query in fuzzy term when the attribute values in a query are continuous values. In this case, the subset of the examples covered by a query is a fuzzy set rather than a crisp set. A user specifies the membership function of the fuzzy set, thus the membership function is utilized in the process of finding interesting complexes. This method is useful because the expression of people's thought is often in fuzzy term.

According to the probability theory for fuzzy sets [11 12] and the theory of statistics, we modify the calculations in formula (1):

$$P(R|Q) = P(Q|R) \times P(R)/P(Q),$$

$$P(Q) = \sum_{x \in \mathcal{D}} \mu_Q(x)p(x),$$

$$P(Q|R) = \sum_{x \in \mathcal{D}} \mu_Q(x)p(x|R),$$

where x is an example in a database, $\mu_Q(x)$ is the membership of example x in fuzzy set Q, the universe of discourse $\mathcal{D}$ includes all examples in a database. $p(x)$ is the probability of example x occurring in the whole database, $p(x|R)$ is the conditional probability of example x occurring in the case of R occurring.

6 Discussion and Conclusion

In practical applications, there is a problem called heterogeneity of multiple databases such as homonyms (using same name for different attributes) and synonyms (using different names for the same attributes). People have provided some techniques called *schema integration* [13] to resolve this kind of schema conflicts. It is not our topic to discuss the schema integration in this paper. So besides utilization of the links of primary keys and foreign keys by which we can explore through many relational databases, we assume that databases have the uniform schema, i.e., the same attributes in different databases have the same name.

A weakness of our method is that it is based on the assumption that data is sufficient to show particularity of the observed event distribution in a subset with respect to the whole set. For example, the condition part of a user's query only covers a few examples in one database and discovered complexes have high values of significance and accuracy, while in another database, the query covers many examples but discovered complexes have relatively low values of significance and accuracy. In the first case, a complex's high accuracy on the training data does not mean high accuracy on future data from a statistical viewpoint, because the calculation of accuracy of a complex is based on a few examples.

There are two alternatives to deal with this problem. The first one is to use estimating accuracy instead of the accuracy in the training dataset as the validity criterion. We can use the *far more pessimistic estimate* method adopted in C4.5 [14] to calculate the estimating accuracy of a complex. Another one is to add another weight P(R) to the formula (1):

$$S = P(R|Q) \times P(R) \times log\frac{P(R|Q)}{P(Q)}$$

$$= P(R \wedge Q) \times log \frac{P(R|Q)}{P(Q)}$$

Thus, the weight before log becomes the joint probability of R and Q. If the number of examples in a database that satisfy Q is too small, the significance of the complexes found in this database are also relatively small. The results of the case study of section 4 is the same after applying the modified significance measure.

Till now selecting the most appropriate parameter mainly depends on the practical application and a user's experience. In the case study of section 4, if we choose smaller threshold value, we can still get the same order of result rules, because complexes with the higher accuracy are reinforced according to definition of the significance. The order of rules sorted by descending significance value is not very sensitive to the choice of parameter, although in some cases adjusting these values may lead to some different results. Another problem is the overlapping of complexes' information. Although information of some complexes is overlapping, we also keep them in the result list because sometimes their accuracy values are different. It's also our future work to derive more concise knowledge which is easy for users to analyse.

Acknowledgements

We gratefully thank Dr Hongjun Lu and Manoranjan Dash for their valuable comments on earlier drafts of this paper.

Reference

1. J. P. Yoon and L. Kerschberg. A framework for knowledge discovery and evolution in databases. In *IEEE Transactions on Knowledge and Data Engineering 5(6)*, pages 973–979, December 1993.
2. J. S. Ribeiro, K. A. Kaufman, and L. Kerschberg. Knowledge discovery from multiple databases. In *Proceedings of KDD-95*, pages 240–245, 1995.
3. B. Liu, W. Hsu, H. Y. Lee, and L. F. Mun. Tuple-level analysis for identification of interesting patterns. In *Technical Report of Dept. ISCS. National University of Singapore*, 1996.
4. W. M. Shen, K. L. Ong, B. Mitbander, and C. Zaniolo. Metaqueires for data ming. In *Advances in Knowledge Discovery and Data Mining*, pages 376–398. AAAI Press / The MIT Press, 1996.

5. U. M. Fayyad, G. Piatetsky-Shapiro, and P. Smyth. From data mining to knowledge discovery: An overview. In *Advances in Knowledge Discovery and Data Mining*, pages 1–34. AAAI Press / The MIT Press, 1996.
6. A. Silberschatz and A. Tuzhilin. On subjective measures of interestingness in knowledge discovery. In *Proceedings of the First International Conference on Knowledge Discovery and Data Mining*, pages 275–281, 1995.
7. G. Piatetsky-Shapiro C. J. Matheus and D.McNeill. Selecting and reporting what is interesting. In *Advances in Knowledge Discovery and Data Mining*, pages 495–514. AAAI Press / The MIT Press, 1996.
8. B. Liu and W. Hsu. Post-analysis of learned rules. In *Proceedings of the Thirteenth National Conference on Artificial Intelligence AAAI-96*, pages 828–834. AAAI press/ The MIT press, August 1996.
9. J. G. Kalbfleisch. *Probability and Statstical Inference.* Springer-Verlag New York Inc., 1979.
10. P. Clark and T. Niblett. The CN2 induction algorithm. In *Machine Learning 3*, pages 261–283, 1989.
11. A. Kandel. *Fuzzy Mathematical Techniques with Applications.* Addison Wesley Publishing Company, 1986.
12. H. Bandemer and S. Gottwald. *Fuzzy sets, Fuzzy Logic, Fuzzy method with Applications.* John Wiley Sons Ltd, 1993.
13. M. Lenzerin C. Batini and S. B. Navathe. A comparitive analysis of methodologies for database schema intergration. In *ACM Computing Surveys 18(4)*, pages 323–364, 1986.
14. J. R. Quinlan. *C4.5: Program for machine learning.* Morgan Kaufmann, 1992.

Rule Discovery:
Error Measures and Conditional Rule Probabilities

K.S.K. JIM, J.S.S. LAI, B. WÜTHRICH
Department of Computer Science, The Hong Kong University of Science and Technology, Clear Water Bay, Kowloon, Hong Kong.

Many promising rule discovery algorithms use their proprietary methods to measure the goodness (or error) of rules. This paper first compares various goodness (or error) measures, including average error, mean square error, probability difference and prediction factor, to evaluate their appropriateness for rule discovery. Secondly, we study a method of estimating conditional probabilities for a single rule and as a novelty, for rule sets. Results regarding how conditional probabilities affect the goodness of the discovered knowledge are presented.

1 Introduction

Many promising rule discovery algorithms have been proposed [1], [4], [11], [12]. Most of these algorithms use their proprietary methods to discover rules and measure the goodness (or error) of rules. On the other hand, these algorithms share some similarities. They mostly use if-then rules to represent knowledge and use a predetermined hypotheses space together with a greedy search approach.

Our aim is to ascertain results on the suitability of various error measures and conditional rule probabilities respectively for rule discovery.

To build an enabling tool for us to objectively compare error measures, we introduce a general rule discovery algorithm, DA-1, based on the similarities of many rule discovery algorithms. While sharing the above similarities with other rule discovery algorithms, DA-1 differentiates itself with the following:

- Aiming to be an enabling tool, DA-1 is designed with minimum inter-dependency between different modules. Various error measures can be plugged-in easily for us to get results on their suitability for rule discovery.
- DA-1 will evaluate the set of conditional rule probabilities in addition to the rule set discovered.

In DA-1, we use Datalog [15] as the rule representation language because of its simplicity and broad usage [8], [9]. However, the concept discussed can be applied to any other database languages such as SQL and FQL* [14].

DA-1 is a general purpose discovery algorithm which can be seen as a generalization of some existing rule discovery algorithms. We will first review two classification algorithms, ID3 and AQ, and one relational learning algorithm, FOIL, in sections 2. In section 3, we describe our algorithm DA-1. We list the notation used in this paper in section 4. In sections 5 and 6, we discuss search space and error measures respectively. Section 7 investigates the conditional rule probabilities for rules. Experimental results are summarized and analyzed in section 8 while the paper is concluded in section 9.

2 Other Discovery Algorithms

One of the techniques receiving much attention is the paradigm of learning classification rules from a set of training examples. [3] nicely summarizes two such algorithms, ID3 and AQ.

The "rules" that ID3 learns are represented as *decision trees*. A decision tree is generated in stages. It starts as a single node, containing all the training examples. If all these examples are not in the same class, ID3 checks every possible attribute test and sorts these tests using a function called *entropy*. Entropy measures how well an attribute test classifies the training examples. The lower the entropy, the better the test. ID3 selects the attribute test yielding the minimum entropy and expands the tree until every leaf node contains examples of one class only.

Unlike ID3, the AQ algorithm generates a set of if-then classification rules. This is useful for expert system applications based on the production rule paradigm. Such rules are often more comprehensible and compact than decision trees [10].

For each class, AQ generates a set of propositional rules. This generation occurs in stages; each stage generates a single rule, and then it removes the examples the rule covers from the training set. This step is repeated until enough rules are found to cover all the positive examples of the chosen class. This whole process is repeated for each class.

To generate a single rule, AQ first selects a "seed" example for the rule to cover and starts with the most general rule "if *true* then predict class C" (i.e., "all examples are of class C") where C is the class of the seed. The rule is then *specialized* by appending further conditions. A rule is repeatedly specialized until it covers only examples of class C and no other examples.

AQ uses a heuristic function to decide which condition is *best* used for specializing a rule. The particular heuristic function used by the AQ algorithm varies from implementation to implementation. One instance of this algorithm uses the "sum of positive examples covered and negative examples excluded" and prefers the condition with the highest score. In the case of a tie for either heuristic, the system prefers the condition with fewest attribute tests.

A relational learning algorithm is an algorithm that learns a representation for relation *R*. The learned representation is supposed to cover all tuples known to be in *R* and to cover no tuples known to be not in *R*. A typical relational learning algorithm, FOIL, is summarized as follows.

The language in which FOIL [11] expresses theories is a restricted form of Prolog. It is essentially the *Datalog* language specified by Ullman [15], except that there is no requirement that all variables in a negative literal appear also in the head or in a positive literal. FOIL interprets *not* using *negation as failure*.

FOIL uses the separate-and-conquer method, iteratively learning a rule and removing the tuples in the target relation *R* covered by that rule. It stops if no uncovered tuples remain. A rule is grown by repeated specialization: starting with the *most general* rule head and adding literals to the body until the rule does not cover any tuples known to be not in *R*.

FOIL repeatedly tries to construct a rule that covers some tuples in the target relation *R* but no tuples that are definitely not in *R*. Such *gainful* literals are evaluated using the information-based heuristic function *gain*.

3 The General Discovery Algorithm: DA-1

Similar to many other data mining algorithms, discovering non-recursive Datalog rules from a set of background information with DA-1 is the process of searching the hypothesis space of rules to find a set of rules which is the *best* representation of the relationship between the *goal* and the predicates in the background information with respect to some measure.

The input to the algorithm is a set of *background information* and a set of *training data*. The set of *background information* contains the known relationships and attributes. The set of *training data* contains some known to be true examples (*positive examples*) and some known to be false examples (*negative examples*).

The output of the algorithm is a rule set and a set of conditional rule probabilities, which represents the expected accuracy of the rule set.

DA-1 is a greedy algorithm. Greedy hill-climbing algorithms with appropriate evaluation functions are among the most successful search algorithms.

After one rule is found, the examples (both positive and negative) it covered are removed from the set of training data and then the algorithm is iterated to find the next rule until no or very few positive examples are left.

Figure 1 shows the discovery algorithm DA-1 which subsumes the rule discovery algorithms discussed in section 2.

```
1 Let R := {} /*  R is the set of rules so far
                  discovered */
2 If |R| = number of rules to be discovered, OR
    no more positive examples left, then
    stop and output R.
3 Otherwise, search a rule as follows.
  3.1 Let the candidate set C be the set of most
      general rules;
  3.2 Q := best(C);
      E := error(Q);
  3.3 Repeat
        Q'  := Q;
        E'  := E;
        C   := Q ∪ children(Q);
        Q   := best(C);
        E   := error(Q);
      until (E ≥ E') and (Q' ⊄ R);
  3.4 Select a rule r from the set  Q' - R; and
      add r to R
  3.5 Delete all positive and negative examples
      covered by r and go back to 2.
```

Figure 1: The General Discovery Algorithm DA-1

4 Notation

In the sequel we use the following notation.

B	denotes the background information;
Ex	denotes the set of training examples;
Ex(ex)	= 1 if and only if *ex* $\in$ *Ex* and 0 otherwise
r(ex)	= 1 if and only if *ex* is deducible by the rule *r* and 0 otherwise
R(ex)	= 1 if and only if *ex* is deducible by the rule set *R* and 0 otherwise
Ex(R)	$= Ex \cap I(R)$

5 Specialization

Specialization is a partial ordering of rules in *H*. A rule *r'* is defined as a *direct specialization* of another rule *r*, denoted by $r >_d r'$, if and only if *r'* can be obtained from *r* by one of the following transformations:

1. *r'* is obtained from *r* by replacing all occurrences of two variables *x* and *x'* in *r* with the variable *x*;
2. *r'* is obtained by appending a positive literal *L* to the body of *r* where all variables in *L* are unique; *L* contains one and only one common variable with *r* and *L* is not identical to any other literals in *L*.
3. *r'* is obtained by appending a negative literal *(not L)* to the body of *r* where all variables in *L* occur in some positive literals in *r* and both *L* and *(not L)* are not identical to any other literals in *L*.

A most general rule is a rule in *H* such that it is not a direct specialization of any other rules in *H*. Formally, the set of *most general rules*, *M* is defined as follows:

$$M = \{ r \in H \mid \nexists r' \in H \text{ s.t. } r' >_d r \}$$

The search network *N* is defined as the union of the following sequence:

$$S_0 = M$$

$$S_1 = \{ r \in H \mid \exists r' \in S_0 \text{ s.t. } r' >_d r \text{ and } r' \notin S_0 \}$$

$$\vdots$$

$$S_{i+1} = \{ r \in H \mid \exists r' \in S_i \text{ s.t. } r' >_d r \text{ and } r' \notin S_0 \cup S_1 \cup \ldots \cup S_i \}$$

i.e., $N = S_0 \cup S_1 \cup \ldots$

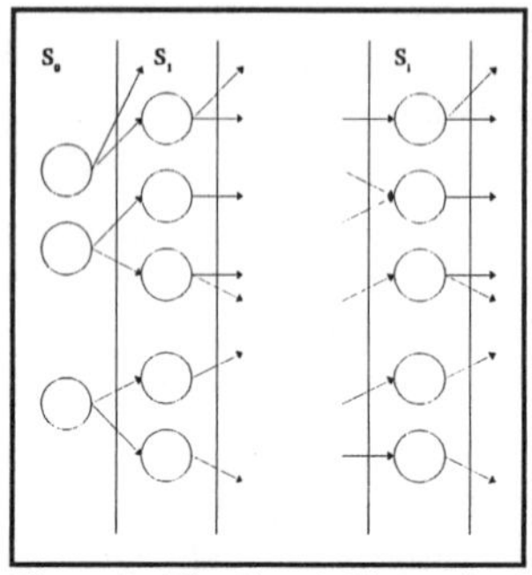

Figure 2: The Search Network of DA-1

Taking testing data set T2 (section 8) as an example, the background information contains several family trees. It includes the predicates *male/1*, *female/1*, *father/2* and *mother/2*. The target relation to be discovered is *husband/2*.

The most general rules are:

```
husband(A, B) :-  male(A), male(B).
```

```
husband(A, B) :- male(A), female(B).
husband(A, B) :- male(A), father(B, C).
husband(A, B) :- male(A), mother(C, B).
husband(A, B) :- female(A), male(B).
    ⋮
```

After evaluating all most general rules, DA-1 finds that the rule

r_1: `husband(A, B) :- father(A, C), mother(B, D).`

has the least error with respect to the error measure *PD* (section 6). It then specializes r_1 and generates the following rules:

```
husband(A, A) :- father(A, C), mother(A, D).
husband(A, B) :- father(A, A), mother(B, D).
husband(A, B) :- father(A, C), mother(B, A).
    ⋮
```

This process is repeated until no improvement is possible. And it stops with:

r_2: `husband(A, B) :- father(A, C), mother(B, C).`

Since this rule covers all positive examples, the algorithm outputs $\{r_2\}$ as solution.

6 Error Measures

In DA-1, an *error measure* (i.e., the smaller the better) is used as the evaluation functions guiding the search engine to locate the correct path and to find the 'best' rule. Four commonly used evaluation functions, namely *average error(AE)*, *mean square error (MSE)*, *probability difference (PD)* and *prediction factor (PF)* are presented in following subsections. They are subsequently investigated using DA-1 to get feed back on their suitability for rule discovery. Our experiments show that using DA-1 with these *error measures* yields correct or good rules without any application specific heuristics. Many papers suggest using heuristics in rule discovery (e.g., [12]). However, in order to make the algorithm and the system widely applicable, as few heuristics as possible should be used.

6.1 Average Error (AE)

When a rule is not perfect, an error occurs when

i) a positive example cannot be deduced by the rule; or
ii) a negative example is deducible by the rule.

The average error (*AE*) is the sum of those error divided by the total number of examples:

$$AE(r)=\frac{\sum_{ex\in Ex}|Ex^{+}(ex)-r(ex)|}{|Ex|} \tag{1}$$

This kind of error measure is used when determining the goodness of association rules [1].

6.2 *Mean Square Error (MSE)*

Mean square error (*MSE*) is a very commonly used error measures [7]. It is defined as follows:

$$MSE(r)=\frac{\sum_{ex\in Ex}(Ex^{+}(ex)-r(x))^{2}}{\sum_{ex\in Ex}Ex(ex)} \quad \textbf{(2)}$$

6.3 *Probability Difference (PD)*

Probability difference (*PD*) is a goodness measure defined as:

$$PD(r)=\frac{\sum_{ex\in Ex^{+}}r(ex)}{\sum_{ex\in Ex^{+}}Ex^{+}(ex)}-\frac{\sum_{ex\in Ex^{-}}r(ex)}{\sum_{ex\in Ex^{-}}Ex^{-}(ex)} \quad \textbf{(3)}$$

In DA-1, *(1 - PD(r))* is used as an error measure.

6.4 *Prediction Factor (PF)*

Prediction factor (*PF*) is a commonly used goodness measure (called *d-weight* in [5]) defined as:

$$PF(r)=\frac{\sum_{ex\in Ex^{+}}r(ex)}{\sum_{ex\in Ex}r(ex)} \quad \textbf{(4)}$$

In DA-1, negative *PF* (*-PF*) is used as an error measure.

7 Conditional Rule Probabilities

7.1 *Confidence Factor*

It can happen that the solution rule set covers negative examples. This occurs because the system stops at a too general rule, be guided to an incorrect path, or, in many cases, because of uncertain data, incomplete data and noise in the data. In these cases, a goal *g* may not be reallly 'true' even if it can be deduced by the solution rule set. Therefore, many applications require the handling of degrees of certainty (most expert systems use some measure of uncertainty as part of their problem-solving strategy). In DA-1, we use the concept of *confidence factor* to handle degrees of certainty. For a ground fact *g*, the confidence factor $cf(g|_R)$ is defined as the probability of *g* being true when deducible from the rule set *R*.

The higher value $cf(g|_R)$ is, the more likely *g* is true. If $cf(g|_R)$ is very high for all positive examples g and is very small for all negative examples g, the predictive power of the rule set is very high.

7.2 Conditional Probabilities for Single Rule

When the solution contains only one rule, i.e., $R = \{r_1\}$, we define cp_1 as the conditional probability that a goal is true when it is deducible from the rule and cp_0 as the conditional probability that a goal is true when it is not deducible.

$$cp_1 = \frac{\sum_{ex \in Ex^+} (r(ex))}{\sum_{ex \in Ex} (r(ex))} \tag{5}$$

$$cp_0 = \frac{\sum_{ex \in Ex^+} (1 - r(ex))}{\sum_{ex \in Ex} (1 - r(ex))} \tag{6}$$

The confidence factor is defined as:

$cf(g|_R) = cp_1$ if g is deducible from the rule.

$cf(g|_R) = cp_0$ if g is not deducible from the rule.

Since DA-1 stops only when there is no or very few positive examples uncovered, cp_0 is normally very small.

7.3 Conditional Probabilities for Two-Rule Solution

Figure 3 illustrates the situation when the solution contains two rules. In the figure, the rectangle covers the training examples Ex, the left circle A covers all examples deducible from rule r_1 and the right circle B covers all examples deducible from rule r_2. The upper half is positive (true) while the lower half is negative (false).

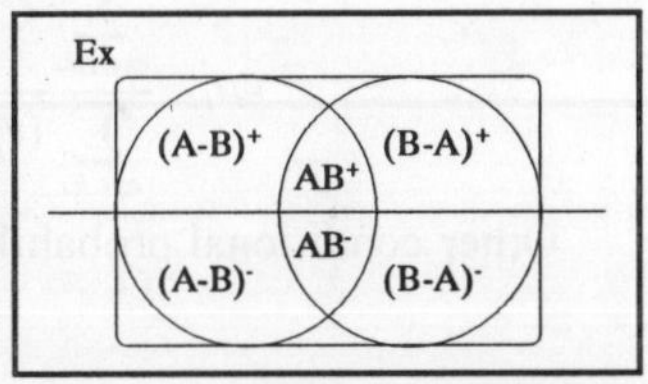

Figure 3: Conditional Probabilities for Rule Set with 2 Rules

Obviously, from the figure, we have

$$cp_1 = \frac{|(A-B)^+|}{|A-B|} \tag{7}$$

$$cp_2 = \frac{|(B-A)^+|}{|B-A|} \tag{8}$$

$$cp_{1,2} = \frac{|AB^+|}{|AB|} \tag{9}$$

$$cp_0 = \frac{|E^+ - (A^+ + B^+)|}{|E - (A + B)|} \quad \textbf{(10)}$$

With these conditional probabilities, the confidence factor is defined as follows:

$cf(g|_R) = cp_1$ if g is deducible from r_1 only but not from r_2.
$cf(g|_R) = cp_2$ if g is deducible from r_2 only but not from r_1.
$cf(g|_R) = cp_{1,2}$ if g is deducible from both r_1 and r_2.
$cf(g|_R) = cp_0$ if g is not deducible from any rule.

7.4 Conditional Probabilities for Multiple Rule Solution

The idea can be easily generalized to multiple rule solution. When the solution contains more than one rule, the confidence factor is determined by how many and which rule(s) are able to deduce the fact g.

To calculate the confidence factor precisely, a matrix of conditional probabilities is required.

For any rule r_i, we define

$$cp_i = \frac{\sum_{ex \in Ex^+} (r_i(ex) * \prod_{k \in \{1..n\}-\{i\}} (1 - r_k(ex)))}{\sum_{ex \in Ex} (r_i(ex) * \prod_{k \in \{1..n\}-\{i\}} (1 - r_k(ex)))} \quad \textbf{(11)}$$

For any rules r_i, r_j, we define

$$cp_{i,j} = \frac{\sum_{ex \in Ex^+} (r_i(ex) * r_j(ex) * \prod_{k \in \{1..n\}-\{i,j\}} (1 - r_k(ex)))}{\sum_{ex \in Ex} (r_i(ex) * r_j(ex) * \prod_{k \in \{1..n\}-\{i,j\}} (1 - r_k(ex)))} \quad \textbf{(12)}$$

Other conditional probabilities, $cp_{i,j,k}$, ..., are defined similarly upto

$$cp_{1,2,\dots,n} = \frac{\sum_{ex \in Ex^+} (\prod_{k \in \{1..n\}} r_k(ex))}{\sum_{ex \in Ex} (\prod_{k \in \{1..n\}} r_k(ex))} \quad \textbf{(13)}$$

The conditional probability cp_0 is defined as:

$$cp_0 = \frac{\sum_{ex \in Ex^+} (\prod_{k \in \{1..n\}} (1 - r_k(ex)))}{\sum_{ex \in Ex} (\prod_{k \in \{1..n\}} (1 - r_k(ex)))} \quad \textbf{(14)}$$

With these conditional probabilities, the confidence factor is defined as follows:

$cf(g|_R) = cp_i$ if g is deducible from r_i only but not from $r_1, \dots, r_{i-1}, r_{i+1}, \dots, r_n$.
$cf(g|_R) = cp_{i,j}$ if g is deducible from both r_i and r_j but not from any other rule.
$\vdots$
$cf(g|_R) = cp_{1,2,\dots,n}$ if g is deducible from each of $r_1, r_2, \dots r_n$.

and
$cf(g|_R) = cp_0$ if g is not deducible from any rule at all

7.5 Error Measures with Conditional Probabilities

All the error measures (goodness measure) discussed above can be extended to measures the error (goodness) of rule sets with confidence factor (conditional rule probabilities) taken into account. The most commonly used measures to compare solution rule sets are the *Mean Square Error (MSE)* and *Average Error (AE)*.

The definition for *MSE* is extended as follows:

$$MSE(R) = \frac{\sum_{ex \in Ex} (Ex^+(ex) - cf(ex|_R))^2}{\sum_{ex \in Ex} Ex(ex)} \qquad \textbf{(15)}$$

The definition for *AE* is extended as follows:

$$AE|_T(R) = \frac{\sum_{ex \in Ex} (Ex^+(ex) - R(ex))}{|Ex|} \qquad \textbf{(16)}$$

where $R(ex)$ = 1 if ex is deducible (i.e., $cf(ex|_R) \geq$ some threshold T)
= 0 otherwise

The next section presents now the experiments and the experimental results.

8 Experiments

We test DA-1 by running it on several data sets. Each data set Ti is briefly described below.

T1: consists of three unary relations a, b, and c; the positive examples are generated by applying the rule `g(x) :- a(x), b(x), c(x).` Random examples not deducible via this rule are taken as negative examples.

T2: consists of several large family trees, *husband* is to be discovered.

T3: is the same as T2, *parent* is to be discovered.

T4: is the same as T2, *grandparent* is to be discovered.

T5: contains data about the currency exchange rate; the goal is to predict whether the value of the US dollar goes *up* against the yen (see [13]).

T6: contains data about patients [2], [17]; each patient is either in class a, s, or i. There are three possible goals, *a*, *s*, and *i*.

T7: is the German credit data used in Statlog (see http://www.up.pt/liacc/MT/statlog/datasets.html); the goal is to detect credit-worthy persons.

T8: is the same as T7; the goal is *not_credit_worthy*; so positive example in T7 now become negative examples and vice versa.

All experiments are carried out with five-fold cross-validation [16]. That is, the training and testing examples are changed five times. Each experiment is therefore run five times. The experiments are run on a PC with an Intel486DX4/100 processor under Windows 3.1. DA-1 is implemented in SWI Prolog 1.9.2.

Tables 1, 2 and 3 show the solution rule sets generated by DA-1 using various error measures.

Tables 4, 5 and 6 provide information about the goodness of the solution rule set found by the various error measures. Table 4 shows *MSE* and *AE* of the solution rule sets without conditional probabilities taken into account. Without probabilities, *MSE* and *AE* are always the same. Table 5 shows *MSE* of the solution rule sets with conditional rule probabilities taken into account. Table 6 shows *AE* with three different thresholds *T*. As DA-1 discovers the perfect solution with any of the error measures for testing datasets T1, T2 and T3, the errors for these datasets are all zeroes and thus are not shown in the tables.

The summary of the findings following from these experiments are provided in section 8.1 and 8.2 respectively.

Table 1: Rules Discovered for T2

	Rule(s) Discovered
T2	
AE	`husband(A, B) :- mother(B, C), father(A, C).`
MSE	`husband(A, B) :- mother(B, C), father(A, C).`
PD	`husband(A, B) :- mother(B, C), father(A, C).`

PF	`husband(A, B) :- mother(B, C), father(A, D), mother(D, E)`
	`husband(A, B) :- mother(B, C), father(A, D), father(D, E)`
	`husband(A, B) :- mother(B, C), father(A, C).`

Table 2: Rules Discovered for T3

	Rule(s) Discovered
T3	
AE	`parent(A,B) :- mother(A,B).` `parent(A,B) :- father(A,B).`
MSE	`parent(A,B) :- mother(A,B).` `parent(A,B) :- father(A,B).`
PD	`parent(A,B) :- mother(A,B).` `parent(A,B) :- father(A,B).`
PF	`parent(A,B) :- mother(A,B).` `parent(A,B) :- father(A,B).`

Table 3: Rules Discovered for T4

	Rule(s) Discovered
T4	
AE	`grandparent(A,B) :- mother(C,B), mother(A,D), father(D,E).` `grandparent(A,B) :- mother(C,B), father(A,D), father(D,E).`
MSE	`grandparent(A,B) :- mother(C,B), mother(A,D), father(D,E).` `grandparent(A,B) :- mother(C,B), father(A,D), father(D,E).`
PD	`grandparent(A,B) :- mother(C,B), mother(A,D), father(D,E).` `grandparent(A,B) :- mother(C,B), father(A,D), father(D,E).`

PF	`grandparent(A,B) :- mother(C,B), mother(A,C).`
	`grandparent(A,B) :- mother(C,B), father(A,C).`
	`grandparent(A,B) :- father(C,B), mother(A,C).`
	`grandparent(A,B) :- father(C,B), father(A,C).`

Table 4: Mean Square Error and Average Error of Solutions without Probabilities

Error Measure	AE	MSE	PD	PF
T4	0.058	0.058	0.058	0
T5: training	0.17	0.17	0.20	0.40
T5: testing	0.38	0.38	0.33	0.67
T6: training				
adm_decs_a	0.30	0.30	0.22	0.55
adm_decs_s	0.18	0.18	0.47	0.18
adm_decs_i	0	0	0	0
T6: testing				
adm_decs_a	0.30	0.30	0.47	0.70
adm_decs_s	0.33	0.33	0.70	0.33
adm_decs_i	0.03	0.03	0.03	0.03
T7: training	0.25	0.25	0.25	0.48
T7: testing	0.23	0.23	0.23	0.60
T8: training	0.08	0.08	0.13	0.15
T8: testing	0.28	0.28	0.35	0.30

Table 5: Mean Square Error of Solutions with Probability

Error Measure	AE	MSE	PD	PF
T4	0.044	0.044	0.044	0
T5: training	0.11	0.11	0.16	0.21
T5: testing	0.32	0.32	0.24	0.28
T6: training				
adm_decs_a	0.21	0.21	0.15	0.19
adm_decs_s	0.15	0.15	0.29	0.15
adm_decs_i	0	0	0	0
T6: testing				
adm_decs_a	0.20	0.20	0.28	0.20
adm_decs_s	0.27	0.27	0.37	0.22
adm_decs_i	0.03	0.03	0.03	0.03
T7: training	0.18	0.18	0.02	0.17
T7: testing	0.18	0.18	0.23	0.18
T8: training	0.07	0.07	0.08	0.12
T8: testing	0.28	0.28	0.29	0.25

8.1 Measure

From the experiments it follows that error measures *AE, MSE* and *PD* work very well with DA-1, especially when a nearly complete set of background information and training examples are provided.

In some cases, *PD* yields a better result than *AE* and *MSE* (T5 measured with testing data, T6 measured with training data and T7) but a worse result in other cases (T5 measured with training data, T6 measured with testing data and T8). It yields the same result as *AE* and *MSE* in T1 to T4. This is due to the difference in the ratio of positive examples to negative examples. When the number of positive examples are roughly the same as the number of negative examples, $PD \simeq (1 - 2AE)$ and *PD* is equivalent to *AE*. When the size of positive examples and negative examples differ a lot, *PD* guides DA-1 into a different path. Suppose we have 100 positive examples and 10000 negative examples and a particular specialization step reduces the positive coverage by 10 and the negative coverage by 30. DA-1 with *AE*

Table 6: Average Error of Solutions with Probabilities

Error Measure	T = 0.25				T = 0.5				T = 0.75			
	AE	MSE	PD	PF	AE	MSE	PD	PF	AE	MSE	PD	PF
T4	0.06	0.06	0.06	0	0.06	0.06	0.06	0	0.12	0.12	0.12	0
T5: training	0.13	0.13	0.20	0.43	0.13	0.13	0.20	0.40	0.13	0.13	0.30	0.40
T5: testing	0.38	0.38	0.33	0.33	0.38	0.38	0.33	0.67	0.38	0.38	0.54	0.67
T6: training												
adm_decs_a	0.30	0.30	0.30	0.30	0.30	0.30	0.22	0.30	0.70	0.70	0.30	0.55
adm_decs_s	0.18	0.18	0.32	0.18	0.18	0.18	0.22	0.18	0.20	0.20	0.22	0.18
adm_decs_i	0	0	0	0	0	0	0	0	0	0	0	0
T6: testing												
adm_decs_a	0.27	0.27	0.27	0.27	0.27	0.27	0.47	0.27	0.73	0.73	0.50	0.79
adm_decs_s	0.33	0.33	0.60	0.27	0.33	0.33	0.53	0.27	0.30	0.30	0.43	0.27
adm_decs_i	0.03	0.03	0.03	0.03	0.03	0.03	0.03	0.03	0.03	0.03	0.03	0.03
T7: training	0.25	0.25	0.03	0.48	0.25	0.25	0.03	0.48	0.68	0.68	0.03	0.48
T7: testing	0.23	0.23	0.23	0.23	0.23	0.23	0.23	0.23	0.73	0.73	0.23	0.60
T8: training	0.08	0.08	0.13	0.15	0.08	0.08	0.13	0.15	0.08	0.08	0.20	0.15
T8: testing	0.30	0.30	0.35	0.30	0.30	0.30	0.35	0.30	0.30	0.30	0.38	0.28

or *MSE* will take the specialization step but DA-1 with *PD* will not.

PF yields the same result as the other error measures in T1 to T3 but worse than the others in other testing data sets. It is because *PF* is too biassed towards rules not covering any negative examples, even though the rules may cover only a few positive examples. This easily leads the system to over-specialized rules. Therefore many systems suggest taking the positive coverage (called *support* in [6]) into account when *PF* is used. Without this, *PF* in general performs worse than the others.

From the experimental result, there is no evidence that one of the error measures is clearly superior to the others.

8.2 Effect of Conditional Rule Probability

From table 4, 5 and 6, it is immediate that conditional rule probabilities considerably improve the quality and hence the prediction power of rules. *MSE* decreases significantly when conditional rule probabilities are taken into account.

For applications that require a binary decision, a threshold is required. From table 6 it follows that an incorrect or badly chosen threshold will only worsen the result. When the threshold is very small, almost all examples are deducible. When the threshold is very large, almost all examples are not deducible. In both extremes, the error will be very large. However, for a rule set with n rules, there are 2^n conditional probabilities. The best threshold is one of these conditional probabilities and can thus be found by exhaustively testing all the 2^n probabilities.

9 Conclusions

Our goal was to attain results on the suitability of various error measures and conditional rule probabilities for rule discovery. We have introduced an enabling tool: a general discovery algorithm, DA-1, for comparing different error measures and assessing the effect of conditional probabilities. Four popular and commonly used error measures have been evaluated and compared with each other. The major findings are as follows:

- *AE*, *MSE* and *PD* work very well with DA-1 and yield good results.
- Whether *PD* or the others are better depends on the ratio of positive examples to negative examples and the actual application.
- *PF* shows better performance in only one of the experiments. *PF* generates the optimal *grandparent* rules. However, in all other experiments *PF* yields lower quality rules then the others. It performs better only if the optimal rules are very specific. Therefore in general, *PF* is not well suited for rule discovery without complement of other measures such as positive coverage.

We also introduced the concept of the confidence factor which is a refinement of the conditional rule probabilities discussed so far in the literature. Conditional probabilities are not only computed for single individual rules, but rather they are determined for the complete rule set. If there are n rules, then 2^n different conditional probabilities are computed. We have also demonstrated that the concept of the confidence factor for rule sets considerably improves the quality of any rule discovery system. We believe that a careful study of our results on error measures can lead to wider applicable and more accurate rule mining algorithms.

Reference

[1] R. Agrawal and R. Srikant, "Fast Algorithms for Mining Association Rules", *International Conference on Very Large Data Bases*, pp. 487-499, 1994.

[2] A. Budihardjo, J. Grzymala-Busse, L. Woolery (1991). "Program LERS_LB 2.5 as a tool for knowledge acquisition in nursing", *Proceedings of the 4th Int. Conference on Industrial & Engineering Applications of AI & Expert Systems*, pp. 735-740.

[3] P. Clark, "Machine learning: Techniques and recent developments", *Artificial Intelligence: Concepts and Applications in Engineering*. pp. 65-93, Chapman and Hall, London, 1990.

[4] P. Clark and T. Niblett, "The CN2 Induction Algorithm", *Machine Learning*,

3(4):261-283, 1989.

[5] J. Han, Y. Cai and N. Cerone, "Data-Driven Discovery of Quantitative Rules in Relational Databases", *IEEE Transactions*, February 1993.

[6] K. Hatonen, M. Klemettinen, Mannila II, P. Ronkainen and H. Toivenen, "Knowledge Discover from Telecommunication Network Alarm Databases", *ICDE'96*, New Orleans, Louisiana, March 1996.

[7] M. Kearns and R. Shapiro, "Efficient Distribution-free Learning of Probabilistic Concepts", *31st Symp. on the Foundation of Computer Science*, pp. 382-391.

[8] J. W. Lloyd, *Foundations of Logic Programming*, Springer-Verlag, 1987 second edition.

[9] S. Muggleton and C. Feng, "Efficient induction of logic programs", *Inductive Logic Programming*, Academic Press, 1992.

[10] J. R. Quinlan, "Generating Production Rules from Decision Trees", *IJCAI-87*, Ca. J. McDermott, Ed., Kaufmann, pp. 304-307, 1987.

[11] J. R. Quinlan, "Learning Logical Definitions from Relations", *Machine Learning*, 5:261-283, 1990.

[12] L. De Raedt, N. Lavrač, and S. Dzeroski, "Multiple Predicate Learning", *Proceedings Joint International Conference on AI (IJCAI)*, pp. 1037-1042, 1993.

[13] K. Sankaran, "A System Forecasting Currency Exchange Rates", *MPhil Thesis*, The Hong Kong University of Science and Technology, Jan 1996

[14] P. Schäuble and B. Wüthrich, "On the Expressive Power of Query Languages", *ACM TOIS*, 12(1):67-91, 1994.

[15] J. D. Ullman, *Principles of Database and Knowledge-Base Systems*, Computer Science Press, Rockville, MD, 1988.

[16] C. J. C. H. Watkins, "Combining Cross-Validation and Search", *Progress in Machine Learning (Proceedings of the 2nd European Working Session on Learning)*, I. Bratko and N. Lavrač Eds., Sigma, Wilmslow, UK, pp. 79-87, 1987.

[17] L. Woolery, J. Grzymala-Busse, S. Summers, A. Budihardjo (1991). "The use of machine learning program LERS_LB 2.5 in knowledge acquisition for expert system development in nursing". *Computers in Nursing* 9, pp. 227-234.

[18] B. Wüthrich, "Toward Formally Comparing KD Techniques", *Workshop on Knowledge Discovery in Databases and DOOD*, pp. 9-16, 1995.

[19] X. M. Zhou and T. S. Dillon, "Theoretical and Practical Considerations of Uncertainty in Automated Knowledge Acquisition", *IEEE Transaction on Knowledge and Data Engineering*, 7(5):699-712, 1995.

Chapter 4

Learning Association Rules and Patterns

INCREMENTAL ALGORITHMS FOR ASSOCIATION GENERATION

RONEN FELDMAN, AMIHOOD AMIR,
YONATAN AUMAN, AMIR ZILBERSTIEN
Mathematics and Computer Science Department
Bar-Ilan University
Ramat-Gan, ISRAEL 52900
feldman@cs.biu.ac.il

HAYM HIRSH
Department of Computer Science
Rutgers University
Piscataway, NJ USA 08855
hirsh@cs.rutgers.edu

Current algorithms for finding associations amongst the attributes describing data in a database assume all the data are available at the start of the data mining session. However, it is often the case that data arrive incrementally, and after some collection of associations has been formed additional data are subsequently obtained. In such cases it has been necessary to rerun the association-finding algorithm from scratch again to generate a new collection of associations from the union of the old data plus the newly arrived data. This paper describes three incremental algorithms for generating associations from streams of arriving data that achieve different tradeoffs between space usage and processing speed. We discuss the time and space complexity of these algorithms and compare their performance on association discovery for a well-known textual database.

1 Introduction

One of the most commonly used techniques in the new emerging field of Data Mining is that of association generation. Associations, introduced by Agrawal et al [1], are rules that represent correlations between two sets of attribute-values that co-occur in the same transaction. Associations have been proven useful in several application areas including analysis of basket data for customized marketing programs (DMA 1992), telecommunications alarm correlation [2] and course enrollment [3].

Several algorithms have been proposed for efficient generation of associations [4,5,6]. The basic assumption common to all these algorithms is that all transactions are given at the time the algorithms are executed. However, in many cases this assumption does not hold. For example, consider a medical database where transactions are patients' medical records, and we try to find associations between treatments and outcomes, between symptoms and medical procedures, between patients' demographic attributes and medical outcome or between patients' initial symptoms and hospital length of stay. The medical researcher is interested in getting results in real time as new records accumulate and the researcher needs to see the associations based on all accumulated data. A second scenario involves finding associations between labels of articles in textual collections [7,8,9,10]. For example, given a collection of newswire articles one can ask for interesting patterns of co-occurrence amongst the topics of articles, such as countries that often appear as a topic of a document whenever some other countries also appear as a topic of the document. A potential user of such a system, such as an economic or political analyst, gets new articles about relevant topics every day. These articles are accumulated in his or her account and the analyst would like to find relevant associations based on all the articles.

In both these examples transactions arrive at different points in time, and there is a need to provide all valid associations at any given moment. Clearly, we can run the same algorithm from scratch again to generate all associations based on the old transactions combined with the new transactions without using the work already done. However, this means that even adding a very small amount of new transactions will require running the association generation algorithm on all known transactions. In order to remedy this problem we need to develop an incremental algorithm for association generation that will be able to take advantage of computations performed on previous transactions. Such an incremental algorithm would let the system avoid processing all the transactions again and instead only perform a small fraction of the work and thereby provide the results in a timely manner.

The major issue in the design of an incremental algorithm is the tradeoff between space and processing time. As we save more intermediate results from previous computation we use more space but reduce the processing time. On the other hand, if we save a minimal amount of intermediate results we use less space but increase the processing time. In this paper we present several algorithms spanning the spectrum of the tradeoff between space usage and processing time. We discuss the complexity of these algorithms and compare their performance on the Reuters 22173 text collection.

2 Association Generation Algorithms

We begin by presenting the definition of associations, based on Agrawal et al. [4] as well as additional definitions and notation that will be useful for the remainder of the paper.

Let $r = t_1,\ldots,t_k$ be a collection of transactions, each containing some subset of attributes from the n-attribute set $R = A_1,A_2,\ldots,A_n$. Given an attribute A and transaction t, we write $t[A] = 1$ to represent the fact that A is one of the attributes in t, and $t[A] = 0$ otherwise. If W is a subset of the attributes in R, we use the notation $t[W] = 1$ to represent the case that $t[A] = 1$ for every attribute $A \in W$. Given a set X

of attributes from R, define $[X] = \{ t \mid t[X] = 1 \}$. $[X]$ is the set of all transactions that are labeled (at least) with all the attributes in X. Given some number σ, X is called a σ-*covering* (or just *covering set*) if $|[X]| \geq \sigma$.

We say that $W \Rightarrow B$ is an association rule over r if $W \subseteq R$ and $B \subseteq R \backslash W$. We refer to W as the left-hand side (LHS) of the association, and B as the right-hand side (RHS) of the association. We say that r satisfies $W \Rightarrow B$ with respect to $0 < \gamma \leq 1$ (the confidence threshold) and σ (the support threshold) if $W \cup B$ is a σ-covering (i.e., $|[W \cup B]| \geq \sigma$) and $|[W \cup B]|/|[W]| \geq \gamma$. Intuitively this says that of all transactions that contain the attributes in W, at least a proportion γ of them contain also the attributes in B, and further, this rule is based on at least σ transactions that contain all the attributes in both W and B.

The key step in all association-generation algorithms is the formation of covering sets, and that is what we focus on for the remainder of this paper. The algorithm in Figure 1 is the core of all covering-set finding algorithms in the literature [4,5,6]. Each L_i maintains candidate coverings sets of size i. Associations are then generated by systematically checking all subsets of all covering sets that have the desired support and confidence.

$L_1 = \{\{A\} \mid A \in R \text{ and } [A] \geq \sigma\}$

$i = 1$

While $L_i \neq \emptyset$ **do**

  $L_{i+1} = \{S1 \cup S2 \mid S1, S2 \in L_i, |S1 \cup S2| = i + 1, \text{All subsets of } S1 \cup S2 \text{ are in } L_i\}$

  $i = i + 1$

end do

return($\{X \mid X \in \bigcup_i L_i \text{ and } |[X]| \geq \sigma\}$)

Figure 1 - The basic algorithm for finding σ-covers

Note that this algorithm differs slightly from those in the literature, in that sets with insufficient support are pruned at the end of the process rather than as sets are generated within the main loop of this algorithm. Our experiments find that the greater number of sets that must be maintained due to this modification is made up for by the fact that pruning at the end can be done with only one database lookup per transaction.

Further, in actuality our implementation begins by generating the set L_2, pruning those elements of L_2 that do not have sufficient support, then proceeds with the algorithm's main loop to create the sets L_3 and on. We do this because our experiments show that most pruning takes place in the set L_2, so pruning here significantly limits the number of items created in sets L_3 and on.

3 Incremental Association Generation

The algorithm in the previous sections looks at all transactions in generating the covering sets for a collection of data. This section presents three algorithms that generate covering sets incrementally, as data arrive over time, with each varying in the nature of the intermediate results maintained between the processing of each new set of transactions.

3.1 Naive Algorithm

Our first approach for the incremental generation of covering sets is to maintain all covering sets, including those that do not have the required support. With each covering set we maintain its support. Then, when we get new transactions, we just update the counters associated with each of the covering sets. We generate associations only from covering sets whose support was changed and exceeds the support threshold.

The algorithm shown in Figure 2 implements this idea. In what follows (and throughout the rest of the paper) T_O will refer to the set of the old transactions, T_N the set of new transactions, T the full set of transactions ($T_O \cup T_N$). The key idea of the algorithm is to compute $X.count(S)$ for each set X occurring in some transaction in S – $X.count(S)$ will maintain how many elements of S have X as a subset of its attributes. (In the case of $T = T_O \cup T_N$ we will simply write $X.count$.) Finally, we use $2^t = \{c \mid c \subseteq t\}$ to designate the powerset of t.

```
forall transactions t∈T_N do
        P_t = 2^t
        forall candidate covers X ∈ P_t do
                X.count++
                if (X ∉ N) and (X.count ≥ σ) then
                        N = N ∪ {X}
                end if
        end do
end do
return(N)
```

Figure 2 - The Naive Algorithm

This algorithm maintains all covering sets with support 1 or greater for all transactions in T_O, then adds those generated from T_N. If there are $k = |T_O \cup T_N|$ transactions, and each has size at most m, in the worst case there will be $k2^m$ sets to maintain – each transaction can generate 2^m sets, and there are k transactions total. We believe this makes the algorithm only feasible in today's technology if m is less than 30 or so. The time complexity for this algorithm is $O(|T_N|2^m)$ – each of the transactions in T_N can require generating 2^m possible covering sets.

3.2 Propagation Algorithm

All existing algorithms for producing associations are exponential in the worst case but use heuristics that hope to limit the time complexity in a typical case. A good example of such a heuristic is utilizing the support to lower the overall time complexity. The larger the support, the faster the algorithm. The main shortcoming of the naive algorithm is that it cannot exploit the support values, saving even covering sets of support 1, which may be prohibitive.

A more sophisticated approach is to not save all covering sets, but only covering sets that satisfy the support threshold. In addition to these covering sets, we save also all *pairs* of elements that co-occur in any of the transactions between the processing of each newly obtained set of transactions. We maintain a frequency counter with each of these pairs. The algorithm starts by generating all element-pairs from the new transactions. We then update the counters of the newly generated pairs by adding to their frequency-counter the frequency-counter of the matching pair in the old covering sets. Using the new pairs whose frequency-counters satisfy the support threshold as the candidate set, we start performing the known association generation algorithms. In the algorithm Pairs(S) gives all pairs of attributes that occur in some transaction in S, i.e., Pairs(S)=$\{\{X,Y\} | \exists t \in S, \{X,Y\} \subseteq t\}$.

$L_2 = \varnothing$
forall pairs $p \in P(T_N)$ do
  $p.count(T_N \cup T_o) = p.count(T_N) + p.count(T_o)$
  if $(p \notin L_2)$ and $(p.count(T_N \cup T_o) \geq \sigma)$ **then**
    $L_2 = L_2 \cup \{p\}$
  end if
end do
Generate sets L_3 and onward using the algorithm in Figure 1
return($\{X \mid X \in \bigcup_i L_i$ and $|[X]| \geq \sigma\}$)

Figure 3 - The Propagation Algorithm

It is possible to prove the correctness of this algorithm formally:

Theorem 1: All covers whose support becomes greater than or equal to σ after processing T_N is added to N by this algorithm.

Proof: What we're trying to show is that given any covering set X that satisfies
1. $X.count(T_N \cup T_O) > X.count(T_O)$ and
2. $X.count(T_N \cup T_O) \geq \sigma$,

then $X \in N$. We will prove this by induction on the size of X.
Base: $|X| = 2$, based on the construction of L_2 all covering sets of size 2 that satisfy properties 1 and 2 will be in L_2 and hence will be in N.
Induction Step: We will prove that if the claim is true for all $k \leq l$, it holds also for all covers of size $l + 1$. Assume we have a covering set X, $|X| = l + 1$, that satisfies properties 1 and 2 above, but does not belong to N. In that case, it must be that there is at least one covering set $X' \subset X$ with $|X'| = l$ (since X is in L_{l+1}, which, by construction, is created from the union of two sets in L_l) and $X' \notin N$ (since otherwise X would have been in N). Clearly X' must satisfy properties 1 and 2, otherwise X will not satisfy them (if X has support σ then X' must have support at least σ) but then we have a contradiction to the induction hypothesis.❑

This algorithm only maintains counts for pairs of attributes that appear in some transaction. Since each transaction has at most m attributes, and there are k transactions, there are at most $O(km^2)$ pairs maintained by this algorithm. If the number of transactions k is large a better bound can be obtained by the fact that there are at most n attributes total, which means there are at most $O(n^2)$ pairs, yielding a space complexity of $O(min(km^2,n^2))$. The time complexity of the main loop in Figure 3 is $O(|T_N|m^2)$, with the complexity of the remainder of the algorithm the same as that for the algorithm in Figure 1, only for $|T_N|$ rather that $|T|$.

3.3 The Delta Algorithm

In this section we present the *Delta algorithm* for generating and maintaining the *large* covering sets (i.e. those with minimum support) in the incremental setting. The algorithm strikes a balance between the *space* necessary for keeping the count of covering sets and the *time* invested in recomputing the large covering sets after each insertion. In the Delta algorithm, we balance these by only keeping the count of the potentially interesting covering sets, i.e. those with a count above or sufficiently close to the minimum support (σ). We call these covering sets *potential* covers. Other covers we call *far.* For the far covers, many transactions must be inserted before their count can possibly reach *s.* Thus, when inserting a transaction, only the count of the potential covers is updated. Clearly, at some point even covers which were initially *far* may grow to have minimum support. At this point we recompute the set of potential covers and their count. Thus, the cost of recomputing the count is amortized over many insertions. We now give the algorithm in detail.

Let σ be the minimum support. The algorithm employs a parameter Δ that defines how far covers can be from σ and still be saved – this parameter can be dynamically adjusted to obtain desired performance. The algorithm maintains a set *P* (*potential*) of all covering sets with support greater than σ - Δ. All new transactions update the supports of these sets. As soon as the support of a set in *P* rises above σ, it is added to the set of covering sets. The difficulty is recognizing the far set elements whose support eventually rises above σ.

There are two approaches to doing this. The first is to create a set *F* (*far*) consisting of all covering sets of T_N with support 1, and when the support of one of them reaches Δ, recompute *P*. This has the potential liability that even a single added transaction of length *m* can add up to 2^m new cover sets with support 1. The second approach is do without *F* and instead simply recompute *P* after every Δ new transactions. If Δ is large, this is a simple and effective method. However, for small Δ it may present only a small advantage over recomputing *P* after every new transaction. Moreover, it is to be expected that it takes much more than Δ new transactions to make a covering set support rise above Δ. We instead propose a hybrid method of these two approaches, as shown in the algorithm in Figure 4 – it creates all covers with support $\Delta/2$ after every $\Delta/2$ transactions, creating a compromise between the two approaches. (The value of $\Delta/2$ was being halfway to

Δ, but other fractions of Δ could be used, depending on the relative cost of recomputing covers as the number of transactions builds up.)

```
procedure init:
        step = 0 ; NewT = ∅ ; F = ∅ ;
        Compute P = {all covering sets of T_O ∪ NewT with support at least σ - Δ}

init
foreach new transaction t ∈ T_N do
        NewT = NewT ∪ { t}
        T_O = T_O ∪ { t }
        step++
        foreach candidate cover X ⊆ t do
                if X ∈ P then
                        X.count++
                        if X.count > σ then
                                N = N ∪ {X}
                        end if
                else
                        if X ∈ F then
                                X.count(NewT) ++
                                if X.count(NewT) ≥ Δ then perform init
                        end if
                end if
        end do
        if step ≥ Δ/2 then
                Compute F = all covering sets of NewT with support at least Δ/2
        not in P
                step = 0
        end if
end do
return( N )
```

Figure 4 - Delta Algorithm

The correctness of this algorithm can be shown formally:

Theorem 2: A cover X has support $\geq \sigma$ iff $X \in P$ and $X.count \geq \sigma$.

Proof:
The if direction is immediate. We prove the only if. It is easy to see that at all times the following two invariants are maintained:

1. For $X \in F$, *X.count*(*NewT*) is the true count of X in *NewT*, and *X.count*(*NewT*) $< \Delta$.
2. P and F are disjoint.

In addition clearly if cover X has support $\geq \sigma$ then *X.count* $\geq \sigma$.
We now prove that if $X \notin P$ then *X.count* $< \sigma$. Hence we can conclude that if cover X has support $\geq \sigma$ then $X \in P$ and *X.count* $\geq \sigma$, which proves the only if direction.

Consider $X \notin F \cup P$. First consider the case of when *step*=0. By construction, either *NewT*=∅ (after init), or F is recomputed. Thus, by the definition of F, the count of X in *NewT* is less than $\Delta/2$. A single step can only rise the count of X in *NewT* by 1. Thus, at all times, the count of X in *NewT* is less than $\Delta/2+step$. Since at all times $step \leq \Delta/2$, we have that at all times if $X \notin F \cup P$, the count of X in *NewT* is less than Δ.

Consider $X \notin P$. Combining the above argument with invariants 1 and 2, we obtain *X.count*(*NewT*) $< \Delta$. By definition,

$$X.count(T_O)=X.count(T_O\text{-}NewT)+X.count(NewT).$$

By construction, since $X \notin P$, *X.count*(T_O-*NewT*) $< \sigma - \Delta$. Thus, *X.count*(T_O) $< \sigma$, as claimed. ❑

Thus, it is sufficient to generate associations using only the large covers from P.

The delta algorithm performs well when σ is sufficiently large (e.g., a constant percentage of database size). In this case, choosing Δ a small fraction of σ, the set P remains small (and in any case not much larger than the set of covering sets with minimum support, which must be retained regardless). The set F stores only the new covering sets, and can be kept small. Thus, the total space the algorithm requires is small. At the same time, the time complexity of the algorithm is also low. Note that during the processing of most of the transactions the database itself need not be scanned, and the time complexity of the operations depends only on the size of P and F, which can be assumed to be small relative to the size of the entire database. Therefore, most operations are fast. The expensive operation is recomputing P. However, **init** is executed only when a covering set of F reaches a count of Δ, and thereafter all counts in F are reduced to 0. Thus, there are at least Δ

insertions between consecutive times P must be recomputed, and the cost of recomputing P is therefore amortized over many insertions. Furthermore, note that Δ insertions is the *minimum* number of insertions that can possibly necessitate re-execution of **init**. In most cases we expect that many more insertions be performed before the count of any specific covering set in F reaches Δ. In this case, the cost of recomputing P is amortized over an even larger number of insertions.

In attempting to achieve some level of tractability, the parameter Δ can be adjusted to obtain desired tradeoffs between space and time. A large Δ gives rise to a faster algorithm but requires more space. A smaller Δ reduces the space requirements, but recomputing P becomes more frequent, and thus the algorithm is slower. (And of course if σ is very small (e.g., < 10) the algorithm is not effective: either Δ is very small and recomputing is frequent, or $\sigma - \Delta \sim 0$, which means that essentially the count of all covering sets are kept in memory.) Finally, we note one possible refinement to the delta algorithm that can help limit its space requirements, that is to execute **init** even if no specific member of F has count $\geq \Delta$, in cases where F grows too large.

4 Experimental Evaluation

The database we used for this paper is the Reuters-22173 text categorization test collection. The documents in the Reuters-22173 collection appeared on the Reuters newswire in 1987. The 22173 documents were assembled and indexed with categories by personnel from Reuters Ltd. and Carnegie Group, Inc. in 1987. Further formating and data file production was done in 1991 and 1992 by David D. Lewis and Peter Shoemaker. The documents were tagged by the Reuters personnel with 135 categories from the Economics domain. There are 5 types of tags: countries, topics, people, organizations and stock exchanges. We treat each document as a single transaction, where the attributes are the keywords with which the document is tagged.

We report here on 2 experiments that we have performed with the Reuters-22173 collection. In each of the experiments we have fixed some documents as the initial transaction set for which all associations were computed and then in each cycle we added a certain amount of new documents and using each of the algorithms computed the set of associations based on the total collection of documents we have accumulated. We have timed each of the cycles and we report here the comparison between the execution time of the above algorithms. We did not implement the naive algorithm due to its huge space complexity and instead used as a reference point the algorithm in Figure 1 that just recomputes from scratch the associations based on the accumulated collection of documents.

In Figure 5, we can see the cumulative execution time (on a Pentium/133 MHz with 32M RAM) for each cycle for the 3 algorithms where the size of the initial set was 3000, and the amount of new documents added in each cycle was 25, and we ran 30 cycles, with $\sigma = 12$, and we used $\Delta = 6$. In Figure 6, the initial size was 10,000, the amount of new documents added in each cycle was 100, and we ran 70 cycles, , with $\sigma = 40$, and we used $\Delta = 20$.

As we can see in Figure 5, the delta algorithm gave the best performance with speedups between 143-182 times compared to the plain algorithm. The propagation algorithm is also a substantial improvement, although far less than the delta algorithm, with speedups between 6-8 times. In this case, the delta algorithm did not get to the point where it had to recompute the *P* set. In Figure 6, we can see that the propagation algorithm gave the best performance with speedups between 13-21 times compared to the plain algorithms that recomputes all the associations from scratch. The delta algorithm average performance suffers from the peaks where is recomputes the *P* set, but for all other cycles its performance is better than the propagation algorithm. The delta algorithms provided speedups between 7-162 times the cumulative execution time of the plain algorithm. We assume that for much larger datasets where the threshold and delta will be quite high, the delta algorithm will deliver much better performance.

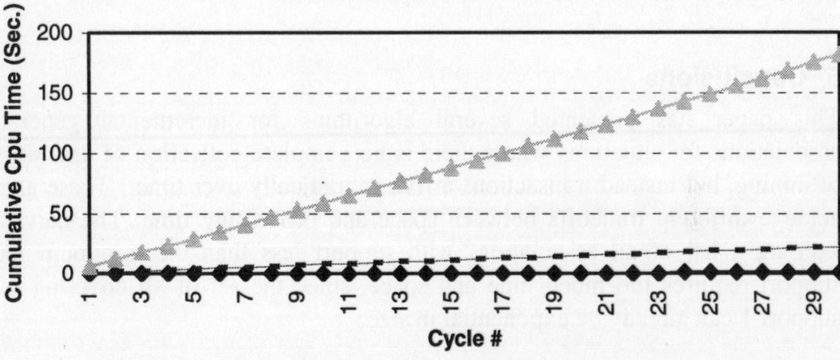

Figure 5 - Performance comparison of the 3 algorithms for $\sigma = 12$, $\Delta = 6$, initial size = 3000, cycle size = 25. (triangles = recompute, diamonds = delta, rectangles = propagate)

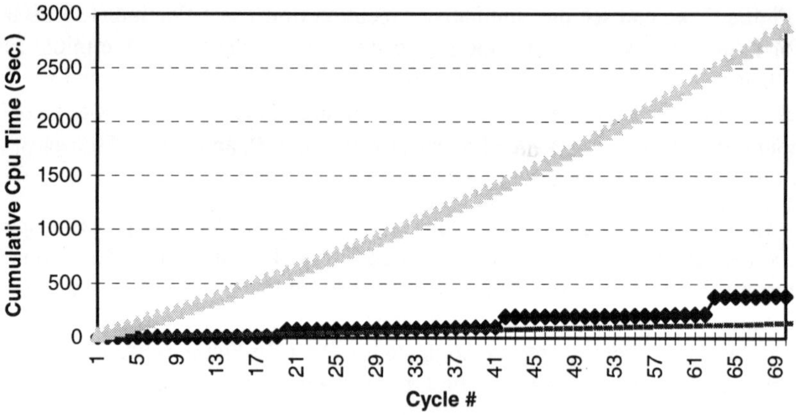

Figure 6 - Performance comparison of the 3 algorithms for $\sigma = 40$, $\Delta = 20$, initial size = 10,000, cycle size = 100. (triangles = recompute, diamonds = delta, rectangles = propagate)

5 Conclusions

This paper has presented several algorithms for incremental generation of associations for situations where there is no complete collection of data at the start of mining, but instead transactions arrive sporadically over time. These algorithms achieve different tradeoffs between space and processing time. The naive idea of keeping a list of all associations with support less than the minimum requested support requires too much time and space, since the set of all covering sets with support 1 can already be exponential in size.

We proposed two ways around this problem. In the propagation method, we filtered the covering sets by keeping pairs of attributes with support greater than or equal to 1. The covering sets were subsequently constructed based on this initial filter. The space requirement was thus manageable and the time was 3-10% of the time it would take to recompute the associations every time new transactions arrive.

The second method we proposed was an amortized method. We save covering sets with support (σ - Δ), and update them when new transactions arrive. We also have a mechanism for checking when covering sets with a smaller support, finally reach a support above (σ - Δ). Our experiments on the Reuters 22173 collection show tremendous savings by the delta method. The amortized time is 0.6-13% of the time for recomputing associations upon arrivals of new transactions. We expect that on huge databases the advantage of using the delta algorithm will be substantial even over the propagation algorithm.

Acknowledgements

This research was partially supported by grant 8615-1-96 from the Israeli Ministry of Sciences and Technology.

References

1. Agrawal, T. Imielinski, and A. Swami. Mining association rules between sets of items in large databases. In *Proc. of the ACM SIGMOD Conference on Management of Data*, pages 207-216.

2. Klemettinen, H. Mannila, P. Ronkainen, H. Toivonen, and A. Verkamo. Finding Interesting Rules from Large Sets of Discovered Association Rules. *In Proceedings of the 3rd International conference on Information and Knowledge Management*, 1994.

3. Mannila, H. Toivonen, and A. Verkamo. Efficient Algorithms for Discovering association rules. In Proceedings of *KDD94: AAAI workshop on Knowledge Discovery in Databases*, pages 181-192.

4. Agrawal, H. Mannila., R. Srikant, H. Toivonen, and I. Verkamo. Fast Discovery of Association Rules. In Advances in Knowledge Discovery and Data Mining, Eds. U. Fayyad, G. Piatetsky-Shapiro, P. Smyth, and R. Uthurusamy, pages 307-328, AAAI Press.

5. Agrawal. and R. Srikant. Fast algorithms for mining association rules. In *Proceedings of the VLDB Conference*, Santiago, Chile.

6. Savasere, E. Omiecinski, S. Navathe. An Efficient Algorithm for Mining Association Rules in Large Databases. In Proceedings of the 21st VLDB Conference. Zurich, Switzerland, 1995.

7. Dagan., R. Feldman, and H. Hirsh. Keyword-Based Browsing and Analysis of Large Document Sets. In Proceedings of *SDAIR96*, Las Vegas, Nevada, April 1996.

8. Feldman, and H. Hirsh. Mining Associations in Text in the Presence of Background Knowledge. In Proceedings of the 2nd International Conference on Knowledge Discovery (KDD-96), Portland, Aug 1996.

9. Feldman, I. Dagan, and W. Kloesgen. Efficient Algorithms for Mining and Manipulating Associations in Texts. In *Proceedings of EMCSR96*, Vienna, Austria, April 1996.

10. Feldman and I. Dagan. KDT - knowledge discovery in texts. In *Proceedings of the First International Conference on Knowledge Discovery (KDD-95)*, August 1995.

AN EFFECTIVE PARTITIONING-COMBINING ALGORITHM FOR DISCOVERING QUANTITATIVE ASSOCIATION RULES*

ZHAOHUI ZHANG YUCHANG LU BO ZHANG

National Lab. of Intelligent Technology & Systems,
Dept. of Computer Science & Technology,
Tsinghua University, Beijing 100084,
P.R.China

Quantitative association rules problem is to discover associations among quantitative attributes. Usually, the approach is to map this problem into the Boolean association rules problem. The quantitative value is first partitioned into intervals and then each <attribute, interval> pair is mapped into a Boolean attribute. Whether to partition a quantitative attribute and how many partitions there should be are the main problem of the mapping. In this paper, we present a clustering algorithm for partitioning quantitative values and a combining algorithm for obtaining a simple rule set. Our method utilizes the distribution of the transactions for each attribute value. It does not need a predefined threshold and only considers those interesting intervals.

1 Introduction

The amount of data collected by some large companies is vast. These data cover many domains. In order to overcome the situation of "data rich and knowledge poor", it is necessary to apply analysis techniques to build models and characterizations of data. Data mining, also called knowledge discovery in database(KDD) in literature, has been recognized as a new area for such research.

The variety of data mining techniques is growing and complicating the choice of an appropriate set. Whatever the technique, the essence of data mining is the nontrivial extraction of implicit, previously unknown, and potentially useful information from data. In this paper, we concern the technique of mining quantitative association rules from a large data set.

The problem of discovering association rules was introduced by Agrawal, *et al.*[1] Given a set of transactions, where each transaction is a set of items, an association rule is an expression of the form X => Y, where X and Y are sets of items. There are two factors associating with the rule. The support of the rule is the percentage of

*This work was supported by National Natural Science Foundation of China.

transactions that contain both X and Y. The confidence factor of the rule is c% which represents that at least c% of transactions that satisfy X also satisfy Y. An intuitive example of an association rule is:" 70% of transactions that contain keyboard also contain mouse; 6% of all transactions contain both of these items." Here, 6% and 70% are the support and the confidence of the rule respectively. The above problem can be viewed as finding associations between the "1" values in a relational table where all the attributes are Boolean. The value of an attribute for a given record is "1" if the corresponding item is present in the transaction, "0" else. This problem can be called BARP — Boolean Association Rules Problem.

However, there are various types of attribute in most business and scientific domains. When attributes are quantitative (e.g. age, price) or categorical (e.g. city scale, building layers), discovering associations among these attributes is more complex than BARP. This mining problem can be called QARP — Quantitative Association Rules Problem. Boolean attributes can be considered a special case of categorical attributes and BARP can be considered a special case of QARP.

BARP is relative easy to solve. Many researchers have designed considerable algorithms for mining such rules[14567]. When QARP was introduced, there is an obvious way to map it into BARP. If all of the attributes are categorical or the quantitative attributes have only a few values, the mapping can be straightforward. That is to use as many fields as the number of values instead of only one field for each attribute. If the domain of values for a quantitative attrbute is large, an obvious approach will be to first partition the values into intervals and then map each interval to a Boolean attribute, then use an algorithm for finding Boolean association rules (e.g. in 4) to find quantitative association rules.

How to partition attributes is a main problem for mapping QARP into BARP. There are two problems with the partition: "MinSup" problem and "MinConf" problem.

If the number of intervals for a quantitative attribute is large, the support for any single interval may be low, this is called "MinSup" problem. If the number of intervals is small (the intervals are large), some rules' confidence will be low. This is called "MinConf" problem.

The first problem can be solved by combining adjacent intervals. The second problem can be reduced by increasing the number of intervals, while simultaneously combining adjacent intervals without encountering the "MinSup" problem. However, the number of items per record's increasing will increase the execution time and the number of uninteresting rules. To mitigate this problem, they restrict the extent to which adjacent values/intervals may be combined by introducing a user-specified "Maximum support" parameter, if the combined support exceeds this value, they stop combining. At the same time, any single interval/value whose support exceeds maximum support still considered.

Although the Equi-depth partition method[3] is very intuitive and uses an partial completeness measure to determine the information loss and the number of interval, it may not work well on randomly distributed data. It deals with all range of the quantitative values regardless that some of the values are unimportant and it doesn't deal with categorical values. In this paper, we use a clustering algorithm to partition quantitative values and those categorical attributes the number of values of which is large. According to the distribution of the values, we first partition the attributes into intervals. If two adjacent intervals are relative, we combine them. Since not all of the quantitative values or categorical values are important, we only consider those salient values and discard some unimportant values while clustering. To different attributes, we use different minimum support thresholds. Although we don't proposed an theory to measure the information lost, the experiment shows the benefit of the clustering method via Equi-depth method.

2 Partial Completeness Measure and Equi-depth Partition

Equi-depth partition method is used to partition quantitative values into equal intervals. To deal with the problem such as whether to partition a quantitative attribute and how many partitions there should be, a partial completeness measure was introduced which gives a handle on the information loss by partitioning and helps make these decisions [3].

The partial completeness measures information loss as follows. Let R be the set of rules obtained by considering all ranges over the raw values of quantitative attributes, R' be the set of rules obtained by considering all ranges over the partitions of quantitative attributes. Information loss is evaluated by measuring the distance between each rule in R and the "closest" rule in R' when we go from R to R'. The distance is represented by the ratio of the supports of the rules.

Let P be a K-complete set[3] with respect to C which is a set of all itemsets. Let Rc be the set of rules generated from C and Rp the set of rules generated from P. The minimum confidence for Rc and Rp are $Minconf$ and $Minconf/K$ respectively.

Then for any rule A => B in *Rc*, there is a rule A'=>B' in *Rp* such that the confidence of A'=>B' is at least $1/K$ times and at most K times the confidence of A => B.

The number of intervals N with equi-depth partition is determined by the following formula:

$$N = (2\times n)/(m\times(K-1))$$

where n is the number of quantitative attributes, m is the minimum support and K is the partial completeness level given by the user.

3 Algorithm

In our method, we cluster some categorical attributes when the number of values is more than a predefined threshold. For quantitative attribute, we partition the values into intervals by using the same clustering algorithm according to the distribution of the transactions. Then we deal with a set of categorical values or a quantitative attribute interval instead of a single value. In the following sections, we first briefly describe the definition of the problem of mining quantitative association rules and then describe the clustering and combining algorithms.

3. 1 Statement

The definition of the problem of mining quantitative rules in this paper is similar to that in. the literature[3]. In this paper, mining quantitative association problem partitions not only quantitative attributes but also categorical attributes. We use some symbols in the literature[3] for comparing conveniently.

In order to treat all of the quantitative attributes and categorical attributes uniformly, we map categorical value (or a set of categorical values) and quantitative value (or quantitative attribute interval) into consecutive integers after clustering. Let $I = \{i_1, i_2, i_3, .., i_m\}$ be a set of attributes, where i_k $(1\le k \le m)$ can be quantitative or categorical attribute. Let D denote the set of transactions, P denote the set of positive integers. Let I_r denote the set $I \times P \times P$. A triple $(x, l, u) \in I_r$ denotes the attribute x with the associated value between l and u, and I_r denotes the set $\{(x,l,u) \mid x\in I,\ l\in P,\ u\in P,\ l\le u \text{ and } l\le x \le u \}$. For any $X \subseteq I_r$, attribute(X) denote the set$\{x \mid (x, l, u)$

$\in X$ }. We say that a transaction record $T \in D$ support $X \subseteq I_r$, , if $\forall (x,l,u) \in X$, $\exists (x,v) \in T$ such that $l \le v \le u$.

A quantitative association rule is an implication of the form X=>Y, where $X \subset I_r, Y \subset I_r$, and attribute(X) $\cap$ attribute(Y) = ϕ. The support and the confidence of the rule are s% and c%, if s% of records in record set D support $X \cup Y$ and if c% of records in D that support X also support Y. In this way, given a set of record D, the problem of mining quantitative association rules is to find all quantitative association rules that have support and confidence greater than the user-specified minimum support (*supp*) and minimum confidence (*conf*) respectively.

3.2 *MAQA algorithm*

MAQA(Mining Association among Quantitative Attributes) algorithm converts a mining quantitative association rules problem into a mining Boolean association rules problem. The simple constructive algorithm is described below.

1. Determine the partition of the quantitative attribute and some categorical attribute by using a clustering algorithm.

2. For categorical attributes and quantitative attributes, map the values or sets of values and intervals (if they have been partitioned) into consecutive integers. All of the <attribute, integer> pairs consist the itemset.

3. Find the interesting items from the itemset to form the frequent itemsets. An item is considered interesting if the number of the corresponding transactions is larger than the user specified minimum support *supp*.

4. Recurrently find the combined items whose support is greater than *supp* from the frequent itemsets and add them to it. Some adjacent quantitative values are combined.

5. Use the frequent itemsets to generate association rules. If ABCD and AB are frequent itemsets, we can determine if the rule AB=>CD holds by computing the ratio confidence= support(ABCD) / support(AB). If confidence $\geqslant$ *conf*, then the rule holds.

6. Determine the interesting rules in the output.

Since step 2 and step 3 are very intuitive and simple and step 5 and step 6 use a typical algorithm[4] , we describe step 1 and step 4 in detail in the following sections.

3.3 Determine the Partition of Quantitative Attributes

If the number of values of an attribute is above a predefined threshold, we partition it into several intervals or sets. We partition categorical attributes as well as quantitative attributes by using samilar clustering algorithm. Here, we assume that categorical values are arrayed according to their meanings.

For each value of an attribute, count the number of transactions, the result form the set I_C. I_C denotes the set $\{(x, v, n) \mid x \in I$, v is the value of attribute x, $n \in P$ is the number of transactions in D$\}$.

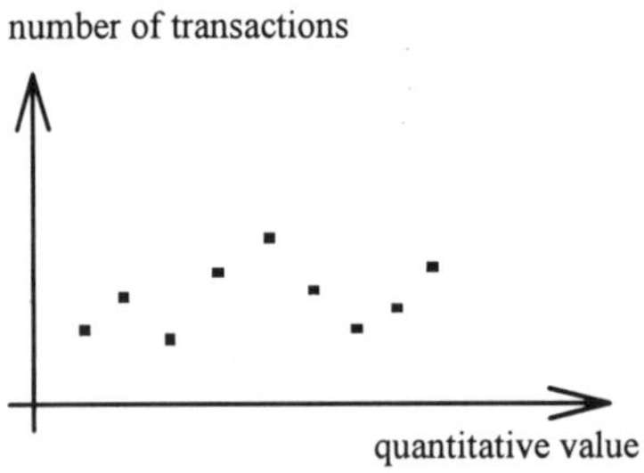

Figure 1 dot graph

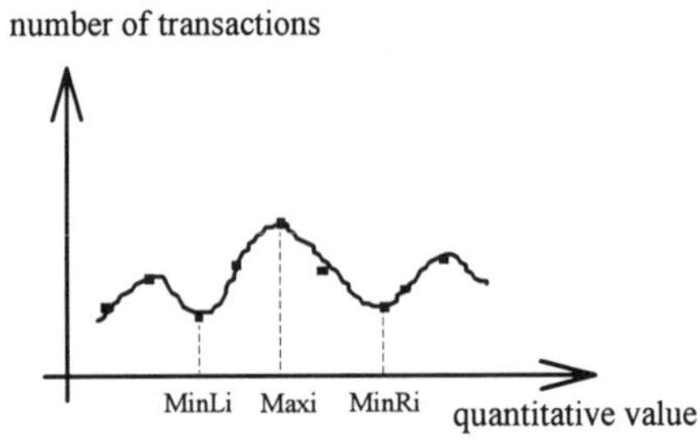

Figure 2 curve graph

For any attribute x, we can map the corresponding set I_C to a two-dimension graph as in Figure 1. The x axis denotes the value of the attribute while the y axis denotes the number of the corresponding transactions in D. If we draw a curve through the dots, we get the graph in Figure 2. The line fluctuates because the number of transactions for different value is different. For each local Maximum point Max_i, there are two local Minimum points $MinL_i$ and $MinR_i$. We get Sum_i by suming all of the number of transactions between $MinL_i$ and $MinR_i$. Then we sum all of the Sum_i and divide the total value S by K which is the number of local maximum point. The *supp* is set to the value $c \cdot S_{ave}$, where c>0 is a real number associating with the problem, S_{ave} is the average value.

In this way, the width of the intervals (or the number of values in the intervals) may be different. If Sum_i is greater than S_{ave}, then we say that the attribute in the interval between $MinL_i$ and $MinR_i$ is interesting. There are three problems with this approach.

1) S_{ave}'s representation. If there is a maximum value Sum_i much more than the others or/and a minimum Sum_j much more less the others, then the average value will not be representative. S_{ave} should not approximate $\max\{Sum_i\}$ or $\min\{Sum_i\}$ when the values of Sum_i distribute randomly.

2) Information loss. If we discard the intervals which have less transactions than the average, there will be much information loss. Although the number of the transactions is few, an attribute interval may be interesting when combining with its neighbors.

3) Value discrimination. If the numbers of transactions in each interval are nearly equal to each other, then each Sum_i approximates to S_{ave}. It is difficult to discriminate which interval is more interesting than others.

For the first problem, we adopt the following method to solve it. Before we compute the average number of the local maximum, we subtract the values $\max\{Sum_i\}$ and $\min\{Sum_i\}$ from the sum S and 2 from K. In this way, the average will usually represent the expected value.

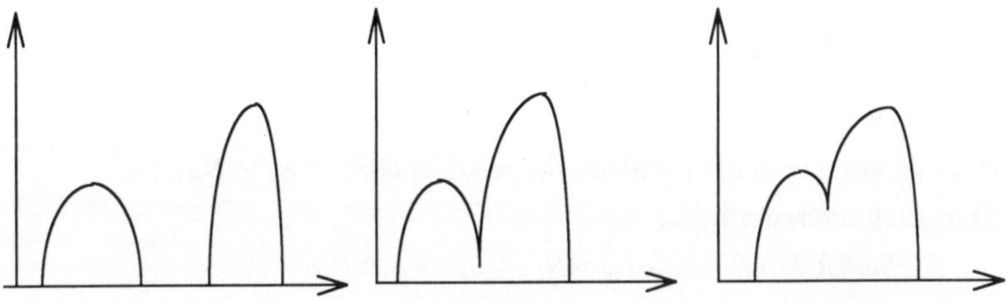

a. Long Gap b. Low Nadir c. Combining

Figure 3 Combining Neighbors

For the second problem, we adopt the method of combining adjacent intervals. If an interval's width is narrow and the interval is close enough with its neighbor and the nadir between them is close to the lower local maximum, then we combine the two intervals. This idea can be intuitively expressed in Figure 3.

There is a tradeoff between information loss and too many intervals which will lead to too many rules. In addition to combining intervals, we can reduce the information loss by keeping more intervals at the cost of increasing the number of rules which are not interesting. Some researchers[345] adopt the method of generating enough rules first, then using some interest measure to delete the uninteresting rules in the output.

For the third problem, we can combine some adjacent intervals and consider the width of the intervals to solve it. The combining method is the same with that mentioned above. The ratio of the number of transactions and the number of values is also considered. If $Sum_i/(MinR_i - MinL_i) > S/(MinR - MinL)$, then we say that the interval corresponding to Sum_i is interesting, where $MinR$ and $MinL$ are the maximum and minimum value that the attribute can have respectively.

The clustering partition algorithm can be briefly described below.

for each attribute (the number of values $> N$) do

1) Count the number of transactions for each value

2) Find all local maximum zeniths among the numbers and their two adjacent nadirs to determine the intervals

3) For each interval i between the adjacent nadirs, compute the number of transactions Sum_i

4) Combine such two intervals that their supports are below *supp* and their width is narrow and they are close enough and the nadir between them is close to the lower maximum

5) Compute all Sum_i except the two values max{ Sum_i } and min{ Sum_i }, conserve to S

6) Compute the average number of transactions and conserve to S_{ave}

7) Find all the intervals that Sum_i is greater than $c \cdot S_{ave}$, where $c>0$ is a real number associating with the problem, the result is conserved to S_{tmp}

8) For each interval j in S_{tmp} do

if $Sum_i/(MinR_i - MinL_i) > S/(MinR - MinL)$

then conserve interval j to S_{res}

Where *MinR* and *MinL* are the max and min value that the attribute can have respectively.

The interesting intervals are all stored in the set S_{res}.

3.4 Combining Adjacent Quantitative Algorithm

Apart from the combining operation used for obtaining enough support as discussed in section 3.3, we also combine some intervals whose supports are above *supp*.

To illustrate the reason why we combine adjacent intervals, let us consider the following rules:

<Age=20..25> => <Cars=1..2> (3% support, 70% confidence)

<Age=26..30> => <Cars=1..2> (4% support, 70% confidence)

At this situation, we can combine the two rules and generate a new one:

<Age=20..30> => <Cars=1..2> (7% support, 70%confidence)

It can be seen that we lose little information and the lost information (the support of some small intervals) is not important. Even if the two rules are a little different, this doesn't significantly influence the information held by the rules. However, the number of rules decreased and the rule set is simplified.

We do not combine the adjacent quantitative intervals whose supports are above *supp* when we determine the frequent items of a single attribute. If we combine the intervals at that time, some information may be lost. For example, A=>C (50% confidence), B=>D (70% confidence), A and B are adjacent intervals of the same attribute, C and D are different attributes. However, if A and B are combined in the early state, we may not get the two rules because the confidence may be lower than *conf* (e.g. 40%), AB=>C (e.g. 28% confidence) AB=>D (e.g. 35% confidence).

Combining adjacent quantitative attribute intervals is applied only when two adjacent intervals of an attribute appear with other same items in an item set. As to the above example, we do not combine the item <Age=20..25> and <Age=26..30> until we have the sets {<Age=20..25>, <Cars=1..2>} and {<Age=26..30>, <Cars=1..2>}. Then we produce the set {<Age=20..30>, <Cars=1...2>}. At the same time, in order to avoid too much information loss, we do not discard the two small interval sets immediately. They may combine with other items and achieve the minimum confidence when generating rules, while the combined set may not.

The combining algorithm can be briefly described below.

at the *k*th step of the algorithm for finding the frequent itemsets

1) Find the tuples which are comprised of same attributes.

2) If one of the attributes is quantitative and the two corresponding intervals are adjacent and other attribute values/intervals are same,

then combine the two tuples

4. Experiment Results

We assessed the effectiveness of our approach by experimenting with a real-life dataset. The data had 8 attributes: 6 quantitative and 2 categorical. The quantitative attribute is: population(pop), average income(avi), high-level-cigarette(hlc), middle-level-cigarette(mlc), low-level-cigarette(llc), age(age); the categorical attribute is: city name, city scale. There are 30,000 records in the data.

When using equi-depth method to partition quantitative attribute, we generate few useful rules because most of the rules are over general. For example, <avi=800..1500> = > <hlc=10..40>(5.6% supp, 85% conf). When we partition the intervals smaller,the number of transactions can't achieve the minimum support *supp*.

Table 1. Number of Intervals(NOI) and Interesting Intervals (II)

algorithm	class	pop	avi	hlc	mlc	llc	qua
Clustering Algorithm	NOI	8	6	5	7	6	5
	II	5	4	3	4	4	3
Equi-depth Algorithm	NOI	7	4	3	6	5	6
	II	4	3	3	4	3	3

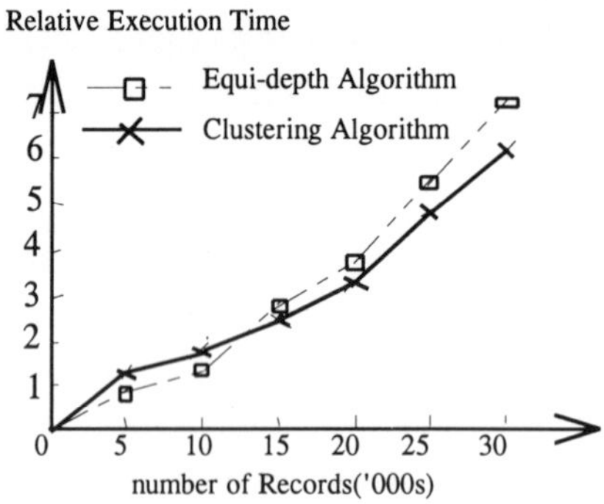

Figure 4. Execution Time

When using clustering algorithm to partition the quantitative attribute, we got many useful rules. Comparing with the above example, we got <avi=1000..1500>=> <hlc=10..18>(4.5% supp, 78% conf). From this rules, we can recognize that most people whose income above 1000 bought high-level-cigarette(hlc) between 10 and 18. Table 1 shows the number of intervals partitioned by the two methods and that of the corresponding interesting intervals (above the supp and not over general). Figure 4 shows the relative time comparing the two methods. Comparing with equi-depth algorithm, the clustering algorithm produces more interesting intervals and more interesting rules (50 to 35) while the running time is comparable.

5 Conclusion

Mining association rules problem was first introduced in 1993[1] and mining quantitative association rules problem was introduced in 1996[3]. The algorithm presented in the second literature has been shown effective. It converts the problem of mining quantitative association rules to the problem of mining Boolean association rules. However, the method for partitioning quantitative values into intervals may not work well on randomly distributed data, especially on highly skewed data. In order to achieve enough support, the algorithm has to combine adjacent values as long as their supports are less than the user-specified minum support. In this way, the partitioned intervals contain the whole domain of the attribute. In this paper, we use a clustering algorithm for partitioning quantitative values. According to the distribution of the number of transactions of each attribute value, the algorithm partitions quantitative attribute into several intervals. Then we use the average number of transactions among all the intervals as the minimum support to choose interesting intervals. In order to simplify the rule set while simultaneously reduce information loss, we combine adjacent quantitative values when generating item sets which contain more than one attribute. This method avoid predetermining a minimum support value and only considering some uninteresting intervals. Moreover, the intervals partitioned by our method are more representative than the equi-depth method. So the clustering algorithm may generate more useful rules than equi-depth algorithm.

Reference

1. R. Agrawal, T. Imielinski, and A. Swami, "Mining Association Rules between sets of items in large databases." In Proc. of the ACM SIGMOD Conference on Management of Data, p207-216, Washington D. C, may 1993.

2. P.R. Limb and G.J.Meggs, "Data Mining- Tools and Techniques". BT Technol Journal, 12, No. 4. p32-41, October 1994.

3. R. Srikant and R. Agrawal, " Mining Quantitative Association Rules in Large Relational Tables". In Proc. of the ACM SIGMOD Conference on Management of Data.

4. R.Agrawal and R. Srikant, " Fast Algorithm for Mining Association Rules". In Proc. of the 20th Int'l Conference on Very Large Databases Santiago, Chile, 1994.

5. R.Srikant and R.Agrawal," Mining Generalized Association Rules". In Proc. of the 21st Int'l Conference on Very Large Databases, 1995.

6. M.Houtsma and A.Swami, "Set-oriented Mining of Association Rules". In Int'l Conference on Data Engineering, Taipei, Taiwan, March, 1995.

7. H. Mannila, H. Toivonen and A.I.verkamo, "Efficient Algorithms for Discovering Association Rules". In KDD-94: AAAI Workshop on Knowledge Discovery Databases P181-192, Seattle, Washington, July, 1994.

EPSILON FOCUSING—A STRATEGY FOR ACTIVE EXAMPLE SELECTION

PARTHA NIYOGI
Artificial Intelligence Laboratory
Massachusetts Institute of Technology, USA

KAH-KAY SUNG
Department of Information Systems & Computer Science
National University of Singapore, Singapore

In most classical formulations of learning from examples, a *passive* learner is presented with examples randomly drawn. Here we discuss the ϵ-focusing strategy to *actively* choose examples for concept learning. We describe the local focused property that functions must have for such a strategy to work. Finally, we develop a heuristic motivated by ϵ-focusing for a practical human face detection task.

1 Introduction

Many problems in machine learning can be cast within a framework where the learner attempts to approximate an unknown target function on the basis of examples provided to it. A formal analysis of such learning problems suggests that the sample complexity of learning is often unreasonably high, i.e., the number of examples the learner would need to collect in order to provably be within an ϵ-width of the target function is much higher than the number of examples typically available in real world learning situations. Crucially, however, the formal analyses typically assume a *passive* learner who is presented examples that are randomly drawn from the space of possible examples. In this paper, we would like to explore the possibility of a more *active* scheme where the learner collects examples that are relevant to the task at hand.

As we shall see, in some cases, knowledge that the function lies within some ϵ-ball (in function space) might directly translate (due to locality properties) into knowledge about the regions of the domain X over which the target function values are uncertain. The learner can then zoom (*epsilon-focus*) in on this region of uncertainty, and sample there. This gives rise to a recursive ϵ-focusing strategy where the learner starts out with a few preliminary examples that provide a loose estimate of the target function. It then derives a region on the domain where it should attempt to collect more examples. These new well chosen examples tighten the learner's estimates and then again allows it to rederive a smaller region of the domain where it should collect examples. The process is repeated in this fashion.

We begin with an illustrative example. We then go on to generalize the approach to arbitrary function classes that share a *local focused* property that allows the epsilon focusing strategy to work. Finally, as a concrete real world application, we describe a face detection system that learns with fewer examples by utilizing such an epsilon focusing strategy in practice.

2 A Simple Illustrative Example

Suppose we want to PAC [7] learn (with (ϵ, δ) accuracy) the following class of indicator functions from $[0,1]$ to $\{0,1\}$.

$$\mathcal{F} = \{1_{[a,1]} : 0 \leq a 1\}$$

Further suppose the distribution P on $[0,1]$ according to which data is drawn is known and is uniform. It is known that a *passive* learner would take at least $\Omega((1/\epsilon)\ln(1/\delta))$ examples to do so. We suggest the following k-step strategy which seeks examples from successively smaller well-focused regions of the domain to learn this class in $\Omega((k/\epsilon^{2k})\ln(k/\delta)$ examples.

2.1 The ϵ-focusing Algorithm (1)

The learning occurs over k (k can be arbitrarily chosen) stages.

1. Draw enough examples to learn the target with $\epsilon^{1/k}$ accuracy with δ/k confidence. Obtain hypothesis $1_{[\hat{a_1},1]}$.

2. Now ask for examples drawn uniformly at random from the region $[\hat{a_1} - \epsilon^{1/k}, \hat{a_1} + \epsilon^{1/k}]$ and try to learn the target function with $\epsilon^{2/k}$ accuracy with δ/k confidence (with respect to this new distribution over the smaller region). Obtain hypothesis $1_{[\hat{a_2},1]}$.

3. Repeat like step 2, i.e., ask for enough examples drawn uniformly at random from the region $[\hat{a_2} - \epsilon^{2/k}, \hat{a_2} + \epsilon^{2/k}]$ in order to learn the target function to $\epsilon^{3/k}$ accuracy with δ/k confidence. Obtain hypothesis $1_{[\hat{a_3},1]}$. In general at the jth step, ask for examples drawn uniformly at random from the region $[\hat{a_{j-1}} - \epsilon^{(j-1)/k}, \hat{a_{j-1}} + \epsilon^{(j-1)/k}]$ to learn the target to within $\epsilon^{j/k}$ accuracy with δ/k confidence. Obtain hypothesis $1_{[\hat{a_j},1]}$.

4. Stop with hypothesis $1_{[\hat{a_k},1]}$.

2.2 The Spirit of ε-focusing

Rather than learn at one step by collecting the requisite number of examples for (ϵ, δ) learning, the method of ϵ-focusing collects a few examples to make a loose ($\epsilon^{1/k}$ accurate) estimate—it then derives a region of interest ($[\hat{a_{j-1}} - \epsilon^{(j-1)/k}, \hat{a_{j-1}} + \epsilon^{(j-1)/k}]$ at the jth step) from where it collects further examples. It keeps refining its estimates by these further examples and eventually narrows down to the target function. For the example considered, the sample complexity is provably reduced to $O((k/\epsilon^{2/k})\ln(k/\delta))$. This is lower than the lower bound on *passive* learning.

There are two useful directions we pursue in the rest of this paper. First, on a theoretical note, we generalize the approach to arbitrary function classes and describe conditions necessary for the provable reduction in sample complexity by ϵ-focusing. Second, on a more practical note, we describe a "boot-strapping" example selection strategy that is motivated by ϵ-focusing to improve the performance of a face detection system.

3 Generalization of Epsilon-focusing

It is of interest to characterize general conditions on function classes for which the ϵ-focusing strategy would yield superior performance. We introduce the notion of localized function classes. These classes which have a *local focusing* property can be learned faster by the method of ϵ-focusing as we show below.

3.1 Localized Function Classes

In the illustrative example provided, the function class had the property that knowledge of the distance between any two functions f and g in $\mathcal{F}$ (in the d_P metric) allowed us to focus in on a region of interest in the domain $X = [0, 1]$ where f and g differ. We formalize this notion to derive a general bound on sample complexity for the ϵ-focusing strategy.

Let $\mathcal{F}$ be a concept class (i.e. class of indicator functions) on some compact domain X. Let P be the uniform distribution on this domain, i.e., the distribution which corresponds to the normalized Lebesgue measure on it. We define the usual $L_1(P)$ distance metric on the space functions by:

$$d_P(f, g) = \int_X |f - g| P(x) dx$$

We define the *local focusing* property of such an arbitrarily defined concept class as follows:

Definition 1 *For a given f belonging to some concept class $\mathcal{F}$ on X, and for any given $\epsilon > 0$, its ϵ-region of interest, $\mathcal{R}_\epsilon(f)$ is given by*

$$\{x \in X | f(x) \neq g(x) \text{ for some } g \in \mathcal{F} \text{ such that } d_P(f,g) \leq \epsilon\}$$

Definition 2 *The concept class $\mathcal{F}$ is said to be locally focused with focusing bound g (g is a real valued function taking values on $[0,1]$) if for every $\epsilon > 0$,*

$$\sup_{f \in \mathcal{F}} Volume(\mathcal{R}_\epsilon(f)) \leq g(\epsilon)$$

Here, $Volume(s)$ for any set $s \subset X$, is simply the volume[a] of that set. We assume that $Volume(X) = 1$. Thus, locally focused classes are those with bounded ϵ regions of interest into which we can focus in the iterative manner of Algorithm (1).

3.2 The General ϵ-focusing Algorithm (2)

The general algorithm to learn such ϵ-focused classes is as follows:

1. Begin with the entire class $\mathcal{F}$, draw examples according to the uniform distribution P on X, (call this P_1) and attempt to learn the target ($f_t \in \mathcal{F}$) to $\epsilon^{1/k}$ with probability at least $1 - \delta/k$. Obtain hypothesis $\hat{f}_1$. Also obtain the reduced set of candidate target functions (version space),

   $$\mathcal{F}_1 = \{f \in \mathcal{F} | d_{P_1}(f, \hat{f}_1) \leq \epsilon^{1/k}\}$$

   Finally, also obtain the ϵ-region of interest: $R_1 = \mathcal{R}_{\epsilon^{1/k}}(\hat{f}_1)$.

2. Draw examples according to a uniform distribution on R_1 (call this distribution P_2) and learn the target to $\epsilon^{2/k}/g(\epsilon^{1/k})$ (according to P_2) with probability greater than $1 - \delta/k$. Now obtain hypothesis $\hat{f}_2 \in \mathcal{F}_1$, the reduced version space:

   $$\mathcal{F}_2 = \{f \in \mathcal{F}_1 | d_{P_2}(f, \hat{f}_2) \leq \frac{\epsilon^{2/k}}{g(\epsilon^{1/k})}\},$$

   and the new ϵ-region of interest $R_2 = \mathcal{R}_{\epsilon^{2/k}}(\hat{f}_2)$.

---

[a] From a more formal perspective, one should really replace $Volume(s)$ by the measure on the set s, i.e., $P(s)$. Clearly, $P(X) = 1$. In our case, we assume that $Volume(X) = 1$. Since P is a uniform distribution, i.e., any point in this set is as likely as any other point, it follows that $P(s)$ is simply $Volume(s)$. We will continue to use this notation, but the reader will easily see that P can be used in general, and in fact, need not even be uniform.

3. Repeat step 2. In general, at the jth step, learn the target to $\frac{\epsilon^{j/k}}{g(\epsilon^{(j-1)/k})}$ (according to distribution P_j), and obtain $\hat{f}_j, \mathcal{F}_j$, and R_j in the obvious way.

4. Stop at the kth step and output hypothesis $\hat{f}_k$.

3.3 Proof of Correctness:

Recall that our eventual goal is to learn the unknown target f_t within ϵ accuracy (according to the distance metric d_P) with probability greater than $1-\delta$.

Consider the first step. The target has been learned to $\epsilon^{1/k}$ accuracy with high confidence. The learner's hypothesis is $\hat{f}_1$. Clearly, with high probability (greater that $1-\delta/k$), the target lies within in an $\epsilon^{1/k}$ ball around $\hat{f}_1$ (this is denoted by $\mathcal{F}_1$). According to our definition, all functions in $\mathcal{F}_1$ agree on the region outside of R_1. So we only need to sample the region R_1 which is what we do in the second step.

In the second step, we learn the target to $\epsilon^{2/k}/g(\epsilon^{1/k})$. This is according to a distribution P_2 (uniform on the region R_1). Again, the target, is within an $\epsilon^{2/k}/g(\epsilon^{1/k})$ ball of the hypothesis at this stage ($\hat{f}_2$). Thus,

$$d_{P_2}(\hat{f}_2, f_t) = \frac{Volume(\{x \in R_1 | \hat{f}_2(x) \neq f_t(x)\})}{Volume(R_1)} \leq \epsilon^{2/k}/g(\epsilon^{1/k})$$

But, $Volume(R_1) \leq g(\epsilon^{1/k})$. Therefore:

$$Volume(\{x \in R_1 | \hat{f}_2(x) \neq f_t(x)\}) \leq \epsilon^{2/k}$$

Clearly,

$$d_P(\hat{f}_2, f_t) = Volume(X \setminus R_1)(0) + Volume(\{x \in R_1 | \hat{f}_2(x) \neq f_t(x)\}) \leq \epsilon^{2/k}$$

Thus, after the second step, we see that the target f_t is within $\epsilon^{2/k}$ accuracy (with respect to our original distribution P). By our definition of the local focusing property, we know that $f_t \in \mathcal{F}_2$, and the points on which f_t and $\hat{f}_2$ disagree must lie within R_2.

In general, before the jth step, the points on which the target and the $(j-1)$th hypothesis disagree must lie within R_{j-1}. Since, we sample according to a uniform distribution on this (P_j), and attempt to learn the target to an accuracy of $\epsilon^{j/k}/g(\epsilon^{(j-1)/k})$, by a similar argument,

$$d_{P_j}(\hat{f}_2, f_t) = \frac{Volume(\{x \in R_{j-1} | \hat{f}_j(x) \neq f_t(x)\})}{Volume(R_{j-1})} \leq \epsilon^{j/k}/g(\epsilon^{(j-1)/k})$$

But, $Volume(R_{j-1}) \leq g(\epsilon^{(j-1)/k})$. Therefore,

$$Volume(\{x \in R_{j-1} | \hat{f}_j(x) \neq f_t(x)\}) \leq \epsilon^{j/k}$$

and

$$d_P(\hat{f}_j, f_t) = Volume(X \setminus R_{j-1})(0) + Volume(\{x \in R_{j-1} | \hat{f}_j(x) \neq f_t(x)\}) \leq \epsilon^{j/k}$$

Thus, after the jth step, the learner has learned the target to $\epsilon^{j/k}$ accuracy. Further, according to our definition of the local focusing property, the points on which the learner and target disagree must lie within the set $R_j = \mathcal{R}_{\epsilon^{j/k}}(\hat{f}_j)$.

Clearly, after the kth step, the learner will have learned the target to ϵ accuracy. The only way in which this would not happen is if the learner failed made a mistake in any one of the steps. The probability of making a mistake in each step is δ/k. The probability of making a mistake in any one is bounded by δ. Thus, the learner would have identified the target to ϵ accuracy with confidence greater than $1 - \delta$. □

3.4 Sample Complexity

By the standard Vapnik Chervonenkis theorem [8] we see that at the jth stage, the learner will have to draw at most $O((g^2(\epsilon^{(j-1)/k})/\epsilon^{2j/k}) \ln(k/\delta))$ examples to satisfy the learnability requirement of that stage. The total number of examples the learner needs would be

$$O\left(\sum_{j=1}^{k} \frac{g^2(\epsilon^{(j-1)/k})}{\epsilon^{2j/k}} \ln(k/\delta)\right)$$

3.5 Remarks

Now we are in a position to re-evaluate our simple example from this general perspective. It is easy to see that

1. **Opening Example:** For an arbitrary $f_a = 1_{[a,1]}$, we see that $\mathcal{R}_\epsilon(f_a) = [a - \epsilon, a + \epsilon]$. Clearly, $g(\epsilon) = 2\epsilon$. The corresponding sample complexity is $O((k/\epsilon^{2/k}) \ln(k/\delta))$.

2. **Box Functions:** Consider the following class of indicator functions on $[0,1] : \mathcal{F} = \{1_{[}a,b] : 0 \leq a \leq b \leq 1\}$. For an arbitrary $f_{a,b} = 1_{[a,b]}$, we see that $\mathcal{R}_\epsilon(f_{a,b}) = [a-\epsilon, a+\epsilon] \cup [b-\epsilon, b+\epsilon]$. Clearly, $g(\epsilon) = 4\epsilon$. The sample complexity $O((k/\epsilon^{2/k})\ln(k/\delta))$ follows.

3. **Extensions to n-dimensions:** Suppose one considers the PAC learning of a concept class of hyperplanes dividing an n-simplex into two regions. Essentially, the hyperplane cuts the simplex at its edges. Consequently, along each edge, the points on one side of the cut are labelled 0, while the points on the other side are labelled 1. Such a problem can then be reduced to n one-dimensional problems and a provable sample complexity of $O((n^2/\epsilon^{1/k})\ln(kn/\delta))$ In view of the fact that we have an effective ϵ-focusing strategy for box functions, we can even address concept classes represented by multilayer perceptrons with two hidden layers.

4. **Handling misclassification noise:** The ϵ-focusing strategy in this part has been developed for a noise-free case. Extensions to cover a situation with a bound on the misclassification noise (the label of the example can be flipped with probability at most η) can be considered as well. In this case, the ϵ-region of interest can be bounded in terms of the misclassification noise η.

Finally, some natural questions arise at this stage. First, given that locally focused classes can be efficiently learned by ϵ-focusing, we need to know what kinds of concept classes have the locally focusing property in the first place? Second, given the existence of the locally focusing property, how easy is it to compute the ϵ-region of interest $\mathcal{R}_\epsilon$ for such concept classes. Further research on these questions is awaited.

4 A Real Application — Learning Human Face Detection

We now describe a real application of the *epsilon-focusing* idea on training a classifier for human face detection [5] [6] Given a digitized image, we want an algorithm that returns the location and size of each human face in the image. For now, we shall just limit ourselves to vertical frontal views of human faces.

Computational efficiency aside, one can reduce the face detection problem to searching an image exhaustively for all square patches having the general structure of Figure 1(a). Our task then, is to train a classifier to recognize such patterns using a well chosen database of positive (face) and negative (non-face) examples. Ideally we would like to train the system with as large a set of "face" and "non-face" examples as possible, in order to attain classification

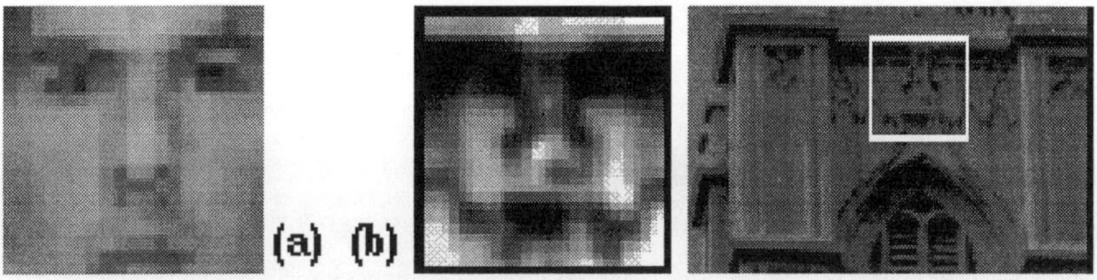

Figure 1: **(a)**: A "canonical" face pattern. **(b)**: An example of a non-face pattern that resembles a human face when viewed in isolation. The *epsilon-focusing* example selection strategy seeks out these patterns with high information value.

with minimal error. Unfortunately, we must constrain the size of our training database because of limited disk space and training time.

How does one build a comprehensive but tractable database of "face" and "non-face"" patterns? For "face" patterns, we simply collect all the frontal views of faces we can find in mugshot databases and other image sources. Because we do not have access to many mugshot databases, the number of "face" examples remains manageably small. For "non-face" patterns, the task is more tricky. In essence, every square non-face window pattern of any size in any image is a valid "non-face" example. Clearly, even with a few source images, our set of "non-face" patterns can grow intractably large if we are to include all valid "non-face" patterns in our training database.

We borrow a few ideas from ϵ-focusing to derive a heuristic training strategy for the problem described above. First, in the spirit of ϵ-focusing, we will not attempt to train the classifier in one step—rather, we break the the training process into several stages. At each stage, if we were to follow ϵ-focusing *exactly* then, we should collect examples from the ϵ region of interest, i.e., $R_j = \mathcal{R}_{\epsilon j/k}(\hat{f}_j)$. Note that this set is essentially the set of points on the domain that are differently classified by some function that is "close" to the current hypothesis $\hat{f}_j$. Points that are classified similarly are of no consequence in the training process and carry no information value. Therefore, we concentrate only on the misclassified examples to retrain our system. Although, we should ideally consider only those misclassified examples that are close to the boundary, in practice we actually consider all misclassified examples. This is because we do not have a formal bound yet on the ϵ-region of interest for our hypothesis class (a class of feedforward RBF/MLP hybrid networks).

This gives rise to the following strategy:

1. Start with a small and possibly incomplete set of "non-face" examples

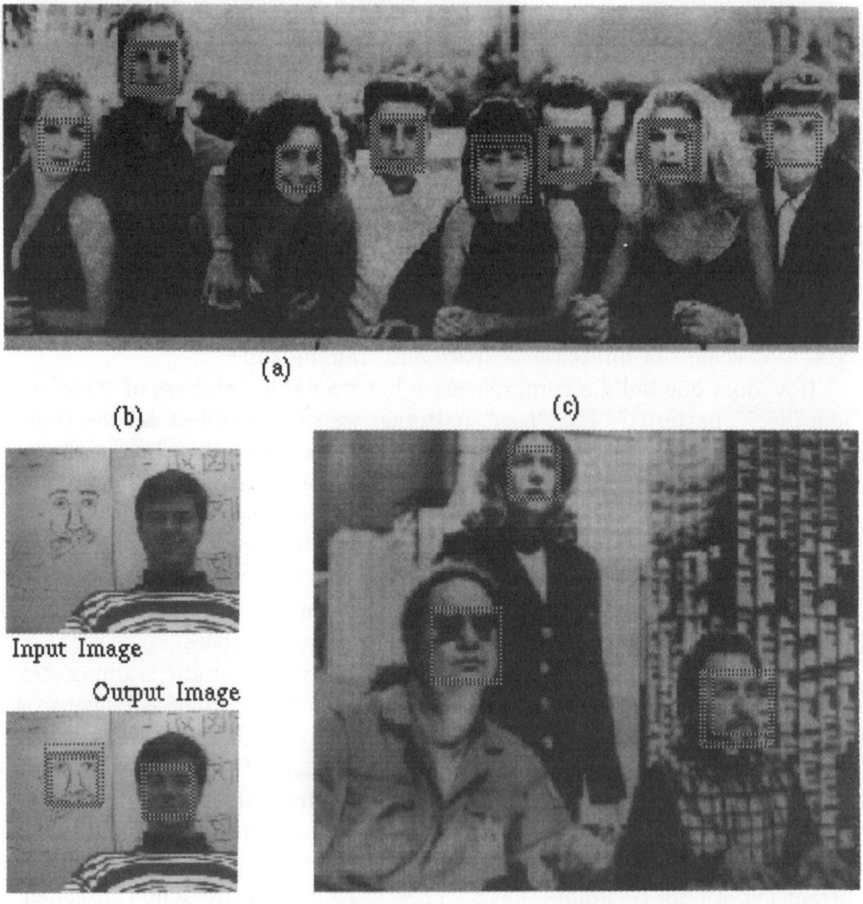

Figure 2: Some face detection results by the (Sung and Poggio 94) frontal view system, trained using a strategy similar to ϵ-focusing. (a): An image with many (8) frontal faces. The system finds all 8 faces successfully. (b): An input-output image pair. The same system detects real human faces and hand drawn faces. (c): The system finds faces successfully over multiple scales. There are no false detects even in a background with complex texture.

System without epsilon–focusing | **System trained with epsilon–focusing**

Figure 3: Face detection results on two images. **Left:** The system trained without ϵ-focusing produces several false alarms. **Right:** The ϵ-focusing system is trained with a better set of "non-face" examples and does not produce any false alarms on both images. Notice that the faces in both output images are enclosed by light dotted-squares, indicating successful detection.

in the training database. Train the neural net classifier with the current database of examples.

2. Run the face detector on a sequence of images with no faces. Collect all the patterns that the current system wrongly classifies as "faces" (see for example Figure 1(b)). Add these mis-classified patterns to the training database as new negative examples. Retrain to obtain updated classification system.

3. Return to Step 2.

We trained one such system in two iterations ($k = 2$). The final database consists of 4150 face patterns and about 40,000 non-face patterns, of which 6000 were selected in the second iteration. On a test set of 23 cluttered images with 147 faces, the system missed 23 faces and produced 13 false alarms. As a control, we trained a second system (without ϵ-focusing) using the same 4150 face patterns and another 40,000 randomly selected non-face patterns. This yielded 15 misses and 44 false alarms.

First note that system trained with ϵ-focusing has a lower total error rate than the control trained without ϵ-focusing. It has a slightly higher miss rate for faces but a much lower false alarm rate for non-faces. This is because we have used ϵ-focusing only to select better "non-face" examples while leaving the "face" examples unchanged. Consequently we are better able to reject non-faces at a slight expense of correctly detecting faces.

5 Conclusions

We have described a general strategy for selecting examples that provably reduces the sample complexity of learning for functions that have a local focused property. We proceeded to develop a heuristic for a real world human face detection problem with superior empirical performance.

References

1. P. Niyogi. The Informational Complexity of Learning from Examples. Ph.D. Thesis, Massachusetts Institute of Technology. 1995.
2. K. Sung and P. Niyogi. Active Learning for Function Approximation. In *Proc. Advances in Neural Information Processing Systems 7.* April 1995.
3. K. Sung and P. Niyogi. Active Learning the Weights of a RBF Network. In *Proc. Neural Networks for Signal Processing.* September 1995.

4. K. Sung and P. Niyogi. A Formulation for Active Learning with Applications to Object Detection. Tech Report AIM-1438, Artificial Intelligence Lab, Massachusetts Institute of Technology, May 1996.
5. K. Sung and T. Poggio. Example-based Learning for Human Face Detection. Tech Report AIM-1521, Artificial Intelligence Lab, Massachusetts Institute of Technology, December 1994.
6. K. Sung and T. Poggio. Learning Human Face Detection in Cluttered Scenes. In *Proc. Intl. Conf. on Computer Analysis of Images and Patterns.* September 1995.
7. L. Valiant. A Theory of the Learnable. In *Proc. of the 1984 STOC.* 1984.
8. V. Vapnik. Estimation of Dependencies Based on Empirical Data. Springer-Verlag, Berlin. 1982.

PATTERN DISCOVERY FROM DATA USING GENETIC ALGORITHMS

M. PEI, E. D. GOODMAN
Case Center for Computer-Aided Engineering and Manufacturing
W. F. PUNCH, III
Intelligent Systems Laboratory, Department of Computer Science
Genetic Algorithms Research and Applications Group (GARAGe)
Michigan State University, 230 Engineering Building, East Lansing, MI 48824
e-mail: pei@egr.msu.edu

In this paper we summarize our research on pattern discovery and classification from high-dimensionality data sets using genetic algorithms. We have developed a GA-based approach utilizing a feedback linkage between pattern evaluation and classification. That is, we carry out pattern discovery by feature extraction (with dimensionality reduction) and appropriate setting of thresholds with classifier design simultaneously, through "genetic learning and evolution." This approach combines a GA with a production decision rule system. We first apply this approach on a binary data set, demonstrating the effectiveness of this approach on real biological data. In further ongoing research, it will be extended to handle a variety of feature types that include binary, nominal, numerical and structural features.

Keywords: genetic algorithms, classification, pattern discovery, feature extraction, production rules.

1. Introduction

The growing glut of data in the worlds of science, business and government create an urgent need for a new generation of automated and intelligent tools and techniques which can analyze, summarize, and extract "knowledge" from raw data [1]. Most of knowledge discovery or data mining tools and techniques are based on statistics, machine learning, pattern recognition and artificial neural networks. The great challenge for data mining comes from huge databases of noisy, high-dimensionality data. Genetic algorithms (GAs) are good candidates for attacking this challenge since GAs are very useful for extracting patterns in multiclass, high-dimensionality problems where heuristic knowledge is sparse or incomplete [2] [3].

The data mining approach we have developed is called the GA/RULE approach--a genetic algorithm combined with a production rule system. This approach is based on the general structure of a Pittsburgh-style classifier system [4] [5], and focuses on discovery of feature patterns by the classification rules. The inductive learning procedure of the GA evolves a rule classifier using a known "training" sample set. The result of training is a small set of "best" classification rules which classify the training set more accurately than other rule sets. By examining these "good" rules, one can discover the feature patterns which are most useful for classification. These patterns of interest, represented as rules, provide information useful to domain experts for evaluating and interpreting the extracted patterns to decide what constitutes "knowledge", then consolidating the knowledge, resolving conflicts with previously extracted knowledge, and making the knowledge available for use in the KDD process.

In the following section we introduce the basic concept of this approach, then apply this approach first to a binary data set, showing the effectiveness of the approach on biological data. In further ongoing research, it is being extended to handle variety of feature types that include binary, nominal, numerical and structural features.

2. Basic Concept of the Approach

In the design of automatic pattern classifiers, feature selection and extraction are crucial to optimizing performance, and strongly affect classifier design. Ideally, the problems of feature selection and extraction on the one hand and classifier design on the other should never be considered independently. Yet, for practical considerations, most researchers make the simplifying assumption that the feature selection/extraction stage and the classification stage are independent. However, the ultimate goal is correct classification, and the intermediate step of feature extraction and dimensionality reduction is, in a sense, subservient to that goal, rather than being an end in itself. It would be better to couple pattern evaluation, including feature extraction, with effective classification techniques [6] [7] [8]. This then implies some sort of classification decision feedback mechanism to modify or adapt the feature patterns. Our research follows this direction.

We have developed a data mining approach based on genetic algorithms (GA's). The basic operation of this approach utilizes a feedback linkage between pattern evaluation and classification. That is, we carry out pattern discovery by feature extraction (with dimensionality reduction) and appropriate setting of thresholds simultaneously with classifier design, through "genetic learning and evolution," as shown in Figure 1.

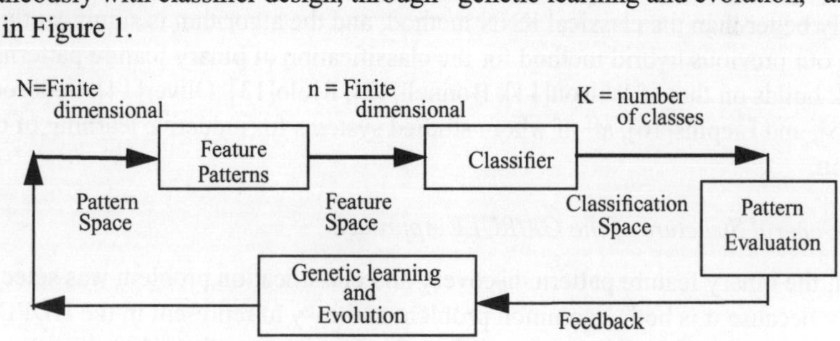

Figure 1. Pattern Discovery and Classifier with GA Feedback Learning System

The objective of this approach is to find interesting feature patterns of certain classes with a feature subset reduced from the original N features such that useful class discriminatory information is included and redundant class information and/or noise is excluded. We take the following general approach. The data's original feature space is selected or transformed into a new feature space with fewer features which (potentially) offers better separation of the pattern classes, which, in turn, facilitates discovery of nearly optimal patterns and improves the performance of the decision-making classifier. The criterion for optimality of the patterns of different classes is usually the probability of misclassification.

This GA data mining approach includes both the steps of selection, cleaning, transformation, projection of data, and pattern extraction -- two major steps in the whole KDD multi-step process [1].

3. GA/RULE Approach

One of great challenge for data mining from high dimensionality data is the computational cost. Algorithms are typically required to meet some acceptable computational efficiency limitations. In our previous research, the computational cost of the GA/KNN method [9] [10] we have used is very high and requires parallel or distributed processing to be attractive for large, high-dimensionality problems. We have explored whether we could decrease computational cost without sacrificing performance by directly generating rules -- i.e,. using a genetic algorithm combined with a production (rule) system. This inductive learning method is simpler to implement than the previous GA/KNN hybrid system, and requires substantially fewer computation cycles to achieve answers of similar quality. The system was developed for application to both classification and pattern discovery by feature extraction of high dimensionality feature patterns. Thus, we named our system the HDPDCS (High Dimensionality Pattern Discovery and Classification System) and first have applied it to two previous biological data sets (containing two species) with encouraging results (the original form was called HDBPCS) [10]. The accuracy of this method is significantly better than the classical KNN method, and the algorithm is significantly faster than our previous hybrid method for the classification of binary feature patterns. Our work builds on that of Wilson[11], Bonneli[12], Riolo[13], Oliver[14], Sedbrook et. al[15], and Liepins[16], all of whom studied systems for inductive learning of classification.

3.1 General Structure of the GA/RULE Approach

First, the binary feature pattern discovery and classification problem was selected for study because it is both a common problem and easy to represent in the HDPDCS. Then, general pattern discovery and classification were studied. As with other inductive learning approaches, this algorithm uses a collection of labeled "training" data to drive learning. What is characteristic of the approach is the "evolution" of classifiers/rules to classify the training data, and subsequent testing of the accuracy of those classifiers on data not used in classifier training.

The results of this process are two: 1) "good" rules are created for classifying "unknown" data, and 2) domain researchers are shown the interesting patterns and those features which are important for the classification, based on the features used by the rules.

Our HDPDCS, like most machine learning systems, performs supervised learning. The characteristics of the HDPDCS genetic algorithm are described in the following sections and in Fig. 2.

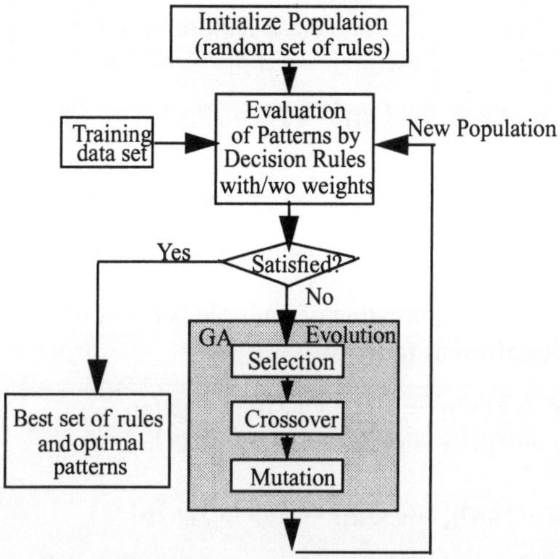

Figure 2: The structure of the GA/RULE approach

The objective of the GA/RULE approach is to find the optimal transformation that yields both the lowest classification error and patterns with smallest number of features. The basic tenet of this approach is to utilize a feedback linkage between pattern evaluation and classification, but in a way much different from GA/KNN [8]. GA/RULE directly manipulates a rule representation which is used for classification and evolving patterns.

3.2 Rule (Chromosome) Structure

Suppose there are k possible pattern classes $\omega_1, \omega_2, \cdots, \omega_k$. A classifier is a production rule which is used to make a decision assigning a pattern x to one of a set of classes ω_j, $j = 1, 2, \cdots, k$. The <condition> part of the rule in HDPDCS is a string which consists of k *class-feature vectors*, where k is the number of classes. Each class-feature vector consists of one pattern of N elements or multiple patterns of N elements in disjunctive normal form, where N is the number of features being used for the classification of that class k. Each pattern of a class-feature vector plays the role of examiner as a classification predicate for the input data pattern. All class-feature vectors are put together to determine which features form useful patterns when used in this rule's decision for classification. The <message> part of the classifier is a class variable ω which indicates into which class the rule classifier places an input data element based on matching against the pattern of each feature vector. A classifier rule therefore takes the following form:

<classifier> : : = <condition> : <message>

The specific form of a rule for a class-feature vector, consisting of one pattern of N elements, is:

$$(\mathbf{y}_{11}, \ldots, \mathbf{y}_{1i}, \ldots, \mathbf{y}_{1N}), \ \ldots, (\mathbf{y}_{j1}, \ldots, \mathbf{y}_{ji}, \ldots, \mathbf{y}_{jN}), \ \ldots, \ (\mathbf{y}_{k1}, \ldots, \mathbf{y}_{ki}, \ \ldots \mathbf{y}_{kN}) : \omega,$$

where $i = 1, 2, \cdots, N$; $j = 1, 2, \cdots, k$, and

where ω is a variable whose value can be one of the k classes.

Class-feature vectors consisting of multiple patterns of N elements in disjunctive normal form as described as follows:

$$(\mathbf{y}_{11}, \ldots, \mathbf{y}_{1i}, \ldots, \mathbf{y}_{1N})_1, \ \ldots (\mathbf{y}_{11}, \ldots, \mathbf{y}_{1i}, \ldots, \mathbf{y}_{1N})_q,$$
$$(\mathbf{y}_{j1}, \ldots, \mathbf{y}_{ji}, \ldots, \mathbf{y}_{jN})_1, \ \ldots (\mathbf{y}_{j1}, \ldots, \mathbf{y}_{ji}, \ldots, \mathbf{y}_{jN})_r,$$
$$\ldots,$$
$$(\mathbf{y}_{k1}, \ldots, \mathbf{y}_{ki} \ldots \mathbf{y}_{kN})_1, \ \ldots \ (\mathbf{y}_{k1}, \ldots, \mathbf{y}_{ki} \ldots \mathbf{y}_{kN})_1,: \omega,$$

The <condition> is a simple pattern matching device. For the binary and nominal types of features, the alphabet of the class-feature vector consists of 0, 1, and a don't-care character; i.e., $\mathbf{y}_{ji} \in \{0, 1, \#\}$.

When the value of a feature is of nominal type, each feature $\mathbf{y}_{ji}$ is a fixed-length binary string which enumerates the nominal values in order. For example, for the set of colors = {white, yellow, black}, a three-bit string feature in turn represents white, yellow, and black as present or not by 0 or 1. When the value of a feature is a numerical type, each feature $\mathbf{y}_{ji}$ is a pair of numerical values represented by a binary string whose length depends on the desired resolution. The pair of values $\mathbf{y}_{ji} = (\mathbf{a}, \mathbf{b})$ represents the upper and lower bounds, respectively, of an interval of the feature on the pattern.

3.3 Training Data

The training data consists of a set X of *training vectors* $\overline{x}$ each of size N (again, N indicating the number of features being used), and each with a known classification label:

$\bar{x} = [x_1, x_2, \cdots, x_i, \cdots, x_N]$. $\qquad i = 1, 2, \cdots, N,$

where $x_i \in \{0,1\}$, or nominal type, or numerical type in a defined range;

and N is the number of features.

3.4 Evaluation of the Rules (Classifiers)

Each rule in the population is evaluated by applying it to classify the training data set. In this procedure, every class-feature vector of the rule's condition is compared with each training vector at every feature position (i.e. every component). For a binary value, a 0 in the class-feature vector matches a 0 in the training vector, a 1 matches 1 and a # don't-care character matches either 0 or 1. For nominal types, the value matches if the value is present in the enumerative set represented by the string of the feature. For numerical types, the value matches if the value is within the interval of the feature represented by the pair of strings (lower and upper bounds). Thus, for a training set with three classes, the training vector would be compared with the three class-feature vectors of each rule. The number of matching features in each pattern of class-feature vector of the rule's condition is counted, and the pattern of the rule's class-feature vector with the highest number of matches determines the classifier's message -- the class of the sample (handling of ties is described below). Since the class of each training sample is already known, this classification can then be judged correct or not. Based on the accuracy of classification, the decision rule can be directly rewarded or punished. Based on this rule "strength," the GA can evolve new rules.

Let us now discuss the use of classifier rules as pattern discriminators. A given data sample $\bar{x}$ of unknown class normally can be assigned to any of the k classes. Thus, we have k possible decisions. Let $R(\bar{x})$ be one of the above rule classifiers -- i.e., a function of $\bar{x}$ that tell us which decision to make for every possible data pattern $\bar{x}$. For example, $R(\bar{x}) = \omega_j$ denotes the decision to assign pattern $\bar{x}$ to class ω_j. During the classification step, class membership needs to be determined based on the comparison of k discrimination functions $g_1(\bar{x}), g_2(\bar{x}), \ldots, g_k(\bar{x})$, or, say, by k matching functions $m(x_i, y_{ji})$ computed for the input pattern under consideration. A discrimination function or matching function for two different cases is defined as follows:

For binary type of feature:

$$g_j(x) = [W]\left[\sum_{i=1}^{N} m(x_i, y_{ji}) = \begin{cases} 1 \; (x_i = y_{ji}) or (y_{ji} = \#) \\ 0 (x_i \neq y_{ji}) and (y_{ji} \neq \#) \end{cases}\right]$$

For nominal type of feature:

$$g_j(x) = [W]\left[\sum_{i=1}^{N} m(x_i, y_{ji}) = \begin{cases} 1\,(x_i \ni y_{ji}) \\ 0\,(x_i \notin y_{ji}) \end{cases}\right]$$

For numerical type of feature:

$$g_j(x) = [W]\left[\sum_{i=1}^{N} m(x_i, y_{ji}) = \begin{cases} 1\,(y_{jilower} \le x_i \le y_{jiupper}) \\ 0\,(x_i \notin [y_{jiupper}, y_{jilower}]) \end{cases}\right]$$

where

$$W = \begin{bmatrix} w_1 & 0 & \dots & 0 \\ 0 & w_2 & \dots & 0 \\ \cdot & \cdot & \cdot & \cdot \\ \cdot & \cdot & \cdot & \cdot \\ 0 & 0 & 0 & w_N \end{bmatrix}, \quad \text{or } \overline{w}^* = [w_1, w_2, \dots, w_N], \qquad \overline{x} = [x_1, x_2, \cdots, x_N]$$

- $w_i \in \{0,1\}$, $1 \le i \le N$.

  When we use only binary values for $\overline{w}^*$, we interpret it as follows: if the *i*th weight component is one, then the *i*th feature was preserved in feature space; otherwise, the feature was discarded from the feature set. Thus we perform feature selection to define an optimal subset pattern and (potentially) reduce the dimensionality of the original data pattern.

- $w_i \in [a, b]$, such as $w_i \in [0.0, 10.0]$, $1 \le i \le N$.

  In this case, we do feature extraction by allowing the values of the weight components to range over some values [a, b], such as 0.0 to 10.0 (presuming that the features are first "normalized" to some standard range). That amounts to searching for a relative weighting of features that gives optimal performance on classification of the known samples. Thus we are selecting for features in a linearly transformed space. Those weight components that move towards 0 indicate that their corresponding features are not important for the discrimination task. Essentially, those features "drop out" of the feature space and are not considered. Any feature that moves towards the maximum weight indicates that the classification process is sensitive to changes in that feature. That feature's dimension is elongated, which probably reflects that an increased separation between the classes gave better resolution. The resulting weights indicate the usefulness of a particular feature, sometimes called its discriminatory power.

It is convenient to assume that the discriminant function $g_j(x)$ uses scalar values and that the pattern $\overline{x}$ belongs to the jth class if and only if

$$g_j(x) > g_i(x), \qquad \text{for } j, i = 1, 2, \ldots, k, \quad i \neq j$$

This is equivalent to

$$R(x) = \omega_j, \qquad \text{when } \; g_j(x) = \max \{g_i(x)\} \quad i = 1, 2, \ldots, k,$$

The decision in N-dimensional feature space between pattern classes ω_j and ω_i is defined by the equation

$$g_j(x) - g_i(x) = 0$$

The above equation represents the decision surface. When a pattern $\overline{x}$ falls on the boundary of this surface, it is ambiguous as to which classification to make. It would be advantageous to allow the classifier to withhold making a decision and reject the pattern. However, in the results described here, the classification of the first pattern to achieve the maximum number of matches is arbitrarily assigned.

3.5 Evolution of the Rule Classifier and Pattern Discovery Using a GA

Running HDPDCS yields a small set of "best" classification rules which classify the training set more accurately than other rule sets. By examining those "good" rules, one can determine those features which are most useful for classification. In order to find the interesting patterns of each class as simply as possible, we must keep the number of features used to a minimum and provide a mechanism by which one can foster not only accuracy of classification, but also minimum cardinality of the feature set used. The problem then becomes a multiobjective or multicriterion optimization problem. One way to address this is to add another term to the fitness function and to choose different proportions of wild cards # (in the binary and nominal value cases) in the rule classifiers of the initial population.

- **Fitness Function**

  Each rule's fitness is based on the classification of the known samples. The form of the fitness function is as follows:

  Fitness = CorrectPats/TotPats + α * n_don'tcare/TotPats.

  where TotPats is the number of total training samples to be examined and CorrectPats is the number of training samples correctly classified by the rule, and n_don'tcare is the number of invalid features (see below) for classification. The constant α is used to tune the two terms of the fitness function, and its value is determined on a problem-specific basis. This fitness function could be used to guide the GA to search out best rule sets as a multiobjective optimization problem, if the GA also searched the space of possible α's.

- **Genetic Operators**

  Crossover was standard one-point crossover. Mutation was standard single bit-modification. Operations were performed only on the condition part of the classifiers/rules. Elitism was used to keep the best solution in the population, and mating was generational, not steady-state. Offspring replaced their parents.

- **Discovering Useful Patterns**

  To keep the complexity of the useful patterns and rules generated to a minimum, an optimization step was applied to remove redundant features

$$\begin{bmatrix} y_{11}, & y_{12}, & \ldots & y_{1N} \\ y_{21}, & y_{21}, & \ldots & y_{2N} \\ \ldots & \ldots & \ldots & \ldots \\ y_{k1} & y_{k2} & \ldots & y_{kN} \end{bmatrix} \Rightarrow \omega$$

For each pattern of different classes of a rule, we arrange the class-feature vectors as a matrix above; then for the binary case, we determine whether every class-feature vector has the same value (1 or 0) or a "don't care" (#) at any feature position (column); for the nominal case, we determine whether every class-feature vector has the same string at any feature position. If either of these situations occurs, the number of the n_don'tcare variable is incremented, as this feature is not contributing to the discrimination of classes; e.g., in the binary case

for any column i,

if $\forall(y_{mi}, y_{ni})\ \{(y_{mi} = y_{ni})$ or $(y_{mi} = \#)$ or $(y_{ni} = \#)\}$,

where m, n =1, 2, . . ., k, $m \neq n$,

then the ith feature is redundant for classification

else valid.

For the case of numerical features, the situation is more complicated. We might, for example, set as a criterion for matching that every class-feature vector have the same interval (i. e., lower and upper bounds) at any feature position, but that appears to be overly restrictive. Instead, one might, for example, require for a match only that the upper bounds are within epsilon of each other, for some given positive epsilon, and that the lower bounds are similarly within epsilon of each other. For other cases we can do same thing to remove redundant features.

After we delete all redundant features, we can easily pick out the useful patterns for the various classes. These patterns provide information useful to domain experts for evaluating and interpreting the characteristics of the classes, which constitutes "knowledge" about them. In the end, near-optimal patterns can be drawn from the best rule which keeps the classification performance at a certain level, and this makes knowledge available for use in tasks of prediction and description.

3.6 A Real-World Problem -- Biological Pattern Discovery and Classification.

We explored pattern discovery and classification of several real-world datasets exemplifying high-dimensionality biological data. Researchers in the Center for Microbial Ecology (CME) of Michigan State University have sampled various agricultural environments for study. Their first experiments used the Biolog© test as the discriminator. Biolog consists of a plate of 96 wells, with a different substrate in each well. These substrates (various sugars, amino acids and other nutrients) are assimilated by some microbes and not by others. If the microbial sample processes the substrate in the well, that well changes color, which can be recorded photometrically. Thus large numbers of samples can be processed and characterized based on the substrates they can assimilate. Each microbial sample described was tested on the 96 features provided by Biolog (for some experiments, extra taxonomic data were also used); the value of each feature is either 0 or 1.

Using the Biolog test suite to generate data, two test sets were used in showing the effectiveness of our approach.

Rhizosphere Data Set

Soil samples were taken from three environments found in agriculture:

1) near the roots of a crop (rhizosphere), 2) away from the influence of the roots (non-rhizosphere), or 3) in a fallow field (crop residue). There are 300 samples in total, 100 samples per area. The data set contains *P. fluorescens* isolates (196 isolates) and *P. putida* isolates (104). These two isolates represent two different species of bacteria which are phylogenetically closely related.

2,4-D Data Set

Soil samples were collected from a site that is contaminated with 2,4-D (dichlorophenoxyacetic acid), a pesticide. There were 3 classes, based on three genetically similar microbial isolates which show the ability to degrade 2,4-D. There were a total of 232 samples.

We applied the HDPDCS to the two datasets described above. The GA parameters used were those that gave the best results over a number of runs. The initial populations were created randomly, with the value at each vector position generated using probability 0.3 for a 0, 0.3 for a 1, and 0.4 for a #. The population size was 200, 40% of individuals (random) survived without change from each generation, elitism preserved the best individual, the crossover rate was 0.6, the mutation rate was 0.005, and fitness-proportional roulette wheel selection was used.

In several runs, the HDPDCS system discovered a reasonable classification rule and corresponding patterns for each data set. The HDPDCS outperformed a standard KNN method in every case, and its performance approached that of the hybrid GA/KNN method in most cases. It is most important to note, however, that the computation time required for the hybrid GA/KNN method running under similar circumstances was about 14 days (if run on a single SPARC I processor), whereas the HDBPCS required only 3 hours, although on a somewhat faster processor. The average accuracy results of six runs and the numbers of valid features after selection are shown in Table 1 below.

The useful patterns we discovered can be listed for every class of each different data set. Here we show the three patterns for *P. putida* isolates (104) of Rhizosphere data in Table 2. In the original data set each data sample has 96 features. After learning, we found patterns for three classes using only 8 features.

		KNN Correctness rate	GA/KNN Correctness rate	HDPDCS Correctness rate	Number of features	Number of valid features
Rhizosphere data	Training	71.00%	82.00%	80.00%	96	23
	Test	68.00%	79.90%	70.00%		
P.fluorescens	Training			86.80%	96	13
P. putida	Training			87.37%	96	8
2,4-D data	Training	93.36%	99.17%	98.61%	96	22
	Test	91.70%	98.00%	96.00%		

Table 1: Classification results using HDPDCS system

Feature index	Feature	9	21	35	41	52	66	81	95
Class 1	rhizosphere	0	0	0	0	1	1	0	#
Class 2	non-rhizosphere	1	#	#	1	0	1	#	1
Class 3	crop residue	0	1	1	0	0	0	1	0

Table 2: Discovery Patterns for *P. putida* data using HDBPCS system

Information about the patterns of the classes such as that shown in Table 2 is particularly important to biological researchers, as it can be used to derive new hypotheses and research efforts. In particular, for our biological examples, it was shown that HDPDCS can indeed distinguish between different bacterial communities on the basis of which substrates are being used -- i.e., 2,4-D degraders -- based on a standardized test that measures substrate uptake. This may help to distinguish what substrates are available in each of the communities, and may have ramifications in determining which bacteria are suitable for bioremediation of particular environments. In practical problems, one can derive several different patterns which includes different numbers of features to characterize the same classes.

Finally, the errors of classification in each class are not uniform across the data sets examined. This information may also provide some hints for research in the domain being studied.

There are some problems of classifiability of high dimensionality data sets noted for the GA/RULE approach. The quality of the data sets -- i.e., whether or not they have overlapping features in some classes, or lack sufficient information for discrimination among the classes -- affects pattern discovery and classification accuracy. The quantity of training samples given, or the ratio of training sample size to dimensionality, are crucial factors in the design of a pattern discovery and classification system. The sample (training) dataset needs to be representative, and it must also be large enough to allow for effective training. Otherwise, it will allow 'false' patterns and rules to be induced, based on a few examples which do not span the space of possible class membership.

4. Conclusion and Future Research

In this paper we have shown that genetic algorithms can be a good data mining tool, and play an important role in pattern discovery and classification for high dimensionality and multiclass data. The basic approach is a classification -- feedback -- pattern evaluation technique. This is an automated pattern search method which utilizes feedback information from the classifier being designed to change the decision space. The GA/RULE does this by modifying the classifier pattern of the decision rule using inductive learning and evolution to improve the performance of the classifier. The results achieved by this approach indicate potential application in many other fields. We plan to go on to test various data sets with different types of features, design appropriate encodings. We also plan to apply parallel genetic algorithms to discover several disjunctive patterns on different nodes (island) and use coevolution to increase the quality of discovery patterns. The final goal is to put this approach into practical KDD systems.

Acknowledgments

This work was supported in part by Michigan State University's Center for Microbial Ecology and the Beijing Natural Science Foundation of China.

References:

[1] U. M. Fayyad, G. Piatetsky-Shapiro, P. Smyth, From Data Mining to Knowledge Discovery: An Overview, *Advances in Knowledge Discovery and Data Mining*, 1996, p1-34.

[2] D. E. Goldberg. *Genetic Algorithms in Search, Optimization and Machine Learning*. New York: Addison Wesley, 1989.

[3] S. W. Wilson, D. E. Goldberg, ACritical Review of Classifier, *Proc. Third Inter. Conf. Genetic Algorithms and their Application* (ICGA), 1989,

[4] S. Smith, A Learning System Based on Genetic Algorithms, *Ph.D Dissertation* 1980 Computer Science, University of Pittsburgh.

[5 K. De Jong, Genetic Algorithms: A 10 Years Perspectives, *Proc. First International Conf. Parallel Problem Solving from Nature*, 1990, 169-177. P244.

[6] Anil K. Jain, *Artificial Neural Networks and Statistical Pattern Recognition.* Editor preface, 1991, Elsevier Science Publishers B.V.

[7] W. Siedlecki and J. Sklansky, On Automatic Feature Selection Internat. *Journal of Pattern Recognition and Artificial Intelligence*. Vol 2, No.2 1988, 197-220.

[8] W. Siedlecki and J. Sklansky, A Note on Genetic Algorithms for Large-Scale Feature Selection, *Pattern Recognition Letters*, 10 1989, 335-347.

[9] W.F. Punch, E.D. Goodman, Min Pei, et al. Further Research on Feature Selection and Classification Using Genetic Algorithms. *Proc. Fifth Inter. Conf. Genetic Algorithms and their Applications (ICGA)*, 1993, p.557.

[10] M. Pei, E.D. Goodman, W.F. Punch, Y. Ding, Genetic Algorithms For Classification and Feature Extraction. 1995 *Annual Meeting, Classification Society of North America,* June 1995.

[11] S.Wilson. Classifier Systems and the Animate Problem. *Machine Learning Journal* 2: 199-2 28, Kluwer Academic Publishers, Boston, 1987.

[12] Bonelli, Pierre and Parodi, Alexandre (1991). An Efficient Classifier System and its Experimental Comparison With Two Representative Learning Methods on three Medical Domains. *Proc. Fourth Inter. Conf. Genetic Algorithms and their Application (ICGA)*, 1991, p. 288.

[13] R. L. Riolo. Modeling Simple Human Category Learning with a Classifier System. *Proc. Fourth Inter. Conf. Genetic Algorithms and their Application (ICGA),* 1991, p. 324.

[14] J. Oliver, Discovering Individual Rules: An application of Genetic Algorithms, *Proc. Fifth Inter. Conf. Genetic Algorithms and their Application (ICGA)*, 1993, p.216.

[15] T. A. Sedbrook, H. Wright, R. Wright, Application of a Genetic Classifier for Patient Triage, *Proc. Fourth Inter. Conf. Genetic Algorithms and their Application (ICGA),* 1991, p. 334.

[16] G.E. Liepins, L.A. Wang, Classifier System Learning of Boolean Concepts, *Proc. Fourth Inter. Conf. Genetic Algorithms and their Application (ICGA)*, 1991, p. 318.

Chapter 5

Visual Data Exploration

A NEW VISUALISATION TECHNIQUE FOR KNOWLEDGE DISCOVERY IN OLAP

HWEE-LENG ONG, HING-YAN LEE
Japan-Singapore AI Centre
Information Technology Institute
11 Science Park Road
Singapore Science Park II
Singapore 117685

In the on-line analytical processing (OLAP) model, a cross tabulation table is often used as its visualisation tool. This paper describes how a modified multidimensional visualisation technique is used to visualise OLAP models.

1 Introduction

Knowledge discovery in databases (KDD) has as its primary objective the uncovering of new and useful knowledge from huge masses of raw data. Our research in KDD has focused on how visualisation can be exploited in the dialectic process of knowledge discovery[6]. Our approach uses a multidimensional data visualisation (MDV) technique that builds upon a refined and improved method of parallel coordinates. We also explore how visualisation can be used synergistically with other techniques such as inductive learning (e.g., C4.5) and hierarchical clustering to harness their respective strengths in KDD. Our recent work investigates whether the requirements for visualisation would differ if the input to the knowledge discovery comprises aggregated data instead of raw unprocessed data. In particular, we concentrate on the multidimensional model, an emerging model for analysis, that underlies the on-line analytical processing (OLAP) concept [2]. The OLAP camp uses the two-dimensional cross-tabulation table as its visualisation tool. We argue that this is inadequate and that a modified MDV can provide superior results for KDD.

2 Visualisation in OLAP

Traditionally, production databases tuned for operational applications with emphasis on transactions efficiency are collectively referred to as on-line transaction processing (OLTP). Because OLTP databases are designed to support updates and transaction processing type applications efficiently, these requirements are unable to provide the flexibility required by end users in manipulating, displaying, and analysing data. This shortcoming has triggered a search for new ways to address the needs of analytical processing, especially with the increasing popularity of end user computing and with the advent of technologies such as client-server and visualisation. This search has given birth to OLAP, which refers to a new way of getting to important information, especially for decision making. The primary objective is to get value out of data by viewing from different perspectives. This requires a powerful and different data model that can support give end users access to data in a multidimensional fashion. The main differences between OLTP and OLAP can be found elsewhere[7,8]. Edgar Codd, the father of relational database technology, argued the need for the OLAP model and has proposed 12 rules for evaluating OLAP products[3].

Underlying the OLAP concept is the multidimensional data model. It principally determines how users will be able to look at the data. A multidimensional data model is one in which the basic unit is a dimension (contrast with record-based models), where a dimension is a set of similar entities. It is the highest level in a consolidation path and represents a specific perspective of the data. For example, a set of all bank employees or a set of all products. Data consolidation is the process of synthesising pieces of information into single blocks of essential knowledge. A series of consolidation levels or steps defined in terms of multi-level parameters is a consolidation path. Such a path determines which details are visible to the end user when he drills down. The data is organised by dimensions into arrays with a vertical dimension, a horizontal dimension, a page dimension, etc. The array contents are the actual values.

An OLAP model is visualised using a two-dimensional cross-tabulation table (Figure 1). This representation is easy to understand; it is the spreadsheet way of representing data in the form of rows and columns. However, the user is restricted to seeing at most three dimensions at a time: using row, column and page to represent a dimension each. In addition, the representation comprises numerical output which is tedious to read. We will show how our MDV approach represents the data visually, allowing the user to see more than three dimensions at a time as well as to quickly find relationships among the dimensions.

REGION	(All)				
Count of GRANTED	TIME				
LOAN TYPE	Q1	Q2	Q3	Q4	Grand Total
Short_Term	135	257	261	145	798
Long_Term	37	51	55	31	174
Mid_Term	16	40	31	13	100
Grand Total	188	348	347	189	1072

Figure 1. Cross-tabulation of Credit Screening Dataset

3 Multidimensional Data Visualisation (MDV)

Parallel coordinates, as originally conceived[4], can be described as:

> "The principle coordinate axes are parallel and equidistant to each other. That is, for an N-dimensional data set, N vertical axes are placed on the plane, so that every two successive axes are one unit part from each other. An N-dimensional data entry is represented by a broken (polygonal) line whose vertices lie on the parallel axes and whose height (y-position) is determined by the entry's attributes, i.e., the value of the first attribute determines the height of the vertex placed on the first vertical axis, etc. A data set, then, is represented by a collection of these polygonal lines." [1]

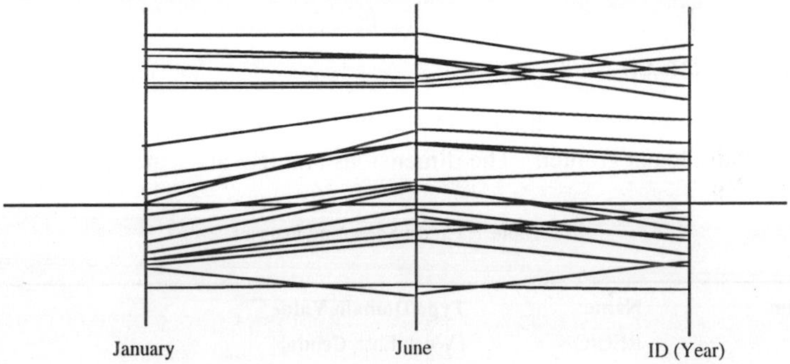

Figure 2. Inselberg's parallel coordinates for USA employment for females in the 16-19 age group between 1960-1981[1]

Figure 2 shows that a dependency between the ID axis and the other two axes exists. Although some negative correlations exist in the data, the number of employed women rises generally over time. Our research in visualisation extends the parallel coordinates concept. We have implemented our MDV technique, an improved version of parallel coordinates in a tool called WinViz[5].

The MDV version of the parallel coordinates, as implemented in WinViz, differs from Inselberg's in several aspects[5]:

a) While the polygonal lines exist, they no longer play a significant role. WinViz supports a polygonal line display toggle whereby the user can select between having a polygonal line to represent a tuple (or database record) or several tuples satisfying the attribute (or dimension) values specified by the user.

b) *Group bars* appear in the place of attribute values on each vertical axis. The group bars reduce the complexity of lines when the dataset gets too big.

c) The concept of *class* is introduced, where a class is a subset of the data. The user can group subjects of interest into classes, and see how they are represented in the dataset and how they correlate with other attributes in the data.

d) *Horizontal histograms* are provided on the right hand portion of group bars when the data is divided into classes. This allows the user to compare against other attributes.

WinViz currently handles datasets comprising records. We will describe how MDV could be applied to OLAP which looks at summary data as input, rather than raw data. The number of records handled by WinViz currently depends on the number of attributes, attribute values and the memory size of the PC. To date, we have tested it on datasets up to 70,000 records with 100 attributes of varying attribute values. As OLAP looks only at aggregate data whose dataset size is much smaller than raw data, it should not have any problems handling larger datasets.

4 MDV for OLAP

In this section, we discuss how MDV will be used in the OLAP model using a dataset on bank loans granted. The dimensions and its values are shown in Table 1.

Table 1. Credit Screening Dataset

Dimension	Name	Type/Domain Value
Region	REGION	{West, East, Central}
Time (in quarters)	TIME	{Q1, Q2, Q3, Q4}
Loan Type	LOAN_TYPE	{Short_Term, Mid_Term, Long_Term}
Applicant's age group	AGE	{21-29, 30-39, 40-49, 50-59, 60-65}
Applicant's gender	SEX	{Male, Female}

The cross-tabulation on the dimensions REGION, TIME and LOAN_TYPE (Figure 1) can be represented using MDV (Figure 3). Each dimension is represented as a vertical column, with the dimension name at the top and its values below. Each rectangular box, known as *group bar*, corresponds to a value in a dimension. For example, the REGION dimension is represented by three bars: *West, East*, and *Central*. The width of each bar corresponds to the number of loans granted for the dimension. The height of a bar has no significance. At a glance, we can see that for the REGION dimension, the *Central* region grants the most number of loans (as indicated by the widest bar for REGION = *Central*). Looking at the TIME dimension, we see that most loans are concentrated in the second and third quarters (as indicated by the wider bars at TIME = *Q2* and TIME = *Q3*). Similarly, we see that short term loans are most popular under the LOAN_TYPE dimension.

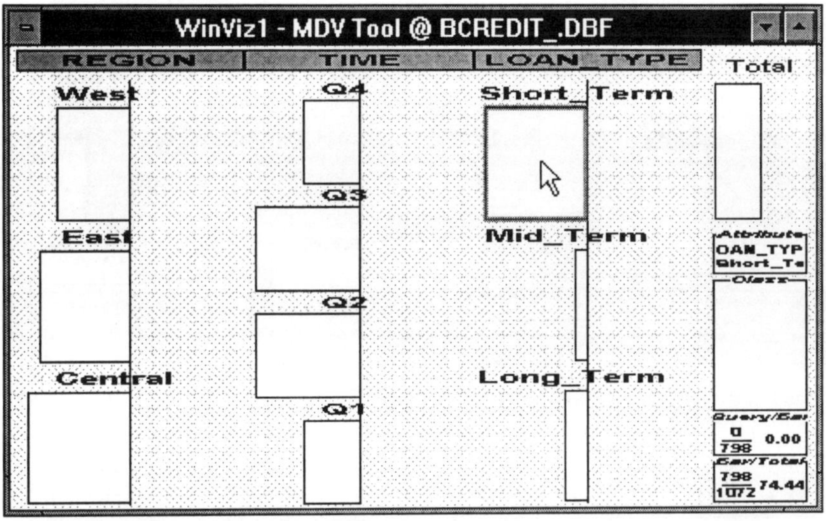

Figure 3. MDV display of REGION, TIME and LOAN_TYPE dimensions

To obtain the numerical values of each bar we move the mouse cursor over each *group bar*, and look at the bottom-most box on the right hand side of the MDV display. From Figure 3, by placing the mouse cursor over LOAN_TYPE = *Short_Term*, we see that there are 798 short term loans out of a total of 1072. This corresponds to the grand totals of the cross tabulation for short term loans in Figure 1.

In comparing Figure 3 with Figure 1, we see that only the grand totals of Figure 1 have been represented on MDV. The grand totals for the REGION which is absent in Figure 1 is now displayed visually. The figures for the loan types for each quarter is lost in this initial MDV display.

To see the loan types for each quarter, MDV allows the creation of *classes*. A *class* is a subset of the data and is represented as *class bars* on the right of each *group bar*. In Figure 4, we have divided each group bar into three classes corresponding to each loan type, and represented them in 3 colours on the right hand side of each *group bar*. Again, by moving the mouse cursor over each *class bar*, we can see its distribution over each value of a dimension. For example, in Figure 4, we have placed the cursor over the first class bar in TIME = *Q1*. The statistics box (on the bottom-most box on the right of the MDV display) shows 135/188. This means that there are 135 short term loans out of a total of 188 loans in the first quarter, TIME = *Q1*. Similarly, we can also examine the distribution of the three loan types for each region by moving the mouse cursor along the REGION dimension axis.

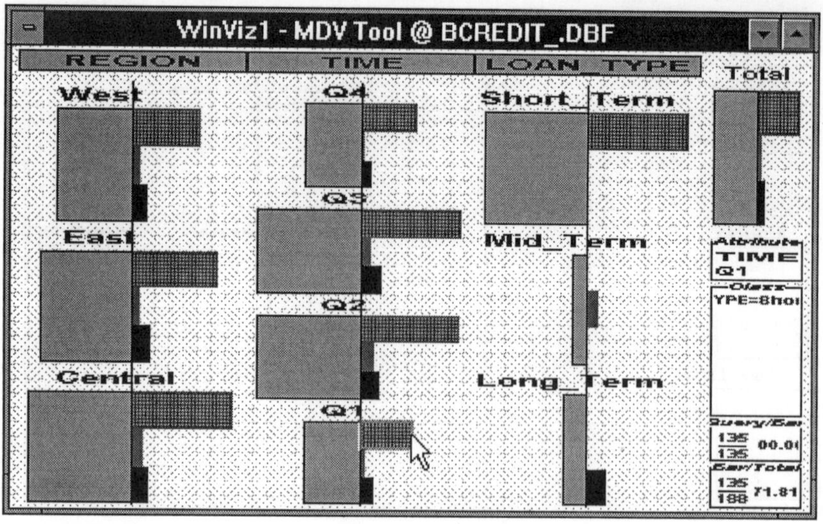

Figure 4. Creating Classes on the MDV display

The OLAP cross-tabulation allows a user to drill down a dimension. For example, the TIME dimension can be further expanded into units of months. Similarly, MDV also provides this capability by expanding a group bar into lower level group bars.

We have shown how the information in a cross-tabulation display is captured using the MDV display. However, MDV provides the following added advantages:

- It is easier to read than the numerical display in a cross tabulation.
- MDV is not limited to displaying just 3 dimensions. In the cross tabulation display, the user has to rotate the display to see the various dimensions. For example, in Figure 1, in order to see how the LOAN_TYPE dimension varies over say, the AGE dimension, the TIME dimension will have to be dropped and replaced by AGE to create a new cross tabulation. On WinViz, we can just load in other dimensions like AGE and SEX (as shown in Figure 5) without losing the TIME dimension. We can now see the distribution of loan types on all the dimensions. MDV provides a global view of all the dimensions at the same time.
- An interactive query capability in MDV allows one to discover potential relationships among the various dimensions. MDV makes use of polygonal lines, from parallel coordinates, to indicate relationships. Figure 6 shows a query on age group *60-65*. If we look down the LOAN_TYPE dimension (the third vertical axis on the MDV display), we see that there are no polygonal lines intersecting LOAN_TYPE = *Mid_Term*. This shows that people in age group AGE = *60-65* do not take any mid-term loans.

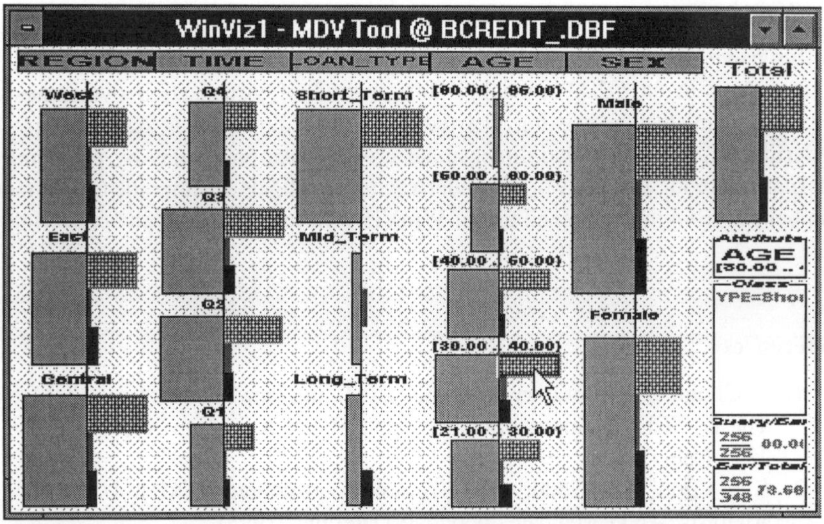

Figure 5. MDV display of 5 dimensions

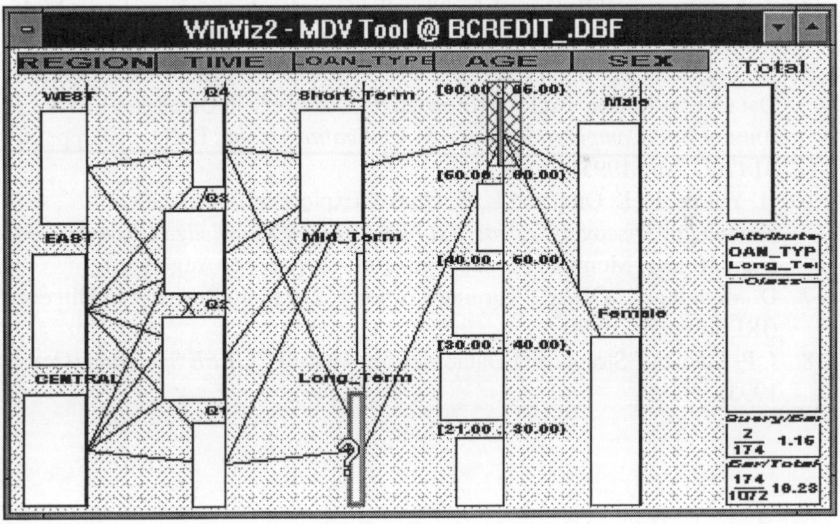

Figure 6. Making queries on MDV

5 Conclusion

In this paper, we have presented how MDV can be used to discover patterns and relationships in an OLAP model. This method of visualisation overcomes the impedance mismatch existing between the multidimensional data model that underlies OLAP and its two-dimensional cross-tabulation display by providing an alternate method. Further work is underway to investigate whether the OLAP model can benefit from the combined use of WinViz with rule induction and clustering for KDD.

References

1. T. Chomut, "Exploratory Data Analysis Using Parallel Coordinates", Msc Thesis, UCLA Computer Science Dept., IBM LA Sc. Cen. Rep. No. 1987-2811 (1987).
2. E. F. Codd, S. B. Codd, and C. T. Salley, "Providing OLAP to User Analysts: An IT Mandate" (Codd & Date, Inc., 1993).
3. E. F. Codd, S. B. Codd, and C. T. Salley, "Beyond Decision Support", *ComputerWorld* (26 Jul 1993).
4. A. Inselberg, and B. Dimsdale, "Parallel Coordinates for Visualizing Multi-Dimensional Geometry", *Proc. Computer Graphics Intl. Conf.* (1987).
5. H. Y. Lee, H. L. Ong, E. W. Toh, and S. K. Chan, "A Multi-Dimensonal Data Visualization Tool for Knowledge Discovery in Databases", *Proc. 19th Annual Intl. Computer Software & Applications Conf.*, Dallas, TX, pp. 26 - 31 (7-11 Aug 1995).
6. H. Y. Lee, H. L. Ong, and L. H. Quek, "Exploiting Visualization in Knowledge Discovery", *Proc. 1st Intl. Conf. on Knowledge Discovery and Data Mining*, Montreal, Canada, pp. 198 - 201 (20-21 Aug 1995).
7. D. Menninger, "OLAP - Turning Corporate Data into Business Intelligence" (IRI Software, 1994).
8. J. P. Stamen, "Structuring Databases for Analysis", *IEEE Spectrum* (Oct 1993).

MULTIDIMENSIONAL HISTOGRAM FOR DATA EXPLORATION AND MINING

JUNPING SUN
SCIS, Nova Southeastern University, Fort Lauderdale, Florida 33314, USA

WILLIAM I. GROSKY
Computer Science Department, Wayne State University, Detroit, Michigan 48202, USA

In this paper, we will present an adaptive data exploration and mining approach in the multidimensional database environment. Our approach uses a technique based on the dynamic quantized space, a dynamic multidimensional data structure developed for the field of motion analysis and other applications. In order to extract the quantitative knowledge from irregularly distributed data in dynamic multidimensional database systems, we developed our adaptive heuristic algorithms to manage and achieve the uniform resolution of data distribution when databases undergo frequent update activities. The approximate associative range rules about the range data in multidimensional space can be derived from the very well-managed dynamic multidimensional data structure to support the multidimensional query processing, and the approximate multidimensional range queries can be fast answered to support the OLAP (on-line analytic processing) and data warehousing.

1 Introduction

The process of knowledge discovery in databases requires various intelligent methods which are different from theses methods developed in the field of artificial intelligence and machine learning. [11] [3] The difficult issues in the field of KDD are that the technologies must deal with the huge amount of dynamic data and support fast derivation of the encoded knowledge. When databases undergo frequent activities of random updates, the derived knowledge from database must be reclassified and reorganized.[6]

In order to reduce the costs of reorganization and reclassification of the derived knowledge from database mining, we use a dynamic multidimensional scheme to keep track of most up-to-date approximate range information and associated knowledge. This can be used to support various applications such as the analysis of financial data and the predication of market information with discovered knowledge. Our main memory based dynamic multidimensional scheme can be used to derive some approximate associative range rules and provide approximate answers to range queries for multidimensional applications such as OLAP (on-line analytical process) and others.

2 Related Work and Background

One of the major tasks in KDD is to extract the certain domain knowledge from databases for various applications. One type of useful domain knowledge is the histogram that represents the data distribution in database systems. Many of early research literatures in the database field have shown that it is very useful to use the domain knowledge from histograms to support the different query optimization strategies.[10] [7] [4] These histogram-based approaches have been used to explore the resolution of irregular data distribution in relational databases, to extract the quantitative knowledge such as estimated selectivities for queries, and to guide the DBMS engine to optimize various type of queries in relational databases.

Both equi-width [10] and equi-depth (multi-dimensional) [7] histogram methods have been proposed to extract the quantitative knowledge of data point distribution in databases. When the data distribution for a specific database state becomes irregular in each of equally divided bin, the discrepancy between the estimated selectivity and the actual selectivity become larger in the equi-width histogram approach. [10]

Although the approach [7] of equi-depth multi-dimensional histogram allevates the problems in the equi-width histogram, its algorithm [7] requires periodic reorganization of the histogram by sorting multidimensional data along each dimension due to the storage structure of H-tree [7] whenever databases undergo frequent updates such as insertions and deletions.

We believe that the histogram can also be used to derive useful quatitative rules about the data distribution to serve the various purposes.

Assume the relational schema $R(A_1, A_2, ..., A_D)$. Let $hb(R)^{c_j}_{A_k}$ be the jth histogram bin for the range $c_{j,k}$ along the dimension A_k and X be a data point, $(x_1, ..., x_D)$, in a D-dimensional hyper-rectangular region where $x_k \in domain(A_k)$ and $1 \leq k \leq D$ such that

$$c_{j,k} = \{(x_1, ..., x_D) \mid (r^{(lo)}_{c_{j,k}} \leq x_k < r^{(hi)}_{c_{j,k}})\} \quad 1 \leq j \leq n \, , \, 1 \leq k \leq D \qquad (1)$$

where $r^{(lo)}_{c_{j,k}}$ and $r^{(hi)}_{c_{j,k}}$ are the low bound and the high bound for the range $c_{j,k}$ (the *jth* bin) along the dimension k, and j is the sequence number for each of the histogram bins along k dimension for x_k.

There are several simple rules can be extracted as follows:

- if $count_{j,k}(X(x_k)) \geq 1$, then at least the rule $\exists(X)((r^{(lo)}_{c_{j,k}} \leq X(x_k) < r^{(hi)}_{c_{j,k}}) \rightarrow count_{j,k}(X(x_k)) \geq 1)$ can be derived.
- if $count_{j,k}(X(x_k)) = 0$, then the rule $\neg\exists(X)(r^{(lo)}_{c_{j,k}} \leq X(x_k) < r^{(hi)}_{c_{j,k}}) \rightarrow count_{j,k}(X(x_k)) \geq 1)$ can be derived.

- The selectivity rules can be derived such as

$$\exists(X)((r_{c_{j,k}}^{(lo)} \leq X(x_k) < r_{c_{j,k}}^{(hi)}) \rightarrow (sel_{(=val(x_k))} = count(X((x_k))/count(A_k)))$$

If there is a select query such that $\sigma(_{(r_{c_{j,k}}^{(lo)} \leq x_k < r_{c_{j,k}}^{(hi)})}(R))$, then the empty answer can be given directly with the support of the rule as:

$$\neg \exists(X)((r_{c_{j,k}}^{(lo)} \leq X(x_k) < r_{c_{j,k}}^{(hi)}) \rightarrow count_{j,k}(X(val(x_k))) \geq 1)$$

In this paper, we will show our adaptive split and merge rules to achieve the uniform resolution of data as well as to keep track of the quantitative knowledge in the multidimensional histogram.

3 The MultiDimensional Histogram Data Structure

There are many applications which require the database engine to support associative range queries. A list of multidimensional data structures have been proposed such as the k-d tree, [1] [2] k-d-b tree,[12] r-tree,[13] and others.[8]

In our approach, we use a multidimensional histogram data structure (MD-HDS) similar to a k-d tree [1] as a dynamic hierarchical structure to store a *histogram* of attribute values in multidimensional space. There will be one such tree for each chosen set of attributes, each logical D-attribute 'tuple' being interpreted as a D-dimensional point. A chosen set of attributes can comprise an individual relation, part of a relation, or part of a join of many relations as a views.

Using C notation, a MDHDS node is described as follows:

```
struct  mdhds_node
    {int    nodetype;
    float   range[D][2];
    union
        {struct
             {int      discriminator;
              float    midpoint;
              struct   mdhds_node *leftson, *rightson;
             } internal;
         struct
             {float  count;
              float  bias[D];
             } leaf;
        } u;
    }
```

The integer, *nodetype*, indicates whether the node is an internal node or a leaf node. The D by 2 dimensional array, *range*, stores both the low bound and high bound values of that node along each dimension in the D-dimensional space. The range information stored at the root node represents the entire range the MDHDS tree covers, and range information stored in each leaf node represents the subrange covered by the node. The *discriminator* in internal node is used for various purposes such as insertion, deletion, splitting, and merging operations. The *midpoint* represents the center of the data distribution along the dimension defined by *discriminator*. The pointers to both **leftson* and **rightson* are used to link the nodes at the next level of the MDHDS tree.

The *counter* in the leaf node stores the number of data points in each subrange (bin) covered by the node. The array *bias[D]* keeps tracks of the data distribution, which is the difference of data points between the high half and low half along each dimension.

3.1 Conditions for Split and Merge in MDHDS

The purpose of split and merge is to maintain the uniform resolution of data distribution with the equi-count of data points in each bin. For a given leaf node, if the value of count is too large or if the absolute value of bias[i] for some dimension i is too large, then that leaf node should be partitioned into two new leaf nodes, with each one covering half of the parent's range. The count of the old leaf node will be distributed to each of its childern based on the value of bias[discriminator] where discriminator corresponds to the split-dimension. On the other hand, a leaf node should be merged with its neighbor(s) leaf node(s) if the resultant merge operation will not generate too high a count and too skewed a bias. Since the split always favors the dimension with the largest *bias* value, the value of *dimension* in each node is no longer systematically cycled. Note that we assume that all fields are integer valued at this time. Our approach can be easily extended for other types of domain.

3.2 Definitions

Definition 3.1 *Suppose c is a D-dimensional hyper-rectangular region such that* $c = \{(x_1, ..., x_D) \mid r_{c,j}^{(lo)} \leq x_j < r_{c,j}^{(hi)},\ 1 \leq j \leq D\}$.

Definition 3.2 *Let* $N(c)$ *be an approximation of the number of tuples in a relation R (real or virtual) which reside in cell c such that* $N(c) \approx |\, R \cap c \,|$.

Definition 3.3 *The low half-cell of c along dimension d and the high half-cell of c along dimension d,* $c_d^{(p)}$ *and* $p \in \{lo, hi\}$, $\forall d\ 1 \leq d \leq D$, *is defined by*

$$c_d^{(lo)} = \{(y_1, ..., y_d) \mid r_{c,d}^{(lo)} \le y_d < \tfrac{r_{c,d}^{(lo)} + r_{c,d}^{(hi)}}{2}, \forall 1 \le j \ne d < D, r_{c,j}^{(lo)} \le y_j < r_{c,j}^{(hi)}\}$$
$$c_d^{(hi)} = \{(y_1, ..., y_d) \mid \tfrac{r_{c,d}^{(lo)} + r_{c,d}^{(hi)}}{2} \le y_d < r_{c,d}^{(hi)}, \forall 1 \le j \ne d < D, r_{c,j}^{(lo)} \le y_j < r_{c,j}^{(hi)}\}.$$

Definition 3.4 *The number of tuples in each half-space is given as:* $N(c_d^{(lo)}) \approx \mid R \cap c_d^{(lo)} \mid$ *and* $N(c_d^{(hi)}) \approx \mid R \cap c_d^{(hi)} \mid$.

The last two quantities in Definition 3.4 are the number of data points residing in a particular MDHDS bin and, as shown, are approximations to the true values. Note also that $N(c) = N(c_d^{(hi)}) + N(c_d^{(lo)})$, $\forall d \; 1 \le d \le D$.

Definition 3.5 *The bias vector value or imbalance of bin c along certain dimension d is defined as:*
$imb(c, d) = N(c_d^{(hi)}) - N(c_d^{(lo)})$.

4 Adaptive Split Rules

The adaptive algorithm to compute the split child cell's *bias* or *imbalance* values critically depends on our approximation of the number of data points in each of *quadrants* of the bin or bucket to be split.

4.1 Bucket Count Splitting Computations

Assume cell c (bin or leaf node) splits along dimension s based on the *imbalance* (or *bias*) $imb(c, s)$ along that dimension. Thus, cell c will have the new split cells $c_s^{(lo)}$ and $c_s^{(hi)}$ which represent the low and the high half-spaces resulting from the split along dimension s. The corresponding adaptive split cell's counts can be given from the above discussions shown as:
$N(c_s^{(lo)}) = \frac{N(c) - imb(c,s)}{2}$ and $N(c_s^{(hi)}) = \frac{N(c) + imb(c,s)}{2}$.

4.2 Adaptive Split Rules for Bias Vectors

Before starting the algorithm to compute the *bias* or *imbalance* vector values, the following definitions will be given for later usage in **Step 3** of **Case 2** of Algorithm 4.1 for computing the *imbalance* vectors.

Definition 4.1 *Let* **lub** *be the least upper bound function defined in the lattice shown in Figure 1(a.), such that* **lub():** $\{\perp, \mathbf{lo}, \mathbf{hi}\}^2 \to \{\perp, \mathbf{lo}, \mathbf{hi}\}$ *as:*
$\forall a \in \{\perp, \mathbf{lo}, \mathbf{hi}\}$ $\mathbf{lub}(a, \perp) = \mathbf{lub}(\perp, a) = a$, $\mathbf{lub}(a, a) = a$; *and also* $\mathbf{lub}(\mathbf{lo}, \mathbf{hi}) = \mathbf{lub}(\mathbf{hi}, \mathbf{lo}) = \perp$.

Definition 4.2 *Let* $u, v \in \{\perp, \mathbf{lo}, \mathbf{hi}\}^D$. *Then u and v are* **compatible** *if,* $\forall j \; 1 \le j \le D$, *whenever* $u[j]$ *and* $v[j] \in \{\mathbf{lo}, \mathbf{hi}\}$, *we have that* $u[j] = v[j]$.

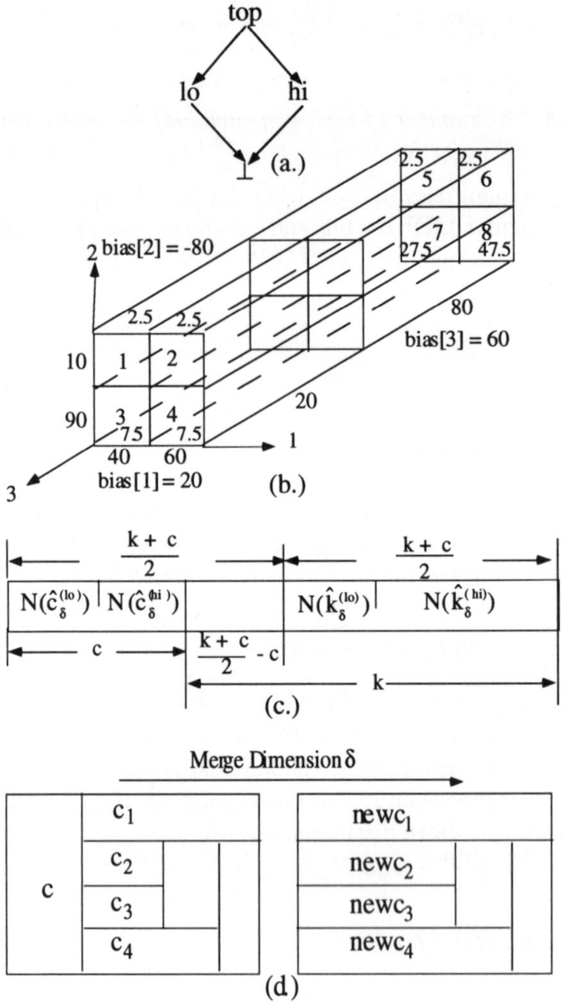

Figure 1: Figure (a.), (b.), (c.), and (d.)

Definition 4.3 *Let* **lub** *be extended to compatible* D *element vectors over* $\{\perp, \mathbf{lo}, \mathbf{hi}\}$ *in the obvious way by defining* $\mathbf{lub}(u,v) = w$, *where* $w[j] = \mathbf{lub}(u[j], v[j]),\ \forall j\ 1 \le j \le D$.

Definition 4.4 *For* $u, v \in \{\perp, \mathbf{lo}, \mathbf{hi}\}^D$, $size(u,v)$ *is defined as:*

$$size(u,v) = \begin{cases} 2^{|\{j|1 \le j \le D \text{ and } \mathbf{lub}(u,v)[j] = \perp\}|} & \text{if } u \text{ and } v \text{ are compatible} \\ 0 & \text{otherwise} \end{cases}$$

Definition 4.5 $\forall d\ 1 \le d \le D$ *and* $q \in \{\mathbf{lo}, \mathbf{hi}\}$, *let* $\alpha_{d,q} \in \{\perp, \mathbf{lo}, \mathbf{hi}\}^D$ *be such that* $\alpha_{d,q}[d] = q$, *and* $\forall\ 1 \le j \ne d \le D, \alpha_{d,q}[j] = \perp$.

$\forall\ 1 \le d \le D$, the computation of imbalance vector values for the new split cells $imb(c_s^{(lo)}, d)$ and $imb(c_s^{(hi)}, d)$ are given by the following different cases as shown in **Algorithm** 4.1 of Figure 2.

In **Algorithm** 4.2 shown in Figure 3, for each value of i, $v_{c,i}$ represents a number of hyperquadrants of the D-dimension space c. The number of new hyperquadrants which haven't been encountered in previous $v_{c,j}$'s is equal to the number of new regions, $number\_of\_new\_regions_{c,i}$, and each of these new regions contains $new\_region\_size_{c,i}$ points.

The worst-case time complexity is again $O(D^2)$, as the number of times the outer **while** loop is executed is proportional to D, while the inner **loop** adds a linear factor.

Example 4.1 *Illustration of* **Step 1** *of* **Case 2** *in* **Algorithm** *4.1.*

Assume that there is 3-D bin in Figure 1(b.) with the following count and bias values for splitting operation: $Count = 100$, $Bias[1] = 20$, $Bias[2] = -80$, $Bias[3] = 60$. So the computed $\{N(c_1^{(lo)}), N(c_1^{(hi)}), \ldots\ldots, N(c_D^{(lo)}), N(c_D^{(hi)})\}$ is as: $N(c_1^{(lo)}) = 40$, $N(c_1^{(hi)}) = 60$, $N(c_2^{(lo)}) = 90$, $N(c_2^{(hi)}) = 10$, $N(c_3^{(lo)}) = 20$, $N(c_3^{(hi)}) = 80$, *and the sorted sequence in ascending order is as:*

$$N_1 = N(c_2^{(hi)}) = 10, N_2 = N(c_3^{(lo)}) = 20, N_3 = N(c_1^{(lo)}) = 40,$$
$$N_4 = N(c_1^{(hi)}) = 60, N_5 = N(c_3^{(hi)}) = 80, N_6 = N(c_2^{(lo)}) = 90.$$

Starting with starting with the first equation: $N(c_2^{(hi)}) = 10$, **Algorithm** 4.2 computes the sequences $\{v_{c,1}, \ldots, v_{c,length}\}and$ $\{new\_region\_size_{c,1}, \ldots, new\_region\_size_{c,length}\}$ for each quadrants.

A trace of **Step 2** of **Case 2** of **Algorithm** 4.1 as shown in **Table** 1.

Example 4.2 *Illustration of* **Step 4** *of* **Case 4** *of Algorithm 4.1 as follows:*

$\alpha_{s,q} = \alpha_{3,hi} = (\perp, \perp, hi)$; $\alpha_{d,hi} = \alpha_{1,hi} = (hi, \perp, \perp)$; $\alpha_{d,lo} = \alpha_{1,lo} = (lo, \perp, \perp)$;
$lub(\alpha_{s,q}, \alpha_{d,hi}) = lub((\perp, \perp, hi), (hi, \perp, \perp))$; (hyerquadrants 6 and 8)
$lub(\alpha_{s,q}, \alpha_{d,lo}) = lub((\perp, \perp, hi), (lo, \perp, \perp))$; (hyperquadrants 5 and 7)
$v_{c,1} = (\perp, hi, \perp)$; $v_{c,2} = (\perp, lo, lo)$; $v_{c,3} = (lo, lo, hi)$; $v_{c,4} = (hi, lo, hi)$;

Thus the computation of imbalance is given as follows.

Algorithm 4.1 *Computing Splitting Imbalance*

Input: *Split dimension s, bias vector and count values of split bin*
Output: *New computed bias vector for the split children*

1. <u>**case 1:**</u> if $d = s$, then $imb(c_s^{(lo)}, d) \;=\; imb(c_s^{(hi)}, d) \;=\; 0$

2. <u>**case 2:**</u> if $d \neq s$, then

   a.) <u>**step 1:**</u> sort the set

   $\{N(c_1^{(lo)}), N(c_1^{(hi)}), ..., N(c_D^{(lo)}), N(c_D^{(hi)})\}$ in ascending order.

   Let the resulting non-decreasing sequence be,

   $N_1 = N(c_{d_1}^{(p_1)}), ..., N_{2D} = N(c_{d_{2D}}^{(p_{2D})})$

   where $p_i \in \{lo, hi\}, 1 \leq d_i \leq D, \;\forall\; 1 \leq i \leq 2 \times D.$

   This step has a worst-case time complexity of $O(D \log D)$.

   b.) <u>**step 2:**</u> Utilizing the lattice shown in Figure 1(a.), execute the **Algorithm** 4.2 in Figure 3 to determine the sequences

   $\{\; v_{c,1}, ..., v_{c,length} \;\}$ and
   $\{new\_region\_size_{c,1}, ..., new\_region\_size_{c,length}\}$

   c.) <u>**step 3:**</u> $\forall\; 1 \leq d \leq D$ *and* $q \in \{\mathbf{lo}, \mathbf{hi}\}$,
   Let $\alpha_{d,q} \in \{\perp, \mathbf{lo}, \mathbf{hi}\}^D$ be such that $\alpha_{d,q}[d] = q$,
   $\forall\; 1 \leq j \neq d \leq D, \alpha_{d,q}[j] = \perp.$

   Define Definition 4.1, 4.3, 4.4, and 4.5.

   d.) <u>**step 4:**</u> For $q \in \{lo, hi\}$, given the split dimension s, definitions in **Definition** 4.1, 4.3, 4.4, and 4.5, and above results, the computation of *imbalance* is given by

   for $(d = 1;\; d \leq D; \&d \neq s;\; d{+}{+})$ **do**

   $$imb(c_s^{(q)}, d) = \sum_{i=1}^{length} [size(lub(\alpha_{s,q}, \alpha_{d,hi}), v_{c,i}) - size(lub(\alpha_{s,q}, \alpha_{d,lo}), v_{c,i})] \times new\_region\_size_{c,i}$$

Figure 2: Algorithm to Compute Split Imbalance Vector

Algorithm 4.2 *NewRegionSize*

Input: *The sorted set* $N_1 = N(c_{d_1}^{(p_1)}), ..., N_{2D} = N(c_{d_{2D}}^{(p_{2D})})$ *where* $p_i \in \{\text{lo}, \text{hi}\}, 1 \leq d_i \leq D, \ \forall\ 1 \leq i \leq 2 \times D.$

Output: *Sequences* $\{\ v_{c,1}, ..., v_{c,length}\ \}$ *and* $\{new\_region\_size_{c,1}, ..., new\_region\_size_{c,length}\}$

Let w be D-tuple, each of whose elements is $\perp$;

$w = \{\perp, ..., \perp\}^D$;

$number\_of\_new\_region\_s_0 = 2^D$;

$i\ =\ 0$;

$continue = \textbf{true}$

do {

$\quad i = i + 1; \qquad v_{c,i} = w;$

$\quad$ **if** $(w[d_i] == \perp)$ {

$\qquad number\_of\_new\_regions_{c,i} = number\_of\_new\_regions_{c,i-1}/2;$

$\qquad v_{c,i}[d_i] = p_i;$

$\qquad w[d_i] = \textbf{reverse}(p_i);\quad /\ *\ \textbf{reverse}(hi) = lo;\quad \textbf{reverse}(lo) = hi\ *\ /$

$\quad$ **else** {

$\qquad number\_of\_new\_regions_{c,i} = number\_of\_new\_regions_{c,i-1};$

$\qquad continue = \textbf{false};$

$\quad$ }

$\quad excess = 0;$

$\quad$ **for** $(j = 1;\ j < i - 1;\ j{+}{+})$

$\qquad$ **if** $(v_{c,j}[d_i] = \perp)$

$\qquad\quad excess \mathrel{+}= new\_region\_size_{c,j} \times number\_of\_new\_regions_{c,j}/2;$

$\qquad$ **else**

$\qquad\quad excess \mathrel{+}= new\_region\_size_{c,j} \times number\_of\_new\_regions_{c,j};$

$\quad new\_region\_size_{c,i} = (N_i - excess)/number\_of\_new\_regions_{c,i};$

} **while** $(continue = \textbf{true})$

$length = i;$

Figure 3: Algorithm for Determining the Sequences $\{v_{c,1}, ..., v_{c,length}\}$ and NewRegionSize

i	*Number of NewRegions*	*NewRegionSize*	d_i	p_i	$v_{c,i}$	N_i	*excess*
0	8	-	-	-	$v_{c,0} = (\perp, \perp, \perp)$	-	0
1	4	2.5	2	*hi*	$v_{c,1} = (\perp, hi, \perp)$	10	0
2	2	7.5	3	*lo*	$v_{c,2} = (\perp, lo, lo)$	20	5
3	1	27.5	1	*lo*	$v_{c,3} = (lo, lo, hi)$	40	12.5
4	1	47.5	1	*hi*	$v_{c,4} = (hi, lo, hi)$	60	12.5

Table 1: Illustration of Algorithm for Computing NewRegionSzie

$imb(c_3^{(hi)}, 1) =$
$[size((hi, \perp, hi), (\perp, hi, \perp)) - size((lo, \perp, hi), (\perp, hi, \perp))] \times 2.5+$
$[size((hi, \perp, hi), (\perp, lo, lo)) - size((lo, \perp, hi), (\perp, lo, lo))] \times 7.5+$
$[size((hi, \perp, hi), (lo, lo, hi)) - size((lo, \perp, hi), (lo, lo, hi))] \times 27.5+$
$[size((hi, \perp, hi), (hi, lo, hi)) - size((lo, \perp, hi), (hi, lo, hi))] \times 47.5$
which is equal to $0 \times 2.5 + 0 \times 7.5 - 1 \times 27.5 + 1 \times 47.5 = 20$

This is the same value as if the difference is taken of the sum of the number of points in hyperquadrants 5 and 7, from the sum of the number of points in hyperquadrants 6 and 8.

5 Adaptive Merge Rules

Both new merged count and bias vector rules are given in this section. Also in computing the merge counts and bias vectors, **Algorithm** 4.1 in Figure 2 is going to be used here again to determine *regionsize* of each hyperquadrant in the multidimensional space. Then both merged count and bias vector computational rules are developed based on the computation of data points in each of these *hyperquadrants*.

5.1 Adaptive Merge Rule for Merge Counts

Suppose cell c merges with cells $c_1, ..., c_n$ along dimension δ, for $1 \leq \delta \leq D$, as shown in Figure 1(d.) In that figure, the horizontal-axis is dimension δ, while the vertical-axis is a generic dimension d. The resulting cellular structure after the merge is also sas shown in Figure 1(d.) After the merge, it is to be shown next how to calculate $N(newc_1), ..., N(newc_n)$ and $imb(newc_1, d), ..., imb(newc_n, d)$, for $1 \leq d \leq D$. Let $k \in \{c_1, ..., c_n\}$ be a generic cell.

Let β and γ be two cells. The following is to derive an algorithm to determine an approximation to the number of points in $\beta \cap \gamma$, $N(\beta \cap \gamma)$. This approximation will be a function of

$N(\beta_d^{(lo)}), N(\beta_d^{(hi)}), N(\gamma_d^{(lo)})$, and $N(\gamma_d^{(hi)})$, for $1 \leq d \leq D$.

Definition 5.1 *A* D-dimensional extent *is a D-element sequence of closed intervals of the real line. The* volume *of extent* $e = < e_1, ..., e_D >$,

$$vol(e) = \mu(e_1)\mu(e_2)...\mu(e_D) = \prod_{j=1}^{D} \mu(e_j), \tag{2}$$

where for $1 \leq j \leq D$, and

$$\mu(e_j) = \begin{cases} b_j - a_j & \text{if } e_j = [a_j, b_j] \\ 0 & \text{if } e_j = \emptyset \end{cases} \tag{3}$$

Definition 5.2 *Let* $e = < e_1, ..., e_D >$ *and* $f = < f_1, ..., f_D >$ *be two D-dimensional extents. Then, the* **intersection** *of* e *and* f, $e \cap f = < e_1 \cap f_1, ..., e_D \cap f_D >$, *for* $e_j = [a_j, b_j]$, $f_j = [c_j, d_j]$, *with the constraints that* $b_j > c_j$ *and* $a_j < d_j$, $\forall j 1 \leq j \leq d$. *We then have that:*

$e_j \cap f_j = [\mathbf{max}(a_j, c_j), \mathbf{min}(b_j, d_j)], \forall j \ 1 \leq j \leq D.$

Definition 5.3 *For* $1 \leq j \leq length$, *the definition of a D-dimensional extent* $e_{\beta,j}$ *corresponding to* $v_{\beta,j}$ *in the previous computation of split new_region_size is as:* $\forall k \ 1 \leq k \leq D$, *let* $e_{\beta,j}[k] = [left_{\beta,j,k}, right_{\beta,j,k}]$, *where*

$$left_{\beta,j,k} = \begin{cases} \frac{r_{\beta,k}^{(lo)} + r_{\beta,k}^{(hi)}}{2} & \text{if } v_{\beta,j}[k] = hi \\ r_{\beta,k}^{(lo)} & \text{if } v_{\beta,j}[k] \in \{\perp, lo\} \end{cases} \tag{4}$$

$$right_{\beta,j,k} = \begin{cases} \frac{r_{\beta,k}^{(lo)} + r_{\beta,k}^{(hi)}}{2} & \text{if } v_{\beta,j}[k] = lo \\ r_{\beta,k}^{(hi)} & \text{if } v_{\beta,j}[k] \in \{\perp, hi\} \end{cases} \tag{5}$$

Corresponding to γ, the definition of a *D-dimensional extent* e_γ, where $\forall j \ 1 \leq j \leq D$, $e_\gamma[j] = [r_{\gamma,j}^{(lo)}, r_{\gamma,j}^{(hi)}]$. The function of $N(\beta \cap \gamma)$ is defined as follows: $N(\beta \cap \gamma) =$

$\sum_{j=1}^{length} number\_of\_new\_regions_{\beta,j} \times new\_region\_size_{\beta,j} \times \frac{vol(e_\gamma \cap e_{\beta,j})}{vol(e_{\beta,j})}$

where β is the cell to be merged away, and γ is a generic cell mentioned previously. Returning now to cells c, and $k \in \{c_1, ..., c_n\}$, we define

$$\hat{c} = \left\{(x_1, ..., x_D) \mid r_{c,\delta}^{(lo)} \leq x_\delta \leq r_{c,\delta}^{(hi)}, \ while \ r_{k,j}^{(lo)} \leq x_j < r_{k,j}^{(hi)}, 1 \leq j \neq \delta \leq D\right\} \tag{6}$$

Then, the new merged count computation of cell $newk \in \{newc_1, ..., newc_n\}$ is as: $N(newk) = N(k) + N(c \cap \hat{c})$.

5.2 Adaptive Merge Rule for Merged Bias Vectors

Based on the new merge count computation, the imbalance vector computation of *newk*, $imb(newk, d)$, for $1 \leq d \leq D$, is given as follows based on two different cases. That is, the computations of the merged bias vectors are treated differently for merged dimension δ, and non-merging dimensions d, $\forall\ 1 \leq d \neq \delta \leq D$. The derivation of formulas to compute the merged *imbalance* vector values is given as follows:
For **Case 1:** if $d \neq \delta$ then,

$$imb(newk, d) = imb(k, d) + N(c \cap \hat{c}_d^{(hi)}) - N(c \cap \hat{c}_d^{(lo)}).$$

For **Case 2a:** if $d = \delta$ and $r_{c,\delta}^{(hi)} - r_{c,\delta}^{(lo)} \leq r_{k,\delta}^{(hi)} - r_{k,\delta}^{(lo)}$ (as shown in Figure 1(c.)),

$$imb(newk, \delta) = N(k_\delta^{(hi)}) + N(k_\delta^{(lo)}) \times \left[\frac{\frac{k+c}{2} - \frac{k}{2}}{\frac{k}{2}}\right] - N(\hat{c}_\delta) - N(k_\delta^{(lo)}) \times \left[\frac{\frac{k-c}{2}}{\frac{k}{2}}\right]$$

$$= N(k_\delta^{(hi)}) + N(k_\delta^{(lo)}) \times \left[\frac{c}{k}\right] - N(\hat{c}_\delta) - N(k_\delta^{(lo)}) \times \left[1 - \frac{c}{k}\right]$$

$$= N(k_\delta^{(hi)}) + N(k_\delta^{(lo)}) \times \left[\frac{r_{c,\delta}^{(hi)} - r_{c,\delta}^{(lo)}}{r_{k,\delta}^{(hi)} - r_{k,\delta}^{(lo)}}\right] - N(\hat{c}) - N(k_\delta^{(lo)}) \times \left[1 - \frac{r_{c,\delta}^{(hi)} - r_{c,\delta}^{(lo)}}{r_{k,\delta}^{(hi)} - r_{k,\delta}^{(lo)}}\right].$$

For **Case 2b:** if $d = \delta$ and $r_{c,\delta}^{(hi)} - r_{c,\delta}^{(lo)} > r_{k,\delta}^{(hi)} - r_{k,\delta}^{(lo)}$ (it is symmetric to that in Figure 1(c.), then by definitions and our assumptions again:

$$imb(newk, \delta) = N(k) + N(c_\delta^{(hi)}) \times \left[\frac{\frac{k+c}{2} - k}{\frac{c}{2}}\right] - N(\hat{c}_\delta^{(lo)}) - N(c_\delta^{(hi)}) \times \left[\frac{\frac{k+c}{2} - \frac{c}{2}}{\frac{c}{2}}\right]$$

$$= N(k) + N(c_\delta^{(hi)}) \times \left[\frac{c-k}{c}\right] - N(\hat{c}_\delta^{(lo)}) - N(c_\delta^{(hi)}) \times \left[\frac{k}{c}\right]$$

$$= N(\hat{c}) + N(k_\delta^{(hi)}) \times \left[1 - \frac{r_{c,\delta}^{(hi)} - r_{c,\delta}^{(lo)}}{r_{k,\delta}^{(hi)} - r_{k,\delta}^{(lo)}}\right] - N(k_\delta^{(lo)}) - N(k_\delta^{(hi)}) \times \left[\frac{r_{c,\delta}^{(hi)} - r_{c,\delta}^{(lo)}}{r_{k,\delta}^{(hi)} - r_{k,\delta}^{(lo)}}\right].$$

6 Application of MDHDS for Knowledge Extraction

The multidimensional histogram data structure is corresponding to a multidimensional tree, in which the root of the tree covers the entire range of the multidimensional data space. Each leaf node (multidimensional histogram bin) in the MDHDS tree covers a subragne of the multidimensional data space and contains both the histogram information such as the number of data points within the subrange and the range information such as low bound and high bound along each dimension.

There are several applications to which the MDHDS could be applied for the approximate knowledge extraction and approximate derivation of answers to range queries in multidimensional data space. With the help of the MDHDS, many approximate associative range knowledge can be extracted from it.

First, in the MDHDS, the approximate associative multidimensional range rules can be easily extracted and maintained in the adaptive and dynamic fashion. The approximate associative rules in the format as follows can be obtained from the leaf node of the MDHDS,

$$\exists(X)(\prod_{j=1}^{D}(r^{(lo)}_{c_k,j} \leq x_j < r^{(hi)}_{c_k,j}) \rightharpoonup count(X)) \quad 1 \leq j \leq D, 1 \leq k \leq n$$

where X is a multidimensional data point $(x_1, ..., x_D)$, the expression $(\prod_{j=1}^{D}(r^{(lo)}_{c_k,j} \leq X(x_j) < r^{(hi)}_{c_k,j}))$ is the conjunction form of $(r^{(lo)}_{c_k,j} \leq X(x_j) < r^{(hi)}_{c_k,j})$ for $1 \leq j \leq D$ and $1 \leq k \leq n$, and the symbol '$\rightharpoonup$' means the implication by approximation.

Second, by introducing the augmented dimensions such as time, geographical dimensions, it could be adopted to the real time applications such as on-line analytical processing and others in data warehousing. By generating multidimensional query boxes and calculating the data points within the intersect regions of the range query box and the MDHDS bins, the real time applications such as associative summarization queries in OLAP can be answered approximately without access to databases on the secondary storage. So the MDHDS could be an alternative of efficient ways to find the quick compact description for a subset of multidimensional data as mentioned in the reference [3].

7 Conclusion

In order to achieve the uniform resolution with respect to quantitative knowledge of data distribution, we developed our adaptive split and merge rules for this purpose. Our experiments have shown that our method provides much better results than the previous approach. [9] Since the MDHDS keeps track of most up-to-date quantitative information for the purpose of approximate knowledge extraction, the cost of reorganization and reclassification of derived knowledge can be reduced if the approximate quantitative knowledge can serve these purposes for some applications in OLAP and data warehouse.

Acknowledgement

The author Junping Sun would like to thank Dean Edward Lieblein, faculty, and staff at School of Comptuer and Information Sciences, Nova Southeastern University.

References

1. J. L. Bentley, "Multidimensional Binary Search Trees Used for Associative Search," *Communications of the ACM,* Volume 18, No. 9, 1975, pp.

509-517.

2. J. L. Bentley, "Multidimensional Binary Search Trees in Database Applications," *IEEE Transactions on Software Engineering,* Volume SE-5, No. 4, July 1979, pp. 333-340.
3. Usama M. Fayyad, Gregory Piatetsky-Shapiro, Padhraic Smyth, and Ramasamy Uthurusamy,*Advance in Knowledge Discovery and Data Mining*, edited, AAAI/MIT Press, 1996
4. William I. Grosky, Junping Sun, and Farshad Fotouhi, "Dynamic Selectivity Estimation for Multidimensional Queries," *Proceedings of 4th International Conference on Foundations of Data Organization and Algorithms*, October, 1993, pp. 231-246.
5. Jiawei Han and Yongjian Fu, "Attribute-Oriented Induction in Data Mining," in *Advance in Knowledge Discovery and Data Mining*, edited, AAAI/MIT Press, 1996, pp. 399-421.
6. Jiawei Han, Yandong Cai, and Nick Cercone, "Data-Driven Discovery of Quantitative Rules in Relational Database," *IEEE Transactions on Knowledge and Data Engineering*, Volume 5, No. 1, 1993, pp.29-40.
7. M. Muralikrishna, and D. J. Dewitt, "Equi-Depth Histogram for Estimating Selectivity Factors for Multi-Dimensional Queries," *Proceeding of 1988 ACM SIGMOD International Conference on Management of Data*, June, 1988, pp. 28-36.
8. J. Nievergelt, H. Hinterberger, and K. C. Sevcik, "The Grid File: An Adaptable Symemetric Multikey File Structure," *ACM Transactions on Database Systems*, Volume 9, No. 1, March 1984, pp. 38-71.
9. Joseph O'Rourke and Kenneth R. Sloan, JR, "Dynamic Quantization: Two Adaptive Data Structures for Multidimensional Spaces," *IEEE Transactions on Pattern Analysis and Machine Intelligence*, Vol. PAMI-6, No 3. May 1984, pp. 266-280.
10. G. Piatetsky-Sharpiro, *A Self-Organizing DataBase System - a Different Approach to Query Optimization*, Ph.D. Thesis, Courant Institute, New York University, May 1984.
11. G. Piatetsky-Shapiro, and W. Frawley, *Knowledge Discovery in Databases*, edited, AAAI,MIT Press 1991.
12. J. T. Robinson, "The K-D-B-Tree: A Search Structure for large Multidimensional Dynamic Index," *Proceedings of 1981 ACM SIGMOD International Conference on Management of Data*, 1981, pp. 10-18.
13. T. Sellis, N. Roussopoulos, and C. Faloutsos, "R+-Tree: A Dynamic Index for Multidimensional Objects," *Proceedings of the 13th International Conference on Very Large Data Bases,* Sept. 1987, pp. 507-518.

Chapter 6

KDD Applications

Discovering User Access Patterns on the World-Wide Web

David W. Cheung, Ben Kao, Joseph Lee
{dcheung | kao | jkwlee}@cs.hku.hk
Department of Computer Science, The University of Hong Kong, Pokfulam Road, Hong Kong

The World-Wide Web provides its users almost unlimited accesses to the documents on the Internet. We suggest to use intelligent agents to assist users to locate documents related to their interests instead of browsing the Web via primitive search engines. We identify a number of key components in such intelligent systems and propose a system architecture. In particular, we have designed a learning agent and the underlying algorithms for the discovery of areas of interest from the user access logs. The discovered topics can be used to improve the efficiency of information retrieval by prefetching documents for the users and store them in a document database in the system. We have also implemented a prototype system to illustrate the various concepts. Experiments are performed which shows that the areas of interest discovered can in fact be used to improve the efficiency of information retrieval on a distributed information system such as the Internet.

1 Introduction

It has been reported that the Web contains more than 30 million Web pages located on more than 275,600 hosts. While new information are being pumped into the Web everyday, large numbers of the old articles are being updated regularly, some at a very high frequency. It is impossible for a human being to keep track of all this information and changes, and there have been proposals on software tools to help users *retrieve, locate*, and *manage* Web documents. We call these software systems Web tools.

1.1 Classifying Web Tools

In general, we can classify Web tools into five levels, according to their intelligence and power.

A level 0 Web tool such as Mosaic and Netscape *retrieves documents for a user under straight orders.* The user has to instruct the tool on *where* the documents are located and *how* they are retrieved by supplying the document URLs.

A level 1 Web tool provides a *user-initiated searching facility* for finding relevant web pages. Internet search engines, such as Alta Vista[1] are examples of level 1 tools. Most of the search engines work by traversing the WWW indexing a large population of the pages. To find out relevant pages on a particular topic, a user supplies keywords to a search engine which describe the concepts. Documents that match the user query will be ranked according to an estimation on the closeness of the documents to the supplied keywords. Information about the matching documents will be sent back to the user.

A level 2 Web tool should maintain users profiles and have *an active component for notifying users whenever new relevant information is found.* Examples of level 2 Web tools include WebWatcher[2] and SIFT[10]. As an example, SIFT automatically matches new Netnews articles with users' standing orders, looking for news that are of interest to the users. Summaries of the relevant news articles are sent to the users via emails.

A level 3 Web tool should have *a learning and deductive component of user profiles.* Example contents of a user profile include topics of interest and browsing patterns. DiffAgent[7] and Letizia[8] are two experimental systems that track a users browsing behavior to infer the users topics of interest and can be considered as level 3 tools.

Finally, to better inform the users of the most up-to-date and relevant information, an intelligent Web tool should also understand the behavior of the information sources. We define a level 4 Web tool to be one that has the *capability of learning the behavior of both information users and information sources.* This knowledge enables the system to match the requirements and behavior of the two sides of the information interchange.

In this paper, we focus on the techniques in designing a level 4 Web tool. A system design and its architecture is proposed. In particular, we study the problem of constructing user profiles from user access history.

2 Related Works

A number of intelligent Web tools with different functionality have been proposed and implemented. In this section we briefly mention three such systems. Interested readers are referred to the literatures[2,3,5,8] for more details.

WebWatcher. Developed at Carnegie Mellon University, WebWatcher[2] is a tool that assists users by interactively giving them navigation advises. While the user is browsing through Web pages, WebWatcher assesses the hypertext links contained in the pages. It then recommends those links that the system guesses is promising in matching the goal of the session.

Letizia. Letizia[8] is an intelligent agent that works with a conventional Web browser such as Netscape. It tracks the users browsing behavior and tries to infer the users goals. While the user is reading a page, Letizia conducts a resource-limited search based on the goals it deduced. Relevant pages found during the search will be recommended to the user upon request. The goal of

Letizia is to automatically perform some of the Web exploration on behalf of the user to anticipate future page accesses.

Besides intelligent systems, another area in which some interesting works have been done is the discovery of useful access patterns from user access logs in distributed information systems like the World-Wide-Web.

A study by Chen et.al.[4] suggests to capture the browsing movement, (forwards and backward), between Web pages in a directed graph called *traversal path graph.* A set of *maximal forward references* which represent different browsing sessions are first extracted from the directed graphs. By using a technique similar to association rule mining in transactional databases, the frequently traversed paths, called *frequent traversal paths*, can be discovered. These frequent paths are the most common traversal patterns of the users.

Another study by Yan et.al.[11] suggests another approach for automatically classifying users of a Web site according to their access patterns. User access logs are examined to discover clusters of users that access similar pages. This technique may discover categories of Web pages that may be useful in application such as designing online catalogues for electronic commerce. Once these page groups are discovered, they may be used to customize the hypertext organization dynamically. The idea is to try and match an active users access pattern with one or more of the categories discovered. Pages in the matched categories that have not been explored by the user and are not adjacent to the users position may serve as a navigational hints.

3 An Intelligent Web Tools and Architecture

In this section, we outline the most important requirements of a level 4 intelligent Web tools, and propose an architecture for such a system. To reiterate, the goal of the intelligent Web tool is to discover the most updated and the most relevant information to its user with the least amount of user effort and system resources required. The requirements are:

1. The system should be able to discover its users topics of interest automatically. The system should also learn about its users shift of interests over time. This knowledge of users interests is used when the system is navigating the Internet on behalf of the user to discover relevant information.

2. The system should learn its users access patterns and information sources update patterns. It should also learn about when the documents are updated at the sources, and retrieve in advance the latest version before the user requests them.

Figure 1: System architecture

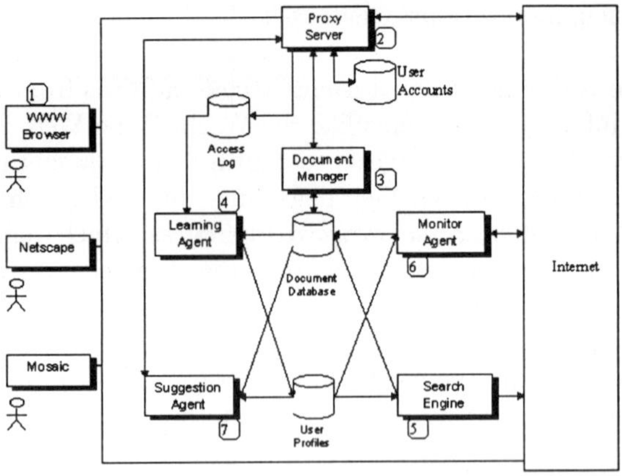

3. The system should make efficient use of network resources. Exhaustive searches that can generate excessive traffics should be avioded. Searching goals of multiple users should be clusterized. Similar goals should be batched together to reduce the number of Web searches conducted.

4. The system should maintain a database and a full-text index on retrieved documents. Data mining techniques [4] can be applied to the saved documents to discover the various types of useful and interesting access patterns.

5. The system should be compatible with most WWW browsers. There should be no extra requirements for a browser to communicate with the system in addition to the standard HTTP protocol.

Here we present an overview of a system design of a level 4 intelligent Web tool which is the model used in our prototype system. Figure 1 shows the system architecture and its components.

WWW Browsers (1). A user accesses the Internet through a conventional Web browser such as Netscape or Mosaic. If the user chooses to use our system, he simply instructs the browser to connect to a Proxy Server maintained by the system. During a session, all HTTP requests go through the Proxy. This mechanism allows the system to maintain a user access log.

Proxy (2). Users communicate with the system via a WWW proxy server. When a user issues a HTTP request, the request is forwarded to the Proxy,

Figure 2: The graphical user interface of the Document Manager.

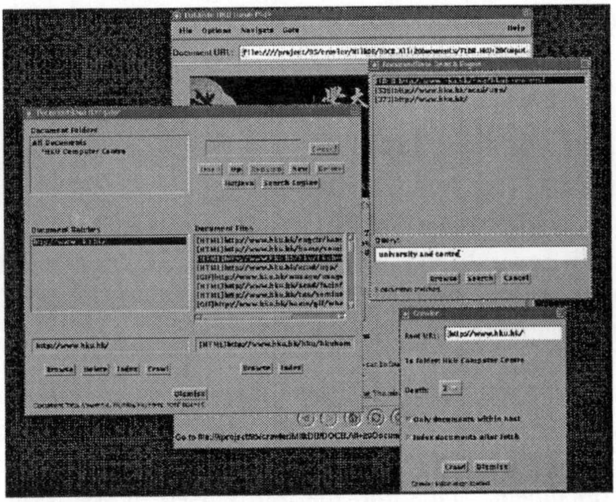

which fetches the desired Web document on behave of the user. The retrieved page is then deposited into the Document Database through the Document Manager (to be discussed shortly). When submitted a HTTP request, the Proxy will first check with the Document Manager and see if the desired document is already cached at the Document Database. If so, the local copy is returned to the user; else, the Internet is accessed. Second, the Proxy knows every document read by every user. This allows logging of user information be performed. In the prototype each user request generates a log record, which consists of the users ID, the URL requested, the time of the request, and the document retrieved. Information kept in the log is used by the Learning Agent to reconstruct the access patterns of the users. We will study how the Learning Agent analyzes this information to deduce the kinds of information sought by the users in Section 4.

Document Manager (3). The Document Manager is the interface for accessing the Document Database. It is responsible for storing and retrieving documents deposited by the system (from both user-initiated and system-initiated HTTP requests). The hypertext structures of the saved documents are preserved by reconstructing some of the links. Besides providing a persistent storage for the documents, the database also maintains a full-text index on the documents. Figure 2 shows the graphical user interface of the Document Manager.

Learning Agent (4). The Learning Agent discovers user access patterns and topics of interest by analyzing the access logs created by the Proxy. It generates a user profile for each user. A profile consists of two types of information:

1. Topics of interest. A topic is a set of weighted keywords and phrases that is of interest to the user. For example, the topic: <Basketball,0.7; Chicago-Bulls,0.4> shows that the user is interested in information about basketball in general (with a weight of 0.7), and the term Chicago-Bulls in particular (with a weight of 0.4). These keywords can be used to drive the Search Engine for information discovery.

2. Time-related access patterns. Some documents are requested by one or more users on a regular basis, e.g., newspaper, stock price quotes. A time-related access pattern records the period and location of a periodically accessed document. This information is used by the Monitor Agent for prefetching documents.

We will discuss in details the algorithms used in generating the user profiles in Section 4.

Search Engine (5). The Search Engine performs robot-based traversal about the Web. Interesting documents encountered during Web exploration is stored and indexed in the Document Database. In the prototype, the Search Engine is implemented as a goal-directed crawler, employing an algorithm similar to the fish-search algorithm. User profiles, in particular, the topics of interest, generated by the Learning Agent are used to drive the crawler, which tries to avoid visiting Web sites and their pages that are irrelevant to the goals.

Monitor Agent (6). The Monitor Agent monitors specific sites and Web pages that are known to contain interesting documents. It serves two functions. First, users can indicate that certain documents should be kept up-to-date. For this type of documents, the Monitor Agent periodically accesses them and learn about the sources update patterns (like how often a page is updated, and when). With this knowledge, the Monitor Agent schedules future retrieval of the pages and keeps them fresh in the Document Database. The second function is to schedule prefectches of pages that are regularly accessed by the users. The agent learns this from the user profiles created by the Learning agent.

Suggestion Agent (7). The Suggestion Agent ranks the newly found documents and assigns scores according to the extent that they match the users profiles. It composes a list of relevant new pages found on users' requests. The Agent also learns from the users feedback to improve the quality of future recommendation.

Figure 3: Discovery of topics of interest from user access log.

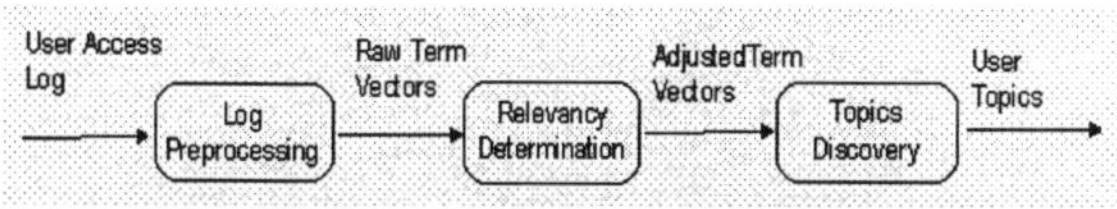

4 Discovery of Access Patterns

The Learning Agent and the Monitor Agent are two important components in our intelligent Web tool. On the client side, the Learning Agent is capable of identifying access patterns from the user access logs, in particular, the topics of interest of the users, while on the server side, it can discover the update patterns of the web pages collected. The Monitor Agent serves the clients by monitoring adaptively the updates on the web pages that the users are interested in.

The documents refereed in the user access logs contain a lot of unpolished information. However, with respect to the discovery of topics of interest, the information are mostly of the lower levels and may not be useful. In order to discover the most interesting topics, we need to identify and extract the most relevant kewords. In this section, we discuss the approach of keyword extraction and describe the algorithms implemented in our prototype system for this discovery task.

4.1 Discovery of Topics of Interests

The mechanism for discovering topics of interest is a 3-phase process (see Figure 3). The input to the process is the user access log. Initially, assume the log records the access history of a single user. We will extend it to cover the multi-users case later. We describe the three phases in detail in the following.

Phase 1. The Learning Agent processes each textual document as recorded in the user access log and produce a term vector of (keyword, weight) pairs. For example, a term vector including the pairs (NBA, 50) and (basketball, 35) may be extracted from a sport document. A modified formula for TFIDF[9] can be used to compute the weight of the keywords.

Phase 2. The term vectors produced in phase-one could be used to discover the users topics directly. However, there is a significant amount of noise in the vectors. For example, some Web pages may not be supplying any information to the user, but are visited simply because they have a large number of reference hyperlinks. Therefore, the learning agent has to determine the relevancy of every document and subsequently adjust the weights of the keywords according to the relevancy of the document from which they are extracted. The following heuristics are very useful for this purpose.

1. A Web page which has a large number of URLs is very likely a directory page of reference links. A document in which the number of hyperlinks exceeds a threshold will be regarded as a reference page and its relevancy is adjusted downward. The weights of the keywords extracted are thus lowered.

2. The amount of time that a user has spent in a document can be estimated from the records in the access logs. A page which is visited for a very short time is very likely a reference page or a pass-by page for browsing purpose. A time threshold is used to identify these pages and their relevancy are adjusted downward to reduce their significance.

3. The documents accessed at the end of a session are mostly visited because of their contents. In order to identify these content-rich documents, a *browse movement graph* which captures the forward and backward browsing relationship between Web pages is constructed from the access log. This graph is similar to the traversal path graph described by Chen[4]. Here, we use it for a different purpose. Every document in the access log is a node in the browse movement graph and an edge is created on the graph if the user has traversed from one document to another. In the browse movement graph, traversal paths can be identified. A traversal path starts from the home of the user and ends when a backward movement is recorded. (A backward movement is a go-back operation in a browser such as Netscape.) All traversal paths can be identified by determining all the backward browsing movement in the access log. A traversal path can be regarded as a browse session and the documents near the end of a session have a high chance of being a content-rich document. To refine this strategy, the time that a user has spent in such a document is also considered. To become a content-rich document, it must be near the end of a traversal path and the user must have stayed on it for a significant amount of time. A document identified as content-rich will have its relevancy adjusted upward to increase its significance.

4. The nodes in a browse movement graph described in point 3 above may have different fan-out. A node that has a high fan-out number represents a document from which many browsing-direction-changes are originated. Therefore, its functionality in the browsing is more like a reference page than a content provider. Hence, its relevancy should be adjusted downward and the weight of the keywords from it should be reduced.

5. Keywords extracted from a document with high **relevancy** are adjusted further according to their functional role in a document. For example, those in a title will have their weights increased the most, following by those extracted from higher level headers. In a HTML document, this adjustment can be performed by searching for the HTML tags such as the title tag <TITLE> and the top level header tag <H1>.

6. URLs that lead to documents which have high relevancy may contain keywords that reflect the users browsinginterest. Thus the keywords found in these URLs should be adjusted with increased weights to reflect their importance.

In summary, the task of the second phase in the discovery process is to use the above heuristics to adjust the relevancy of the raw term vectors extracted in the first phase. The output of the second phase is a sequence of term vectors with their weights adjusted.

Phase 3. The last phase of the discovery process is to produce the topics of interests from adjusted term vectors. Clustering techniques are being used to form the topics. The output is a small number of ***topic vectors*** truncated to a small predefined length, such as (NBA, basketball, stadium, arena). Note that this topic vector represents an area of interest of a user. In fact, the keywords in this topic vector can be input into a goal-directed search engine to retrieve documents that have a high chance of matching the users browsing habit.

In our prototype, the ***reallocation method***[6] is applied on the set of adjusted term vectors in order to generate clusters of similar vectors in the second phase. The distance between any two term vectors is measured by their similarity. The higher the similarity is, the smaller the distance would be. The similarity $s(v_1, v_2)$ between two term vectors v_1 and v_2 is given by the normalized inner product of v_1 and v_2. When a new term vector is added to a pool of clusterized vectors, its distance from the centroid of all the clusters formed so far will be measured. The new vector will be absorbed by the closest cluster unless their distance is longer than a certain threshold, in which case the new vectors form a new cluster by itself. The centroid of a cluster is a term vector which is the mean of all the vectors in the cluster. If too many clusters are formed with a threshold, clustering will be repeated with a smaller similarity threshold, (a larger distance threshold), until the number of clusters formed is small enough.

The last step of this phase is to convert the clusters into topics. Since the term vectors in a cluster are very close to the centroid, it is reasonable to use the centroid to represent all the term vectors in deriving the topic from a cluster. However, a centroid in general may have too many keywords and many of them may carry relatively small weights. A further selection of keywords

Figure 4: A sample document. Underlined words are those appear in the term vector.

```
<HEAD>
<TITLE> Bourne Again SHell (bash)</TITLE>
</HEAD><BODY> <H1> Bourne Again SHell (<SAMP> bash </SAMP>)</H1>
<P>This is a public domain shell written by the Free Software Foundation under their GNU initiative. Ultimately it is
intended to be a full implementation of the IEEE Posix Shell and Tools specification. This shell is widely used within the
academic community.</P>
<P> bash provides all the interactive features of the C shell (csh) and the Korn shell (ksh). Its programming language
is compatible with the Bourne shell (sh).</P>
<P>If you use Bourne shell (sh) for <A HREF="/UNIXhelp/scrpt/index.html"> shell programming </A> consider
using bash as your complete shell environment.</P>
<UL><LI>
<A HREF="/UNIXhelp/shell/ovie1.1.html">Summary of features</A></LI></UL>
</BODY></HTML>
```

within a centroid is performed. The centroids can be truncated with respect to a predefined length threshold or the keywords in it can be filtered against a weight percentage threshold. At the end, the output will be a small number of topic vectors such as (CFL, football, Tigers) and (NHL, hockey, Canada, Oilers).

4.2 An Example of Discovering Topics of Interest

In this section, an example is presented to illustrate the above algorithm. Figure 4 is a document recorded in an access log. In the first phase, raw term vectors from this document are extracted. Once the keywords are identified, their weights are calculated by using the TFIDF method. In the second phase, the heuristics proposed are used to adjust the weight of the term vectors. For example, the HTML tag are used to modify the weight of the keywords. Those in the title with the tag <TITLE> will have their weights increased, while those in the header under the tag <H1> will receive a smaller increment, all other keywords in different sections of the document are modified in a similar fashion. Also, this document is identified in the browse movement graph as a content-rich document, and the keywords weight are further increased. The resulted term vector of this document is ((shell, 0.2994), (bash, 0.2425), (bourne, 0.2379), ...).

In the last phase, the term vectors with adjusted weights are input into the clusterization process for the discovery of areas of interest. The similarity threshold used in this example is 0.1. The following URLs represent a cluster generated

http://theory.uwinnipeg.ca/unixfiles/Unixhelp/shell_oview2.5.html
http://www.fnal.gov/cd/UNIX/unixhelp/environment_exmp_bash.html
http://www.chernikeeff.co.uk/data/doc/lightstr/r2_1/hp_os/gnubash.htm
http://www.lib.ox.ac.uk/internet/news/faq/by_category.unix_faq.shell.html
http://www.ilap.com/UNIXhelp1.3/Pages/shell/ovew2.2.html

Table 1: Number of term vectors from each users

User #	# term vectors	User #	# term vectors	User #	# term vectors
0	364	1	299	2	365
3	642	4	1044	5	1044
6	213	7	213	8	511

Figure 5: Number of clusters vs similarity thresholds.

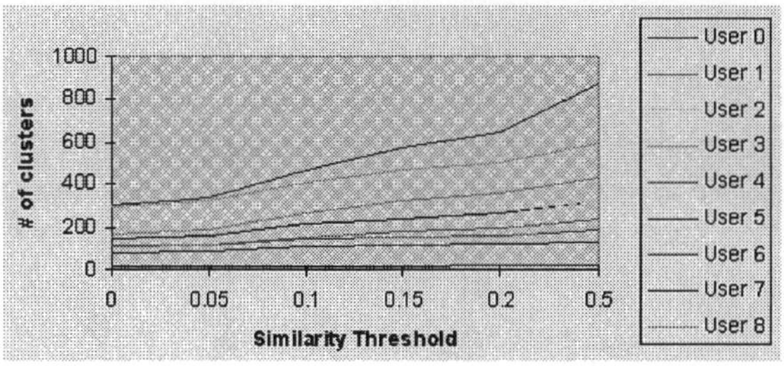

The centroid of the above cluster calculated from its term vectors is the vector ((bash,0.2881), (shell,0.2792), (bourne,0.2312), (unix,0.1138), (csh,0.1024), (z-shell,0.08673), (tcsh,0.03126),...). Finally, the keywords in the centroid of this cluster with small weight are truncated to produce the topic vector ((bash, 0.2881), (shell, 0.2792), (bourne, 0.2312)).

We have described the algorithm for discovering topic vectors from the log of a single user. The same algorithm can be applied to a log recording the access history of multiple users. The topic vectors discovered would be the common areas of interest among them. If these topic vectors are used by a goal-directed search engine, the retrieved documents would match the common interest of these users.

The Learning Agent can provide the system with the topic vectors which reflect the users areas of interest. Moreover, the Monitor Agent described in Section 3 can adaptively determine when these useful and interesting documents should be checked for updates. Together, these two agents provide an integrated and intelligent service to bring to the customers the documents and information that they need.

5 Experimental Results

Our prototype system has been implemented on AIX on an IBM 410 RS/6000 workstation. The proxy is a CERN httpd server. Nine volunteers have been

Table 2: Size and number of clusters generated vs threshold values.

Threshold		0.00	0.05	0.10	0.15	0.20	0.50
User 3	Max	24	22	12	8	7	4
	Mean	2.18	2.02	1.57	1.39	1.27	1.08
	# clusters	294	318	408	461	504	597
User 4	Max	34	28	24	24	23	21
	Mean	3.40	3.05	2.24	1.84	1.62	1.19
	# clusters	307	342	467	568	643	879

accessing the WWW via the proxy for a month. We have collected the user access logs from these volunteers. The logs are then submitted to the Learning Agent in the system to discover the topic vectors and subsequently the areas of interest. Table 1 shows the number of unique term vectors generated for each users.

One of the major steps in the discovery of the users topics of interest is to identify the clusters. The similarity threshold is an important parameter in the determination of the clusters. A smaller threshold would generate less but larger clusters, but they may not reflect a very focusing topic. A larger threshold would produce more clusters in total and each one of them would be better focused, but smaller in size. Figure 5 is the number of clusters discovered against different similarity thresholds for all the nine users in our experiment. When the threshold is set to 0, any two term vectors having an overlapping keyword would be treated as similar. Therefore, the least number of clusters will be generated in that case. We have observed that the number of clusters increases faster when the threshold is near the end of our test range.

In Table 2, we have recorded the clustering results of three selected users for different thresholds. For each user, the first row (Max) is the size of the largest cluster. The second row (Mean) is the average cluster size. The third row is the number of clusters generated.

It is also informative to investigate the distribution of the clusters for different thresholds. Figures 6 and 7 are the distributions of the clusters against their sizes and similarity thresholds. The distribution of user 4 is shown in Figure 6. This user has the largest number of documents, the clustering effect can be seen on all the threshold values. However, the effect is more visible when the threshold is around 0.1 or less. User 3 is an average user is our experiment, the number of documents in his log is close to the average. The distribution of the clusters of these user is shown in Figure 7. Among all the users in our experiment, it can be observed that the cluster distributions are more visible when the threshold is less than or equal to 0.1.

Figure 6: Cluster size distribution of user 4.

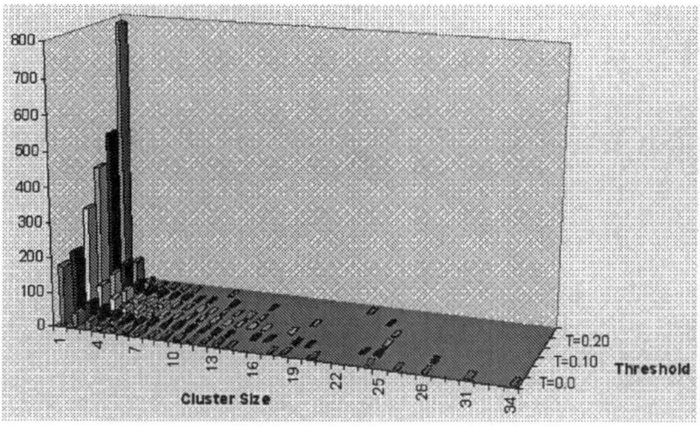

Figure 7: Cluster size distribution of user 3.

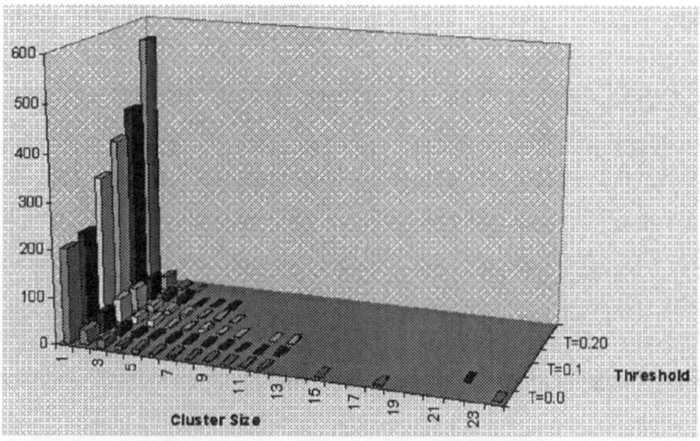

6 Discussion and Conclusion

In this study, the architecture of a level 4 Web tool has been described. The Web tools can discover the users access patterns and bring in documents that users are anticipating. An algorithm for the discovery of topic vectors and areas of interest from user access logs has been proposed. The key in the discovery process is to identify the relevancy of the documents and their keywords in order to select those that have higher influence in the determination of relevant topics. Several important techniques have been adopted in the adjustment of document relevancy. Clustering technique is used to find out topic vectors from term vectors whose weights are adjusted. To prove its feasibility, we have built a prototype system to demonstrate the ideas proposed in this study. The algorithm for mining the users topic vectors from their access logs has been implemented in the prototype and the result shows that the areas of interest discovered are relevant and meaningful. In the future, more learning capability will be introduced into the Learning Agent. It is very likely that there are hot page groups and hot page access sequences, and the Learning Agent can be enhanced to discover these types of access patterns.

References

1. http://altavista.digital.com
2. Armstrong et al. WebWatcher: A Learning Apprentice for the World Wide Web. *Working Notes of the AAAI Spring Symp.: Information Gathering from Heterogeneous, Distributed Environments.* AAAI Press, 1995, pp.6-12.
3. De Bra and R.D.J. Post. Information retrieval in the World-Wide Web: making client- based searching feasible. *Proceedings of the First International World-Wide Web Conference*, R. Cailliau, O. Nierstrasz, M. Ruggier (eds.), Geneva, 1994.
4. M. S. Chen, J.S. Park and P.S. Yu. Data Mining for Path Traversal Patterns in a Web Environment. *Proceedings of the 16th International Conference on Distributed Computing Systems*, Hong Kong, May, 1996, pp385-392.
5. O. Etzioni and D.S. Weld. Intelligent Agents on the Internet: Fact, Fiction, and Forecast. *IEEE Expert*, Vol. 10, No. 4, August, 1995, pp.44-49.
6. W.B. Frakes, R. Baeza-Yates. *Information Retrieval: Data Structure and Algorithms.* Pentice-Hall, 1992.
7. D.H. Jones and D. Navin-Chandra. IndustryNet: A Model for Commerce on the World Wide Web. *IEEE Expert*, October 1995, pp.54-59.
8. H. Lieberman. Letizia: An Agent that Assists Web Browsing. *International Joint Conference on Artificial Intelligence*, 1995.
9. G. Salton. *Automatic Text Processing: The Transformation, Analysis, and Retrieval of Information by Computer.* Addison-Wesley, Reading, MA. 1989.
10. T.W.Yan and H.Garcia-Molina. SIFT-A Tool for Wide-Area Information Dissemination. *Proceedings of the 1995 USENIX Technical Conference*, 1995, pp.177-186.
11. T.W. Yan et. al. From User Access Patterns to Dynamic Hypertext Linking. *Proceedings of the Fifth International World-Wide Web Conference*, Paris, France, May 1996.

BAYESIAN NETWORK LEARNING MODEL
FOR REAL-TIME TELE-MARKETING OPERATIONS

JAE-HYEON AHN
AT&T Laboratory, Room 7E-530, 600 Mountain Avenue, Murray Hill,
NJ 07974, USA

KAZUO EZAWA
AT&T Laboratory, Room 7E-523, 600 Mountain Avenue, Murray Hill,
NJ 07974, USA

This paper presents a Bayesian network learning model for real-time tele-marketing operations. Based on the Bayesian network learning model, a prototype decision support system is further developed for the AT&T Customer Contact Employee to provide a recommendation regarding the promotion of a telephone discount plan. The system integrates Bayesian network learning model (knowledge discovery process) and decision-making technique (influence diagrams) to provide real-time decision support. The probability of a customer's future response is predicted by a Bayesian network learning model based on promotional history/response. An Influence diagram framework is used to integrate the predicted probability with the cost and benefit related to the possible actions. By linking the Bayesian network learning model with rigorous decision-making technique; such as influence diagrams, the decision support system developed in this paper was shown to improve decision making capability.

1 Introduction

As corporations amass huge amounts of data from their daily operations, utilization of the collected data becomes one of the most important corporate activities. To satisfy customers and win the business in the ever-changing market place, it is necessary to understand the data and extract valuable information from them. The extracted information could be used in all stages of corporate activities; from idea generation, product planning and design to targeted marketing and advertisement.

However, it is a very difficult task to extract information from data as the number of variables and volume of the data become large and interactions among the variables become complex. For example, there are more than 90 million AT&T customers, and for each customer, there are many disjointed customer records in hundreds of databases AT&T currently manages. On top of that, new information is generated every second as streams of electronic information are pumped into the AT&T network by the users. It means that over 200 million new data points are generated every day in the AT&T operations. With this extraordinarily huge amount of data and their complex inter-relationships, it is a challenge to understand customers at the proper market segment level, not to mention at the individual customer level. To understand and improve this challenging process, a field *Knowledge Discovery in Databases* attracted considerable attention from many diverse fields such as statistics, information technology, machine learning, knowledge-based systems, database management, etc.

Knowledge discovery in databases (KDD) is a process of discovering previously unknown patterns in large data bases. Also known as data mining in statistics, KDD is a highly interactive and iterative process which includes 1) selection, cleaning, transformation, and projection of data, 2) mining the data to extract patterns, 3) evaluating the patterns to decide what constitutes "knowledge", 4) consolidating the knowledge, 5) resolving conflicts with previously extracted knowledge, and 6) making the knowledge available for use on the KDD system[1].

Even though many KDD systems were developed for applications in the area of finance, insurance, marketing, medicine, geology, astronomy, etc[2], few systems[3,4] address the use of knowledge in the decision-making processes explicitly. Once the knowledge becomes available from the KDD system, patterns or knowledge identified from the KDD process can be used in the decision-making processes. Most of the KDD systems developed so far, however, focused on how to discover knowledge but not on how to use it. Therefore, the link between knowledge discovery process and applications of the discovered knowledge has been either least emphasized or ignored as a different subject. Knowledge is valuable when it is applied appropriately in the decision-making processes. In this paper, an attempt was made to link the knowledge discovery process (Bayesian network learning model) and decision-making process. Based on the information extracted from the Bayesian network learning model, a prototype decision support system was developed for the real-time tele-marketing operations in the telecommunications industry. An influence diagram framework was used as a *decision engine* or *problem processing system* in Bonczek's term[5] to recommend the best action to take.

Decision Support System for Tele-Marketing

AT&T Customer Contact Employees (CCEs) make several million customer contacts each day. Whenever they make contact with customers relating to billing questions, inquiries, subscription of new services, complaints, etc., they can promote special telephone services which customers don't have but may like. A *Telephone Discount Plan* or TDP is one of them. Additionally, in the near future, services such as local services, wireless services, entertainment services, internet services can be promoted.

A TDP is a plan where telecommunication charges are discounted over the regular rates depending on the customer's calling pattern and usage level. At this time, it is not required for the CCE to offer it to new customers or existing customers who don't have it. However, it is believed that by offering the service they can increase customer satisfaction with the telecommunications provider and improve the customer retention. Unfortunately, it is costly to promote it because the CCE has to spend time explaining the characteristics of the plan, how it works, how much money customers can save, etc., sometimes at the expense of other customers waiting on the line to be served. Because there are tradeoffs between offering TDP and serving next customers, it is not obvious for the CCE to decide to promote it on a real time basis at the time of customer contact.

An intelligent decision support system recommending the best action will be useful in this problem, and it will increase the productivity of the CCEs and profitability of our business. In this analysis, a prototype decision support system for a specific TDP promotion decision was developed. The goal was to maximize the effectiveness of the tele-marketing activities by minimizing the time spent on unsuccessful promotion. Theoretically, it can be done by predicting and promoting the TDP only to the people who would subscribe to it. The major problem was uncertainty related to the customer's response regarding the promotion of the TDP. To predict the probability of rejecting the TDP promotion, a Bayesian network learning model was developed from a pre-classified training data set. The training data set had the customers' responses for previous random promotions of the TDP. Then, a decision support system described in this paper provided the best recommendation for the CCE depending on the predicted probability from the Bayesian network model and other factors related to the promotion.

2 Bayesian Network Learning Model for Probability Prediction

To provide intelligent decision support regarding the TDP promotion, it is necessary to predict the customer's response for the TDP offering. An approach would be to predict the customer's response based on the knowledge from previous customer contact results in the databases. To extract good predictors of customer responses, we used a machine learning system called APRI (Advanced Pattern Recognition and Identification) developed at AT&T Bell Labs[6]. It extracts knowledge from databases and represents it in the Bayesian network framework. In the following, we provide a brief explanation of the Bayesian network and the APRI system.

2.1 Bayesian Network

A Bayesian network is a directed acyclic graph where each node represents a random variable. A typical Bayesian network used in our analysis is shown in Figure 1. In the network, we use a special structure for the purpose of classification and later make a recommendation based on the belief which are updated by the new observations. We denote a node that we are interested in predicting as π or by a *prime node*. Other variables in the model are variables explaining customer profile, which is denoted as $X = (X_1, X_2, \ldots, X_n)$ or *field nodes*. Field nodes are connected depending on the probabilistic relationships between them. Probabilistic information is stored in the form of marginal distribution on the prime node and conditional distributions on the field nodes. Assessing $p(\pi|X)$ directly is often infeasible due to data and storage limitations. However, conditional probability $p(X|\pi)$ and the marginal probability $p(\pi)$ are easier to assess by analyzing a pre-classified training data set. Then, conditional probability $p(\pi|X)$ can be calculated by applying Bayes' rule.

Once we develop a Bayesian network, we predict the customer's response for the TDP offering based on the available customer-specific information. Historically, the actual implementation of the *Bayesian Classifier* was infeasible because of the size of the data set. However, recent advances in evidence propagation algorithms[7,8,9,10,11] and computer hardware allow us to *approximate* the ideal Bayesian classifier by using Bayesian network models[12,13,14]. For the use of APRI for the classification and comparison with other methods, see Ezawa and Schuermann[15].

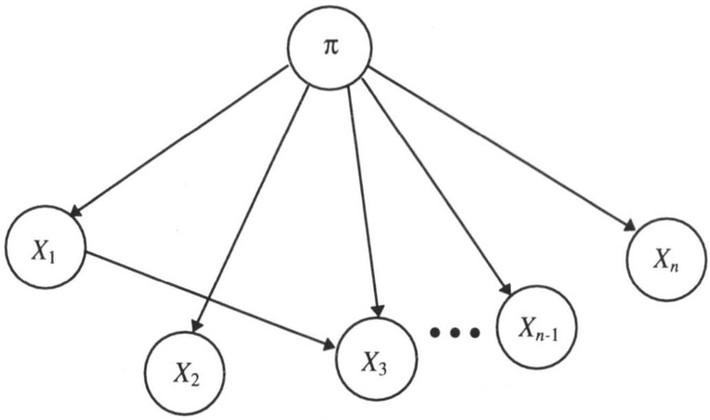

Figure 1: A Bayesian network.

2.2 APRI System

The APRI (Advanced Pattern Recognition and Identification) system was developed primarily for learning Bayesian network models with very large data sets of the telecommunications industry. It is a supervised machine learning system. It uses a heuristic approximation to the full Bayesian classifier in the Bayesian network paradigm using entropy measure (mutual information) to perform variable and dependency selections[16]. In order to obtain a useful approximation of the full conditional probability structure, the APRI system uses mutual information both for variable selection and dependency selection between each pair of the selected variables. This approach was chosen to reduce training time with special emphasis on limiting repeated reading of the training data, which can be a critical factor for generating large data sets. To select variables and dependencies, it uses two parameters $T_{\pi x}$ and T_{xx} both ranging from 0 to 1. $T_{\pi x}$ is a parameter for the selection of variables (field nodes) and T_{xx} is a parameter for the selection of dependencies between field nodes in the Bayesian network. The two parameters $T_{\pi x}$ and T_{xx} will be iteratively selected by the user to achieve the maximum discrimination power. APRI constructs a graphical Bayesian network model in four steps.

Step 1: APRI parses the input database and characterizes its variables. If the prime mode is continuous, APRI first defines the class outcomes either by discretization or kernel density estimation. APRI then scans the database to identify the outcome sets for each variable. For continuous variable, it either estimates the kernel density or information-based discretization.

Step 2: APRI chooses variables to be in the Bayesian network model. The choice is based on the mutual information calculation. If the mutual information between the prime node and any other node or $I(\pi;X_i)$ is zero, then it implies that the variable X_i doesn't help to classify the prime node. On the other hand, $I(\pi;X_i)$ will take higher value if π and X_i have functional relationship. From this reasoning, we select variables in the order of the highest mutual information until the sum of the mutual information of the selected variables doesn't exceed $T_{\pi x}$ times the total mutual information.

Step 3: APRI selects the dependencies among the variables selected in the Step 2. In particular, it computes the conditional mutual information $I(X_i, X_j|\pi)$ between pairs of the previously selected variables. These candidate links are rank ordered and the highest ranked links are selected until the cumulative value doesn't exceed T_{xx} times the total conditional mutual information. Directionality of these links is based on the mutual information variable ranking determined in the Step 2, with higher ranked variables pointing toward the lower ranked ones.

Step 4: APRI estimated $\Pr(\pi)$ and $\Pr(X_i \mid C(X_i))$ using frequency counts, where $C(X_i)$ represents the parents of the prime node X_i.

APRI reads the database from secondary storage which is quite different from other analyses which assumes that data is stored in fast random-access memory[12]. With the big size of data, typically gigabyte size, the assumption is not applicable in our problem. APRI is very efficient in this regard, reading the data set no more than 5 times.

3 Bayesian Network Learning Model

To develop a Bayesian network learning model predicting customer's response for the TDP promotion, we followed three stages. First, we prepared a data set to train a Bayesian network from an existing database (data processing). Second, we trained a Bayesian network learning model using APRI (model training). Finally, we measured the discriminating power of the Bayesian network learning model (performance evaluation).

3.1 Bayesian Network Learning Model Development

In this analysis, an AT&T marketing database was used to develop a data set because it contains prior history of customer responses for the TDP promotions as well as customer profiles. From the marketing database, we collected 37,124 TDP promotion records during the first half of 1995 in a specific region. It was expected that the data set would contain "good" predictors which can effectively discriminate *Takers* and *Non-takers* for the TDP promotions.

We called those customers who took the offer, *Taker*, and those who declined it, *Non-taker*. Out of a total 37,124 customers in the data set, 26,172 customers took the offer and 10,952 customers didn't take the offer yielding a 29.5% unconditional probability of being a Non-taker[a].

---

[a] We estimate the probability of being a Non-taker because they are the customers we want to avoid.

Data Processing

The marketing database used in this analysis contained almost 300 variables for each customer. Out of those, 30 variables were pre-selected for the data set development as the most relevant variables (field nodes) to extract the pattern regarding TDP subscriptions. For those 30 variables, there were continuous variables (e.g., monthly telephone usage in dollars) and categorical variables (e.g., geographical location, date information). The information on whether a specific customer is a Taker or Non-taker (prime node) was also included in the data set as a binary variable.

Model Training

Once a data set was prepared, the data set was separated into two different data sets; *training data set* and *test data set*. The *training data set* was used to develop a Bayesian network learning model using APRI. The *test data set* was used to check the performance of the developed Bayesian network learning model. In our analysis, we randomly selected 90% of the data set for training and 10% for testing. So, the training data set contained 33,411 records and the test data set contained 3,713 records with Non-taker's probability being equal to 29.5% for both data sets. After performing 10 fold cross-validations, the most promising result (the most discriminating power which will be discussed later) was obtained by constructing a Bayesian network with 12 variables and parameters $T_{\pi x} = 0.95$, $T_{xx} = 0.25$.

Performance Evaluation

Based on the Bayesian network learning model developed above, the probability of being a Non-taker was predicted using the test data set. That is, the customer specific information from the test data set was used to propagate the information through the Bayesian network, and the probability of being a Non-taker was predicted.

In many practical problems, a perfect prediction is not possible. To evaluate the usefulness of the prediction, it is necessary to measure the discriminating power of it. To evaluate the performance of the prediction based on the Bayesian network model, the test data set was ordered in descending order depending on the estimated probability of being a Non-taker. For each decile, the average predicted probability was calculated (3rd column in Table 1). Then, the number of Non-takers (4th column in Table 1) was counted and the fraction of Non-takers (5th column in Table 1) was calculated for each decile of ordered data set. The 6th column in Table 1 was calculated by dividing the 5th column by 29.5% to show the degree of discrimination in each decile. The cumulative index showing the percentage of captured Non-takers was also calculated (7th column in Table 1).

If we can make a perfectly discriminating prediction, all the Non-takers would belong to the upper part of the ordered data set. Table 1 shows that, for the first decile in the ordered data set, the percent of Non-takers was 60.1% (the percent of the Non-takers in the training data set was 29.5% yielding a lift of 203.8%) which was considered impressive. Also, it showed that we can capture almost 71% of the Non-takers up to the fifth decile of the ordered data set.

Table 1: Gains Table.

Decile	Observation per group	Average Predicted Pr.	# of Non-takers	Non-taker Rate	Non-taker Index	Cumulative Index
0-10%	371	0.681	223	60.1%	203.8%	20.4%
10-20%	371	0.486	189	50.9%	172.7%	37.6%
20-30%	371	0.387	144	38.8%	131.6%	50.8%
30-40%	371	0.320	115	31.0%	105.1%	61.3%
40-50%	371	0.268	105	28.3%	96.0%	70.9%
50-60%	371	0.223	89	24.0%	81.3%	80.0%
60-70%	371	0.183	75	20.2%	68.5%	85.8%
70-80%	371	0.144	69	18.6%	63.1%	92.1%
80-90%	371	0.102	55	14.8%	50.3%	97.2%
90-100%	374	0.056	31	8.3%	28.1%	100.0%
Total	3713	0.295	1095	29.5%		

Note: (Column 6) = (Column 5) / 29.5%.

3.2 Misclassification Probability and Misclassification Cost

The Bayesian network learning model can be used for classification based on the probability prediction. If the classifications are perfect, then it is easy to recommend the optimal decision based on them. That is, if a customer is classified as a *Taker*, then offer the TCP. If a customer is classified as a *Non-taker*, then do not offer it. We can save costs from unsuccessful promotion. Therefore, with perfect classification capability, the Bayesian network model can be used as a decision support system directly. In reality, perfect classification procedures are hardly obtainable.

One way of judging performance of any classification procedure is to calculate misclassification probability. Suppose that we classify a customer as *Taker* or *Non-taker* based on the predicted probability. That is, if the predicted probability (of being a Non-taker) is greater than the "threshold probability", then we classify the customer as a "Non-taker". If the predicted probability is less than the threshold probability, then we classify it as a "Taker". Label the Non-taker's population π_1 and the Taker's population π_2. Let's denote prior probability of population i as $p(\pi_i)$, and the probability of classifying population i given that it is actually from the population j as $p(i|j)$, i, j=1,2. Note that $p(i|j)$ is different depending on different threshold probabilities. Then, the misclassification probability is calculated as the weighted sum of the false negative rate and the false positive rate weighted by their prior probabilities, or $p(2|1)\ p(\pi_1) + p(1|2)\ p(\pi_2)$. The misclassification probability was calculated to be minimum at the threshold level 0.5. Therefore it would be good to use threshold level 0.5 for classification if we want to minimize the misclassification probability.

On the other hand, suppose that we were interested in minimizing the Expected Misclassification Cost (EMC) of the classification procedure. Let's denote the cost of classifying Non-taker (population 1) into Taker (population 2) as $C(2|1)$ and cost of classifying Taker into Non-taker as $C(1|2)$. Then the EMC is expressed as

$$\text{EMC} = C(2|1)\, p(2|1)\, p(\pi_1) + C(1|2)\, p(1|2)\, p(\pi_2).$$

Suppose that $C(2|1)$ is two times larger than $C(1|2)$, then the threshold probability minimizing EMC is calculated as 0.4. This is because the cost of misclassifying Non-takers as Takers is high (for example, the time spent for customer contact), it is better to classify customers aggressively as Non-takers. On the other hand, if $C(1|2)$ is two times larger than $C(2|1)$, then the threshold probability minimizing EMC is calculated as 0.8. This is because the cost of misclassifying Takers as Non-takers is high (for example, poor customer satisfaction and possible change of companies), it is better to classify customers conservatively as Non-takers. If C(1|2) is same as C(2|1), then EMC criterion gives the same threshold probability as minimizing misclassification probability.

As was shown above, if there exists an asymmetric misclassification cost structure, a classification procedure depending only on the misclassification probability criterion may provide misleading input for the decision-making process. It doesn't consider the cost related to the classification. If the misclassification cost is different for each customer and uncertainty is attached to the misclassification cost structure, even EMC criterion does not provide sensible input on the individual customer level. Therefore, it is better to use the predicted probability directly as an input in the decision-making process rather than the classification result. That is, regardless of the objective in the decision problem (whether it is minimizing misclassification probability or misclassification cost), the predicted probability will be used directly in the decision-making process. Because the Bayesian network learning model is based on probability theory, the predicted probability from the model can be perfectly linked with the influence diagram framework which is also based on probabilistic decision theory.

4 A Prototype Decision Support System Development

In the previous Section 3, it was shown that decision support based only on the Bayesian network model can be misleading depending on the objective of the decision problem. So, it is linked with rigorous decision-making tool to provide an intelligent decision support. In this section, the Bayesian network learning model and influence diagram framework were integrated to develop a prototype decision support system. The Bayesian network learning model developed by the APRI system was used to predict the probability. And, the influence diagram framework[16] was used as a decision engine for the CCE to make recommendations based on the probability prediction and other related factors to the TDP promotion decision.

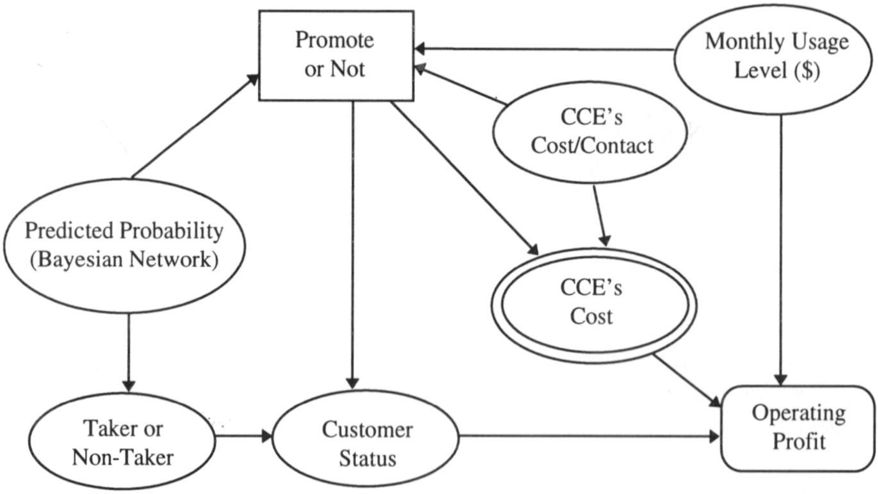

Figure 2: Prototype decision support system for the TDP promotion.

Figure 2 shows a prototype decision support system based on the influence diagram framework recommending whether the CCE should promote the TDP or not. Once a Bayesian network model predicts the probability of being a Non-taker, the information is represented as a node "Predicted Probability" in Figure 2.

The Bayesian network learning model predicts the probability in a continuous scale and later it is discretized to be used in making a recommendation. The node

"Predicted Probability" in Figure 2 is dynamically linked to the Bayesian network learning model described in Section 3. The event of being an actual Taker or Non-taker is represented as the node "Taker or Non-Taker" given the node "Predicted Probability". The probability of being a Non-taker ("Predicted Probability" node) is calibrated using the actual Non-taker's ratio in each decile (5th column in Table 1). An arrow from the node "Predicted Probability" to a decision node "Promote or Not" implies that the predicted probability is available at the time of the decision. A node "Customer Status" represents the uncertainty that the customer may leave AT&T depending on whether an TDP plan is offered or not, and the customer is actually a Taker or a Non-taker. The actual cost of CCE's time is represented as "CCE's Cost" determined jointly by whether the TDP is offered or not and the CCE's cost per contact. The node "Monthly Usage Level ($)" is used to represent the revenue impact related to the decision. The value function we want to maximize is dependent on the cost of offer and the expected revenue from a customer.

Based on the relationships among the variables shown in Figure 2, a decision support system was implemented on a Sun SPARC Station 10. The interface is designed so that the AT&T Customer Contact Employee (CCE) can use the system without ever knowing either Bayesian network or influence diagrams. When a customer contact is made, the customer's profile is automatically retrieved from the relevant databases. The Bayesian network learning model, if necessary, predicts the probability of being a Non-taker based on the customer profile. Then, the decision support system recommends the best action for CCE whether to promote the plan or not. If there is missing information on the customer profile, then the CCE may ask customer questions to better predict the probability. The missing data are shown in the order of importance (based on the mutual information calculation), and as far as it is possible, it is recommended to ask questions in that order because more uncertainty can be resolved in that order. The system then makes a new recommendation based on the new customer information.

Table 2 summarizes the recommendations regarding the TDP promotion. It shows the following. If the average monthly bill size (international charge) is large (more than \$$X_2$/mon.), then offer the TDP regardless of predicted probability and the cost of offering because the potential benefit of keeping this customer outweighs the cost of offering[b]. If the monthly bill size is moderate (from \$$X_1$ to \$$X_2$/mon.), then i) offer it when the cost of offering is small (\$$Y_1$), ii) offer it only when the cost of offering is moderate (\$$Y_2$) and the predicted probability (of being

---

[b] The cost of offering would be dependent not only on the expected CCE's time to spend, but on how many customers are waiting in queue to be served.

a Non-Taker) is less than Z_2, and iii) do not offer it if the cost of offering is high ($\$Y_3$). If monthly bill size is small (less than $\$X_1$/mon.), then offer it only when the cost of offering is small ($\$Y_1$) and the predicted probability is less than Z_1.

Table 2: Optimal recommendations.

Monthly bill \ Cost of offer	$\$Y_1$	$\$Y_2$	$\$Y_3$
0 - $\$X_1$	Offer only if predicted probability $< Z_1$	Do not offer	Do not offer
$\$X_1$ - $\$X_2$	Offer	Offer only if predicted probability $< Z_2$	Do not offer
> $\$X_2$	Offer	Offer	Offer

Note: $X_1 < X_2$, $Y_1 < Y_2 < Y_3$, and $Z_1 < Z_2$.

Those recommendations have some implications on how to implement this decision support system. For example, if a specific customer's bill size is large, then don't bother to predict probability from the Bayesian network learning model, but promote it all the time. If a specific customer's bill size is small, then run the Bayesian network model to predict probability only when the cost of offering is small.

For the purpose of the analysis in this paper, we have chosen a simplified version to demonstrate how the decision support system really works. In the real implementation, more factors should be considered such as 1) the effect of stimulated usage because of the TDP subscription, 2) reduced revenue because of discount due to TDP subscription, 3) a more sophisticated assessment of the customer's life with or without the TDP.

5 Conclusion

We developed a decision support system based on the Bayesian network learning model and influence diagram framework. The system was specially developed to make recommendations for a Telephone Discount Plan (TDP) promotion. In Section 3, it was shown that decision support based only on the Bayesian network learning model can be misleading if there are different objectives in the decision problem. So, it was linked with a rigorous decision-making tool to provide an intelligent decision support.

To do that, a Bayesian network learning model was used to predict the response probability for the promotion, and the influence diagram framework was used to integrate the predicted probability with the cost and benefit related to the possible actions. In this paper, it was demonstrated how the knowledge (predicted probability) was extracted using a Bayesian network learning model and linked to the decision support system. The Bayesian network based knowledge discovery process was useful in finding patterns out of the customer's response, and it was fed into as an important input to the decision support system. Because the Bayesian network learning model was based on probability theory, the predicted probability from the model was perfectly linked with the influence diagram framework which was also based on probabilistic decision theory.

In this paper, a real-time decision support system using a Bayesian network learning model was presented for a special TDP promotion decision. However, this approach can be equally useful to target customers in providing services such as wireless service, internet service, entertainment service, banking service, local service as well as our traditional long-distance service.

Acknowledgments

We want to thank Ann Skudlark for her helpful comments on this paper.

References

1. Fayyad, U. M and Uthurusamy, R., *Proceedings of the First International Conference on Knowledge Discovery & Data Mining* (AAAI Press, 1995).
2. Fayyad, U. M., Piatetsky-Shapiro G., Smyth, P., and Uthurusamy, R., *Advances in Knowledge Discovery and Data Mining* (AAAI/MIT Press, 1995).
3. Chaturvedi, A. R., "Supporting Complex Real-Time Decision Making through Machine Learning", *Decision Support Systems*, Vol. 10, 213-233 (1993).
4. Shaw, M. J., "Applying Inductive Learning to Enhance Knowledge-based Expert Systems", *Decision Support Systems*, Vol. 4, 319-332 (1987).
5. Bonczek, R. H., Holsapple, C. W. and Whinston, A. B., "Future Directions for Developing Decision Support Systems", *Decision Sciences*, Vol. 11, 616-631 (1980).

6. Ezawa, K. J. and Norton, S., "Knowledge Discovery in Telecommunication Services Data", *Proceedings of the First International Conference on Knowledge Discovery & Data Mining*, (AAAI Press, 1995).
7. Shachter, R. D., "Evidence Absorption and Propagation through Evidence Reversals", *Uncertainty in Artificial Intelligence*, Vol. 5, 173-190, (North-Holland, 1990).
8. Lauritzen, S. L., and Spiegelhalter, D. J., "Local Computations with Probabilities on Graphical Structures and their Application to Expert Systems," *J. R. Statistics Society, B*, Vol. 50, No. 2, 157-224 (1988).
9. Pearl, J., *Probabilistic Reasoning in Intelligent Systems*, (Morgan Kaufmann, 1988).
10. Jensen, V., Olesen K. G., and Anderson S. K., "An Algebra of Bayesian Universes for Knowledge-Based Systems," *Networks*, Vol. 20, 637-659 (1990).
11. Ezawa, K. J., "Value of Evidence on Influence Diagrams", *Proceedings of the Tenth Conference on Uncertainty in Artificial Intelligence*, 212-220 (Morgan Kaufmann, 1994).
12. Cooper, G. F. and Herskovits, E., "A Bayesian Method for the Induction of Probabilistic Networks from Data", *Machine Learning*, Vol. 9, 309-347 (1992).
13. Langley, P. and Sage, S., "Induction of Selective Bayesian Classifiers," *Proceedings of the Tenth Conference on Uncertainty in Artificial Intelligence*, pp. 399-406 (Morgan Kaufmann, 1994).
14. Singh, M. and Valtorta, M., "Construction of Bayesian Network Structures from Data: a Brief Survey and an Efficient Algorithm", *International Journal of Approximate Reasoning*, Vol. 12, 111-121 (1995).
15. Ezawa, K. J., and Schuermann, T., "Fraud/Uncollectible Debt Detection Using a Bayesian Network Based Learning System: A Rare Binary Outcome with Mixed Data Structures," *Proceedings of the 11th Conference on Uncertainty in Artificial Intelligence*, 157-166 (Morgan Kaufmann, 1995).
16. Cover, T. M. and Thomas, J. A., *Elements of Information Theory* (John Wiley and Sons, 1991).
17. Shachter, R. D., "Evaluating Influence Diagrams", *Operations Research*, Vol. 34 (6) 871-882 (1986).

TACKLING THE CROSS-SALES PROBLEM USING DATA MINING

S. S. ANAND, J. G. HUGHES
Northern Ireland Knowledge Engineering Laboratory, Faculty of Informatics,
University of Ulster, Northern Ireland BT37 0QB

D. A. BELL
School of Information and Software Engineering, Faculty of Informatics,
University of Ulster, Northern Ireland BT37 0QB

A. R. PATRICK
Northland Computer Services, Northland Road, Derry, Northern Ireland BT48 7HX

In this paper we discuss the use of Data Mining to provide a solution to the problem of cross-sales. The cross-sales problem is defined and analyzed and a methodology developed for solving this problem. The methodology developed is a hybrid based on the discovery of characteristic rules[6] generalised to allow uncertain characteristic rules and deviation detection[11]. We discuss a mechanism for filtering out interesting characteristic rules based on deviation detection and discuss its use for different types of data types. The effect of domain knowledge within the interestingness filter is discussed and techniques for refining the domain knowledge to increase the interest in different rules is studied. The developed methodology is applied to a real world cross-sales problem within the financial sector. The results of this application are also presented in this paper. Though the application described is in the financial sector the methodology is generic in nature and can be applied to other sectors as well.

1. Introduction

Data Mining, the semi-automated search of hidden, previously unknown and interesting knowledge has over the last decade been an area of great interest to academia as well as to the industry[8]. Already a number of real-world applications of Data Mining exist in different sectors of the industry from basket analysis[2] to space exploration[7].

In this paper we discuss the use of Data Mining in the previously unexplored area of customer cross-sales. The methodology developed for this purpose is a hybrid that uses uncertain characteristic rule discovery and deviation detection. Although the application area discussed in this paper is cross-sales in the financial sector, the methodology developed is general and can be used in other applications for which only positive examples are available.

The structure of the paper is as follows: In section 2 we describe the cross-sales problem in detail and analyze it in section 3 to develop a methodology for solving it using Data Mining techniques. In section 4 we discuss the techniques used to discover knowledge while in section 5 we discuss the interestingness filter that is used to filter out non-interesting knowledge. In section 6 we discuss the effect of domain knowledge on the discovered knowledge and how automated techniques along with user guidance can be used to refine the domain knowledge to discover more interesting knowledge. In section 7 we describe how the discovered knowledge can be refined as new data is collected by the organization, making the methodology incremental in nature.

2. The Cross-Sales Problem

In the present cut-throat competitive environment within the service industries, retaining customers and making better use of a customer base have become as important as, if not more important than, attracting new customers. Most companies are involved in providing more than one service or product. Since they know more about their existing customers through data collected about them, targeting those customers with appropriate products that they do not already have is seen as a way of reaping quick profits. There is also an urgent need for effective targeting of prospective customers as the competition is out to woo those customers to buy their competitive products instead.

Cross-Sales is the term given to the problem of attempting to sell a product to existing customers of the company who are not already customers for that particular product (see Figure 1). A customer base of a company can be sub-divided into a number of customer groups based on the product they have purchased. Consider a company that sells four products: Household Insurance, Mortgage Protection, Indemnity Bonds and Commercial Contents Insurance. Cross-Sales is the targeting of customers for Household Insurance who bought one of the other products, namely, Mortgage Protection, Indemnity Bonds or Commercial Contents Insurance, and vice-versa. Now, clearly not all customers of the other products would be suitable for targeting for Household Insurance and the company can incur large savings if only a subset of the rest of the customer base, that are more likely to buy Household Insurance, are targeted for that product.

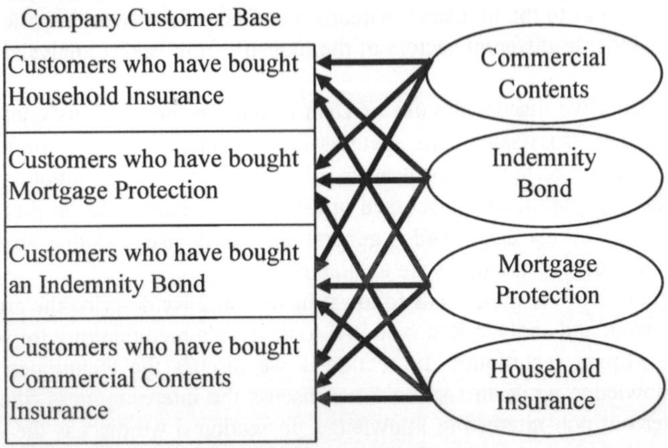

Figure 1: The Cross-Sales Problem

However, customer databases can be very extensive in large organizations and manually sifting through them is difficult. Thus automatic techniques that can incorporate domain expertise and discover useful knowledge for the domain expert can help solve cross-sales problems. In the next section we analyze this problem of cross-sales with a view to using Data Mining techniques to discover such knowledge from the customer base. Such an analysis is essential to ensure that the most appropriate Data Mining methodology is chosen which is imperative for the success of any Data Mining solution[5].

3. Problem Analysis

Consider the following scenario. A Bank wants to promote a product A by targeting existing customers who are not already customers for product A. At present most marketing departments are groping in the dark, targeting some of their customers based on certain hunches held by their marketing experts or sometimes in a totally random manner. Within their customer database, the bank has two types of customers:

Customer Type 1: Those that have product A

Customer Type 2: Those that do not have product A

At first glance this seems like a simple classification problem but on closer examination it is obvious that the problem at hand is actually not a classification problem at all. For a classification problem what is required is three types of customers:

Customer Type 1: Those that have product A

Customer Type 2: Those that have refused to purchase product A

Customer Type 3: Those that do not have product A but have not refused to purchase product A

The first type of customers form the positive examples, the second type of customers form the negative examples and the third type form the target data set.

For our problem at hand we only have positive examples and a target data set. Thus, rather than using a classification algorithm we need to use an association algorithm to discover characteristic rules. These rules define those characteristics that are prevalent in a particular group of records which in our case is the group of records that pertain to customers who have product A. Given these rules, customers in the target data set with similar characteristics can be targeted with sales campaigns.

Characteristic Rules are not as accurate as classification rules would be as classification rules take both the negative and positive examples into account when discovering the rules and are discriminatory in nature. However, Characteristic Rules have the benefit of providing domain experts an insight into how their business plans are working in the real-world, possibly identifying areas within the customer base that seem to be responding less favorably to their present policies of targeting customers. Based on this discovered knowledge experts may intensify their efforts to targeting these parts of the customer base.

The next stage in the process of cross-sales would be the exploitation of the discovered rules by the targeting of the customers, from the target data set, picked using the characteristic rules. At this stage the bank can keep a record of those customers that were targeted but did not buy the product and use these records to refine the characteristic rules making them more accurate or they can use these records as negative examples and then use a classification algorithm to discover classification rules.

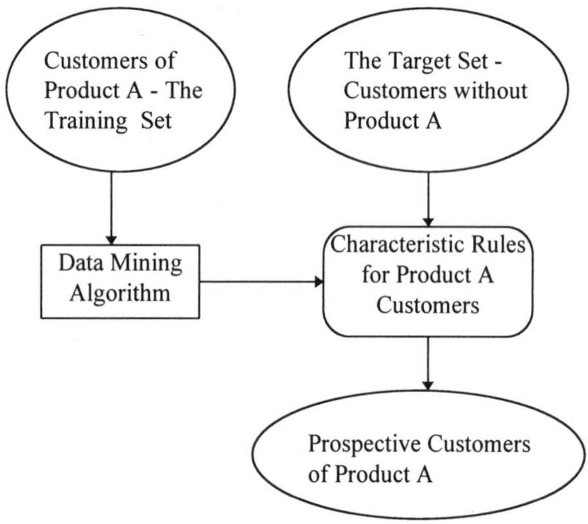

Figure 2: Cross-Sales using Data Mining

4. Discovery of Rules

Recently, the authors have been working in conjunction with a financial institution in Ireland on a project involving such a Cross-sales problem. The client wanted to find characteristic rules defining the type of customers who would buy their various financial products, from the data held within their Customer Information File. The Customer Information File contains over 100,000 customer records with over 80 attributes stored for each customer. The attributes consisted of the customers personal data (e.g. Age, Marital Status, Occupation etc.), properties about the customer generated based on the service record with their financial institution and information about various products/services[a] bought by the customer. An

[a] Confidentiality agreements require us not to disclose the data used or rules generated. We are therefore using pseudonyms for the products and attribute names in our discussions. As specific rules

association rule discovery algorithm based on Evidence Theory, the EAR (Evidence Based Association Rule) algorithm[4] was used to mine the clients data.

The EAR algorithm is a generalization of earlier Association algorithms [AGRA94] and therefore allows the incorporation of support and uncertainty thresholds and syntactic constraints[1]. In addition to the simple syntactic constraints of the type defined by Agrawal et al.[1] EAR allows the definition and consequently the incorporation of *Attribute Dependency constraints*. For example, a rule that contains an expression pertaining to the *Account Average Balance* of a customer is only valid if it also contains an expression regarding the *Account Type* as well. In addition to this, the EAR algorithm can discover knowledge from multi-valued attributes rather than just binary attributes as in the case of previous algorithms[2]. It allows the incorporation of domain knowledge and can handle missing values in the data. The EAR algorithm requires attributes to be discrete. Therefore, interval bands were provided by the domain expert for continuous variables. Also domain specific hierarchies were provided by the domain expert for a number of other attributes. Use of such hierarchies makes knowledge more "visible". However, its use can also have a detrimental effect on the discovery. We discuss this aspect in section 4 and provide a novel method for adjusting this domain knowledge to improve the quality of knowledge discovered.

For each product or service provided by the financial institution, the positive subset of records from the Customer Information File was extracted, i.e. those records where the corresponding customer had bought the product. Each of these subsets were then mined separately for discovering characteristic rules for the corresponding product.

The number of characteristic rules discovered by EAR can be controlled using a threshold of minimum support that the rules must have to be considered as useful[b]. The higher this threshold the fewer is the number of rules discovered. The procedure followed by us was to initially set the threshold value for support as high and then to reduce it iteratively and constrain the rules discovered to those attributes that seem interesting through knowledge discovered in previous iterations.

The first product of interest was Household Insurance. The number of positive examples for household insurance within the Customer Information File was over 8000. For our first discovery iteration, the support threshold was set to 0.8 i.e. for a rule to be useful it must satisfy 80% of the data. The number of rules discovered was low. However, this iteration provided us with an insight into problems within the data set chosen for this cross-sales exercise. Firstly, it was found that a number of attributes within the data set had a single value appearing in them for over 90%

---

are not of interest within our discussion we feel that this does not reduce the relevance of this paper in any way to others interested in the cross-sales problem.

[b] Note that when characteristic rules for a particular product are being discovered from the subset of positive examples for that product, the uncertainty and support values for the rules are equivalent as the support for the antecedent of the characteristic rules (e.g. Product = Household Insurance) is always equal to 1.

of the customers. This was due to the fact that these attribute values were the attribute's default value or were obvious to the expert as they were a prerequisite for the product. These lead to a number of attributes being removed from the data that were not adding any value to the data due to their "obvious" nature. The number of attributes was reduced from 80 to 43 for the Household Insurance data set.

For the second iteration the support threshold was reduced to 0.2. This lead to an explosion in the number of rules discovered. Over 4000 rules were discovered with the size of the rules being constrained to a maximum of four attributes in the consequent. The number of rules presented to the expert clearly causes a problem in their ability to find the real "nuggets" amongst them. Therefore there was a need for a technique to filter out the non-interesting information automatically.

In the next section we describe the filtering technique developed by us for this purpose. We also investigate the effect of domain knowledge on the discovery of interesting rules and discuss a way to automatically refine or generate the domain knowledge to maximize the interest.

5. Using Deviation to Discover Interesting Rules

As outlined in Section 3, Characteristic Rules describe the characteristics of a particular data set consisting of just positive examples. There are two problems with basing cross-sales on such rules. Firstly, the number of such rules that can be discovered using an association rule discovery algorithm like EAR[4] is exponential. Secondly, in the absence of negative examples, the discovered characteristics may also be characteristics of the complete data set as they represent the necessary but not the sufficient condition for the membership of the positive example set. Therefore, it is important to use a filtering system that reduces the number of rules generated as well as limits the rules to only the interesting or useful ones. The development of such a filter is the topic of this section.

The number of rules generated can be reduced by setting a threshold on the support of the rule in the data set, by using domain knowledge, for example, Hierarchical Generalisation Trees and Attribute Relationship rules[3], syntactic constraints and by defining an interestingness measure and setting a threshold on it.

The interestingness measure used is normally dependent on the problem at hand[9, 10]. In cross-sales, we clearly do not want to base our targeting of a product based on its characteristics that are actually characteristics of the companies customers in general. Thus, the interestingness measure we use is based on the deviation of the characteristic rules discovered for the product being targeted from the "norm". The "norm" in our case is the support for these characteristics within the complete customer base of the company i.e. a characteristic rule is interesting if it is a characteristic of the customer of a product rather than the customer base in general. Thus, we define the interestingness measure for characteristics c, $Interest_c$, as:

$$Interest_c = \frac{S_p - S_o}{max\{S_0, S_p\}}$$

where, S_p is the support for the characteristics, c, in the positive example data set, S_o is the support for the characteristics c in the complete customer base. The expression, $max\{S_0, S_p\}$, is called the normalising factor as it normalises the interestingness measure onto the scale [-1, 1].

Using a threshold of 0.15 for the absolute measure for interest, the number of rules presented to the user was reduced to 20. Of these the expert was now able to focus on the most interesting rules based on his domain expertise.

Consider the following example rules discovered from a positive example data set of 8268 tuples out of a customer base of 100162 tuples:

if Household Insurance = Y
then Marital Status = M and Joint Customer = Y
and Commission Agent = No Broker
with support = 68.30% and interest = 0.194
and
if Household Insurance = Y
then Marital Status = S and Joint Customer = N
and Commission Agent = No Broker
with support = 21.30% and interest = -0.251

This first rule states that 68.30% of the customers of Household Insurance are Married, have Joint accounts and have bought their mortgage directly from the financial institution. The interestingness measure is a calculation of the difference between this value and the support for these characteristics within the complete customer base divided by 68.3 as the interestingness is positive in this case. Therefore only 55.02% of the records in the complete customer base satisfy these characteristics.

The second rule states that 21.30% of the customers of Household Insurance are Single, without Joint Accounts and have bought their mortgage directly from the financial institution. In this case 28.44% of the records in the complete customer base satisfy these characteristics resulting in a negative interestingness value.

The conclusion arrived at by considering these rules together is that the mail shots for Household Insurance seem to get a better response from Married customers with joint accounts as compared to Single customers without joint accounts. This could be due to the way the Household Insurance product is being pitched that makes it seem to be less attractive to Single customers. Changing this could lead to substantial gains in the sales of Household Insurance.

6. Effect of Domain Knowledge

In this section we discuss the effect of domain knowledge on the interestingness measure described in section 5. In particular we discuss the effect of domain knowledge on the three different types of Attributes: Discrete Un-ordered Attributes, Discrete Ordered Attributes and Continuous Attributes.

6.1 Discrete Un-ordered Attributes

Consider the example distribution in Figure 3. The Post Code attribute has no order associated with it due to the nature of its data type. However, based on domain knowledge we can impose a geographical structure on it as shown in Figure 4. At the lowest level of the hierarchical structure are individual post codes whose distribution in terms of "percentage occurrence" is shown in Figure 3. Based on the hierarchy if we were to group together the Post Codes we would get the following deviations between the overall customer base and the positive example set:

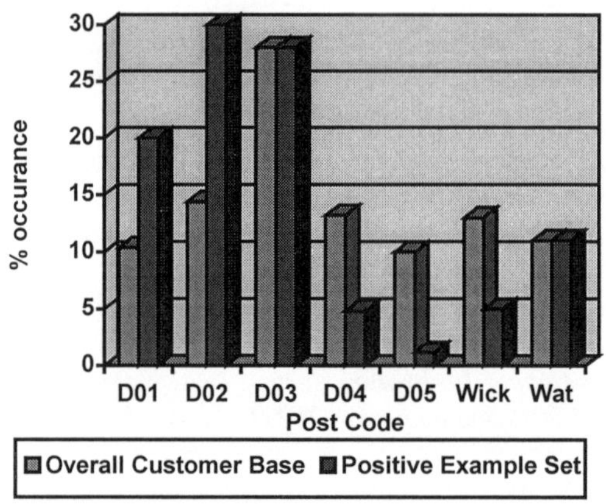

Figure 3: Interest Measure for a Discrete Un-ordered Attributes

Dublin: 0.09; Wicklow: -0.615; Waterford: 0

Often the interest can be lost due to the domain dependent hierarchies and intervals provided as domain knowledge by the domain expert aimed at reducing the number of rules generated. We now show how the interestingness measure discussed in the previous section can be used to refine the hierarchies provided by the domain expert. It is clear from Figure 3 that

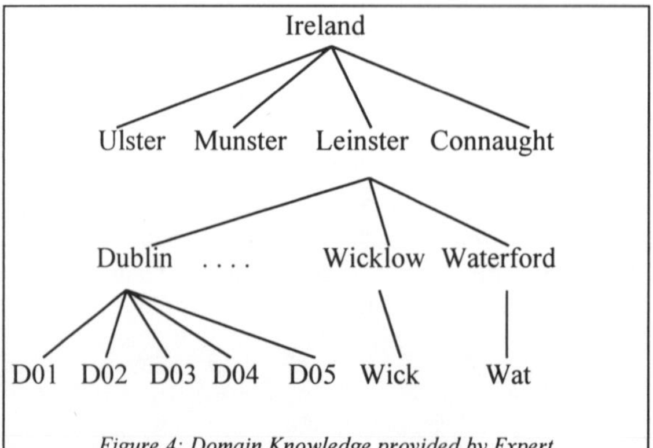

Figure 4: Domain Knowledge provided by Expert

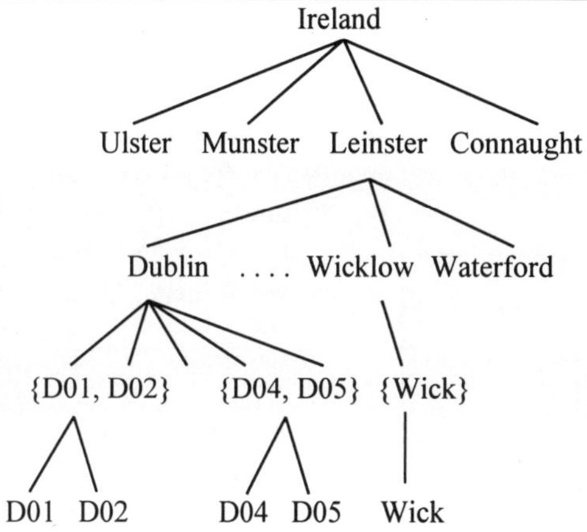

Figure 5: Refined Domain Knowledge

the Post Codes can be divided into three categories: those where the deviation is positive (i.e. the "% occurrence" in the positive example set is greater than that in the overall data set), those where the deviation is negative (i.e. the "% occurrence" in the positive example set is less than that in the overall data set) and those where there is no deviation (i.e. the "% occurrence" in the positive example set is equal to that in the overall data set). The categories for the example data sets are {D01, D02}, {D04, D05, Wick} and {D03, Wat}. Of the three categories, only the "Positive Deviation" and "Negative Deviation" categories are of interest. We, therefore, can ignore the Post Codes in the "No Deviation" category. The hierarchical structure in Figure 3 can now be refined based on this knowledge to that shown in Figure 5. Note that the Post Code "Wick" is kept separate from the set {D04, D05} due to it belonging to a different sub-tree within Figure 4 based on its geographical location. There may be a case for merging the two sub-sets {D04, D05} with {Wick} based on Expert Knowledge about the geographical or demographic features of these sets of Post-Codes. This would further refine the Hierarchical Generalisation Tree in Figure 5.

Using the refined hierarchical structure we now find the following deviations within the post codes:

{D01, D02}: 0.504; {D03}: 0; {D04, D05}: -0.741; {Wick}: -0.615; {Wat}: 0

Thus, the new hierarchy has lead to the discovery of two new interesting subsets of the customer-base based on post code where the deviation from the norm is substantial for the set of positive examples. A negative interestingness measure is interpreted as the characteristic reducing the likelihood of a customer buying the product or that the products targeting has not been effective for customers with that characteristic. A positive value for the interestingness measure is interpreted as being a characteristic of customers of the product being considered for cross-sales.

6.2 Discrete Ordered Attributes

In the case of an Discrete Ordered variable, the domain knowledge need not be provided initially by the user. In bands for the variable can be created directly by the algorithm using the frequency information as shown in Figure 6. In this case, the attribute domain is partitioned into three sets of intervals : those with positive interest {[0, 1], [4]}, those with negative interest {[2, 3], [5, 6]} and those with no significant interest {[7]}. The initial iteration of the algorithm is performed using the individual intervals. If the support for the individual intervals is lower than the support threshold provided by the user, the discovery can be performed on the sets defined above instead or subsets of the sets based on Domain Knowledge provided at this point by the user. For the example in Figure 6, the deviations for the individual intervals discovered are:

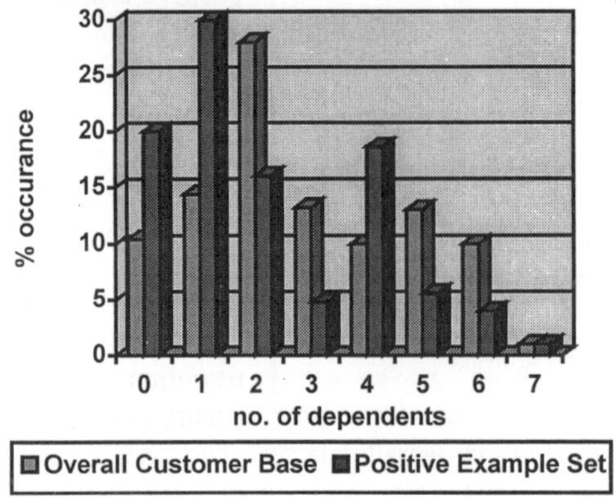

Figure 6: Interest Measure for a Discrete Ordered Variable

[0, 1]: +0.504; [2, 3]: -0.495; [4]: +0.408; [5, 6]: -0.582; [7]: 0

Here, three of the intervals seem to have significant interestingness values.

The reason for not using just two sets consisting of Positive Deviation Intervals and Negative Deviation Intervals is that this could lead to over-generalization and unnecessary loss of information[6].

6.3 Continuous Attributes

Finally, we have a look at employing a similar technique to continuous variables. Once again no intervals are required from the domain expert though if the expert desires, the intervals that he provides may be taken into account and be refined in an interactive fashion as in the case of Discrete Ordered variables. In Figure 7 we show an example of the distributions of a continuous variable 'Balance'. Clearly, the points where the distribution curves for the Overall Customer Base and Positive Example Set intersect are the optimal points for splitting the domain of Balance as it is at these points that the deviation or interestingness changes signs. Thus, the optimal intervals to be generated in the example in Figure 7 are [0, 3000], [3001, 20000] and [20000, 30000]. Clearly, In the example shown in figure 7, the areas shaded a lighter shade of grey are areas of negative interestingness while the darker shade of grey indicates a positive interest. Mathematically, the interestingness measure can be calculated for each area as $\int_a^b [f(x) - F(x)]$ where f(x) is the distribution function for the Positive Example Set, F(x) is the distribution function of the Overall Customer Base and [a, b] is the interval for which the interestingness value is sought.

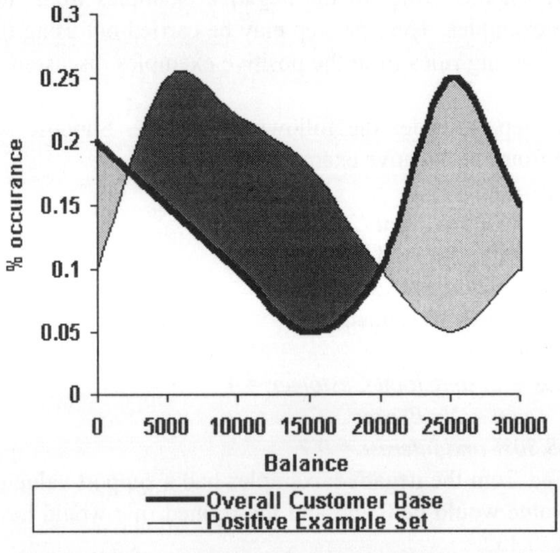

Figure 7: Interest Measure for a Continuous Variable

Based on the techniques described above the domain knowledge for the Age attribute in the customer base of the financial institution was refined from [0, 20], [21, 25], [26, 30], [31, 35], [36, 40], [41, 45], [46, 50], [51, 55], [55,60], [61, 65], [66, 70], [71, 100] to [0,21], [22, 37], [38, 38], [39, 39], [40, 40], [41, 46], [47, 47], [48, 48], [49, 100] resulting in a great improvement in the quality of rules being discovered. For example, before the domain knowledge was refined no rules that combined Age with Family_Income_Protection were discovered. However, after refining the following rule was discovered:

if Household Insurance = Y
then Age = [22, 37] and Family_Income_Protection = Y
with support = 39.11% and interest = 0.971

The high Interestingness measure proves the usefulness of domain knowledge refinement.

7. Refining Characteristic Rules

In section 3 we described why the cross-sales problem cannot be solved using a classification algorithm. We also suggested that after using a characteristic rule discovery approach, customers could be targeted in a sales campaign the results of which, including negative responses, could be stored in the database. This new database can now be used to generate a classification tree. However, we also pointed out certain advantages of the characteristic approach i.e. the fact that these rules provide the expert with insights into their customer base that are not in general provided by the classification algorithm. In this section we discuss how the Characteristic Rules discovered may be refined to take into account the negative examples.

Refining the Characteristic rules generated from the positive examples consists of two steps: Discovery of Characteristic Rules for the negative examples and discovery of deviation of the Characteristics of the negative examples from the characteristics of the positive examples. The first step may be carried out using the same techniques used for discovering rules from the positive examples discussed in sections 3 and 4.

To illustrate the second step, consider the following example. Suppose we discovered the following rule from the negative example set:

if Household Insurance = N
then Marital Status = M and Joint Customer = Y
and Commission Agent = No Broker
with support = 20.45% and interest = -0.628

The example rule in section 4 will now be refined to:

if Household Insurance = Y
then Marital Status = M and Joint Customer = Y
and Commission Agent = No Broker
with support = 68.30% and interest = 0.7

However, if the rule discovered from the negative examples had a support value of 75.02%, the interestingness value would be 0.266 and the refined rule would have an interestingness measure of -0.132.

Thus a positive interestingness measure for rules from the negative example set reduces the interest in the corresponding rule from the positive examples as it signifies the characteristics to be those people who have refused the product being targeted. Similarly, a negative interestingness value implies that the characteristics are in fact that of customers of the product, thus, the interest in them increases.

8. Conclusions

In this paper we have discussed the cross-sales problem and analysed this problem from the view to solving it using Data Mining techniques. The Data Mining solution is based on the discovery of characteristic rules, generalised to allow uncertain rules, from the set of positive examples (customers of the product being targeted). We have highlighted the need for filtering the discovered rules based on what rules are interesting and presented a novel technique based on deviation detection for this purpose. We also discussed the negative effect that domain knowledge can have on the discovery of interesting rules and introduce a method for the refinement of the domain knowledge using the interstingness filter. We showed how the characteristic rules may be refined to more accurate rules if negative examples are made available through subsequent data collections.

The approach discussed in this paper has been applied to a real-world data mining application in the financial sector and results of its application are also provided. In general, the methodology developed for providing a Data Mining solution to the cross-sales problem results in useful knowledge being discovered from the customer database and has great potential for exploitation within the services sectors other than finance as well.

References

1. R. Agrawal, T. Imielinski and A. Swami. Database mining: A performance perspective. IEEE Transactions on Knowledge and Data Engineering, Special issue on Learning and Discovery in Knowledge-Based Databases, 1993.
2. R. Agrawal, R. Srikant. Fast Algorithms for Mining Association Rules in Large Databases. Proc. of the 20th VLDB Conference, Pg. 487 - 499, Chile, 1994.
3. S. S. Anand, D. A. Bell, J. G. Hughes. The Role of Domain Knowledge in Data Mining. Proc. of the 4th International Conference on Information and Knowledge Management (CIKM'95), November, 1995
4. S. S. Anand, D. A. Bell, J. G. Hughes. Evidence-Based Discovery of Association Rules. Internal Report, Faculty of Informatics, University of Ulster, 1996.
5. S. S. Anand, A. G. Buchner, D. A. Bell, J. G. Hughes. Real-World Data Mining. Workshop on Data Mining in Real World Databases at the 1st International Conference in Practical Aspects of Knowledge Management, 1996.
6. Y. Cai, N. Cerecone, J. Han, Attribute-Oriented Induction in Relational Databases, Knowledge Discovery in Databases. Pg. 213 - 228. AAAI/ MIT Press. 1991.
7. U. Fayyad, N. Weir, S. Djorgovski. Automated Analysis of a Large-Scale Sky Survey: The SKICAT System, Workshop on Knowledge Discovery in Databases, AAAI, 1993.
8. U. Fayyad, G. Piatetsky-Shapiro, P. Smyth, P. Uthurusamy. Advances in Knowledge Discovery and Data Mining, AAAI/ MIT Press, 1996.
9. M. Kamber, R. Shinghal. Evaluating the Interestingness of Characteristic Rules. 2nd International Conference on Data Mining and Knowledge Discovery, 1996.
10. C. J. Matheus, G. Piatetsky-Shapiro, D. McNeill. An Application of KEFIR to the Analysis of Healthcare Information. Workshop on Knowledge Discovery in Databases, AAAI-94, Pg. 441 - 452, 1994.
11. G. Piatetsky-Shapiro, C. J. Matheus. The Interestingness of Deviations. Workshop on Knowledge Discovery in Databases, AAAI-94, Pg. 25 - 36, 1994.

Improving Forward Selection with Background Knowledge: Finding Interesting Multiple Regression Models for Sales Prediction

Oliver Büchter, Michael Müller, Josef Schneeberger
Bavarian Research Center for Knowledge-Based Systems (FORWISS)
Am Weichselgarten 7, D-91058 Erlangen, Germany
orbuecht|mueller|schneeberger@forwiss.uni-erlangen.de

Abstract

Data mining has to combine two procedures: one procedure to find a hypothesis and a second to test a hypothesis for interestingness. Multiple regression is a common method within data mining to test hypotheses expressed as a function. Sales can be predicted with multiple exponential regression models. While testing a hypothesis with multiple regression and fitting the regression function to the data is a well-understood procedure; finding a good or even the best hypothesis is difficult. We show that model search for interesting hypotheses can be structured with the aid of domain knowledge in a way which enables us to perform automatic model search. A difficult problem from marketing research has been chosen as a case study. For this problem, no existing model search technique was applicable. Our system MSA solves the previously intractable problem of finding a good regression model for sales prediction in the presence of multicollinearity and many irrelevant variables.

Keywords Interestingness, Subjective Relevance Estimation, Use of Prior Domain Knowledge, Multiple Regression, Marketing

1 Introduction

Data mining systems explore data in search for interesting patterns [2]. Such a pattern provides information about some featuresr [a] present in the data. Furthermore, this information may be used to explain the past characteristics of that feature or to predict its future development. For example, we have used data from market research—so called panel data—to explain sales figures of a certain product with respect to the pricing or promotion activities in the past. Similarly, we use panel data to predict the sales e.g., with respect to a marketing campaign of a direct competitor.

In order to discover any interesting development of a variable (e.g. sales changes) a hypothesis, i.e., a set of additional variables (like pricing or promotion) from the panel data is generated and tested subsequently. In other

[a] We use the terms attribute, variable, and feature synonymously throughout the paper.

words, a hypothesis is the trial to explain one variable with respect to others. A successfully explaining set of variables is also referred to as a model. There are many methods from statistics and machine learning which can be used to evaluate a (set of) hypothesis. However, any detectable pattern in the (panel) data will only be as good as the selected hypothesis.

Data mining has to combine two procedures: one procedure to generate hypotheses and a second to test a hypothesis for interestingness. Selecting the best model according to some interestingness measure is called an interestingness filter.[7] Obviously, exhaustive search is not efficient at all since every possible subset of variables forms a hypothesis and has to be tested. In realistic domains there are easily hundreds or thousands of variables.

Multiple regression [b] is a common method to test hypotheses expressed as a function. Sales are often predicted with multiple exponential[c] regression models. While testing a hypothesis with multiple regression and fitting the regression function to the data is a well-understood procedure, finding a good or even the best hypothesis is not. We propose a procedure for generating and improving a multiple regression hypothesis guided on the one hand by domain knowledge about variables and the user's preferences and on the other hand by testing intermediate hypotheses using the multiple regression procedure. As the procedure is guided towards good hypotheses the number of computed regression models is very low. This approach has been called interestingness engine[7].

Our system reflects the separation into two procedures: the *Markensimulator*[d] tests a hypothesis with multiple exponential regression. It is used by a market research institute to predict sales figures from their monthly ascertained panel data. We have implemented the *Markensimulator Assistant (MSA)*, which proposes hypotheses with the aid of a knowledge base and evaluates them by invocation of the Markensimulator. The results of the evaluation change the domain knowledge such that the hypothesis is improved.

Finding and improving hypotheses is called model search[2]. We show that model search for interesting hypotheses can be structured with the aid of domain knowledge in a way which enables us to perform automatic model search even with a large set of variables containing multicollinearity (see below) and lots of irrelevant variables. In the following section we outline our procedure for multiple regression model search and compare it to related work like for-

---

[b]Regression approximates the values from input data by determining the coefficients of a function which maps the variables of the hypothesis onto the target variable. Regression is called multiple if a hypothesis contains more than one predicting variable.

[c]Regression is called exponential if the function which maps the predictors onto the target variable is the exponential function (instead of a straight line or a polynomial).

[d]English: "Brands Simulator"

ward selection. The third section describes the case study with marketing data and the fourth section depicts knowledge that helps to guide the search. In section five the key ideas of our search strategy in regression model generation are presented. The sixth section proposes a representation and an update procedure for preferences among sets of variables. Finally, we discuss the results of our system and compare them with the results that were found by human experts.

2 Related Work and Model Search Procedure

The search for the best multiple regression model is a relevant practical problem. Because handcrafting a model incrementally is not very exciting for the user, there are some approaches from statistics to loop over the regression procedure. The user has to define a list of attributes to be potentially contained in the regression model and a criterion for removal/inclusion of attributes. In *backward selection* the entire list of attributes is adopted as initial model. Next, the model is evaluated according to the criterion and the worst attribute is removed. This step is repeated until all remaining attributes fulfill the criterion. In *forward selection* the initial model is empty and the attribute that complies best with the criterion is added. This step is repeated until there is no attribute left that meets the criterion. Usually the F statistic or the significance of F are used as a selection criterion.

This kind of purely data-driven greedy search to find the best regression model has often been criticized [5,1,4]. At least three problems outlaw the application of these techniques for our sales prediction. If the data contain chance correlations the corresponding attributes are built into the regression model. Apparently, the blind optimization of statistical criteria leads to theoretically suspect results and a lack of predictive power [5]. Another problem is multicollinearity [6]: in a regression model two predictors measuring the same influence will be collinear and hence disturb each other, such that they loose their significance. A third problem—particularly for data mining—is that these approaches are not efficient in the presence of hundreds of irrelevant variables.

All three problems are attacked within our approach (cp. Fig. 1). We implement a variant of forward selection. It includes one attribute at a time according to the user-defined preferences (1) but removes all attributes that do not meet a statistical criterion. This meets the golden rule that hypotheses must not be found in the same data they are tested with: The MSA selection algorithm uses a data structure that contains knowledge about the user's preferences to determine the best attribute that is included into the regression model. The regression is computed in order to evaluate the model (3),

```
preferences := initial_preferences;
REPEAT
          best_attribute := max_inclusion_evaluation(preferences);     (1)
          model := model ∪{ best attribute };                           (2)
          evaluation := regression(model);                              (3)
          bad_attributes := {a_i| removal_criterion(a_i,model)};        (4)
          model := model - bad_attributes;                              (5)
          preferences := update(preferences);                           (6)
UNTIL     the model is interesting enough for the user;
```

Figure 1: The MSA Model Search Procedure

particularly to evaluate the statistical removal criterion for all the attributes (4). Bad attributes according to the criterion are removed (5). Finally, the preferences are updated (6). The knowledge gained by testing the hypothesis changes the preferences according to some heuristics. For example, the removal of an attribute reduces its own interestingness.

3 A Case Study: Regression Models for Sales Prediction

At the german market research institute *Gesellschaft für Konsumforschung* (GfK) the Markensimulator, a regression-based statistical tool for explaining the market share of a given brand using several variables, has been developed [9,10]. The regression models describe the causal influences on the market share of a target brand and their interaction (as far as they are contained in the panel data) over time and submarkets.[e] The product manager of the target brand uses the generated regression model for short-time predictions and what-if-analysis [8,9,10].

The everyday data-mining-quest at the market research institute is model search: to find a combination of five to twenty essential influences on the market share, which is interesting for the marketing manager. Therefore, the search space consists of $\sum_{j=5}^{20} \binom{N}{j}$ possible regression models, where N is the number of variables available in the data. A usual value for N is 2000. The variables contain multicollinearity, a lot of irrelevant ones, and a lot of chance correlations with the target attribute. Apparently, neither exhaustive search with an interestingness filter nor forward/backward selection can be applied to this problem.

[e] Values of time and submarkets constitute the points for the regression method.

4 Knowledge for Organizing the Model Search

A product manager has a strong feeling which influences are relevant for the market share and which are not. However, this feeling is far from being exact or complete knowledge. He typically states propositions like "the price of brand X is very important". This means that the price of brand X effects the market share in practice, in the setting of all important attributes, and plays a main role in the product manager's causal theory. The only way to find out if the proposition is true or false is to construct an entire plausible causal model and to compute the corresponding regression model. Since the proposition may be false, the knowledge has to be handled with care. It is rather a guess than knowledge. This is due to the marketing domain where causal relationships are unstable: competitors always try to change the market to their own favor. In consequence, model search cannot be restricted to models that are consistent with prior knowledge, since prior knowledge may have to change. Our approach is to structure the model search space with the aid of domain knowledge. We distinguish five types of knowledge:

(1) **Market knowledge** tells us which brands are sold in the examined market, about rivalry between brands, about the brands' identity or profile, about related markets, and so on. This information can be summarized and formalized as preferences on attributes concerning certain brands or markets. A marketing manager knows best about all this and he should be asked to acquire this knowledge. This knowledge module is the only one which has to be replaced or updated if we change the data to be analyzed *within* marketing.

(2) **General marketing knowledge** deals with the ontology of marketing and describes the most important domain concepts. It is valuable for different markets. A useful aspect for data mining is to find taxonomies of attributes within marketing textbooks. For example, we can classify the given attributes into distribution-, promotion-, price-numbers etc. Distribution numbers contain information about a brand's availability within the segment's stores. Promotion numbers describe the manufacturer's actions to increase the sales. Some numbers are always expected to be better than others. Therefore, we can describe their relevance by default. Market knowledge adapts these relevance defaults to the examined market.

A brand's market share is predicted with a set of *attributes* that are described by naming the *market object* and a particular *number* (like 'price'). A market object is either a *brand* or a *market*. The brands in the data are of different importance for predicting a target brand's market share. Experts know a variety of those brands' characteristics (like color, taste, or design) which are not reflected in the data but which help to select the right predictors (i.e., those variables predicting the market share properly). For the purpose of variable selection, brands may be grouped according to their image. Brands with a similar image as the target brand are called *main competitors*, the others simply *competitors*. A main competitor's variable receives a higher relevance than the same variable concerning a competitor. This leads to a preference of main competitors while generating a new model.

(3) There is **statistical knowledge** about how to use regression. It is needed to integrate the already existing statistical multiple regression tool (Markensimulator) as a black box into the knowledge based search process. The knowledge defines the interface to the black box: how can a specific statistical result be interpreted and what are promising selections for the black box's input.

(4) **Result knowledge** contains the information which pattern has been produced by Markensimulator. Result knowledge is purely *local*: it only concerns one hypothesis and completes it to a regression model. During model generation, result knowledge is only an interface to the regression black-box output.

(5) Under favorable conditions, results concern the whole search process giving global information about the data. For example, one could find out that the price of brand B is irrelevant for explaining the market share of brand A. This kind of knowledge is called **discovered knowledge** and gets asserted by interpreting a statistical result. In order to evaluate the significance of a variable's influence on the target brand's market share within a given regression model, this variable's t-value is examined. [6] [f] Hence, the t-value can be used to learn about the facts and to build up beliefs on their relevance in a meaningful regression model in order to improve the interestingness assessment. The MSA adds to the discovered knowledge base one of the following propositions: [g]

(1) If $t \notin]-2, 2[$ then the considered variable v is **relevant** denoted by $relevant(v)$: it is recommended for further analysis because it takes part in the explanation of the market share.

(2) If $t \in [-1.5, 1.5]$ then the considered variable v is **irrelevant** denoted by $irrelevant(v)$: it can be excluded from further elaboration of the model.

[f] In general, the empirical value t_{emp} is compared with a critical value depending on the sample size n and the level of significance α: we can accept the hypothesis, that there is a connection, if $|t_{emp}| > |t_{n-2,\alpha/2}|$ [6].

[g] The predicates 'irrelevant', 'relevant', and 'weak' have been acquired from the statisticians of the market research institute. Surprisingly, John et.al. have introduced just these three predicates to classify features for decision tree induction [3]. A main difference is that they infer these predicates from classification quality of the whole feature set, while our heuristics use the single variable's (feature's) significance within the model (set).

(3) Otherwise, the considered variable v is **weak** denoted by $weak(v)$. We cannot predict once and for all whether a variable is promising or not. If we replace one distribution variable by another, the model changes and a considered variable may change from a weak to a relevant one.

A model which contains only relevant facts is called a **valid model**.

5 Correlated Spheres of Influence and Smart Path Model Search

The central action performed by a data mining system is the selection of a hypothesis. What we could ascribe to such a system are knowledge and preferences. An intelligent system should learn from previously tested hypotheses and change both knowledge and preferences according to its observations. Using regression, this only works if the system stays on a path of meaningful models. The key idea to avoid foolish hypotheses is (a) to group correlated attributes into so-called 'correlated spheres of influence' (CSI) and (b) to build only meaningful hypotheses (including only one attribute per CSI and adding only one attribute per step).

A marketing manager explains to himself the share of the market with a set of influences. For example, he may consider a price reduction, a successful promotion of a competitor, or a holiday that influences the sales. An influence is indicated by one or more variables. They vary in the degree to which they reflect the influence. Variables that measure more than one relevant influence of the domain theory are not desirable: a more detailed model enables more possibilities for simulation and prediction and results in a more transparent explanation. For example, instead of having a single variable combining age and salary of customers we prefer separate variables.

In a regression model two variables measuring the same influence disturb each other, such that they loose their significance. This is one of the traps for data mining systems. To avoid this effect—called **multicollinearity** [6]—the MSA first chooses a list of the most interesting influences and then refines each of the influences by introducing the most promising variable(s) measuring this influence. The concept 'correlated sphere of influence' (CSI) can be regarded as a general way to structure the search space in order to reduce the search effort and to avoid faulty results: A **CSI** is a set of variables which the domain expert expects to correlate by definition, because they measure the same influence.[h]

[h] If the knowledge about influences is incomplete or vague it is sensible to assume that perhaps two variables measuring this influence do not correlate because the definition is bad. In this case observations have to be generalized carefully and two variables from the same CSI may be combined within a single regression model. This vagueness can be stated in the MSA knowledge base by saying that the 'breadth' of an influence is larger than 1.

In contrast, variables that measure different influences will only correlate if there is 'real' interrelation between them.

A **meaningful model** is a model that (i) contains the most relevant influences according to the prior knowledge, (ii) contains no multicollinearity *by definition*, and (iii) contains no foolish variables. [i] The construction of meaningful models can be forced when—with the aid of domain knowledge—the set of all attributes is partitioned into subsets according to influences and only one variable per influence is integrated into the model. If we add to the relevant attributes of a meaningful regression model only one additional attribute of a different influence, we can conclude from the variable's t-value in the new regression model whether it shall be recommended for or excluded from further elaboration of this model. This proceeding is called a **smart path**: a sequence of meaningful models, so that the successor of every model m contains all the variables which have been relevant in m plus only one additional variable.

The discovered knowledge about the relevance of variables is used to avoid redundant findings. However, it can be used to introduce beliefs about the relevance of *other* variables measuring the same influence and, hence, can improve future hypotheses. For example, the more variables that measure an influence X are weak, (believe that) the less relevant is influence X. In the following section the representation, the utilization, and the update of preferences are introduced.

6 Representation, Utilization, and Update of Preferences

The adequate estimation of interestingness for KDD is still an open research issue. As interestingness has many facets like novelty, potential usefulness, relevance, and validity [2] the integration within a single value is sometimes suspect. But it is necessary to achieve a selection decision. Within the MSA the most interesting model hypothesis is the combination of the n most interesting CSIs. Estimation of interestingness for CSIs is the key functionality to add a single attribute to the last hypothesis. We use the facets relevance and complementarity.

6.1 Defining the Relevance of CSIs and of Attributes

Every influence is possibly relevant. But there are different degrees of relevance that evolve from the initial knowledge about the market. For ex-

[i] In terms of pure statistical criteria the best results are achieved by explaining the market share with itself or with simple linear transformations or with another brand's market share, because two market shares correlate over market segments and time. But this is useless and trivial.

type of market object	attribute type distribution	price	actions	stocks
target	1	1	1	0.9
main competitor	0.8	0.8	0.8	0.6
competitor	0.7	0.7	0.7	0.4
other markets	0.5	0.5	0.5	0.1

Table 1: A priori Relevance Estimations for Selected Types of CSI

distr_dm_display	1	distr_gew_ek	0.5
distr_gew_vk	1	distr_num	0.5

Table 2: Preferences among attributes of type 'distribution'

ample, main competitors are more relevant than other competitors. Each influence is characterized by an influence type and the market object it belongs to. For example, it has the type *price* and belongs to *brand A*. In the MSA, types of influences are associated with an a priori relevance degree $R_i^{apriori} \in [0,1]$ that reflects initial believes. These believes lead to preferences for the inclusion of attributes into a hypothesis. Table 1 shows an example of plausible definitions. Types like `main_competitor` may be instantiated with every main competitor contained in the data, for example `main_competitor('X')`. Instances initially get their type's relevance estimation, but every instance's relevance estimate is updated individually. For instance, the CSI `main_competitor(distribution,'X')` gets the initial relevance estimation 0.8.

Variables grouped into an attribute type may be of different interest because they vary in the degree to which they measure the named influence. In order to express preferences on attributes we define their a priori interestingness $I_f^{apriori}$. Table 2 shows preferences among randomly chosen attributes characterizing the distribution of a brand. The preferences could be stated in general for every brand, but the estimations have to be updated for every instance individually. These estimations guide the construction of the model hypotheses in a two-step-process: In order to generate a hypothesis, a given number of most relevant CSIs is selected according to Table 1 at first. These are only influences related to the target brand and to the two main competitors, because their CSIs are rated most relevant. They are refined with the most relevant attribute (cp. Table 2). The generated hypothesis is shown in Figure 2. Please note that the preference scores are defined as numbers but that they are not added, subtracted, multiplied, or divided. Only when a score is up-

```
-----------------------------------------------------------------
object    attribute type     | sphere of influence
-----------------------------------------------------------------
target:   dis_gew_vk         | distribution(target)
target:   preis              | price(target)
target:   imp_anteil         | actions(target)
target:   best_display       | stocks(target)
'X':      imp_preis          | main_competitor(price,'X')
'X':      distr_dm_display   | main_competitor(distribution,'X')
'X':      imp_anteil         | main_competitor(actions,'X')
'Y':      imp_anteil         | main_competitor(actions,'Y')
'Y':      preis              | main_competitor(price,'Y')
'Y':      distr_dm_display   | main_competitor(distribution,'Y')
-----------------------------------------------------------------
```

Figure 2: A First Model Hypothesis

dated, it is multiplied by a constant or another constant is subtracted. So the differences between the scores should be chosen according to these constants. The update of relevance scores is presented in the following section.

6.2 Updating the Relevance Estimates

After the regression method has finished the parameter search, the model is evaluated by computing R^2 and the t-value for every attribute. The t-values are interpreted by the MSA and for every attribute f one of the following facts is asserted to the knowledge: $relevant(f)$, $weak(f)$, $irrelevant(f)$.

Let F denote the set of attributes, I the set of all CSIs; let $i(f) : F \rightarrow I$ be a function which selects the CSI that is measured by a given attribute f; let $R_i^{apriori} \in [0,1]$ be the a priori relevance of CSI i and $F_i := \{f | i(f) = i\}$. In addition, we define the sets

$$\begin{aligned} WEAK_i &:= \{f | f \in F_i \wedge weak(f)\}, \\ IRR_i &:= \{f | f \in F_i \wedge irrelevant(f)\}, \\ REL_i &:= \{f | f \in F_i \wedge relevant\_in\_the\_last\_model(f)\}. \end{aligned}$$

and the function $refinable(i) := \begin{cases} 0 & if\ |WEAK_i| + |IRR_i| = |F_i| \\ 1 & otherwise \end{cases}$.

Every influence in the causal model has to be represented in the regression model by the most interesting variable[j] that measures this influence and is

[j] The computation of a separate interesting measure for attributes (instead of working off a list) has been chosen because it is flexible enough to allow alternative strategies. For example,

contained in the data. The current interestingness of every variable is updated according to the following equation:

$$I_f^{current} := \begin{cases} 0 & f \in IRR_i \\ 1 & f \in REL_i \\ I_f^{apriori} - c_3 & f \in WEAK_i \end{cases} \quad (1)$$

Observations that lead to inclusion of f into REL_i or IRR_i dominate the a priori interestingness while c_3 should be chosen smaller (e.g. 0.1). The desired behavior for the facts' agenda is constancy: A selected fact is kept in the current model if it is relevant accordingly. If a selected fact turns out to be irrelevant, it should be excluded from further analysis. A weakness should only lead to a slight relapse toward the agenda's end. The relevance estimation for spheres of influence must be updated in the search process according to the following heuristics:

- If a variable is known to be relevant then we know that the influence measured by the variable is relevant. The relevance estimation must increase significantly: the influence is doubtlessly relevant.
- If we observe that a variable is irrelevant then we believe that the measured influence is not as relevant as we believed before.
- If we observe that a number of variables which all measure the same influence are weak then we also think that this influence is less relevant than we thought in the beginning.

The increment for a CSI i—i.e. the current relevance—is computed as a modification of the a priori relevance according to the following formula:

$$R_i^{current} := R_i^{apriori} * c_2^{|IRR_i|} + |REL_i| - c_1 * \frac{|WEAK_i|}{a_i} - refinable(i) \quad (2)$$

This formula is rather complicated because it has to summarize the effect of all we know about any attribute within the CSI i. The constants c_i are weights for the impact of discovered knowledge about irrelevant and weak facts concerning the influence. In the test run c_1 has been set to 0.1 and c_2 to 0.5. While an observation of weakness results in a single step downstairs the influence rank every irrelevant variable may even halve the current relevance estimation. The constants a_i represent the knowledge of a given influence's breadth usually

one may think of refining brand A's distribution with a different distribution number than brand B's distribution in order to minimize correlation between the independent variables.

chosen between one and two. If we admit that an influence breadth is more than one we should consider to change our influence terminology and split the corresponding influence. Apparently, $R_i^{current}$ only changes if the influence i has been selected for the previous model (dependingon changes of the sets $WEAK_i$, IRR_i and REL_i). The terms $|REL_i|$ and $refinable(i)$ are defined such that they dominate the equation. A relevant fact leads to the integration of the corresponding influence into the model and a lack of variables leads to a sudden lack of interest for the influence respectively.

In our example all attributes of the main competitor gained a t-value that showed their irrelevance within the regression model. The attribute `distr_dm_display` for `'Y'` has been considered weak. These four attributes are excluded and one new attribute will be included into the next hypothesis. Previously the results affect the relevance estimations for the attributes that are observed to be weak or irrelevant within this model as follows. The interestingness of the three attributes of brand `'X'` is set to zero. The interestingness of the weak attribute is reduced by the constant $c_3 = 0.1$. According to table 2 it's now less interesting (for brand `'Y'`) than `distr_gew_vk`, but still more interesting than `distr_grew_ek` or `distr_num`.

But these results also change the relevance estimations for the influences. For example, the attribute `imp_preis` of `X`, which belongs to the CSI `main_competitor(price, 'X')` has been irrelevant. Its relevance estimation is now divided in half and set to 0.45. The weak influence `main_competitor(distribution,'Y')` is only degraded by 0.1 to 0.8. Table 1 shows that no more relevant descriptions of the main competitors are available. Other competitors may now be integrated into the model hypothesis.

6.3 Integrating Complementarity as an Additional Bias

An interesting regression model should cover a broad range of possible influences. A human analyst tries to integrate different influences and he asks himself what is missing in the current model. A simple checklist could contain the following items: target brand, main competitors, other competitors, other markets, price, distribution, actions. If an influence fills a gap on this checklist it should reveive a complementarity bonus in order to be preferred over other influences with nearly equal relevance. An influence fills a gap if it belongs to one of the influence classes on the checklist that no other influence in the last model belonged to. The interestingness estimations for influences are computed according to equation (3):

$$interestingness := relevance\ estimation + complementarity\ bonus. \qquad (3)$$

7 Evaluation

The MSA has been tested by carrying out an analysis that has recently been done by the market research institute for a client. We first produced our own result and then compared it with the experts' original regression model. Only twenty iterations of the MSA model search procedure have been computed. The surprising effect was the construction of a very good initial hypothesis with R^2=0.9376 that could only slightly be improved in the following iterations up to R^2=0.9448. Regarding R^2 as a main quality factor for a model that was not assembled blindly, the model that has been developed by our experts (R^2=0.9496) has nearly been reached. The experts' model and the MSA's model could be combined such that the certainty factor R^2 raised from 0.9496 to 0.9507. The experts acknowledged that at least three quarters of the model generation work could be done by the MSA and that some of the contained facts are considered 'idea lightnings'. The MSA changes the work process at the market research institute significantly. Instead of testing all hypotheses by hand (usually about 80-100) the market researcher can start with a nearly finished regression model which only needs little refinement.

Until now the problem of overfitting has not been tackled and the data have not been divided into a training set and a test set. Our approach is unlikely to overfit the data for the following reasons. The knowledge based search tests reasonable hypotheses first and only a small number of models is tested at all. Furthermore, the number of variables within a model is limited and the algorithm does not optimize nor even use R^2. The problem of overfitting also seems of minor practical relevance for our case study, because the generated models mainly have to be comprehensible; only then the statistician may use and improve them. Transfering our approach on to other data requires further examination of the search effort and error rate on a separate testset when using less complete or correct knowledge.

8 Conclusions

We have shown that model search for interesting hypotheses can be structured with the aid of domain knowledge. This enables us to perform automatic model search with a special forward selection type procedure even when a large number of variables are present in the data containing multicollinearity and lots of irrelevant variables. A difficult problem from marketing research has been chosen as a case study. No existing model search technique was applicable to this problem. We have presented the knowledge available and a way of translating this knowledge into preferences. We have also introduced a method for determining a hypothesis from these preferences and a method for updating the preferences after the hypothesis has been tested. Besides, our model search procedure has got a second advantage: the search strategy can be explained to the user in terms of his domain and every search decision can be justified with the knowledge.

References

1. Norman Richard Draper and Harry Smith. *Applied Regression Analysis.* John Wiley and Sons, New York a.o., 2nd edition, 1981.
2. Usama M. Fayyad, Gregory Piatetsky-Shapiro, and Padhraic Smyth, editors. *Advances in Knowledge Discovery and Data Mining.* AAAI Press, 1996.
3. George H. John, Ron Kohavi, and Karl Pfleger. Irrelevant features and the subset selection problem. In William J. Cohen and Haim Hirsh, editors, *Machine Learning: Proceedings of The Eleventh International Conference*, pages 121–129, San Francisco, CA, 1994. Morgan Kaufmann.
4. Alan J. Miller. *Subset Selection in Regression.* Monographs on statistics and applied probability. Chapman and Hall, London a.o., 1990.
5. Kristian S. Palda. The evaluation of regression results. In David A. Aaker, editor, *Multivariate Analysis in Marketing: Theory and Application*, pages 35–39. Belmont, 1971.
6. Bernd Rönz and Erhard Förster. *Regressions- und Korrelationsanalyse. Grundlagen - Methoden - Beispiele.* Gabler, Wiesbaden, 1992.
7. Avi Silberschatz and Alexander Tuzhilin. On subjective measures of interestingness in knowledge discovery. In Usama M. Fayyad and Uthurusamy Ramasamy, editors, *Proceedings of The First International Conference on Knowledge Discovery & Data Mining*, pages 275–281, Menlo Park, 1995. AAAI Press.
8. Ulrich Vossebein. Einsatzmöglichkeiten von Scannerdaten. *Jahrbuch der Absatz- und Verbrauchsforschung*, 1, 1993.
9. Raimund Wildner. Simulation and prognosis: New ways for getting more information out of integrated panel data. In *New Ways in Marketing and Market Research, EMAC/ESOMAR-Symposium, Athene, 24-27*, October 1990.
10. Raimund Wildner. Nutzung integrierter Paneldaten für Simulation und Prognose. *Jahrbuch der Absatz- und Verbrauchsforschung*, 2:114–130, 1991.

Index of Authors